The Search for a Method

The Search for a Method

Focus Groups and the Development of Mass
Communication Research

DAVID E MORRISON

UNIVERSITY
UP *of*
LUTON PRESS

British Library Cataloguing in Publication Data

A catalogue record for this book is available from the British Library

ISBN: 1 86020 540 2

Published by
University of Luton Press
University of Luton
75 Castle Street
Luton
Bedfordshire LU1 3AJ
United Kingdom

Tel: +44 (0)1582 743297; Fax: +44 (0)1582 743298
e-mail: ulp@luton.ac.uk

Typeset in Van Dijck MT
Printed in United Kingdom by Whitstable Litho, Whitstable, Kent

Contents

For my daughter Lucy

Acknowledgements

In writing this book I owe a debt to many people, some of them, such as Paul Lazarsfeld, John Marshall, and Bernard Berelson are now long dead. Of the living I would particularly like thank Julie Firmstone, not only for her insightful substantive comments on the manuscript, but also for relieving me of duties at the Institute beyond a level that I had any right to expect. Michael Svennevig, my close colleague at the Institute, deserves special thanks not simply for the support offered by friendship, but for his long patience in discussing points made in the book with me, indeed, for making many of the points in the book. Without his assistance in assuming a research load at the Institute greater than one would have thought possible by a single individual, this book would have been a lot longer in coming. My colleague, Paul Statham, who gave a very detailed reading to the first draft of the manuscript contributed more to the final structure of the book than he perhaps realises – I am indebted. Although it is many years since I was a colleague of Graham Murdock, the early part of the book owes much to his guidance and insistence on an historical approach to knowledge. I would like to thank Paul Croll, for reading sections of the manuscript and for his comments on methodology, and also for his encouragement throughout the years for the survey side of my research. David Docherty's hand is more present in the book than he might realise, for it was David who first introduced me to focus groups when we were both on the research staff of the Broadcasting Research Unit at a time when the method did not have the presence that it now has in academic communication research. Of the staff members of the Institute I would like to thank David Gauntlett for his literature search on focus groups, along with Nicholas Pronay, Philip Taylor and Robin Brown for their general enthusiasm for the project and kind support. I would also like to thank Christine Bailey for initial proof-reading. James Halloran, as ever, was helpful in never failing to give me intellectual encouragement, and political advice. Thanks must also go to those within market research – Simon Chadwick, when at Research International, for showing me what management of a large market research company entails; Julian Bond, of Research International, for demonstrating the statistical expertise that exists within market research companies; and Nick Moon, of NOP, for offering an example of the closeness of market research to academic endeavour. Mike Cooke, of NOP Numbers, is to be thanked for reading sections of the manuscript and making substantive points. I would especially like to thank the buyers of research within the media industry and regulatory bodies for actively demonstrating points that I make concerning the possibility of co-operation between academics and the industry. For their enlightened attitude I would like to thank Robert Towler of the Independent Television Commission, Andrea Millwood Hargrave and Stephen Whittle of the Broadcasting Standards Commission, Colin Shaw, the previous Director of the Broadcasting Standards Council, Robin McCron and Robin McGregor, of the BBC, Tony Hopewell-Smith, of Carlton Television, and David Brennan, of Flextech Television. Sheila Byfield, of Ogilvy and Mather, deserves my absolute thanks not simply for her enthusiasm for research, and appreciation for University-based learning, but for allowing me a view of what a really pressured (but friendly) work environment looks like.

To say thanks to my editor Manuel Alvarado is not enough. It is refreshing to have an editor who is as receptive to ideas as he is, and one as keen to foster knowledge. Edward Buscombe also helped magnificently in assisting editorially to make the book more readable than it would otherwise have been.

Introduction

The background to this book is quite simple: it stems from an interest in methodology, and a concern about the rise in the popularity of focus groups within media research. It is not that I have an objection to focus groups as a methodological tool, far from it; but I do worry that they have gained a position for themselves in the lexicon of the language of research without sufficient attention having been given to their nature, practice and application. If this is the immediate concern which prompts the writing of this book, my more general interest in doing so stems from a long-standing fascination with the institutionalisation of knowledge that is part personal and part intellectual.

This intellectual interest in the institutionalisation of knowledge derives from my early work on Paul Lazarsfeld, one of the founding fathers of mass communication research, and a leading figure in the development of the quantification wing of sociology, especially through survey methodology. Lazarsfeld's prominence in the history of social research owes much, however, to his position as an institutional innovator, especially through his establishment of the Bureau of Applied Social Research at Columbia University in New York in the 1940s. The training given in the methods of quantification at the Bureau to generations of students who then went on to establish or populate other such centres helped cement the position of empirical sociology within sociology in general, and at the same time helped provide mass communication research with a firm base in quantification. Indeed, one can talk of a Lazarsfeldian sociology, and a Lazarsfeldian mass communication research. Although such sociology and such mass communication research have not been without their detractors, Lazarsfeld had an appreciation for a wide range of methods, and it is through the work of the Bureau that focus groups owe their origination, more specifically through Lazarsfeld's close colleague, Robert Merton.

Although the biographical work on Lazarsfeld as an institutional innovator was completed while I was at the Leicester Centre for Mass Communication Research, established by James Halloran, and itself an innovation in higher learning within mass communications in Britain, my involvement in Lazarsfeld's work was fed by my interest in the history of ideas. Only when I interviewed Lazarsfeld over many months in New York, and researched in Vienna, where in 1926 Lazarsfeld established the Österreichische Wirtschaftsforsocialforsung Forsungstelle, the first such research centre of its kind, a cross between a market research centre and an academic research institute, did my interest in the organisational structure of knowledge begin. The fact that this interest developed while at the Centre in Leicester owed nothing to any first-hand reflection on how organisational forms structure knowledge, and how certain forms of knowledge 'demand' certain organisation structures for its completion. I did not connect the intellectual and personal aspects of my working life together at all. Coming to understand how Lazarsfeld established the Bureau of Applied Research, the difficulties he faced and the manoeuvrings he engaged in to have research centres accepted as a rightful institutional part of a university, did not then lead me to make the connection that I had in some small way been part of a similar enterprise undertaken by James Halloran.

Of course, Halloran's Centre had been set up in the 1960s with the full blessing of the parent university and was not seen as some kind of wayward child as was the case with Lazarsfeld's Bureau and Columbia University, but the role of managerial scholar, which Lazarsfeld had created, involved Halloran in similar strains and similar conduct, most notably, the raising of research funds for expensive empirical work. This was research as an enterprise; not one where the central rational was the generation of profit, but an enterprise nevertheless, where ideas had to be sold if livelihoods were to be maintained. It was not until much later, having helped Michael Tracey, along with David Docherty, to establish and build the now defunct Broadcasting Research Unit, that I began to fully appreciate what Lazarsfeld and Halloran, along with numerous other research directors running similar outfits, had done.

The BRU[1] had core funding provided by the Markle Foundation in America, the BBC and the Independent Broadcasting Authority, with free office space provided by the British Film Institute. Moneys for projects, and the bulk of staff salaries, were raised from the media industry, government departments and

---

1   The Broadcasting Research Unit was established under the chairmanship of Richard Hoggart in late 1979 – early 1980 and grew out of Elihu Katz's commission in 1975 by the BBC to prepare an 'agenda for new projects of social research in the field of broadcasting'. The resulting report of Katz was published as 'Social Research on Broadcasting: Proposals for Further Development' by the BBC in 1977. History is rarely neat, but it would seem that Kenneth Lamb was the key figure in commissioning Katz. What is more certain is that it was Lamb, reflecting on Katz work, who became the main mover inside the BBC to establish a new, and independent, research centre. Tony Smith, then Director of the British Film Institute, became involved with Lamb in planning the future of such an enterprise. The BFI committed itself to providing office and administrative support, with the BBC, along with Independent Broadcasting Authority, now the Independent Television Commission, providing financial support. At some point in 1980 Smith managed to persuade Lloyd Morrisett of the American Markle Foundation to give financial support also. As well as having this core of operating funds, the BRU raised money for individual studies from external sources – government departments, local authorities, the television industry, and foundations. Not surprisingly, given what has been said earlier about the perceived usefulness of quantifiable knowledge by policy makers, all the studies for which money was given had a statistical component to them. It might seem, given the heavy empirical nature of the Units work, that Hoggart was a strange choice as Chairman. From the outset, however, the BBC, probably in the personage of Lamb, insisted that if it was to financially support the Unit then there had to be an independent chairman, and it is difficult to imagine a more independent person or personality than Hoggart.

philanthropic foundations. It was a stressful and precarious existence, an enterprise but one which sold ideas to ensure continued existence, and not one grounded in the generation of profit. It was, however, at least in its orientation, much more 'commercial' than the Leicester Centre, and much more locked into the policy concerns of the industry from where the bulk of its support came. Although always independent, and with a management structure under the Chairmanship of Richard Hoggart which ensured such independence, it was in truth a half-way house between a market research company and a university research centre.

The necessity to pay ourselves undoubtedly saw us 'chase' money that if left to our own volition we probably would not have gone for, but the financial imperatives of existence at least ensured that the BRU never became removed from concrete political and economic concerns. In the end, though, the BRU could not survive once its core funding was removed: it was never designed to exist as a commercial enterprise, neither did the staff have the skills, or one might say desire, to operate on such a basis.

Having worked in a university research centre, in a university teaching department as a research fellow, and in a hybrid research unit, I then for two years worked as Head of Media in a thoroughly commercial research enterprise, Research International, one of the largest market research companies in the world. Although the research undertaken there was of high quality, there was no disguising the fact that the name of the game was profit, and profit was to be gained by aggressively selling the services of the company to clients, and making sure, once accounts were won, that the needs of clients were satisfied. The company was structured to ensure that this happened. The buying, or funding, of research, call it what one will, is an inextricable part of the production of knowledge, which has often being over-simplified in terms of the implications for the type of knowledge produced.

Max Horkheimer, in looking at the operations of the Frankfurt School during its exile in New York, with its need to attract research funds following a downturn in its fortunes, considered, rather bitterly, that the 'School' had become a *Betrieb* – a business. (Jay 1973:342) A *Betrieb* (Research Enterprise) or not, the situation the Frankfurt School faced whilst in New York saw its most productive period of empirical research. Of course, the Frankfurt School never lost its abiding commitment to theory, and Adorno had a very uneasy relationship with Lazarsfeld whilst working on the Rockefeller Foundation-funded Princeton Radio Research project that was to form the basis for Lazarsfeld's establishment of the Bureau of Applied Social Research. Adorno was there, so to speak, at the birth of focus group research, and was most scathing of the Lazarsfeld-Stanton programme analyser that was used to 'focus' respondents in the groups to the research in hand. Whatever the criticisms of Adorno towards the type of work Lazarsfeld engaged in, Lazarsfeld himself recognised the existence of the audience at other than a theoretical level, and wished to engage with people through an empirical language in a way resisted by Adorno. And part of that language of research – methodology – was the focus group.

The history of focus group research is a story about the relationship of a method to the organisation of knowledge. First developed in 1941 by Robert Merton, then working at the 'Bureau' with Lazarsfeld, the use of focus groups formed part of university-based knowledge, but then was lost to sight within that domain, to be later taken up and taken over by market research, only to be rediscovered by academia, in particular by researchers into the media audience. Why this should be so will become clear as the story unfolds. I wish, however, to tell this story in a particular way, fed by my interest in the institutionalisation of knowledge, and by my personal experience of working in a variety of organisational research settings. I will argue that the career of focus group research cannot be truly appreciated without understanding research as practice. To do this, however, especially from within a media research perspective, a bigger tale needs to be told than a straightforward narrative account of the passage of the method from academia to market research and back to academia again. The lesson is that as a short-cut towards understanding the audience, media research is in severe danger of adopting a method that, like all methods, has limitations. I will also claim that the over-ready adoption of focus groups by media researchers is dangerous, because the logic of the method has been misunderstood. This misunderstanding is not wilful, but stems from confusions within communications research between qualitative and quantitative research. The culprits for this state of affairs, and they are many, will become obvious as the story unfolds.

This book is not offered in the hope of a rapprochement between traditions. Sermons are rarely effective in changing beliefs if one cannot state what a state of grace would be, and there is no methodological holy grail. The hope is to offer insight into the basic grounding of a practice, and by doing so encourage those who wish to use focus groups to restrict their claims for the method to areas of operation where they might satisfactorily be applied. A basic aim, therefore, is to protect against an over-enthusiastic and unreflective use of focus groups. The hope is that the practitioner will appreciate more fully where the method sits within the language of research, and how the method has developed. The story, as I have set it within the institutionalisation of research, moves along very much as an insider's view of research culture, and as a commentary on important episodes of communication research history.

I have had in mind when writing the book that increasingly, especially in Britain, universities must now pay for themselves, and also that increasingly researchers who wish to engage in empirical work must look for support outside traditional forms of funding such as research councils, to other, often commercial, bodies. It is government policy to have academia move its research efforts closer to the interests of industry. The university has increasingly become a *betrieb*. This may, for some, be a cause for lament, for others a source of invigoration. Whichever, focus group research owes its life to direct contact between researchers and agencies outside the academy, and its flowering within commercial research owes much to the benefits which market research agencies saw for using the method to answers their clients' questions.

Robert Merton considers that market researchers have 'abused' the technique that he developed. In recent correspondence with him he reflected on the present position of the method: '... in ultimate irony, the practice of actually ignoring the core idea originally basic to the focused interview by failing to have members of the group focus on actual materials to facilitate their responses. In short, I've simply been urging social researchers to put the "focus" back in focus group research'.[2] My own position is that although market researchers may have 'misused' focus groups, they have not done so to the extent that academic researchers have. The reasons for using focus groups by market research are often different from the use academics make of them; it is academics who demand too much from the method, and lack rigour in how they apply it, not market researchers.

The fact that focus group research is valued and employed on an extensive scale by the media and media-related industries means that here is a source of research funds for the academy in the pursuit of knowledge. As with all courtship, the relationship between the academy and industry is not without its tension, but my position for the moment is that, unlike the case of survey research, the university is well placed to compete with market research companies in obtaining funds from the media industry. To develop this point I have found it necessary to compare and contrast different research settings, to examine what I have called the industrialisation of knowledge by market research companies with the research setting and research practices of the university. In doing this I have taken the opportunity to lay out some of the early history of communications research and relate part of the story of the institutionalisation of communications research through one of its founding fathers, Paul Lazarsfeld.

The relationship of the university to the outside world of commerce and politics can undoubtedly be productive, but it can also be destructive. One of the weaknesses of communication research has been the small scale, and often parochial nature, of its studies, something recognised by the recent Economic and Social Science Council research initiative in the area.[3] My own feeling is that the 'parochialism' of much communication research will only be added to by the developing use of the focus group as a way of knowing the audience. I am not for a moment, however, suggesting a Lazarsfeldian model of funding research, or at least not suggesting the model without offering insight into what reliance on external funding for large-scale projects can entail.

Because of its necessarily expensive operations, Lazarsfeld's love of mathematics and the statistical component of his work, his survey research,

---

2   Letter from Robert Merton – 18 April 1995.
3   ESRC Media Economics and Media Culture Research Programme.

pushed him into seeking funds from whatever source would provide them. The media industry was one. While not claiming that Lazarsfeld's operations can act as a model to current researchers strapped for cash, there can be no denying that Lazarsfeld's links with commerce proved extremely productive. The manner of Lazarsfeld's operations and his views on the conducting of research raise substantive questions about the nature and purpose of social research, perhaps no better illustrated than his peregrinations with Adorno and the difficulties that Lazarsfeld faced by having Adorno work with him.

It is not my purpose to correct myths about Lazarsfeld and C Wright Mills's castigation of him as the doer of 'abstracted empiricism', but to provide, by looking at Lazarsfeld's life, a wider history to the method of focus groups. The 'ownership' of the focus group is rightly to be given to Robert Merton, but the setting in which it occurred is the story of Paul Lazarsfeld. Out of respect for Lazarsfeld the methodologist, and in recognition of Robert Merton's insistence on methodological rigour being applied to focus group research, I have been at pains in the course of the book to comment on methodological procedures beyond that of focus group research. Indeed, methods tend to acquire their significance through consideration of other methods that might have been used to address a research question but were not. The question of why some methods are used by particular researchers and others are not has not been left at the purely intellectual level of internal methodological debate. Instead, I have attempted to explain why certain types of people might more readily adopt one method rather than another, and why certain areas of intellectual enquiry have so readily seized upon the focus group as an appropriate method for their ambitions. I single out here media studies and cultural studies, and offer warning that focus groups are an incomplete method – that they cannot finish what they set out to do.

The criticism of the focus group method is handled in a variety of ways, but most notably by offering a guide to its practice. This is undertaken not in the sense of a 'how to do' research manual, although there is instruction, but on an issue basis. I have paid much more attention to the problems of doing focus groups, what is required, the dangers of moderator demand, and the status of the knowledge that they generate, than is associated with research manuals. Finally, political consideration is given to the ethics of such work, and issue taken with those who wish to use focus groups as a consciousness-raising exercise. This section is used not only to warn of the dangers of politicising university research, of having research geared to immediate political gain rather than have it inform general political debate, but to show, by the manner in which some scholars worry about the political implications of the exchanges that take place within the focus group, how focus groups have been misconstrued in terms of their use and their effectiveness.

It is now just over half a century since Robert Merton first developed focus groups. It has been a long journey to their current popularity among media researchers, but I am far from sure that the distance travelled has been very great. The avenue for social understanding that they offered is in danger in the hands of current practitioners of turning into a cul-de-sac. If, however, focus groups are going to form a central part of media research, it is time to examine them in some detail in an effort to try and gain a perspective on their benefits and drawbacks. Sonia Livingstone, writing in the 1973 volume of the Journal of Communications dedicated to a review of the past decade of media research, commented, after stating that methodological development of the field was 'sorely needed':

> Two 'new' methodologies – which, of course, are both very old - have been used enthusiastically in recent audience research: the focus group and ethnography. Undoubtedly, these methods have demonstrated that viewers are active interpreters of texts and that viewing contexts vary widely in their impact on these interpretations. It is time for a sober assessment of these methods, given the problems that are raised through their use, and for their development and integration with other communication research methods. (Livingstone 1973:7)

I find it difficult to disagree with Livingstone's statement. A 'sober assessment' of the focus group method is certainly needed.

One

A Focus on History

In the summer of 1990 the *European Journal of Communications* produced a special double issue dedicated to examining communications research in Europe. The volume was timely. The communications scene was changing rapidly, and communications scholarship was being transformed as it attempted to provide understanding to the changing situations of its subject area. If excitement was in the air, James Curran in a considered piece on the new revisionism, which challenged the dominant radical paradigms of the late 1970s and early 1980s, cast cold water on the revisionists' claims to innovatory thought. Ever the historian, Curran castigated the revisionists for their ignorance of the past, suggesting that the new school of thought had more than a tinge of revivalism to it. Considering David Morley (1989) to be one of the key revisionists, he rounded on him for his characterisation of the effects tradition as dominated by the hypodermic model of influence, before the 'uses and gratifications' approach put forward the idea of the active audience. Curran's obvious annoyance rested on the exalted position that the new revisionists, with their stress on audience autonomy, claim for their 'new' thinking by falsifying or mythologising the history of mass communication research. Though he noted Morley's critique of 'uses and gratifications', and his view that although an advance on the hypodermic model, the theory's reliance on individual differences of personality and psychology to explain differential responses to media content is severely limited, Curran could no longer contain himself, especially in light of the claim that only the new revisionism offers a more satisfactory and rounded account:

> This is a breath-taking, though often repeated, caricature of the history of communications research that writes out a whole generation of researchers. It presents as innovation what is in reality a process of rediscovery. This mythologising also has the effect of obscuring the multiple lines of intersection between past media research in the pluralist tradition and the new revisions emerging out of the radical tradition. Effects research cannot be said in any meaningful sense to have been 'dominated' by the hypodermic model. On the contrary, its main thrust

since ever since the 1940s was to assert the independence and autonomy of media audiences and dispel the widespread notion that people are easily influenced by the media. It did this by developing many of the same insights that have been proclaimed afresh in the recent spate of 'reception' studies, albeit in a different technical language and sometimes with less subtlety. (Curran 1990: 146,147)

It is not as if Curran sees no advantages in the revisionist approach to the study of communications; rather, he questions its over-blown claims to superiority. He does consider, for example, that the revisionist approach has given a more focused attention to the text than past approaches, and has provided 'a much richer and fuller understanding of interdiscursive processes in audience reception and, above all, locates these in a more adequate sociological context'. But at the same time Curran considers that the revisionists' reluctance to quantify is 'a backward step'; indeed, he rounds on the revisionists for their 'over-reliance on group discussions'. (p150)

It is not for nothing that Curran entitles one of the sections of his article, 'Rediscovering the Wheel'. Curran wishes to signify that what looks new and innovatory in communication research has all been done before. Had he wished Curran could have extended his criticism of the revisionists' 'over-reliance on group discussions' by pointing out that the methodology of group discussions was first developed and used by the very group of researchers that the revisionists would wish to categorise as 'effects' researchers. The difference between then and now is that the 'old' researchers – Robert Merton, Paul Lazarsfeld, Marjorie Fiske, Patricia Kendall – were not only methodologically sophisticated, but tolerant of a whole variety of methodologies. They were skilful combiners of qualitative and quantitative analysis. Not for them the righteousness of a single method or approach to understanding, nor ignorance of the history of methods.[1] Ellen Wartella in her commentary on qualitative research quotes Paul Rock's observation on the lack of historical awareness among symbolic interactionists as a warning to mass communications research: 'A sociology which forgets its past may be committed to the continuous rediscovery of old ideas. When the provenance is unknown, authorship can be claimed by those who lack any proper title to it.' (Rock 1979:45 quoted in Wartella 1987:109)

David Morgan is a noted figure in focus group research. He is author of one of the two handbooks on focus group research that Sage Publications produced in 1988, marking the 'arrival' of academic focus group research. In 1993 he edited a volume entitled *Successful Focus Groups*, with the subtitle *Advancing the State of the Art*, clearly indicating that focus group research had now moved beyond the earlier handbook stage. The opening lines of his editorial introduction to the book read: 'Just five years ago, few social scientists had heard of focus groups, yet

---

1   See in particular the collected essays of Lazarsfeld, *Qualitative Analysis: Historical and Critical Essays* (Lazarsfeld 1972) to gain a good grasp of Lazarsfeld's astonishing range of range of knowledge and his appreciation for a variety of approaches and methodologies.

now they are the subject of widespread interest.' The articles in the book grew out of a conference - the Menucha Conference – whose purpose appears to have been to take stock of developments in focus group research, and at the same time to advance its development. Morgan says: '...we set ourselves the long-term goal of achieving a level of sophistication that would give focus groups a permanent place within the range of social research methods'. (Morgan 1993:1X)

The excitement of the 'discovery' of this new method is plain to see in the enthusiastic writing of the contributors to the volume, yet what is surprising is that Morgan in an article in *Qualitative Sociology*, written with Margaret Spanish, also well known in focus group research, entitled 'Focus Groups: A New Tool for Qualitative Research', states the origin of focus group techniques to be in market research. (Morgan and Spanish 1984:254) This is simply not the case, although it is a general mistake that focus groups began in the commercial rather than academic sector of research. A few years later, however, Morgan locates the beginning of focus group research not in market research, but 'in sociology'. (Morgan 1988)

This offers an insight into the development of focus groups as a now accepted research tool of the social sciences, in that in common with the establishment of any field, a point is reached when historical excavations of its beginnings takes place. Morgan says that within 'the social sciences the earliest published work on focus groups is by Robert Merton and his collaborators', (Morgan 1988:11) but a few pages earlier he states that the focus group technique 'has a long history that extends to Lazarsfeld's Marienthal studies in the thirties'. (Morgan 1988: 5) This is not actually so, but as I will document, Lazarsfeld, in developing the research setting from within which focus group research emerged, is vital to an understanding of their origination and subsequent development. In tracing the history of focus group research, one traces an important episode in the general history of mass communication and social research. Given that the question of methods is central to any social enquiry, in discussing the method of focus group research, I have been forced to comment on media research as such and document a significant tract of its history.

Methodology is often seen as sterile, even boring; the methodology section of any book or article is quickly glanced at on the way to reading the results or theorising about the issue at hand. This is a pity, but probably stems from the way that methodology is taught and discussed – as a technical issue, or as a set of procedures, and not as a struggle for meaning. Yet what language we use shapes the nature of the conversation we can have with, and about, the world. Methodology is, in other words, the fundamental part of our story-telling technique, and as such is more than technical: it is the very language of research, quite simply how we go about doing things.

Given that methodology, the procedural language we chose to adopt, is the basic building-block in the construction of our narrative account of the world, I have sought to show in an interdisciplinary way, through an historical enquiry, the factors that have shaped the development of one particular method, namely, that of focus groups. In doing so I have tried to humanise the technical, that is, to breathe some life into the development of a procedure by paying attention, at times a great deal of attention, to those who developed the method.

Too often in communications research a nod is made towards history to explain a current condition, when what is required is a detailed excavation of events. One can address the history of ideas from a variety of perspectives, and ignore the individuals associated with the ideas under discussion, but history never did anything, only people. Even though no individual can be said to make history, if history is taken to encompass broad changes in human association over time, with the creation of an idea, then the individual as a single actor becomes a rightful focus of attention. In other words, ideas or methods do not come *ex nihilo*, but are created by people, operating within conditions that have not necessarily been of their own direct making. Yet in providing any account what one includes and excludes depends not simply on the information one has access to, but on the point one wishes the story to tell. In my case, in the early part of the book dealing with Paul Lazarsfeld, the intention is to show, in detail, the forces that made him what he was. Even there, however, I have been selective in what to include, in my decisions over what is and is not important to the story of his development. All history must be selective; of all the rivers Caesar crossed, only the Rubicon was considered worthy of special mention.[2] The significance of crossing the Rubicon only emerges if placed within an understanding of the political upheaval of Rome of the late Republic. Similarly, my account of Lazarsfeld and his years in Vienna only makes sense if one has some understanding of his place in a particular moment of Austrian history. The fact that Lazarsfeld was a middle-class Jewish socialist is not sufficient to understand his work without understanding the position after the collapse of the Hapsburg Empire of the whole class to which he belonged, the nature of Austro-Marxism, the position of the Jew within the Social Democratic Party, and the position of the Jew within the Austrian state. Due weight must be given to each of these to know what the statement, 'middle-class, socialist intellectual Jew' means, and how this helps provide an account of Lazarsfeld's journey, as both a scholar and as a person, and an understanding of his importance in the development of a methodology in communication research.

The founding fathers of communications research, Paul Lazarsfeld, Kurt Lewin, Harold Lasswell and Carl Hovland all came from distinct disciplines. Lazarsfeld came from sociology, Lewin from psychology (small-group dynamics), Laswell from political science and Hovland from experimental psychology . Perhaps the description 'distinct disciplines' is the wrong term, and it would be better to say recognised disciplines. For an area of activity to be considered a discipline means little more than that a critical mass develops within which each shares in a common recognition that they are addressing similar issues using a similar approach, and that this critical mass is recognised by those outside as constituting an identifiable activity. This activity, or discipline, is then awarded

---

2   See EH Carr 1961 for this point and illustration.

status, depending on the value attached to the activity. At some point the activity is institutionalised, thus cementing its hold further on the claim to the title 'discipline'. But most disciplines, even the most tightly defined, borrow from others, or as knowledge develops the discipline fragments to form sub-areas of activity which take on the appearance of separate disciplines. Thus the idea of discipline should not be held too rigidly. Indeed, Bernard Berelson's reference in his controversial article, 'The State of Communications Research', written in 1959, to the 'withering away of mass communications research' brought the sharp response from Wilbur Schramm that mass communications research was not a discipline, but a 'field' and thus was not subject to the decline that Berelson foresaw. That is, that the boundaries of communication research were so wide that it was difficult to make a precise commentary on its health.

All the founding fathers moved out of communications research once their interests in the area had been exhausted. Despite the standing of such individuals, by the time they had left the area communications research had not managed to become established as a discipline in the manner indicated above, nor has it since. Thus, Schramm (Schramm 1952) is indeed right to call it a field. But perhaps more than most 'fields' communications research crosses many disciplines, and indeed other fields. It has borrowed a whole variety of approaches and methods when and where they were needed. It has always, therefore, been open to the challenge that it has been somewhat eclectic in its methodological approaches. Nevertheless the development of communications research was firmly rooted in the tradition of the social sciences, and as such paid heed, although by no means exclusively, to methods of quantification and experimentation.

The rapid growth of communications/media studies has meant that if it was once possible to have a discussion about whether or not it was a discipline, it no longer is. It is difficult now to discern even the nature of the field. One thing is for sure; there has been a rapid influx of people into the field whose background is not social science, but the humanities, drawing heavily on literary and cultural criticism for their analytical approach, where theory is pre-eminent. If in its formative period communications research borrowed from a whole variety of social science disciplines to force an understanding of the communications process, then those in the humanities have raided the world of ideas – Gramsci, Barthes, Foucault, Baudrillard, Bourdieu, Derrida and so on[3] – in a search of a

---

3   For a good and extremely amusing account of the mix of ideas that have gone to make up culture studies, see Ellis Cashmore 1994. He begins his chapter, 'The Meaning of Cultural Studies' by writing: 'Cultural Studies has the air of a subject created on a dare. What, someone might have asked, if we studied popular media, like film, magazine and television, with techniques borrowed from structural linguistics, using words that few people understand and arriving at conclusions that totally contradict everyone's expectations? Then, with a nod to post-modernism, we tell everyone our conclusions are not true? One might be tempted to suggest that the subject would be regarded as esoteric, if not inconsequential. Not so: cultural studies has become a most influential approach to the study of popular culture, blending Marxist structuralism, semiotics, post-structuralism and other schools together in a heady mixture'. It is Cashmore's conclusion that 'cultural studies' success owes more to mannerism than meaning'. (Cashmore 1994:43)

focus for their activity. It is dizzy stuff, and such scholars have largely concentrated on textual and linguistic analysis and the symbolic meaning of the text. Thus the meaning of Madonna could function just as happily as a subject of enquiry as the main evening news bulletin. Yet at some point there is recognition that the audience ought to be included in the framework of analysis. Not to do so was to have theory spiral out of control as the language of explanation become ever more arcane, as theory set new problems without resolving basic issues, which at the end of the day were really empirical questions, the answers to which were not to be found in the text, but in people. Thus focus group research for those with a background in the humanities forms a good bridge between the empirical and the theoretical: one still has the text and one can insert people. But empirical research, for most in this humanistic tradition, remains at the level of qualitative research. There is little appreciation for, or understanding of, quantitative methods. What is not understood is not liked, and what is not liked, as we shall see, becomes rejected.

Cultural production is always political struggle, in that it involves a contest for definitions of the meanings by which we wish to live. But media research has been, and will remain, especially political. The reasons for this are not hard to find: the media at a symbolic expressive level shape how we view the world, and world views, and which view is to be dominant, are always political questions. The political nature of the field is something that most scholars working in the area recognise and live with, and some even enjoy. But the explosive growth of media studies, allied to the rise of feminist scholarship, has produced a new front in the battle over the language of research. At its most extreme, going well beyond media studies and into the realms of philosophy itself, the attack is on the whole tradition of western science and the notion of scientific rationality. Quantification, seen as part of this rationality, is rejected. Some feminists, as we will see later, whether or not they object to western scientific rationality, even consider that survey research is masculine, and therefore not to be entertained. This I cannot understand. I can accept the methodological argument that survey research may not capture the feelings of women, but only if it is granted that survey research may also fail to capture the feelings of men. Otherwise one is left in the peculiar position that men and women do not belong to the same species. One might mount an argument that survey research is not good at addressing aspects of the human condition that feminist researchers are interested in, but it does not logically follow from this that survey research is masculine. It is not masculine or feminine, it just is.

The focus group as a way of understanding the audience is old, indeed practically as old as modern mass communications research itself, dating back to the early 1940s, but the current popularity of the focus group is in danger of becoming a new methodological imperialism. Focus groups fit the requirements of a breed of media researchers operating within the tradition of humanistic social enquiry, and in a sense this is what any methodology does, namely, fit the requirements of the intellectual tasks that are set, but the danger is that focus groups will come to form a comfort blanket by which to resist further empirical engagement with the audience than that bounded by one specific and limited method. The real danger is that having found a form of empirical enquiry that allows the humanistic researcher to make claims about what people think, feel and so on, and thus give the researcher an authority that his or her own pronouncements alone would not have, the researcher has also lighted upon a method that is closed to public inspection. One can have theory and one can have empirical enquiry, with the best research tending to be marked by both, but in the seclusion of the focus group one can have theory and one can have empirical enquiry and neither may engage with the other. In other words one can keep one's theory – or political ideology – intact through an apparent engagement with others, which in fact is no more than the reproduction of that which one had hoped to hear. And my suspicion is that if a moderator is sufficiently shocked to the point of wishing to intervene when hearing statements they find offensive, this is not just a question of a sensitivity to abuse, but a difficulty of incorporating a world that does not coincide with that of the researchers.

I raise this worry because time and again in presenting survey data one is greeted with strong protest by media studies scholars at findings that they object to because they make for an uncomfortable ideological fit. Groups that they wish to 'celebrate' have exhibited opinions that are not a cause for celebration. One cannot, indeed one does not get, such a response in presenting data to the more established or traditional disciplines. It is as if the field of communications or media studies has not felt the necessity to check its own progress through rigorous examination of the language of research. Instead it has shown itself content to grab the latest piece of excitement, be it an idea from some other area of intellectual life, or some bit of methodology. If, therefore, focus groups are going to form a central part of media research it is time to examine them in some detail in an effort to try and gain some perspective on the benefits and drawbacks of the method.

Long History

Although focus groups have become much favoured by those working within the realm of qualitative research, the fact is that the focus group developed not out of the tradition of qualitative or interpretative sociology, but out of quantification. Focus groups begin with Robert Merton in 1941. However, to understand the development of the method it is necessary to understand the intellectual ethos and situation which nurtured its development. This takes us back to a particular history, the rise of quantification within sociology and the contribution made by Paul Felix Lazarsfeld (1901-1976) to such a development. This is not to say that Lazarsfeld has greater claim to the development of focus group research than Robert Merton, but the social situating of focus groups, or the historical bedding of them, owes much to Lazarsfeld's career and his appreciation for a variety of research approaches.

To the untutored eye it might seem strange that the noted statistical scholar Lazarsfeld, and the noted theoretical scholar Merton, could ever have formed a strong research alliance. In fact, as will be shown later in the story, the joint appointment of Lazarsfeld and Merton to professorships at Columbia University in the 1940s was intended to perpetuate the divide within sociology between its quantitative wing and its speculative or theoretical wing. Yet rather than keep the separation going, Lazarsfeld and Merton joined forces to present social sciences with a formidable partnership. Furthermore, had Lazarsfeld been an abstracted empiricist, as restricted in his vision of research as frequently suggested, then it is difficult to see how he could ever have worked with someone such as Theodor Adorno, the critical theorist. That the collaboration between the two men eventually proved a disaster owes little, as often thought, to Lazarsfeld's intellectual falling out with Adorno. Though Adorno felt uncomfortable working within the empirical setting created by Lazarsfeld, a setting out of which the focus group method of audience research grew, Lazarsfeld had little intellectual disagreement with Adorno. In terms of his intellectual respect for Adorno and the Frankfurt School, and for diverse approaches to knowledge, the following conversation with Lazarsfeld is illuminating. I was aware of his statement on 'Administrative and Critical Communications Research' (Lazarsfeld 1941) that had appeared in the Frankfurt School's own journal, *Studies in Philosophy and Social Science*, but wished to know whether that article represented his actual feelings or whether it was more of a public statement giving legitimisation to his operations. I questioned the sincerity of his relationship to the Frankfurt School.

> No, no that was very serious. To somehow come to terms with something which seemed to me to have a core of intellectual integrity and at the same time seemed to be foolish and irresponsible. It was always a mixture of curiosity, respect and irritation. So anything, any contact with the Institute was always quite a sincere quality.

> There is a famous joke which I have remembered now for forty years because it completely reflected [my position].... During the first Roosevelt election, Roosevelt had three very famous advisors: Smith... Governor of New York, a devout Catholic, Morley who was a Protestant, and a professor of economics at Columbia, and the famous Baruch, a Jewish businessman. And the story went that the three men on this campaign have to sleep in one room, and on the Sunday morning Morley and Baruch are snoring, and Smith gets up to go to morning mass at seven o'clock and as he staggers out, sleepy, he says, 'wouldn't it be Hell if they were right and I was wrong'.

Lazarsfeld was, at least in his intellectual position, far from the mere measurer of worlds. For him social life did not live just in mathematical tables as often claimed. Far from being interested solely in quantification, Lazarsfeld had a fine appreciation of interpretative sociology, and Morgan in noting the development of focus groups themselves traces their history to 'Lazarsfeld's Marienthal studies in the thirties'. (Morgan 1988:5)

This reference to Lazarsfeld's Marienthal study demonstrates the complexity of dating practices in the history of ideas. The Lazarsfeld study referred to is *Die Arbeitslosen von Marienthal*, a study of unemployment in Marienthal, a small town some twenty miles outside Vienna. It was first published in 1933, but was quickly consigned to the bonfires of the National Socialists, despite the protection it was hoped might be afforded by not putting the Jewish-sounding names of the authors on the title page (Jahoda, Lazarsfeld and Zeisel).[4] The people of Marienthal were entirely dependent for their livelihood on the town's only cotton mill, which when it closed created total unemployment and dreadful poverty amidst the generally miserable conditions in Austria in the 1930s. To read the study is deeply moving. It is not only a first-rate piece of ethnographic writing, but also excellent ethnography. Files were created on 478 separate families, with each family member having their own separate file; life histories of 32 men and 30 women are included; time sheets were kept by the unemployed documenting their day's activities and time allocated to them; reports and complaints that people made to industrial commissions were examined; school essays set for primary and secondary school children on subjects such as 'what I want most of all' 'what I want to be', and 'how I see my future' were collected; meal records were kept by 40 families for one week and a record kept of the packed lunches made for the children; statistical data collected on births, marriages, deaths; accounts kept at the co-operative store were examined; money spent at the tavern, the butcher's, the shoe-maker's were recorded; the buying of newspapers documented and so on. Observational data were also collected on such things as visits to the library and even the speed of walking in an attempt to judge the impact of unemployment on purposive behaviour.

Given Morgan's reference to techniques of focus groups having 'a long history that extend to Lazarsfeld's Marienthal studies', and not remembering any reference to focus group research when I had first came into contact with the study years ago, I carefully re-read the work for evidence of such a method. I could find no reference to it by name – but then that is not surprising given that the name attached to the method was created by Merton years later – but no indication that anything approximating a focus group methodology was adopted. Certainly interviews were conducted with family members, often in their homes, and other interviews which look like 'chance conversations' took place in a variety of public spaces, but not group discussions.

My purpose in taking time with Morgan's observation is not to criticise him, especially given that his own focus group research is a model of procedure, and at the substantive level enlightening, as is his methodological writing on the topic, but because in tracing the history of focus groups one needs to separate out the ideas that fed into the approach, and the establishment of the approach itself. It may be that the sociographic approach (as it is called in translation and which I have referred to as ethnography, to use a more modern description,) adopted for the study of Marienthal did feature as an influence when in 1941 Lazarsfeld asked

4 The study was only translated into English in 1971, under the title, *Marienthal, the Sociography of an Unemployed Community* (Jahoda *et al* 1972).

Robert Merton to sit in on some 'experiments' he was conducting into the impact of radio programmes, and from which focus group research directly developed. But it is difficult to see why one would feature Marienthal as the root of focus group research rather than a host of other studies using a distinctly qualitative and 'sociographic' approach. Indeed, there is a very good appendix to *Die Arbeitslosen von Marienthal* on the history of sociography, deliberately written to give a historical context to the study and in which the work of the Chicago School, amongst others, features heavily. This being the case, and in the absence of evidence that focus group methods were used in the Marienthal study, all one can talk about is a general intellectual milieu of appreciation for systematic qualitative research that fostered a climate of enquiry not antagonistic to the development of the method. *Marienthal* was part of a history of qualitative research which includes the Chicago School studies, and Robert and Helen Lynd's classic study of *Middletown*. (Lynd 1929) The inclusion of a lengthy bibliography of sociographic studies shows, furthermore, that the Viennese researchers were aware of the tradition within which they were working: that they were not establishing something entirely new, although the study itself was certainly a departure, in some ways, from what had been done before.

The original intention of the study had been to examine not unemployment, but leisure, for 'reasons I cannot remember' as Lazarsfeld commented. (Lazarsfeld 1969:751) However, Hans Zeisel, a colleague of Lazarsfeld at that time, mentions that it was the intervention of Otto Bauer, leader of the Austrian Social Democrats, that pushed the researchers to focus on unemployment. Commenting on the work of the *Forschungsstelle*, Zeisel records:

> The style of life and the culture of the Austrian proletariat, and more particularly the Viennese proletariat, occupied an extraordinary part of our activities and we had conceived a plan to furnish it with scientific documentation. We wanted to give concrete form to the idea of social accounting by researching into exposing the real aspects of the new forms of the organisation of leisure...When we told Otto Bauer of our plan to study the organisation of leisure he was annoyed and told us, 'you want to study leisure in a country which has suffered for a number of years from heavy unemployment. It is inconvenient if you want to do research; why don't you look at the consequences of unemployment in the long run?'. (Ziesel 1968:8)

It was Otto Bauer in fact who suggested to the members of the Forschungsstelle that Marienthal would be an ideal location for their study. Although most of the studies undertaken by the *Forschungsstelle* were ignored by the socialists as having little to say of political significance, Marienthal was the exception. It contributed directly to the socialists' stock of knowledge. Marie Jahoda (Lazarsfeld's first wife) informed me:

> When the work on Marienthal started going on we reported to the class [a social-intellectual club under the leadership of Otto Bauer which used to meet every second Sunday] and discussed it with various people. You

see before Marienthal came out there were two theories in the Austrian socialist Party abut what unemployment would do to people. On group said it would lead to revolution because people wouldn't take it, and the other group said it would lead to apathy and destruction. The debate was really solved by Marienthal which showed very clearly that it leads to apathy. So it was very highly regarded in political circles and anybody interested in social science'. (Jahoda conversation 26.9.73)

History of Lazarsfeld

Before commenting on Lazarsfeld's Vienna days it is worth noting his intellectual interest in the institutionalisation of knowledge, since, as I will show, the origin of focus groups is to be located within the activities of the Bureau of Applied Social Research that Lazarsfeld established at Columbia University in the 1940s. The Bureau represented not simply the vehicle whereby he would find a place for himself in a major university at a time when anti-Semitism, according to Lazarsfeld, made an appointment at Columbia difficult, but a break with the departmental organisation of research. The 'Bureau' represented a new organisational form of intellectual life, and one more appropriate for large-scale empirical social research that the traditional structure of a teaching department.

Through biography, and intellectual interest in the institutionalisation of knowledge, Lazarsfeld was keenly aware of the role of organisation in the propagation of ideas. The chosen title, for example, of his presidential address to the American Sociological Society was 'The Sociology of Empirical Social Research', in which he reflected on the fortunes of the Chicago School during its prime in the 1920s under such notable figures as Park, Burgess, Small, Thomas and Ogburn. At that time Chicago sociology held a dominant position, yet its influence waned rapidly in the face of intellectual competition from other graduate faculties. Commenting on this, Lazarsfeld noted: 'It is my guess that a more formal organisation for social research would have extended the influence of those great Chicago leaders after other graduate schools began to make their bid'. (Lazarsfeld 1962:763)[5]

---

5   Many factors were responsible for the decline of the Chicago School's position, not least of which were shifts in American society itself. James Coleman, who had gained is doctorate in sociology from Columbia University, but spent most of his professional life at the University of Chicago comments: 'The decline in the Chicago School was not merely a decline in the powerful personalities who shaped it. It was a decline in the kinds of problems that the Chicago School had focused on. Immigration had declined, urban life had become somewhat more ordered, the marginality of men decreased.' (Coleman 1980 quoted in Rogers 1994:195.) Coleman also points the rise of the Columbia School of Lazarsfeld and New York as the centre of the emerging communications industry, advertising industries and national marketing companies. As Everett Rogers comments: 'Instead of studying local community problems like the adaptation of European immigrants in Chicago and marginal or deviant subcultures that ensued, Lazarsfeld and the Columbia scholars were replaced and Park and the Chicagoans on centre stage of American sociology emphasised national-level research problem like the effects of mass media communication.' (Rogers 1994:195).

Lazarsfeld's knowledge of the history of education was such that he was well aware of the structural innovations that have occurred in higher learning as a response to new forms of knowledge. He also recognised that structural changes feed back into 'knowledge' itself: that there was a reciprocal process whereby new organisational forms, prompted by new forms of knowledge, produce in themselves new methods of analysis:

> The technical and organisational nature of empirical social research leads formal ideas to distinctions and inter-connections relevant for many well beyond the realm of strictly empirical research. My position is akin to the kind of sociology of knowledge which Marxists employ when they stress that new tools of production are reflected in new ways of intellectual analysis. (Lazarsfeld 1962:760)

Drawing on his own experience as a Bureau director, Lazarsfeld elaborated this point, arguing that the administrative need to make roles explicit in a research institute, to assign each individual specific tasks and to link those tasks to each other, generates in turn a need to make underlying methodological procedures themselves more explicit, and that as a result: 'The research operation can provide the model which helps to clarify and unify problems that arise in spheres of enquiry far removed from empirical research in the narrow sense. (Lazarsfeld 1962:760) The basic point, however, is the one already stressed, that new forms of knowledge often require a new institutional form to accommodate them. As Raymond Boudon, writing on the 'fit' between forms of knowledge and institutional frameworks, points out:

> The history of French sociology is suggestive on this point: after the decline of the Durkheimian school, in which scholarly work was entirely consistent with academic structure, the development of the social sciences after the Second World War led to institutes outside the universities, such as the 'Centre national de la recherche scientifique or L'Ecole practique des Hautes Etudes. These institutes were successful, because they modelled themselves 'Laboratories', a structure much more appropriate to the development of 'empirical sociology' than faculty positions. It is undoubtedly for this reason that, within a few years, 'empirical sociology' became the ideal for the new generation of French sociologists. (Boudon 1972:423)

In addition to appropriate institutional forms, the growth of new forms of knowledge also requires new forms of training to initiate new disciples and thereby ensure the form's continuation and extension. New institutional forms are usually accompanied by new teaching methods.[6] Take just two examples. The sixteenth century saw the integration into the university of humanistic studies as a new form of learning, characterised most specifically by the founding of the College of France and the establishment of the method of disputation as a way of training. It was the nineteenth century, however, that saw the creation of the

6 For a discussion of this see Lazarsfeld 1961.

modern integrated university, for which Germany led the way, the pattern being set by the University of Berlin, which initiated the seminar and the conducting of research under the guidance of a master.[7] The twentieth century has increasingly witnessed the teaching of the social sciences utilising the 'laboratory' model, and the Bureau of Applied Social Research was a prime case of this. It is not suggested that formal structures are always necessary for the continuation of a school of thought, but they do bestow considerable advantages, and indeed, one of the keys to the success of the Bureau in securing a firm place within American sociology was the fact that its structure included provision for student training. This formalisation of knowledge in the research institute, and the rigorous training provided at the Bureau under Lazarsfeld's direction, furthered the rise of the quantification wing of sociology, leading to the types of attacks upon its influence engaged in by such as C Wright Mills. Yet it was not as if Lazarsfeld, and also his colleague Merton, wished to turn out a generation of scholars bent on measuring the world through survey research. The triumph of the tradition, as with the dominance of any set of ideas, is a complex matter, but it is true that survey research proved useful to corporate, military, and civic interests. Measurement meshed with wider social ideas about the function and place of knowledge, but above all empirical sociology could demonstrate its usefulness, and what is useful is usually a good definer of what valid knowledge is considered to be. Funds thus flowed in the direction of empirically quantifiable research, further enhancing the prestige of such operational knowledge. Yet in accounting for the rise of quantification, and the extension of quantification within sociology, place ought also to be given to the fact that the techniques of quantification could be more readily taught than those of qualitative or more subjective research procedures.

In discussing the rise of empirical social research, Lazarsfeld was clearly impatient with the charges made against him that he was only interested in quantification. He admitted to me: 'I always found it silly, this scientism... to say that quantification is always better... than what you cannot count.' He went on for some time in such vein, and then in a half-apology said: 'The reason I want to take your time on this is I want to know how so many people get such a fixation [about me].' It was put to Lazarsfeld that perhaps one of the problems he faced was in the teaching of methods; given his interest in training students for research, it was much easier to pass on quantitative techniques than qualitative skills:

> That is quite likely...yes. The question of how to teach and even how to learn. You see if you take such masters as Erving Goffman... He is unable to say what he is doing and he isn't interested. Ask Goffman, could you give a course even on your own work, explaining what you do and how you do it – you'll find that a waste of time. (Lazarsfeld conversation 19.7.73)

---

7   The dissertation in German Universities, although under a 'master', was not guided in the modern sense of close supervision. Indeed, the student worked very much in solitary.

It is not suggested that one could ever, even if it was desired, turn out a generation of Goffmans, but one could turn out, if not exactly a generation of Paul Lazarsfeld's, then at least a generation of Lazarsfeld-type of researchers. Clearly Lazarsfeld, judging by his above comments, would agree with the possibility of this, and in practice that is what happened. In the 1940s the institutional framework for the training of graduate students in quantification had been established through the emerging research bureaux or institutes, often modelled on Columbia, that became attached to the graduate faculties of American universities. Furthermore, the social sciences, at least the quantification wing – and this includes focus groups that the Bureau undertook as part of war effort research – had demonstrated its worth to government during World War II, and the empirical wing of sociology was an increasing recipient of moneys after the War from philanthropic foundations such as Carnegie, Rockefeller, Ford and so on. In fact, such is the scale of giving engaged in by the American foundations that if it were not for expensive empirical work then it is hard to see, if they wished to support social research, how else they would rid themselves of such large sums of money.

It was the rise and dominance of quantification within sociology that horrified C Wright Mills and prompted his scathing and influential attack in 1959, in what was an attempt to inject what he felt was some much needed humanism back into sociology. (Mills 1959) Lazarsfeld was paraded as the arch-villain of sociology, but at the level of theoretical sociology Talcott Parsons came in for no less an attack, on the basis of his abstract or grand theorising. Maurice Stein had been a student of Lazarsfeld and saw fit to attack what he saw as the one-sided training he received whilst at Columbia. In one passage he states:

> The issue, however, is not evaluating the survey method, because that is impossible. For certain purposes, obviously, the survey method is the only way to obtain data, but it should never become the only kind of data that sociologists gather, for if it does thought is stopped before it starts. In fact, however, survey logic lends itself to such a thought-stopping role, as indeed does the logic of any method if it is consciously or unconsciously presumed to be the necessary or exclusive method. One of my favourite fantasies is a dialogue between Mills and Lazarsfeld in which the former reads to the latter the first sentence of *The Sociological Imagination*, 'Nowadays men often feel that their lives are a series of traps'. Lazarsfeld immediately replies, 'How many men, which men, how long have they felt this way, which aspects of their private lives bother them, do their public lives bother them, when do they feel free rather than trapped, what kinds of traps do they experience, etc etc etc.' If Mills succumbed, the two of them would have to apply to the National Institute of Mental Health for a million dollar grant to check out and elaborate that first sentence. They would need staff of hundreds and when finished they would have written *Americans View Their Mental Health* rather than *The Sociological Imagination*, provided that they finished it at all, and provided that either of them cared enough at the end to bother writing anything. (Stein 1964:215,216)

Lazarsfeld never really bothered to reply to his critics, but writing in his *Memoir* one finds the rather weary passage, which could be an exact rejoinder to Stein: 'Some critics oppose survey research as restrictive and one-sided, pointing to the Columbia tradition as an evil influence. It is useful to point out that, from its very beginning, this tradition stressed the importance of a diversified approach. Legitimisation, like women's work, seems never to be done.' (Lazarsfeld 1969:283)

John Rex, in a not too dissimilar vein to Wright Mills and Maurice Stein, casts Lazarsfeld as the 'guilty man of history'. Rex viewed Lazarsfeld as a man driven by a desire to turn sociology 'truly scientific':

> Neither Lundberg or Popper, however, was to have a truly lasting influence on sociology. The man who was to have such an influence was Paul Lazarsfeld. Lazarsfeld came to the United States having been brought up in the most profound European theoretical tradition, but became convinced that the social survey, already an established element of American political and commercial life, was the means whereby sociology could be rendered truly scientific.... What Lazarsfeld now envisaged, however, was the opening up of vast new fields of investigation through the specially designed survey which was committed to a quest for kinds of knowledge which no census could aspire to. The improvements of statistical techniques to take account of large numbers of variables, coupled with the technological revolution in data-processing equipment, made the prospects opened up by the new empiricism even more appealing. (Rex 1973:111-112)

Although it would be difficult to disagree with Rex's observation concerning the impact of Lazarsfeld on the development of empirical sociology, it is a definite mistake for him to argue that Lazarsfeld was 'convinced that the social survey could render sociology truly scientific'. Lazarsfeld was enthusiastic about empirical methods, but it was never a philosophical commitment. As Raymond Boudon correctly notes: 'Lazarsfeld would undoubtedly be the last to insist that all research should make use of questionnaires and proceed by the route of survey research'.[8] (Boudon 1972:424) In support of his assertion Boudon cites the passages in Lazarsfeld's *Memoir* in which Lazarsfeld summarised his Austrian research experience, and laid down his 'rules' of method as documented by him in 1933:

> For any phenomenon one should have objective observations as well as introspective reports. Case studies should be properly combined with

---

8 At Lazarsfeld's memorial service at Columbia University Robert Merton said: 'Throughout his working life, Paul took it as his "moral duty" to demonstrate the value and, in the social sciences, the frequent necessity of combining quantitative enquiry with qualitative insight. More than once, as he confronted overly-zealous sociometricians persuaded that numbers are all, Paul could be heard intoning the monitory words of St Augustine "So it is O Lord my God, I measure it and know not what it is I measure"'. (Merton 1979:20)

statistical information. Contemporary information should be supplemented by information on earlier phases of whatever is being studied. One should combine 'natural' and experimental data. By experimental, I meant mainly questionnaires and solicited reports, while by natural, I meant what is now called 'unobtrusive measures' - data deriving from daily life without interference from the investigator. (Lazarsfeld 1969:282-3)

Commenting on the above rules, Lazarsfeld wrote:

Mere description was not enough. In order to get 'behind' it a variety of data had to be collected on every issue under investigation – just as the true position of a distant object can be found only by looking at it from different sides and directions. (Lazarsfeld 1969:283)

It is dangerous intellectual history, such as that engaged in by Rex, to posit the presence of group of thinkers, the Vienna Circle of logical positivists in this case, in a particular location at a particular time, and then draw inference because of similarities of their thought to others outside the circle and deduce direct influence between the 'school' and that individual. The advantage of doing so, of course, is that one can then ignore the individual and simply criticise the school of thought, and even worse, collapse the complexities of the school of thought into some central tenets, in this case positivism, and discuss the 'related' individual in terms of such tenets. The effect of such a manoeuvre is to turn intellectual discussion into a political harangue without the need to address the individuals' ideas as such, and without the need to examine the merits of their ideas. It is also to give a philosophical or political position to an individual where one may not have existed.

Lazarsfeld did not have a philosophical position on quantification, and certainly never wished to turn sociology 'truly scientific' in the manner suggested by Rex. Rex's mentioning the presence of Karl Popper and Ludwig Wittgenstien in Vienna as somehow related to the ideas of Lazarsfeld is spurious. To begin, with Popper and Wittgenstein were never members of the *Wiener Kreis*, but then to see the Vienna Circle as a coherent school of thought is mistaken; it was more a loose amalgam of individuals sharing similar philosophical interests who came and went.[9] One can identify a core circle, but one has to appreciate the intellectual ferment and cafe atmosphere of Vienna in the early part of the century, where a whole variety of learned meetings took place without participants aligning themselves to the body of

---

9   Hans Zeisel (1979:11) does include Wittgenstein in the *Wiener Kreis*. He says of his days in Vienna with Lazarsfeld '...it was a memorable group of men: Schlick, Wittgenstein, Gödel, Waismann, Feigl, the socialist Otto Neurath. But in those days Carnap was the great event. His introductory lecture into philosophy was an unforgettable intellectual adventure. Students from all over the university were packing his lecture hall, having their first encounter with critical analytical philosophy that did not claim to know what is true, good, or beautiful, but limited itself to the modest analysis of what was meant by statements in science, aesthetics, and ethics.

ideas being discussed by the core members. Lazarsfeld certainly knew many of the inner members of the *Wiener Kreis*, but that does not make him a member, or even suggest that he was in any way primarily influenced by them. Although one can see in the quantification aspects of Lazarsfeld's work an alliance with the spirit of logical positivism, it must be noted that the positivism of the *Wiener Kreis* was not 'conservative' in the way that is often cast. Their list of approved thinkers included Marx, admittedly not Marx the philosopher, but Marx the historian, with his attention to facts that might be capable of verification.[10]

The process of verification was important to Lazarsfeld, but not by a single method, and certainly not by quantification alone. It was Lazarsfeld's absolute fascination with mathematics that 'drove' him, and not his desire to turn sociology 'truly scientific'. His interest in mathematics, furthermore, was not unusual among the circle of young socialist intellects at that time in Vienna. The convergence of intellectual interests between Lazarsfeld and the *Wiener Kreis* owed itself more to a common background than to any direct influence. It was the prestige of mathematics among the intellectual circle of Austro-Marxists that Lazarsfeld was deeply involved with that formed his interest in measurement and explication, and not logical positivism as such. In other words, Lazarsfeld's fascination with mathematics can be accounted for in many ways, and does not have to be traced to any philosophical school. To do so gives the impression that Lazarsfeld had a philosophical position on quantification. If that was the case then much that I will have to say later concerning his relationship with the Frankfurt School, and his appreciation of qualitative work, is hard to account for.

Fascination with Methods

The methods researchers select are in many ways a product not just of their own intellectual training, or decision about which method is best suited to the task, but a matter of personality. There is a impersonality about survey research that is missing from the warm exchange often generated within the close personal setting of a focus group. Lazarsfeld said that he himself had often puzzled over this question, and recounted that the psychoanalyst, Siegfried Bernfeld, had once questioned him as to why he wasted his time with statistics. He was unable to answer, and Bernfeld offered his own conclusion that Lazarsfeld's 'obsession' with statistics indicated a basic fear of people. Lazarsfeld was, without doubt, a complex person, yet his

---

10   As well as Otto Neurath – an economics sociologist – the *Wiener Kreis* also included mathematicians, philosophers and physicists. Moritz Schlick is considered the founder, but Rudolf Carnap was its most eminent member. The circle wished to contest metaphysical thought. They wished for a unified science to break with the strong Germanic tradition of a distinct separation of the natural and social sciences and humanities. They claimed that only two types of knowledge existed – the purely formal and the empirical. Empirical knowledge for these logico-positivists had to be capable of being put to scientific test to have philosophic validity. All other knowledge, although it might have meaning, was meaningless.

fascination with statistics cannot be reduced simply to Bernfeld's observation.[11]

Bernfeld, along with Erich Fromm and Wilhelm Reich, was one of the left Freudians who attempted to combine the Freudian theory of instinctual drives with Marx's class theory. Bernfeld was a student of Freud and director of the Children's Home for War Orphans (*Kinderheim für Kreigswaisen*) founded in Vienna in 1919. He was also influential on Lazarsfeld through organising holiday camps for children and young people in the Social Democratic Labour movement. (see Wiggershaus 1994:166) Indeed, Paul Neurath, the son of Otto Neurath, the polymath and a key figure in the formation of the *Wiener Kreis*, informed me that the first time he came into contact with Lazarsfeld was when his father took him along to one of these youth camps and he heard Lazarsfeld, as a socialist youth leader, deliver a moving speech to the assembled camp. Yet, despite his knowing Lazarsfeld well, and despite his training, Bernfeld's estimation for the reasons why Lazarsfeld should bother himself with statistics and quantification is, I feel, mistaken. If a psychological interpretation is needed, a more plausible one can be found. In the course of one discussion with Lazarsfeld I asked him to trace his fascination with statistics:

> Look, I have often thought about this fascination... it's like someone saying the first time they heard a violin play and they had to become a professional violinist, and you don't quite know why. Look, the anthropologists claim they saw a picture of some specific island and from then on all they were interested in was anthropology. I really don't know to what extent non-artists [feel this], to what extent non artists have this [feeling]. How would one call it, this experience of the only thing worthwhile doing... the composer, the first time he hears a piano and he's lost.

Yet, with what must be one of the great methodological ironies, Lazarsfeld informed me, 'and you know, this fascination with methods, it can't even be quantified'.

I asked Lazarsfeld to search his life for illustrations of this fascination. Three examples will suffice. Standing in front of a bookstall in Vienna when he was about nineteen years old he noticed a book which on the outside had a scatter diagram, the type one might use to illustrate a correlation. This caught Lazarsfeld's eye: 'I didn't know quite what it was, but I found it so exiting, God knows... like seeing at that age the photograph of a nude girl or something'. On another occasion, in about 1928 in Hamburg, he saw some ecological tables which Andreas Walter had brought back from a visit to Chicago. He commented, 'they were coloured by income levels. That had the same fascination for me, and I cannot trace behind that'.

Finally, and I think this reveals most about Lazarsfeld's mind:

---

11   It was not uncommon in Lazarsfeld's Viennese circle to be psychoanalysed. For example, his wife, Marie Jahoda, undertook psychoanalysis, but Lazarsfeld never did, or so Elizabeth Schilder, a close friend of Jahoda, thought.

I was in a meeting of the Socialist Young Workers Party and someone handed out questionnaires to show how miserable people were. He had got back questionnaires from two or three hundred people and suddenly I had this feeling... but why doesn't he code them, and I got the questionnaires. It never occurred to this man... he was just interested in misery, you see.

Whereas this man was only interested in misery, Lazarsfeld was interested in something else – order. How many men are miserable, which men are miserable, how long have they been miserable? Bernfeld's conclusion about Lazarsfeld, that he was afraid of people, may have some merit. There are peculiarities about his personal interactions that characterised the running of the Bureau and other research centres, such as always feeling more comfortable with people younger than himself, preferring their presence to that of older and more established figures; but then, in organisational terms, having been raised in the socialist youth movement of Austria, where as head of a *horde* of the *Rote Falken*, (Red Falcons) he became familiar with a style of leadership that was characterised by a loose hierarchy bound together by strong personal ties, and the subordination of members to the leader, who was usually slightly older than the rest of the group. Commenting on his early organisational experiences, Lazarsfeld said:

I was very active in the socialist youth movement. I had a ready-made group of satellites or knights. It was really... it was almost transferring my clique of younger people... by young I mean one or two years younger than I was... into this whole [research] activity.

He talked at some length about his days running a *horde*, and his subsequent administrative style:

Look, you have to get two things. The dominant theme for me was methodology and I could trace that back to when I was 17 or 18 years of age, but the second theme is the desire to build up the 'Bureau', which has guided my interests. The 'Bureau' was a social event. The joke - I was in the socialist children's organisation the *Rote Falken* – the Red Falcon – and I was running the children's group – it corresponds to a boy scout leader, and I have always had the feeling that I never stopped being that. So the 'Bureau' is just an extension of my experiences of running boy scouts – socialist boy scouts. (Lazarsfeld 15.7.73)[12]

12   The *Rote Falken* – Red Falcons – covered the age range 12-16 and were organised into *Horde* of not more than 10-12 members, although groupings of Horden did take place. An important factor of the *Rote Falken* was their mode of organisation or operation. The segmented leadership structure associate with the boy scouts movement was rejected in favour of the direct subordination of every *Falken* to the orders of their leader. At the zenith of the movement in 1932 it had a membership of 15,117. (Gulick 1948:Vol 1:609) Lazarsfeld was a leader of a Hordan, and he is probably right to characterise his administrative research style by reference to his time as such a leader where the atmosphere within the Horde was one of closeness and companionship, but always run on subordinate lines. Indeed Lazarsfeld informed me: 'Look, when I go back to Vienna now, they are all (ex *Falken*) ministers and Chancellors and such. They still classify themselves as belonging to this group. It has such a power over them'. (Lazarsfeld 25.5.73)

One of the strengths of the Austrian Socialist Democratic Party was the impact that it had on those who lived under its embrace and protection. Not only did the Party construct a semblance of order out of the chaos left by the imperial collapse, but in addition it brought purpose and direction to thousands of its supporters through its vast administrative apparatus.[13] The years that Lazarsfeld spent as an active member of the Austrian Socialist Party not only provided him with organisational expertise but, more important, a heightened sensitivity and appreciation of the benefits of organisation. It should not be imagined, however, that such experiences were consciously articulated or that they provided an explicit model for the running of the *Forschungsstelle* and other research centres, but rather that the manner of organisation of the *Forschungsstelle* was a logical extension of his experiences in a socialist youth organisation. To an Austrian socialist such as Lazarsfeld, the idea of collective team work, leadership and hierarchy seemed perfectly 'natural'.

Lazarsfeld's comment that I had 'to get two things' about him clear, his interest in methodology and his interest in building the 'Bureau', is not unrelated. Evidently every Christmas the graduate students at Columbia gave concerts in which the members of staff would be portrayed. One year Lazarsfeld was depicted as a would-be father, and at one point in the scene, according to Lazarsfeld, 'a student steps forward and asks me, 'Is it the child a boy or a girl' and I say, 'I don't know, I'm only interested in the method'. After recounting this story, he said:

> I know that is hard for you to believe. This interest of mine in the process of research, or any kind of research as a question of procedure, has since my student days been so dominant. It has always over-shadowed any substantive part of what I did, you see. (Lazarsfeld 15.6.73)

This interest in methods and statistics, was not, as Bernfeld suggests, a matter of being afraid of people, but a desire for order. His fascination with mathematics and anything to do with the expression of 'abstract' relationships stemmed, to some extent, from the chaos of his own life, both in an historical sense, and in a much closer sense. His personal life, to quote one close friend, 'was always such a mess'. In mathematics and its methodological offshoots he could engage a world where sense reigned and order was distilled by the power of his intellect. He found an order there that was missing elsewhere. That is why he grew excited by ecological maps coloured by income level, that is why he thrilled at the sight of a scatter

---

13 Hitler was not only impressed by the effectiveness of the Christian Socialists leader Karl Leuger's anti-Semitism, but also impressed during his Vienna days with the Social Democrats organisation. He described his response to watching the mobilisation of its member as one of awe: 'With what changed feeling I now gazed at the endless columns of a mass demonstration of Viennese workers that took place one day as they marched four abreast. For nearly two hours I stood there watching with bated breath the gigantic human dragon slowly winding by'. (Hitler 1968:38)

diagram and, intellectual reasons apart, that is why he liked the neat sorting of the Hollerith machine,[14] and why he so admired the organisation of facts within Samuel Stouffer's work, and could not understand what Robert Merton, his close colleague and friend, missed in Stouffer.

Disorder in the Empire

If at the individual level of operations Lazarsfeld's life was 'always such a mess' that it might have prompted the desire for 'order', then, following the collapse of the Empire, Austria itself was a 'mess'. True, the Socialist Party beloved of Lazarsfeld gave a semblance order in Vienna, but Vienna was surrounded on all sides by provinces hostile to her 'Jewish Socialism', and was relatively isolated as a consequence.

Apart from Warsaw and Budapest, Vienna in 1918 had the largest Jewish population of any European city, a population swelled even further by the thousands of Galician Jews who sought refuge there after the Russian invasion of Poland, and by the Hungarian Jews who flocked to Vienna after the fall of Bela Kun in 1919. According to the Census of 1934, nine tenths of all the Jews in Austria lived in Vienna, where they formed around a tenth of the city's total population.[15] More significant than their simple numerical presence, however, was their disproportionate influence on professional cultural affairs. 'Vienna was the city of Freud, Adler, Schnitzler, Kafka, Mahler, Reinhardt and Stefan Zweig... and 1,200 of the lawyers and 1,500 of the doctors, for whom Vienna was famous, were Jews'. (Bentwick 1967:467)

Jealousy of this manifest cultural sophistication and dominance lay at the root of a good deal of the resentment and bitterness that the Austrian lower middle class harboured towards the Jewish bourgeoisie. Norman Bentwick (1967:467) mentions that when Hitler marched into Vienna on 13 March 1938, the Austrian Nazis engaged in 'outrages' against the Jews which far surpassed anything witnessed in Germany. Indeed, 'anti-Semitism and anti-intellectualism were rolled into one abhorrent ball'. (Fischer 1974:135) Nevertheless, despite the rising tide of anti-Semitism Jews had some reason to feel at home in Vienna; the city was after all controlled by the Social Democratic Party, of which most Jews were members. But assimilation was far from complete and consequently a sense of estrangement remained. Jews were, in Peter Gay's apt phrase, permanently in the position of 'outsiders as

---

14 The Hollerith machine was patented in 1884 by Herman Hollerith. The machine involved a method which converted the information on punched cards into electrical impulses which in turn activated mechanical counters. The basic idea was that wire would go through the hole in the card and make an electrical connection with the mercury placed beneath. The resulting electrical current then activated a mechanical counter. Hollerith's system was first tested on tabulating mortality statistics in Baltimore, New Jersey and New York City, and was in use by the time of the 1890 US census.

15 Figure taken from Bentwick 1967:467.

insiders'.[16] This question of Jewish marginality was commented upon by Marie Jahoda:

> The intellectual professional class in Austria was a class alienated. It wasn't alienated individuals, because you know we ate together, and talked, and we felt very 'groupie'. We knew hundreds of people... we talked to artists, musicians, mathematicians and psychologists, and whoever you want to name – and economists. But the whole class was alienated from that impossible situation in which Austria was left after the 1918 revolution, and particularly in Vienna. Vienna could be the capital of a great empire, but as the capital of seven million people it was just out of proportion, and without a recognised function in Austria. (Jahoda 1973)

For the professional intellectual class, to which many Jews belonged, the collapse of the Empire brought not only the curtailment of function noted by Jahoda, but also a marked shrinkage in their social world. It was in this situation of being in a city and a social group increasingly isolated and driven in on itself, that the socialist Party became a key point of reference, identity and comfort for Viennese Jews, and Jewish intellectuals in particular. Thus, on the one hand one has Lazarsfeld, for reasons of personality, appreciating order, and on the other hand there was a world where order was constantly threatened, indeed, where the order established by the Social Democratic Party, was, in historical terms, false in that the certainty that had been created was, and this was obvious to most at that time, only temporary, or at least could not be sustained without a firmer political underpinning.

The similarities between Lazarsfeld's intellectual operation and the logical positivism of the *Wiener Kreis* was due to a common background, and not due to direct contact with members of the school. Before making acquaintance with members of the *Wiener Kreis* he was already teaching statistics at the Psychology Institut ('Institut', in Germany and Austria is the same as 'Department' in England or America). at the University under the patronage of Karl and Charlotte Bühler. The Bühlers had been brought to Vienna in 1923 specifically to develop systematic psychology. Statistics hardly existed in sociology or psychology at the University at that time, and it was Lazarsfeld who introduced the work of the English statistical psychologist Charles Spearman, as well as the statistical writings of Louis Thurstone into the Institut.

Despite his obvious cleverness, Lazarsfeld's position at the Psychology Institut was very junior, but it was the only position really available to him within an anti-semitic university, and one where sociology was very under-developed. In so far as the academic climate of the University was concerned Lazarsfeld had little room for manoeuvre, and it is this lack of scope that propelled him to establish a research institute – the *Forschungsstelle* – away from the University.

---

16 Although Gay (1969) uses this phrase to describe the alienation of the 'intellectuals' in Weimar Germany, it is similarly appropriate when applied to the Viennese intellectuals between the wars.

Nevertheless, Lazarsfeld's work is seen as important to the development of sociology within Austria, and by extension, through Lazarsfeld's own exile, for American sociology. Leopold Rosenmayr, professor of sociology at Vienna University in the 1970s, noted in researching the history of sociology in Austria:

> The development of sociology in Austria can only be rightly understood if one shows that in the central European sphere, after interesting speculative theoretical beginnings at the turn of the century, it lasted more than a quarter of a century before empirical research really developed which today forms an insoluble reciprocal bond with theory. Neither in France, nor in Germany, Poland or in the United States was this relationship missing to the same extent as in Austria. Nevertheless, empirical sociology which had its beginnings in Vienna around 1930, particularly through the work Paul Lazarsfeld, has enriched and helped methodologically improve American social research, and thus had its influence in the United States and beyond. (Rosenmayr 1966:12)

Although Rosenmayr's description of the position of Austrian sociology is correct, it should not be assumed that the contribution of Lazarsfeld to it was recognised at the time, or even for many years after. For example, a major history of Austrian sociology between 1918 and 1938 contains no reference to Lazarsfeld. (Knoll 1959) Ferdinand Westphalen, (1953) in what is an otherwise thorough historical overview of Austrian sociology, also fails to mention Lazarsfeld's work. Indeed, in an interview Rosenmayr confessed that before beginning his research on the history of sociology in Austria he was unaware of the existence of the *Forschungsstelle*. Where Lazarsfeld's work during this period is mentioned, as for example by Rene Konig, a false impression is given of its status at that time. Discussing the relative ease with which Lazarsfeld was assimilated into American sociology, Konig writes:

> Incidentally, we would like to mention that for most of the Austrian colleges the situation in this regard was quite different [from the Germans] in so far as the Austrian tradition, both in social science and in methodology, is completely incomparable with German conceptions in this field. Therefore the Austrian refugees and immigrants did not have to undergo the same changes as the German refugees. On the contrary, the continuity of their work has remained extraordinarily strong. This is the case for Lazarsfeld, Marie Jahoda, Hans Zeisel and others from the same group. Since their first report on *The Unemployed of Marienthal* from 1932, they have indeed contributed in the most impressive way to the development of empirical research in sociology. But this achievement, for them, was much easier to attain, since the Austrian logic of science has always been very different from German philosophical logic, in science in general and in social science as well. (Konig 1959:781-782)

Konig's view of the situation is based on the mistaken assumption that Lazarsfeld's work was representative of the mainstream tradition within Austrian sociology, when in fact it constituted a radical departure from that tradition. The Forchungsstelle stands out as a lone outpost of empirical sociology within Austria.

Although Max Adler held a chair of sociology at Vienna, and Max Weber gave visiting lectures, sociology was underdeveloped as a discipline, and what little that did exist was heavily weighted towards theory.[17] According to Knoll, the major figure within Austrian sociology was the economist Othmar Spann, who was, as Konig points out, a grand theorist and an implacable opponent of empirical research. In the course of discussing the search for sociological theories capable of encompassing the totality of social being[18] and the corresponding denigration and dismissal of 'middle range' theories, Konig notes:

> One of the most extreme cases of this attitude is to be found in Othmar Spann and his organic universe. For him, any attempt to do empirical research conveys the attribute of 'individualistic', the most severe condemnation in his vocabulary'. (Konig 1959:785)

The interesting fact about social enquiry in Austria is that it had a lengthy tradition of work in both sociology and in statistics, yet there was no collaboration between the two, despite occasional calls for rapprochement. In 1912, for example, a lecturer in statistics at Vienna, Frans Zizek, had published a book, *Soziologie und Statistik*, in which he lamented the lack of co-operation between the two disciplines and proposed that future collaboration should be a main priority for both. However, as Rosenmayr notes:

> Despite all this, another 15 years were to elapse since the publication of his work until the first conscious application of statistical methods in sociology. Not before the late 1920s did the interest in quantitative analysis of social problems which were studied with specifically devised methods, come to the fore. (Rosenmayr 1956:277)

In the meantime, sociology remained fragmented and underdeveloped as an academic specialism. Lazarsfeld went so far as to say that during his initial time at the university, there was no sociology. Earlier, however, the prospects of establishing a strong university discipline had looked distinctly promising. Wilhelm Jerusalem's book, *Soziologie des Erkernnes*, published in 1909, had been met with widespread acclaim within the emerging European sociological community, including a favourable review by Durkheim in the *Année Soziologique*.[19] Austrian sociology, however, failed to live up to its early promise.

---

17 For a good concise discussion of the emergence of sociology in Austria see Torrance 1976:185,219. Reflecting on his student days in Vienna at that time, Hans Zeisel (1979:11) says '....in those years empirical, quantitative research in the German-Austrian orbit; sociology was, in the main, still an armchair science'.

18 For a discussion of Othmar Spann and his school, see Landheer 1958.

19 See Rosenmayr 1965:275.

With the devastation brought by World War I, and the ensuing disintegration of the Austro-Hungarian Empire, the demand was for approaches that would contribute towards illuminating and solving the multitude of social, economic and political problems that confronted Austria. These problems, however, 'could no longer be solved with speculative attempts like those of Ludwig Gumplowicz and Wilhelm Jerusalem', (Rosenmayr 1965:276) and Austrian sociologists failed to respond to the changed situation by adopting empirical methods as part of their procedures. It was the social irrelevance of speculative sociology when faced with the new state's problems that was undoubtedly a factor in limiting the development of sociology within Austria, but it must also be noted that financial restrictions also militated against any move away from speculative and theoretical work into the realm of the empirical. The financial difficulties facing the new state were reflected in the universities' extreme impoverishment:

> The financial situation of the University of Vienna was in a critical state, and many professors could hardly exist on the miserable salary they received. An appeal was made to those who had amassed fortunes during and shortly after the war, and had so far done little to help their country, to come forward and assist the University. (Bullock 1939:105)

Arthur Koestler in discussing the controversy of the 'midwife toad' that enmeshed Kammerer and his theory of inherited characteristics and which ran counter to Darwin's theories of natural selection, noted the impoverishment of the Austrian professoriat: 'Within a few months the Kammerer family fortune had melted away. Worst hit, of course, were the white collar workers, including academics, reduced to starvation. Kammerer's salary amounted, in 1923, to the equivalent of £150 a year...'. (Koestler 1974:82) So bad was the financial situation that gripped the University of Vienna during the bitter winter of 1921-22 that the university had to be closed down because of lack of heating; the roof of the university had not been repaired since 1914.

Within such a situation, had empirical work been wished for, no money could have been found to fund it, certainly not extensive and expensive empirical work. Thus, not only was there no tradition of empirical sociology within Austrian sociology for Lazarsfeld to attach himself to, but no money to fund empirical studies. If empirical work was to be conducted it was not to be within the confines of the university, and, if Lazarsfeld himself was to 'advance' it was not to be within the university either.

For a person such as Lazarsfeld, coming as he did from a middle-class Jewish intellectual background,[20] entry into university was a matter of course, but a career within the University was not so easy, nor was the life of a Jewish student, once enrolled, comfortable.

---

20 Lazarsfeld's father, Dr Robert Lazarsfeld, was author of a book on Jurisprudence, *Das Problem der Jurisprudenz*, Vienna, 1908. In addition, his mother, Sofie Lazarsfeld, had written a book based on knowledge gained whilst working in one of the marital advice bureaux fostered by the Social Democrats (*Rhythm of Life: A Guide to Sexual Harmony for Women*, London 1934.

The Position of the Jew in Austria

The Social Democratic Party was the natural home of the Jew. Apart from the Communist Party, a small and ineffectual group until after the failed uprising launched by the Social Democrats in 1934, there was nowhere else for them to go. It was, as Karl Stadler notes, 'in this party that the great majority of Austrian Jews found their political home, and to which they gave some of its most brilliant leaders, like Otto Bauer,[21] Max Adler, the young Friedrich Adler and many more.'[22] (Stadler 1968:139) The party welcomed and valued Jewish intellectualism. In addition to providing a good proportion of the leadership, Jews filled a great number of the jobs calling for intellectual talents and professional skills, such as financial advisers, party lawyers, and authors of party literature. Jews, in fact, wrote the bulk of the trade union press and provided ninety per cent of the editors of the famous *Arbeiter Zeitung*.[23] (Buttinger 1953:80) In addition to the sense of purpose and security that committed membership bestowed, the Socialist Party also afforded points of contact with the social world of the working class, contacts moreover which were underpinned by an ideology of brotherhood and internationalism which acted as a buffer against the expression of anti-Semitism. According to Peter Pulzer:

> The worker did not see the Jew with the same eyes as the upper and middle classes. If they were exploited by a Jewish employer they generally knew that conditions in gentile establishments were no better; and the financier and the broker seemed a less immediate enemy than the capitalist. They did not fail to notice that there were many Jews... including some who could have led a more comfortable existence had they chosen to, who had taken up their cause. (Pulzer 1964:280)

This description is somewhat idealised, for although overt anti-Semitism might have been absent within the Party, undercurrents of tension lay not far beneath the surface, as this extract from a conversation with Elizabeth Schilder, a party activist and friend of Marie Jahoda, makes clear:

> D Morrison: Would you say that there was much antagonism between the Jewish intellectuals in the party and the workers?

---

21 Julius Braunthal, who became a leading figure in the party, records of the first time he was confronted with Bauer: 'When I listened to him for the first time -.in awe and admiration of course - I felt at once that from now on my life was bound to his, that there was no escape for me from the domination of his genius.' (Braunthal 1945:73) Buttinger mentions that Bauer was the only one who 'even before the World War I could stand up to Kautsky, Plekhanov, Mehring and Rosa Luxemberg in international socialist discussion.' (Buttinger 1953:170)

22 The principal Austro-Marxists were: Friedrich Adler, Max Adler, Vicktor Adler (not related to Max), Otto Bauer, Adolph Braun, Robert Danneberg, Julius Deutsch, Gustav Eckstein, Rudolf Hilferding, Karl Renner and Therese Schelinger. See Bottomore and Goode (1978) for biographical notes on the principal figures and for a very good overview of Austro-Marxism along with translations of some of the leading thinkers' writings.

23 The *Arbeiter-Zeitung* was the main daily newspaper of the SDP, founded in 1891 by Viktor Adler, the founder of the SDP, and was edited from 1862-1931 by the illustrious Friedrich Austerlitz.

E Schilder:	No, not really. Bauer you see, it was... these leaders of the party were intellectuals.
DM:	But you said earlier that there was a slight antagonism.
ES:	It was, yes... there was a sensitivity in the party at the Jewish people, for instance, and at the role of the Jewish people. They were big in the party. There existed anti-Semitism among the students at the university. Of course that's all changed now - nobody dares.
DM:	Was the anti-Semitism such that a Jewish socialist intellectual would experience such pressure?
ES:	Well, I didn't know enough of Paul Lazarsfeld - he was by his exterior a type of Jew, his movements always were very Jewish. An intellectual Jew, and it is possible that he had the feeling not to be... that he had not a chance to be a leader of the party by his Jewishness.

Marie Jahoda had no doubts that the fact that Lazarsfeld was a Jew hampered his political career within the Party:

> Well, Paul was very political. When I eventually came to know him closely, he had great political ambitions, you know, the youth movement, and I think the great dream of his life would have been to be Foreign Minister for Socialist Austria one day, but much more in the political party, because of the terrible never-disappearing anti-Semitism in Austria. You know, Paul was so obviously Jewish and he just didn't have a chance in the political party. You know, other young people did make a spectacular career in the Social Democratic Party, but for Paul it was difficult because he was so very intelligent that nothing on the second level would have suited him, and the fear of general reaction to a Jewish dominant figure in the party was very strong. (Jahoda 26.9.73)

Jahoda should have said, reaction to 'another' dominant Jewish figure in the Party, since its leadership was heavily Jewish. However, it was really only after the failure of the 1934 rising and the defeat of the *Republikanische Shutzbund*, the armed wing of the Party - there was even an *Akademische Republikanische Schutzbund* - that the undercurrent of distrust towards Jewish presence in the Party which blocked Lazarsfeld's political ambitions turned to outright resentment. The Jewish leadership was held responsible for the tactical blundering of the *Schutzbund* and for the dragging of feet for years over the issue of armed conflict, when it was clear that civil war was in the long run inevitable. Of the 20,00 members of the *Shutzbund* who reported for action to the Party labour settlements, and other pre-arranged meeting places, only 10,00 saw combat and even they fought in isolated groups without a coherent plan and with inadequate communications. (See Gulick, 1948: Vol. 2. 1278) The bad military planning was certainly a factor in the failure of the uprising, but it was the failure of the called-for General Strike that finally sealed its fate.[24] The intellectual make-up of the leadership of the Party was rounded upon by the workers and mocked for scurrying off to Prague to write more revolutionary pamphlets. Up until that time anti-Semitism within the Socialist Party, although undoubtedly present, remained covert and implicit. Outside the Party's orbit of influence, however, Jewish members were exposed to the full virulence of anti-Semitism, and nowhere more conspicuously so than at the University of Vienna.

If the Jewish intellectual was somewhat cushioned from anti-Semitism within the Social Democratic Party, such protection did not extend as far as the university, within whose precincts Jewish students, and particularly socialist Jewish students, were subject to frequent abuse and attack. Indeed, the University of Vienna was probably the most anti-semitic in the country. Anti-Jewish demonstrations and attacks were greatly facilitated by the autonomy of the university: anti-semitic students could beat up Jewish students with impunity from police intervention. Ironically this privilege of autonomy had been bestowed on the university as a reward for the students' participation in the liberal revolution of 1848, in which Jewish students played an important part. Reflecting on his own days at the university, just prior to the World War I, Martin Freud remembered:

> At high school I had been used to Jews being in a large minority, but this did not apply to the university, of course. The students came from all parts of the vast Austrian empire, those from the German Alpenlander being convinced German nationalists. They were organised into societies *Burschenschaften* mainly on the pattern of the German universities. It happened often enough that they broke into lecture halls shouting *Juden hinaus* and kept it up until the Jews and the

---

24 If there was a time to fight it was certainly before February 1934, possibly in March of 1932 when Dollfuss abolished representative government when many rank and file members wished to fight, or really in July 1927 when a clash between the *Frontkampfervereinigung* – a paramilitary force of the right – and the Schutsbund resulted in killing of at least one member of the Schutbund and a child. The trial of the *Frontkampf*, who were hated by the Republicans for their wishing to join with Hungary, led to the acquittal of the *Frontkampf* members. A demonstration followed and 89 worker were killed by government forces and 1057 were wounded. Although some Shutzbund members uncovered arms and attacked police stations, the SDP leaders failed to give the call for insurrection. If that was possible in 1927, by 1934 the SDP was in no real position to fight. Raids on the armouries of the *Shutzbund* had severely depleted the SDP's weaponry, but of more significance is that in the opening hours of the battle key figures responsible for the distribution of weapons were captured. Not knowing the exact location of the hidden weapons many of the *Schutzbund* remained unarmed throughout the entire three days of the battle. But the SDP's continued failure to take a stand against Dollfuss had left many rank and file members disheartened. Thus, Konig, president of the Railway workers Union had voted at the time of the uprising against a call for a general strike, fearing that his members would not respond. (Gulick 1948: Vol. 2: 12281). In fact, the railway workers had some six months previously joined Dollfuss's Fatherland Front (Buttinger 1953:75) illustrating some of the disintegration that had already set in within the Party. The general strike was thus only half-hearted.

very few Jewesses had gathered up their books and filed out in despondency. (Freud 1967:206,207)

Koestler gives a rather similar account of his days at the university in the mid-twenties. He comments that about half the students wore colours; that is, they belonged to one of the duelling fraternities (*Burschenchaften*). Relics of medieval times, 'strange fossils', as Koestler calls them, they still dominated the University during Lazarsfeld's time there. Rather like the *Wandervogel*,[25] or youth hiking clubs, they retained too much independence of spirit to be tolerated by a Fascist state and were banned by the National Socialists, even though in many respects the ethos of both was close to National Socialist sentiment. The socialist students, for example, never formed *Burschenchaften*, but the Jewish students did. Indeed, singled out for duels by the Pan German Korps, the Jewish *Burchenchaften* not only became remarkable skilled at duelling, but developed a great enthusiasm for such combat, to such an extent that fearing their ability, the Weidhofen resolution was passed ruling that because Jews were devoid of honour, no satisfaction could be attained by duelling with them. As a result the traditional form of institutionalised violence collapsed and the University of Vienna became the scene of a series of bloody and undignified riots. Martin Freud recounted the occasion when he was barred from entry to the university by the mayhem of such riots:

> One day when I arrived at the university, the entrance was cordoned off by police and I could not get in. The police were there because a gang fight was going on between the balustrades which edge the two broad sloping approaches to the university. The adversaries were German-Austrians and Jewish students. They fought with sticks and fists. (Freud 1976:207)

This anti-Semitism was not restricted to the student level, but was present among sections of the staff at the university; although doubt was cast on this

25 The German *Wandervogel* represented a revolt against authoritarian schools, parental education and to a large extent society – although the movement itself was not particularly articulate about such matters. It was basically a middle-class phenomenon beginning in 1896 and ending in 1914 or 1933 depending on how one characterises the essence of the movement. It was always a movement of a minority, and although accurate figures do not exist, the membership of the movement proper probably never exceeded 60,000. (Crossman 1962:9) The movement encouraged a spirit of adventure and freedom from the restraints of adult society. It set great store on upon comradeship and self-organisation, engaging in outings to the woods and mountains, often very long trips indeed. A strange feature of the movement was the replacement of rejected adult values with values abstracted from the tectonic myths of the past. Attachment to glorified myth of the middle ages with knights, vassals and guilds gave the *Wandervogel* an air of unreality. As Walter Laquer comments: 'Their return to nature was romantic, as were their attempts to get away from a materialistic civilisation, their stress on the simple life, their rediscovery of old folk songs and folklore, their adoption of medieval names and customs.' (Laquer 1962:6) Although some of the mysticism and romanticism, plus elements of asceticism can be seen as a precursor of some aspects of Nazi ideology it would be wrong to consider that the Hitler Youth Movement was a continuation of the *Wandervogel*.

in conversation with both Professor Berta Karlick and Professor Rosenmayr. Karlick had been a friend of the Jahoda family and had studied mathematics with Lazarsfeld. Asked if there was much anti-Semitism at the University, she replied:

> *B. Karlick:* No, I shouldn't say there was. There was strong tension among the students. There were certain groups who felt very nationalistic and anti-semitic. These groups were a provocation to other students who gathered together in other groups - for example, the socialist groups, and there were actually unpleasant fights among the groups.

> *D. Morrison:* Very savage?

> *BK:* Yes, people thrown over the balcony, but this was almost always at the student level. There were some young assistants who were also sympathetic with the anti-semitic groups. I had no contact with such groups, but maybe there was, there was certainly a very liberal spirit among the professors. The professor of this Institut [physics] who was my professor, and the director – he was Jewish – and the second professor of the Institut under whom Marie Jahoda's brother worked for his thesis was also Jewish, and there were several Jewish assistants in the university. I was non-Jewish, you see. This was perfectly uninteresting to the group of professors. (Karlick 19.10.73)

This image of the professoriat as relatively liberal and untouched by prejudice was endorsed in an interview with Professor Rosenmayr. He argued strongly that Lazarsfeld's Jewish background would not have hampered his academic advancement, and gave as evidence the fact that one of the university's most celebrated professors – Sigmund Freud – was a Jew. The facts do not support the case.

Ernst Fischer, writing about the famous Jewish editor-in-chief of the *Arbeiter Zeitung*, Friederich Austerlitz, comments that it was Austerlistz's secret hope that on the occasion of his sixtieth birthday he would be awarded an honorary doctorate by the Faculty of Law - it never happened. Fischer adds the biting comment to the sorry tale that 'At the University of Vienna even Sigmund Freud got no further that a professor *extraordinarius*'. (Fischer 1974:138) In the Austrian university structure a professor *extraordinarius* is not a very powerful or prestigious position. It is not true that Freud never made Professor Ordinarius; he did, but he never truly enjoyed the full status normally associated with such a position. (Jones 1953: Vol. 1, p375) Also, he had been at one time in the junior position of *Privatdozent* for the extraordinarily long time of twelve years. He only achieved his professorship, furthermore, through the system of *Protektion*, which was rampant, when one of his patients, Marie

Ferstel, gave the Minister of Education a famous painting that he badly wanted. (Jones 1953: Vol. 1,p374) So frequently had Freud been passed over for promotion in favour of younger people that he had considered leaving the university altogether. As Freud's biographer, Ernest Jones, notes:

> The anti-semitic attitude in official quarters would have been decisive in itself but Freud's reputation in sexual matters did not further his chances. Against these considerations, the splendid work he had done in neurology, and his European standing as a Neurologist, counted for nothing. (Jones Vol. 1,373)

Perhaps it is not surprising that Karlick and Rosenmayr should consider anti-semitism to be absent among the professoriat, but prevalent among the students. One was more visible than the other. No matter how anti-semitic the individual, one would not expect a full professor to engage in throwing Jewish students over a balcony, but one might expect such anti-semitism to manifest itself in blocking the career of a Jewish student or young Jewish assistant. Pulzer points to the prevalence of anti-semitism among the staff, and points to the demand for introducing a quota system on the number of Jews attending the university.

Radical anti-semitism among Austrian students was almost universal – beatings-up of Jewish students at Vienna were regular. The Austrian students enjoyed the sympathy of many of the teaching staff, who joined them in demanding a quota system on the models of Hungary and Poland. Indeed, only the intervention of the law court prevented the implementation of new statutes drawn up along those lines. (Pulzer 1964:08)

Such was the anti-semitism among the staff at the university that the academic senate of the university did pass a population quota of the type mentioned by Pulzer, but the *Verfassungsgerichtshof* (the court which ruled on constitutional matters) ruled on 20 June 1931 that such a move was counter to the Republican constitution. Although a repeated attempt was made by the Minister for Education, Czermac, who introduced it to parliament, it never actually became law despite passing its first reading on 30 June 1932. (Siegert 1974:36) There is evidence that as early as 1925 Czermac was involved with the 'Spann Circle' to limit the number of Jews at the university. The transcript of a meeting of the 'Spann Circle', at which Czermac was present and took notes, reveals interesting evidence of the anti-semitism among some staff, but also of their anti-liberal feeling and of the relationship between the two. Commenting on the transcripts Michael Siegert notes: *Den Feind nannte man die Ungeraden, ein Geheimwort für Juden, und der Jude wieder ein Deckbild für den Liberalen.* (Siegert 1974:35) [The enemy has been called the 'Ungeraden, (odd or non-conformist), a cover word for Jews, and the Jew was a cover picture for the liberal'.] Although Othmar Spann was Professor of Economics, because of the structure of the university he dominated sociology, although as stated, sociology was underdeveloped. In terms of the presence of anti-semitism within the social sciences it is noteworthy, therefore, that the notes made by Czermac reveal that

Spann attacked his fellow professor of economics, Mayer, for supporting the *habilitation* of two Jews – Wiesser and Schlesinger – and Mayer himself for liberal tendencies within his own teaching.[26] It is difficult not to conclude that anti-semitism within the University of Vienna was endemic at all levels, and it undoubtedly restricted Lazarsfeld's career. For example, the *habilitation* referred to above was a necessary condition for becoming a *Dozent* (lecturer), but in order to *habilitieren* one not only had to submit advanced post-doctoral work, but, of special importance in the present context, it was essential to have the sponsorship of a professor.

When Lazarsfeld was interviewed in New York, he made only passing reference to his position as a Jew within the University of Vienna, but did say that it was an important fact in his leaving for America. Perhaps it was an oversight on my part, but I never really pressed him about his student days as a Jew within an anti-semitic university, as likely as not because at that time I was unaware of the depth of anti-semitism within the university. However, I took the opportunity to follow up his comment when visiting Vienna and talking with his past associates, although it was impossible to check statements given by documentary evidence in Lazarsfeld's own case. Nevertheless, it has to be assumed, as a starting point for enquiry, that Lazarsfeld was not somehow unique and escape the effects of such prejudice. The whole question was taken up with Dr Gertrud Wagner:

26   Othmar Spann was an influential figure on the extreme right. His ideas of society as an organic unit certainly had affinity with the idea of a Corporate State. (See Bottomore and Goode 1978:69) Indeed, he appears to have been 'intellectually' of assistance to the *Heimwehr*, the miliarty force which assisted Dollfuss to power. The *Heimwehr* had come into being during the winter and spring of 1918 as voluntary defence units to protect their homes and property from marauding bands of ex-soldiers, and in areas such as Carinthia against attacks from the Yugoslavs. As they developed, however, these units were used not only against foreign enemies but also against Marxists, the enemy 'within'. This in turn led to political, military and ideological links with similar movements in German such as the Stahlheim, a paramilitary force of the far right and a source of trouble to the Weimar Republic. The material support for the Heimwehr was provided by Seipel, leader of the Christian Socialists with aid from the large banks, and by Mussolini, but rising as it did from the ranks of the peasantry, and led by members of the petty bourgeoisie, plus an assortment of faded aristocrats and pensioned-off officers, it lacked firm ideological underpinnings. It was Spann who furnished the Heimwehr's lose beliefs with a groundwork of theory onto which both purpose and respectability could be grafted. Although it is doubtful how much grasp the *Heimwehr* had of Spann's ideological system, it seized on the concept of the corporate state. As Jedlicka notes: 'Groups of influential intellectuals, such as the German club in Vienna, intervened in this discussion about the *Heimwehr's* programme. The club, a meeting place for businessmen academicians belonging to radical and German national groups, arranged a series of lectures in which both Professor Spann and Dr Richard Steidle, and well as representatives of the German Stahlheim took part to discuss a programme. Its first objective was to alter the constitution; the ultimate aim was to set up a new type of state... Walter Heinrich, a colleague of Spann's, was the main proponent of the idea of a corporate state. (Jedlicka 1966:137) What was wanted was a rival of the stand, which in this context is best seen as a state structured according to occupational status – *Standestaat*.

D Morrison: In conversation Professor Lazarsfeld seemed to be very aware of his Jewishness and the part that it played in his life. How far would it be correct to consider that he would have had great difficulty in gaining a senior post at the university because of the existence of anti-semitism?

G Wagner: Well, it's true, he couldn't have.

DM: Rudolf Carnap was a professor and Carnap was a Jew.

GW: Yes, and Charlotte Bühler was a Jew herself or at least partly Jewish. Well, he couldn't have at that time... Carnap [one of the leading figures of the *Wiener Kreis*] was much older, you see. Paul was not only Jewish, he was a social democrat. His family was a very well known socialist family – very friendly with Friedrich Adler. For him it would in fact have been impossible to even get 'Habilitation' and there might be all sorts of difficulties. I don't know. Karl Bühler, who was the main professor there – he would have had to have him put forward because Charlotte Bühler was only assistant professor, and Karl Bühler couldn't do it.

DM: Why was that?

GW: Oh, he wouldn't do it, he was afraid of that. One could say... now I interpret... I don't know because he never said to me. His wife was a Jewess, or at least... and he managed to get her a post. One couldn't refuse to let her teach and he probably thought – well, that is all my colleagues at the senate will allow me and I can't put forward any other Jew because in his Institut there existed – the main assistants were two women Jews. I don't know whether Paul spoke about it to you – a woman named Wolf. She became a professor in America but is dead now, and a woman named Else Frenkel, and she got married to a professor but I can't remember his name. Anyhow, Wolf was the main assistant of Karl Bühler and he did make her... I feel either he really couldn't anymore at this stage – they wouldn't accept it or he was frightened to. (Wagner 9.10.73)

The 'professor' whom Else Frenkel married was not in fact made a professor, but only appointed to the post of *Privatdozent*. His name, which Wagner had forgotten, was Egon Brunswik. The significant point is that he was a gentile. Although Else Frenkel (Brunswik) was passed over for promotion due to her being a Jew, she later became famous as Adorno's co-author on the authoritarian personality studies in America. Fortunately, following the Wagner interview, I saw Lazarsfeld again, and took up Wagner's account. According to Lazarsfeld, Bühler believed that there was a blacklist at the university against Jews, and because of that he promoted Brunswik rather than Lazarsfeld. Whether there was an actual blacklist is difficult to say, but there was certainly a political culture that operated against the possibility of Jewish scholars becoming established within the university, and that included Lazarsfeld. Yet Bühler was a 'patron' of Lazarsfeld, and no doubt would have promoted him if he could have, or felt it wise to attempt to do so. Lazarsfeld appreciated Bühler's position and informed me that his own feeling was that by way of consolation Bühler recommended Lazarsfeld to the Rockefeller Foundation for a travel fellowship - the fellowship that was to launch his career in America.

The fact that Lazarsfeld was a Jew did make for difficulties at the university, and at the same time produced a sensitivity and awareness of his marginality. However, the marginality that Lazarsfeld always felt existed beyond the psychological level. His background and training made him marginal to his environment in many other ways. Marie Jahoda made an insightful comment:

> You know, Paul says he is a marginal character – he's right because he was really in his research style an American long before he went to America. But he had the advantage of the much more deep and broad intellectual education that one used to get on the continent. Researchers in America are trained in statistics and question-asking and they go ahead and they are technicians. While Paul for many years was familiar with all the major strains of thought in Austria of his time - and so he brought this extra, not just methodological technician thing with him to America. (Jahoda 26.9.73)

Two

Lazarsfeld, Politics, Mathematics and Social Research

W hat one sees in Lazarsfeld is creativity in marginality, together with blocked aspirations in both the most personal and the wider sense, that a collapsing social world could not accommodate the dream of a whole class, and a particular social strata – the liberal middle-class intellectuals. On the opening page of his magisterial work tracing the political history of Austria from the Hapsburgs to Hitler, Charles Gulick states:

> To a degree unique in the history of nations the story of Austria between the world wars, particularly between 1918-1934, was that of the fight for and against the aspirations and achievements of the working-class movement. Otherwise stated, this struggle was that between democracy on the one side and reaction and Fascism on the other in political, economic and social fields. The decisive majority of the democratic element was composed of workers. As long as it was possible they and some of the middle class and peasant allies fought by democratic means... on the floors of city councils, through the printed page and over radio... but when Chancellor Dollfuss succumbed to the temptation of authoritarian ideology and began the installation of a native-born Clerical Fascism, they continued the battle in the streets, in the courtyards and on the staircases of the municipal apartments of Vienna as well as in other localities. (Gulick, Vol. 1. 1948:1)

Excluded from the possibility of high office within the Social Democratic Party, and excluded from attaining a place within the university, Lazarsfeld's creative energy was channelled into social research that whilst not overtly political helped form a bridge to social action. It was, however, the prestige of mathematics within Vienna, especially within socialist circles, that pushed him in the direction of quantitative social research:

> You see, in the socialites in Vienna there was a sub-set, and we were very influenced by the importance of mathematics... the sub-set of Friedrich Adler. So there was a convergence of social science and some kind of mathematics... it could easily be Wittgenstein and positivism, or it could be econometrics or relativity theory and Mach. Mathematics had a great prestige. (Lazarsfeld 25.5.73)

The Friedrich Adler referred to by Lazarsfeld was the son of Viktor Adler, the founder of the Social Democratic Party. Friedrich Adler became a revolutionary hero for his assassination of the Prime Minister, Count Stürgkh in 1916, whom he held accountable for much of the slaughter during the war. In reflecting on the history of the Austrian labour movement Otto Bauer, leader of the SDP, called the assassination 'the turning point in the history of the labour movement' in that 'to the masses, who had lived in hopeless and inactive despair, he became a hero who had offered his life to avenge their suffering'. (Bauer 1925:30) After Adler had been sentenced for the murder of Count Stürgkh a demonstration of popular sympathy erupted in the court and carried on out into the street. Lazarfeld was among the demonstrators, and arrested along with thirteen others for his part in the ensuing fracas.

Adler epitomised the atmosphere within which Lazarsfeld grew up in Vienna, with its peculiar combination of political dedication and academic scholarship.[1] During his student days Adler had been a friend of Einstein and in 1908 competed against him for a professorship in physics at the University of Zurich. There seems little doubt that Adler would have been appointed over Einstein due to the socialist leanings of the Zurich Canton's education board if Adler had not informed the board: 'If it is possible to obtain a man like Einstein for your university, it would be absurd to appoint me. I must quite frankly say that my ability as a research physicist does not bear even the slightest comparison to Einstein's'. (Florence 1971: 44-45)

Adler was the organiser of the Karl Marx Association in Vienna, which had always taken an internationalist and anti-war stance, but he was also a scholar, and after his sentence of death he continued, whilst in prison, to work on relativity theory. Lazarsfeld, in the company of his mother, Sofie, who was a family friend of Adler's, was a frequent visitor to the fortress of Stein where Adler was being held. In his biography of Adler, Ronald Florence writes of this period in Adler's life:

---

1   The close knit nature of the academic circle of Vienna at that time can be gathered from Zeisel's note that he and Lazarsfeld '...knew Alfred Adler well'. Zeisel goes on to comment on Adler's influence on psychoanalysis and then mentions, '...before he turned to curing souls, he was a paediatrician; Paul and I had been his patients'. Freud evidently remained outside this close knit circle of academics. Zeisel states: 'Freud remained for us, for Vienna generally, an outsider, almost a mystical figure, although on my way to school I passed his home in the Berggasse almost everyday'. (Zeisel 1979:11)

> Fritz was relatively happy in prison...each week he was allowed two visitors, and the regular visits of Viktor [father] and Emma [mother] or of Sofie and her children were the perfect interludes in his studies. With Paul and Elizabeth, Fritz would discuss their school work or books they had read. He convinced Paul that mathematics was a good foundation for any future studies. In turn Paul helped Fritz by typing the smuggled manuscripts. (Florence 1971:278)

For Lazarsfeld, to visit Adler imprisoned in Fortress Stein, some forty miles up the Danube, was undoubtedly exciting, and he recounted the encouragement Adler provided to continue with his mathematics:

> Well, here you know you have a rather glorious hero. Adler corresponded with me. I have a letter... I reported to Adler my progress in school and I have a letter from Adler in 1916. I was 15... 'Dear Paul, I'm glad to hear that you are doing well in mathematics. Whatever you will do later mathematics will always be useful to you'. You see that undoubtedly is of considerable interest if a glorious murderer wrote it to you from jail, to stick at doing mathematics. (Lazarsfeld 25.5.73)

It would not seem, however, that Lazarfeld applied himself to his studies. In fact when he first arrived at the University of Vienna he did not immediately specialise in mathematics, but enrolled for a variety of subjects, in particular, *Staatswissenschaft*. When seen in its cultural context *Staatswissenschaft* is possibly best translated as 'state-craft', although its modern equivalent would be political science. It combined law with economic and political theory to provide a basis for entry to the civil service. Describing his career as a student, Lazarsfeld commented:

> One term I was enrolled in a social science course and then the next term I was doing *Staatswissenschaft* and then sociology... and the next term I was enrolled in mathematics and so on. But I didn't do much work in any, as I was so politically active. (Lazarsfeld 25.5.73)

With Vienna in political ferment it is perhaps not too surprising that Lazarsfeld never gave himself over to his studies in any especially serious way. This was confirmed by one of his fellow students, Berta Karlick: 'I think he was more interested in social problems than in studying physics and mathematics'. (Karlick 9.8.73) Gertrud Wagner provided further information about Lazarsfeld's time as a student:

> Paul studied physics and mathematics because he was a very bright young man — what would he chose? — he didn't know exactly what to chose. I think he wanted to become a teacher. You see, he was an ardent socialist with educational interests and he wanted to become a teacher. So what subjects should he chose? Well, if he is bright and he has good marks in physics and mathematics, why not them? As a matter of fact he really left physics and mathematics as his field of interest in the middle of his study and he only ... it took him one or

two years longer than it needed... he only finished it because of his mother. She was a very strong person and insisted that he finished it off. (Wagner 9.8.73)

He did eventually graduate in mathematics but, as he noted in his *Memoir*, after several years studying mathematics and staatswissenschaft, 'It was almost accidental that I ended up with a doctorate in applied mathematics'. (Lazarsfeld 1969:274) In discussion it transpired that when a choice finally had to be made as to which subject to follow for his doctorate, mathematics was selected for the pragmatic reason that he simply had more credits in that area than any other area.

Although Marie Jahoda did say that 'Paul's interest in mathematics was simply irrepressible', his political involvement and concern over social issues did not make for single-minded pursuit of mathematics at the university. However, despite Lazarsfeld's deep political commitment whilst in Vienna, the work undertaken there was not overtly political.[2] Marie Jahoda said of the work that Lazarsfeld's group undertook on the life-style of Viennese beggars:

> We just walked up to the beggars and said, 'Can I buy you a cup of coffee?' Then learned of their profession in unstructured interviews. Then we did another study during the Abyssinian War. We went to the general population and let them draw a map of Africa, and Abyssinia comes out as three quarters of Africa... you know, highlighted perception in response to public events. We did a lot of studies of this nature. Small interesting studies which inherently are of social interest, but this is no more and no less political than all social science has to be and I think Paul had a little conflict in his life over, or had at least in those years, over his political ambition, and the impossibility of fulfilling it in the Austrian situation. So a personal solution was to be concerned with social affairs whilst not influencing them in a leading fashion. I think to that extent the work was political, but if I try to see the contribution objectively, I see him all the time as an outstanding methodologist, and never its content. (Jahoda 26.9.73)

If there was conflict in his life between the desire to occupy a formal position within politics, and the inability to do so, which was resolved by undertaking social enquiry, his background in revolutionary politics was not entirely absent from his work. For example, while working on *Jugund und Beruf* (Youth and Occupation) Charlotte Bühler, although appreciating the work, heavily criticised Lazarsfeld for the importation of ideology to the style of reportage:

---

2 Lazarsfeld did write, however, for *Der Kampf Sozialdemokratische Monatschrift*, the monthly journal of the SDP. It was founded in 1907, and edited by Otto Bauer, Adolf Braun, and Karl Renner, and then later by Friedrich Adler who in 1924 became its main editor. Contributors at various times included: Kautsky, Trotsky, Ernst Fischer, Julius Braunthal, Otto Neurath, Alfred Adler, Adolf Sturmthal, Hendrick de Man. (See Bottomore and Goode 1978:296)

...she objected strenuously to the tone in which my section on proletarian youth was written. I was, indeed, full of compassion, talking about exploitation by the bourgeoisie society.... I could not deny this fact, and finally rewrote it. None of the argument was omitted but the tone became descriptive and naturalistic instead of critical. (Lazarsfeld 1969:285)

According to Lazarsfeld this episode affected his subsequent writing and was 'a contributory factor to the debate on the role of sociology led by C Wright Mills', but also, I would argue, led to confrontation with Adorno over his 'critical' style of writing while working for Lazarsfeld on the Rockefeller Radio Research Project. And the Marienthal study, although a moving account of the effects of unemployment, and a politically important work in the sense of answering questions about forced idleness on political consciousness, has none of the stridency of language that marked the first draft of *Jugund und Beruf*.

In terms of political engagement with social questions through research, the original intention of Lazarsfeld was not to examine unemployment at all, but leisure, and it was only the rather angry intervention of Otto Bauer that resulted in the Marienthal study. Although the members of the Lazarsfeld group, 'knights' as he called them, were undeniably political the research undertaken was informed by a background of political influence rather than the outright entry of politics into the *Forschungsstelle*'s operations. There could be no escaping the brute facts of political life in Austria following the collapse of the Empire and the struggle for existence of the First Republic as it fought for survival amidst the growing development of the corporate state, and there was certainly no escape from politics for those embraced by the structure of the Social Democratic Party. Malcolm Bullock goes so far as to say, 'That for a worker to exist it was necessary for him to be a Social Democrat and to belong to a trade union, and all employers had to deal with the unions'. (Bullock 1939:114-115) Indeed, up until 1927 a worker could be dismissed for not belonging to a union, and the Party's influence stretched well beyond the place of work and into every crevice of existence.

From the very beginning, as already noted, the Party laid great store on unity and on presenting a unified front to the outside world. As Mary McDonald notes, 'They tried with this end in view, to prevent the members of the Party from coming into contact with people of other opinions who might influence them and draw them away from the Party orbit'. (McDonald 1946:72) Such isolation was only possible because the Party looked after the worker's every need. Intellectual needs were all satisfied within the Party; it provided his flat, a kindergarten for his children, social and leisure clubs and protected him at his place of work. For Lazarsfeld and his circle of intellectual middle-class socialist friends, to be a member of the SDP was to breath the very air of radical politics, as active participants in the unfolding drama of Austria between the Wars. This was especially so in Lazarsfeld's case through his family's close friendship with the Party's leaders and principal thinkers. For example, in discussing his 'living in the custody of Rudolf Hilferding' (Lazarsfeld 1969:284) in the summer of 1916, Lazarsfeld referred to the leading thinkers of the Party: 'These people were all, so to say, my uncles in some way. When I was 13 or 14 the first serious book I read was probably a book by Kautsky' which Hilferding had given him. (Lazarsfeld 15.6.73) Despite this close personal involvement with leading Marxist thinkers, and his embrace of the Party, one would look in vain in Lazarsfeld's work for the type of political intervention through scholarship that is the associated mark of academics who are Marxists.[3] Nevertheless, his work can be seen to 'float' on a residue of socialist sentiment. Indeed, there was a political ambivalence to Lazarsfeld in that his socialist background does not automatically support the likelihood of a close association with corporate America.

In the course of one interview, where his relationship with the Frankfurt School was raised in the context of the debate surrounding mass culture, Lazarsfeld explained himself and his position by saying:

> Look, you have to understand that I had no interest whatsoever in mass communications. I mean – everything in a way is interesting to a methodologist, but I certainly didn't find that in the beginning an important topic at all. It was exclusively that it [the Rockefeller Radio Research Project] was a rather spectacular job, and then my conviction that anything you do research on is interesting. But the way I got interested, really interested in the mass culture debate was my ambivalence. On the one hand I got money from the industry – everything depended on that – and on the other hand I was tied to a team – my union card as a socialist. So I continually tried to mediate between the culture critics. (Lazarsfeld 15.6.73)

The ambivalence, as he calls it, deriving from his socialist 'union card' stamped while in Vienna, and his financial entanglement with the culture industry in America, is clear to see in his introduction to the collection of essays *Culture for the Millions* (Lazarsfeld 1959), where he adopted an intermediary position between the leftist critics and the straightforward managerial apologists. His socialism, while not impregnating his work to any marked degree remains, nevertheless, as a point of consciousness and even conscience. Clearly the manner of his management of research when in America shows an incorporation and acceptance of extant social arrangements that is missing in his Austrian days. But then, the historical situation faced by Austria was one that drew its citizens into fundamental questions concerning political arrangements, and Lazarsfeld, along with his whole group, could not fail to be affected by the ambivalent position that the SDP itself faced. At the objective level the Austrian Socialist Party was

---

3   John Torrance says of Lazarsfeld: 'Lazarsfeld and his colleagues were no doubt humanitarian social democrats rather than doctrinal Marxists.' (Torrance 1976:200)

suspended between success and failure, which at the subjective level lent an air of unreality to life in Vienna.

Splendour and Disintegration

Prior to the collapse of the Empire in 1918, the working class of Austria had little effective political voice.[4] The end of the old social order was swift and sudden when it came, but it had been preceded by premonitions of its own demise which gave proceedings a certain ethereal air. This atmosphere was at its strongest in the imperial showpiece of Vienna which 'on the surface had never seemed more vital than when it was dying'. (Crankshaw 1974:328) As Ernst Fisher wrote of the city:

> For a couple of decades, however, Vienna was in fact one of the most interesting cities in the world: the Vienna school of medicine, of music, of political economy, positivism, Austro-Marxism, psychoanalysis, Sigmund Freud, Gustav Mahler, Arnold Schoenberg and Karl Kraus. As a rule things tended to come to Austria later than elsewhere; not so the premonition of impending catastrophe, the heightening sensibility, the loss of reality. Something was coming to an end... not only the monarchy, not only the century but a whole world, 'fawned by decay'. (Fischer 1974:76)

The 'decay' was the rotting of the structural support upon which the empire was built, eaten away by the nationalistic aspirations of its peoples outside German-Austria, which eventually pushed Austria towards war in an effort to maintain its imperialistic grip. The Empire was not destroyed through social revolution by the German-Austrian or even Magyar proletariat, but rather by the national revolutions of the Czech, Polish and Yugoslav bourgeoisie. The proletariat did not offer a particular threat to the Empire's continued existence; it was only after:

> ...the Slav nations broke away from the Empire, only when the collapse of the Empire had become inevitable and was imminent, did the proletariat in Austria and Hungary revolt. The Empire was not disrupted by the proletariat revolution, but the disruption of the Empire awakened and unchained the proletariat revolution. (Bauer 1925:74)

The desertion from the Empire of its various national parts thus provided both the opportunity and the impetus for the Austrian working class to seize the remnants and, in particular to capture Vienna. Imagining the Vienna of Straus and the Waltz, it is easy to overlook poverty as a bed-rock feature of the lives of most who lived in the city. For example, Vienna had the highest death rate from tuberculosis of any city in Europe.[5] Although written for propaganda purposes, Hitler's description of the slums of Vienna when he

---

4   See Buttinger (1953: 70) for the lack of political influence of Austrian labour before 1918.

5   See Bullock (1939: 110-111) for the conditions of the Viennese working classes.

lived among its populace prior to World War I offers a good account of conditions:

> Even more dismal in those days were the housing conditions. The misery in which the Viennese day labourer lived was frightful to behold. Even today it fills me with horror when I think of those wretched caverns, the lodging houses and tenements, sordid scenes of garbage, repulsive filth and worse. (Hitler 1973:27)

The culture most normally associated with Imperial Vienna was the culture of a narrow strata, but before the First Republic it was the cultural capital, not only of the German-speaking people, but of South and East Europe also. The culture was, however, 'the decadence of a remarkable civilisation centred on the rich administrative capital of a disintegrating Empire'. (Crankshaw 1974:325) This decadence was that of a specialised culture deriving from a limited ruling elite of nobility and higher bureaucracy; an elite that was possibly more tightly knit than anywhere else in Imperial Europe. Restricted as this elite was, it had nevertheless made an art form out of social grace and charm, and had stamped Vienna with a distinctive gloss. In its support for the arts, the theatre and the opera, it offered a splendid display of talent, yet this group was in decline even before World War I. As a social group it was overwhelmed by the rising middle classes of its own empire, with their thrusting national self-determination, and finally by its own working class. The unfolding of these forces pushed up against the ruling elite to create ripples in society that lapped against the confidence and security of other classes.

Its obvious decline affected very closely the mood of the middle classes, who for so long had identified the court and the great families with the Empire itself; this alone would have been enough to induce in the thoughtful a mood of uncertainty and self questioning. Uncertainty all to easily turned into defeatism in face of apparently insoluble problems posed by the nationalities and their drive for self-expression. (Crankshaw 1974:325)

Accompanying this defeatism in politics went a mood of desperation in the arts, a last thrust which injected life into a dying capital. This appearance of cultural vitality could not banish the harsh political realities that would soon consume Vienna. However, the changing order of relationships within the Empire which were beginning to resonate as waves of alarm for the ruling elite refracted as hope for the determined organisation of labour. It was against this political backdrop, but in particular the sheer deprivation of the working classes, that the Social Democrats made rapid progress in becoming a mass party; indeed, Hitler looked on with admiration at the ability of the Social Democrats to mount huge political demonstrations and parades, and drew important lessons concerning the management of emotion that he would later successfully apply in Germany.

Although the working class were emerging as a serious political force before World War I, it was the War itself which gave the necessary dynamic twist by the injection of militancy and which also provided political opportunity. The War not only compounded the deprivation of the working class by the increased militarisation of the economy to meet the needs of its unforeseen length, but the appointment of military overseers in industry produced conditions of primitive servitude; summary punishment for non-performance of tasks became commonplace.[6] This increased hardship transformed itself into political anger which, when added to the military defeats inflicted upon Austria towards the closing stages of the war, when the hard-pressed German military machine could no longer offer its assistance as it had so often done in the past, saw a radicalisation of labour. With the Italian offensive and the breakthrough in the Bulgarian sector, the front began to collapse and in doing so took the Empire with it. The returning soldiers, many of whom still retained their guns, forced the establishment of the Republic. As Otto Bauer, well positioned to observe, noted: 'The social revolution which arose out of the war proceeded from the barracks rather than from the factories.' (Bauer 1925:56)

With the final secession of the various non-German territories of the Empire and the ensuing collapse of the monarchy the position of the Austrian working class was transformed from a struggling movement to that of inheritors of a revolutionary situation. The disappearance of the monarchist structure meant that practically overnight the old ruling elite of archdukes, ministers and courtiers became redundant. As Karl Stadler (1971:81) comments: 'The Habsburg Empire went to its doom, leaving behind no constructive idea, but only memories and unsatisfied longings'. So far as the monarchists were concerned their world was fractured beyond redemption, and the bourgeoisie, although not broken, were, amid the economic destruction accompanying defeat in war, a class stripped of power and confidence. The real power had been transferred into the hands of the workers and soldiers councils.

The new Republic was the collapsed rubble of a once great empire. The treaty of St Germain which was imposed by the allies in a somewhat similar spirit to the imposition of the Treaty of Versailles on the Germans, reduced the Hapsburg Empire from fifty million people to a mere six and a half million, of which two and a half million lived in Vienna.[7] The newly established state was, in Clemenceau's words, 'that which was left over after the break-up'.[8]

In describing his harrowing return from the battle front, and the situation that greeted him in Vienna, Ernst Fischer recorded: 'When the end did come and the new social order installed, no one believed in the new state's viability. Everyone regarded it as an interim measure'. (Fischer 1974:76) The social and economic disruption produced by the shattering consequences of a lost war produced a

---

6   See Gulick (1948 Vol. 1:36-37) for the description of the militarisation of society, particularly the harshness of conditions in the key war industries. Being drafted to the 'front' was a not uncommon response for industrial disobedience.

7   See Bullock (1939:68) for these figures and for a discussion of the consequences of such a drastic reduction in the population.

8   See Stadler (1971: 106) for this quote and for a discussion of the Treaty of St Germain.

state of uncertain longing. The monarchists, filled with contempt for the 'social rabble' that had replaced the old ruling court circle, cast glances back to a glittering past, the Pan-Germans wished for a rightful home among the German Volk, and the Social Democrats looked for their socialist ambitions to be fulfilled among the powerful German labour movement. All these forces worked together to discourage any firm belief in the future of the new state, a lack of commitment to which produced a stark provincialism.

Far stronger than any loyalty to this new and strange republic was the local patriotism which their distinct history, dialect and mixture of blood had engendered among the inhabitants of each province. When the unifying power of the Hapsburgs had gone, every man felt himself a citizen of his province: a Styrene, a Carinthean or a Viennese. (McCartney 1926:94)

Such was the imperial legacy that the Austrian Social Democrats had to work with, and it may be added, against. The poverty, the vacuum of power, the radicalisation of the working class, and to some extent the peasantry, offered favourable conditions for a left revolutionary party to build its membership and extend its influence. The old order was not simply fractured, to reveal glimpses of a possible future order, but exploded wide open so that new possibilities were clearly visible to the rank and file. The leadership of the Party, however, distanced by their intellectual training from the immediacy of events, perceived the dangers of possible failure and drew back from testing the opportunities presented. Bauer, reflecting on this period and his role as leader of the Party, noted:

> Large sections of the proletariat did not realise these dangers. It was the duty of Social Democracy to see them. Thus, a double task devolved upon Social Democracy; on the one hand, by taking advantage of powerful revolutionary agitation among the masses and the severe shocks which the capitalist social order had suffered, to capture for the proletariat the strongest and most permanent positions in the state and in the workshops, in the barracks and in the schools; but on the other hand, to prevent this revolutionary agitation from developing into civil war and open collision with the superior forces of the Entente imperialism, which would have opened the gates of famine, invasion, and counter-revolution. (Bauer 1925:91-92)

The fact remains that by only 'capturing for the proletariat the strongest and most permanent positions in the state' and not actually capturing the state itself, the Austrian Social Democrats dug their own graves. Even if Bauer's analysis of the situation was correct and defeat would have followed from an attempt to push through the revolution, the decision to draw back merely postponed defeat; it did not prevent it, only the executioner and the time of execution was changed. What ought not to be overlooked, however, is that in the interim period social changes did take place that would not otherwise have occurred. It was the whirlwind of social reform following the establishment of the Republic that Lazarsfeld was caught up in. The socialism of Austria was peculiar among the socialist movements of that time, in its intensity, its success, and its lived expression. Henry Brailsford, reflecting on his life within socialist movements, notes of his time spent in Vienna:

> It has been my good fortune to see something of several continental socialist movements, in Moscow, Budapest, Madrid and Salonica as well as in Paris and Berlin. I can recall several talks with Jean Jaurès and it was for years my habit to read everything this humane and generous thinker wrote in his organ *L'Humanité*. Much of it I still remember clearly. I shared the respect which all who knew them felt for the organising talent and the disciplined steadfastness of the Germans. But it was among the Austrians that I felt most happily at home. More ardently and steadily than any other continental party they lived socialism as a creed that covers the whole of life. It was for them so much more than a political tactic and an economic programme. (Brailsford 1945:8)

The Party's strength lay in its combination of hope for the millennium with the benefits of hard pragmatism and concrete social improvements. For those who embraced the Party its influence was deep, and indeed, lasting. Lazarsfeld was duly affected. Some of his passion and affection for the Party can be gauged from a small but unpublished paper on methodology which he delivered not long after his arrival in America, entitled 'An Index of Class Consciousness'. John Marshall of the Rockefeller Foundation had organised a discussion just prior to the outbreak of World War II. The topic was the measuring of socio-economic status, in the course of which Lazarsfeld said that he could not agree with Lloyd Warner's psychologistic point of view because he considered himself a 'Marxist on leave'. One passage reads:

> ...there were certain songs which made your heart beat more quickly, the sight of the Red Flag at the big demonstrations, the wearing of the Party button at all possible occasions. This element of being demonstrative about one's Party affiliation and emotionally attached to it is almost impossible to recapture in this country, where no major labour movement exits which could elicit such reactions.

Lazarsfeld's attachment to the Social Democratic Party is clear enough, but the new state itself, in so far as the German-Austrians were concerned, was seen as 'Provisorium and Transitorium, and not the culmination of their hopes'. (Stadler 1971:106) The Treaty of St Germain had not only torn away 43.5 million people from the Empire, but in doing so had robbed it of its economic viability, a fact that was to have disastrous consequences for the future success of the Social Democrats' Programmes. Dr Karl Renner,[9] a Social Democrat and the first Chancellor of the new Republic, protested to the Supreme Council of the Reparations Commission in Paris about the conditions imposed on Austria, not only documenting the appalling distress being suffered in Vienna, but

---

9   See Kann (1951: 243-249) for a brief discussion of Karl Renner.

warning of the dire consequences that might follow if nothing was done to relieve Austria of the burden that had had been imposed in defeat. He warned:

> If this mission fails and if it were impossible to feed the people, the coalition government, which was chosen by a democratic parliamentary election with five-sixths of the population behind it, would not remain in office. Only a Bolshevist adventurer would dream of assuming power in succession to it. (Quoted in Bullock 1939:79-80)

The reference by Renner to Bolshevist adventurers captures the reformist nature of Austro-Marxism. Indeed, the sympathetic biographer of Dollfuss somewhat mockingly said of the Social Democrats: 'They were even in those days among the oddest and most unsatisfactory of Lenin's disciples to be found anywhere on the continent'. (Shephard 1961:29) Strictly speaking the Social Democrats never were, or even claimed to be, disciples of Lenin; although the make-up of the Party meant that many rank and file members were sympathetic, especially at the Republic's founding, to the military revolutionary seizure of power. The Communist Party, although numerically small, was both noisy and vigorous, constantly pushing for the dictatorship of the proletariat. They were not without a certain success, and met the Social Democrats on equal footing in the workers' and soldiers councils. Their agitation resulted in several bloody clashes with government forces. For example, encouraged by the proclamation of the Bavarian Soviet on 18 April 1919 the Communists launched an assault on the parliament building which resulted in loss of life. With the failure of this attempt to seize power, Bela Kun sent Ernst Bettleheim to Vienna with instructions to succeed where others had failed. A much more threatening situation faced the Republic since the only force at its disposal was the *Volkswehr* (People's Army), which had been hastily recruited by Julius Deutsch, the Under Secretary for the Forces, and later the creator of the *Republikanische Schutzbund* – Defence League of the Social Democratic Party – to protect the Republic. The *Volkswehr*, however, was extremely unruly and was pervaded by revolutionary ideas.[10] Even so it was the bullets of the *Volkswehr* that put down the next and most serious attempt at insurrection, leaving twenty dead and eighty wounded. The defeat of the Communists clearly demonstrated the ineffectuality of its propaganda among the *Volkswehr*, and its real lack of inroad into the support that the Social Democrats had established among the soldiers and the workers as well.[11] However, so long as Bela Kun remained in power in Hungary the Communists within the Austrian Republic derived both sustenance and hope. It was only with the fall of the Hungarian Republic and the crushing of the Munich Soviet that the Austrian Communists' chance of fermenting revolution collapsed

---

10 See Braunthal for a very good first-hand account of the militancy of the *Volkswehr*, especially the 41st battalion known as the Red Guard, and their visit to his office in the Ministry to insist on the creation of a Socialist Republic.

11 See Braunthal (1945:232) for a good account of the attempted seizure of power and the loyalty of the *Volkswehr* to the Republic.

entirely. Furthermore, the spectre of counter-revolutionary violence, and the fear of the internecine fighting between left forces that had swept Germany in 1918, produced a salutatory effect among the left revolutionary romantics, pushing them back into the folds of social democratic influence.

Although the Republic was a coalition of political forces consisting of the Social Democrats, Christian Socialists and German Nationalists, the Social Democrats controlled Vienna. This gave the rank and file supporters a false sense of their own power, but the slogan '*vom rotem Wien zum roten Österreich*' (Red Vienna never did become Red Austria) never became a reality. Vienna was surrounded by a hostile countryside, although originally the peasantry was not especially antagonistic to the Republic. For many their experience in the War had ruptured their organic conservatism, with considerable numbers joining the soldiers' councils. It was on return to village life, disillusioned with the directional shifts of the Republic, and once more under the influence of the Catholic Church, that their revolutionary spirit melted away. Hostility towards the proletariat, who they had to feed, grew with time and found encouragement not only from the Church, but also from the urban trading class who shared the peasant's dislike of the centralised food distribution system that had been created to feed a starving Austria. It was this alliance between the petit and middle bourgeoisie and the rural peasantry, eventually transformed into a genuinely reactionary movement, that formed the backbone of opposition to the Social Democrats and eventually crushed the Republic.

It is difficult to say what the course of Austrian history would have been had the Social Democrats been a genuinely revolutionary movement, but even if they had been, they could not have withstood the forces of reaction that were developing outside their borders in Germany. But from the very first, Austria was not in control of its own fate; or at least, at the subjective level, the leaders of the Social Democrats did not believe that they were in total control. As McCartney notes: 'as statesmen they could do nothing; as socialists only so much as would not call down a stoppage of supplies.' (McCartney 1925:103) As much as revolutionary fervour swept Vienna, the leadership of the Party was always cautious to remain within the bounds of reforms acceptable to the entente powers. Fear over a stoppage of supplies was only one fear; another was the fear, not unreasonable, of direct military intervention by the entente should Austria opt for a Bolshevik-style Republic. Otto Bauer writes bitterly of this period:

> Immediately after the armistice, the Austrian government had addressed a petition to Wilson, to facilitate the import of foreign foodstuff into the starving country. On the 24 November, Wilson's answer reached us. It promised the import of foodstuff upon one condition: that 'peace and order' were maintained. Wilson's note of the 18 October had unchained the national revolution. Wilson's note of the 24 November demanded the closure of the social revolution. The Western powers now confronted the proletarian revolution in Austria as the protectors of bourgeoisie peace and order. (Bauer 1925:80)

Austro-Marxism was a product of a specific historical situation and encompassed an amazing mixture of hybrids. It contained elements of enthusiastic Messianism combined with sober Fabianism, especially after 1903 with the founding of the Fabian-type society *Zukunft*, which, according to Norbert Leser, 'exerted a lasting and widening influence on the entire structure and performance of Austrian socialism'. (Leser 1960:117-118). To complicate matters further it managed to combine revolutionary Marxism with reformist trade unionism.[12] Party unity, however, formed a central goal of the Social Democrats, a unity that produced its own contradictions. Such was the history of the Austrian labour movement that the appeasement of warring factions had been central to its development from the start. The Social Democratic Party of Austria had only began officially in 1889 in lower Austria. This late arrival of a working-class party to Austria was due largely to the splintering of the working class into moderate and radical factions, to such an extent that unified development was severely hindered. The tasks of unity, of gelling the working class into a coherent movement, fell to Viktor Adler. Using his weekly paper, *Gleichheit*, to the full Adler made constant appeals for rapprochement with the left. The memory of those early days never left the Austrian Social Democratic Party, thus there was never for them the pain of Leninist splits, but rather the exercise of a 'permanently synthesising influence on polarised elements of Marxist thought'. (Leser 1960:21)

However, the competing points of reference that constituted the Party, added to the sturdy pragmatism of Otto Bauer himself, ensured that the Party tripped and stumbled with each fresh turn of events; yet always waiting with insistence for the right 'objective factors' to pronounce the 'real course of history'. The ghosts of old fictional battles were never fully exorcised. They hovered over the Party, making it a poor tool of true revolutionary change. But the threat of intervention by the entente should Austria not curb the ardency of socialists elements within the country was real enough. Even so, the fact is that for a whole variety of reasons, despite the far-reaching social reforms that were enacted by the Social Democrats, private capitalism emerged unscathed from the threatening transitional period of Empire into Republic.

The Social Democrats never in any fundamental sense altered property relationships. Legislation was passed to bring under public control the largest feudal estates, but its impact was small. In addition, several state-owned corporations which had been for the most part orientated to the war effort were brought under a new form of management (*Gemeinwirtschaftliche Anstelle*) whose aim was to rescue those industries facing difficulties over transition to a peace-time economy. These organisations, run jointly by the workers in conjunction with the State and replacing the old imperial bureaucratic administration, left industry, as did the nationalisation laws of 1919, basically in private hands. It was this failure of a thorough-going nationalisation scheme, especially the failure to nationalise the important *Österreichicher Alpine-Montanggesellschaft*, that had far reaching repercussions and according to Leser was 'destined to seal the fate of the Republic'. (Leser 1966:126)

---

12   See Braunthal (1945:17).

Indeed, the *Alpine-Montanggesellschaft* was Austria's most important heavy industrial combine, and a rabid opponent of organised labour, from which the Christian Socialists launched the para-military *Heimwehr* in their final assault on the Republic.[13] The failure, also, to nationalise Austria's most important banks which in the main controlled all the crucial industries undermined the Social Democrats' ability to hold back the forces of reaction, and led Trotsky to deride the Social Democrats as 'the guardian angles protecting the Vienna *Kreditanstalt*'.[14] (Trotsky 1965: Vol 111: 913)

The position of the Social Democratic Party in Vienna, controlling the city and pushing through social reforms, in particular massive slum clearance and the establishment of huge housing projects, but yet not securing absolute dominance of the state apparatus, nor being able to push through the transfer of ownership of the means of production to the proletariat, thus fundamentally altering property relationships, gave to the Party an air of 'suspended success'. Viewed through the lens of history, Leser's judgement is that: 'It was Austro-Marxism's tragedy to neither have heeded Renner's plea for unequivocal acceptance of parliamentary democracy, nor to have forgone the pleasures of brainstorming revolutionary rhetoric and of supplementing it with dedicated action'.[15] (Leser 1966:130) In reflecting on the political achievements of the Social Democrats and their massive building programme, Shepherd, perhaps somewhat unkindly, comments, 'Breitner's Vienna tenement houses and Bauer's universal pipe dreams were socialism in the end; there was nothing in between'.[16] (Shepherd 1961: 30)

---

13 It should be pointed out that the socialists' failure to nationalise the *Alpine-Montangesellschaft* did not result from an oversight or even lack of socialist zeal, but was due to the failure of the socialisation commission which, under the direction of Professor Emil Lederer, and with the connivance of Professor Schumpeter, let the combine fall into the hands of Italian shareholders. From that point there was no possibility of nationalising without direct allied intervention occurring, and since the Republic was not in a strong enough position to face such an eventuality the socialisation plan had to be dropped. See Bauer (1948:155-157) for a detailed discussion of this 'failure'.

14 The Vienna *Kreditanstalt* was one of the most important banks in Austria.

15 Karl Renner was an authority on government, constitutional law and administration.

16 Breitner was municipal treasurer. Before the war, out of 555,000 dwellings in Vienna, one half consisted of apartments of two rooms only, a situation which worsened during the war since no house building took place. Through massive municipal spending the Social Democrats by 1934 owned nearly half the city. See Bullock (1939:108-110) for a discussion of the housing achievement. Although Johnson, a critic of the social democrats, accuses them of 'gerrymandering' by dotting the city with municipal houses in previously conservative areas. See Johnston (1972:75). The big tenement blocks such as the Goethe-Hof, the Engles-Hof and the Karl Marx-Hof were considered by the right to have been built by the Social Democrats as forts to strategically lay down fire in the city. It is true that the Schutzbund drilled in the huge enclosed courtyards, and that weapons were hidden in some of the blocks, but no military strategist would have considered using them as fortresses, especially the Karl Marx-Hof since it was over-looked by the *Hoher Warte* (a football field) from which the governments cannon could, and did, fire directly down onto the complex in 1934.

Lazarsfeld's comments on the Social Democrats, while still holding great fondness for the dreams of that time, were not that far removed from Shepherd's more deliberately critical observation:

> It never took a stand on the work system... the Party was more important than what it did. And if you look back at the history of the Austrian Party the great idea was the unity of the Party... but this unity was bought, as one can see now in retrospect, by complete ineffectuality. The Party became bigger and bigger, and everyone lived in it, but it had no influence on political events. (Lazarsfeld 25.5.73)

Lazarsfeld even referred to the period just after the war as the 'failed revolution', and said that that 'those of us on the socialist side were very much affected by this ambivalence', that is, living in what looked and felt like a transformational socialist period, but which was not:

> I remember we had this joke. I quoted somewhere that a rising revolution needs economists, the victorious revolution needs engineers, the defeated revolution needs social psychologists. And in one way or another that was quite an obvious thing to do. (Lazarsfeld 25.5.73)

The 'obvious thing to do' is a reference to the establishment of the *Forschungsstelle*, which, he informed me, enabled 'this whole defeated socialist group' to transfer to 'a new activity which was close enough to social reality and had some academic glamour'. When it was put to Marie Jahoda that Lazarsfeld's interest in 'action' (*handlung*) stemmed from his political background in Austro-Marxism, particularly his interest in voting[17] and how the individual comes to the point of decision-making, she replied:

> I think so. Not in a completely articulated fashion, but you know all the time Paul was in Vienna and was Director of the *Forschungsstelle* it was still a time that he was very conscious that if he only could, he would be in politics rather than social research, so you know I don't recall a conversation in which he said 'look we are fundamentally interested in politics and this is why we have to study "action"', but obviously... (Jahoda 26.9.73)

---

17 From a very early age Lazarsfeld was interesting in voting procedures, indeed, the mention of Hilferding giving Lazarfeld a book by Kautsky to read was that Lazarsfeld had asked Hilferding to explain electoral systems and Hilferding finding that rather childish said he would do so on condition that Lazarsfeld read Kautsky. But his academic interest in voting behaviour stemmed from his working with Charlotte Bühler upon how people developed their occupational plans. Evidently Lazarsfeld was obliged to substitute the occupational study for a voting study since the conservative university of Vienna made it unwise for a member of staff to engage in an unbiased study of people's voting decisions. However, he was then presented with the difficulty of analysis which was only resolved with the aid of Lotte Danziger who had knowledge of American market research techniques. Given that occupational choice was a much more complicated phenomenon, because if its longitudinal nature, than consumer choice, Lazarsfeld at first concentrated on the latter in order to tackle the former. As Lazarsfeld, in his Memoir, noted: 'Such is the origins of my Vienna market research studies: the result of the methodological equivalence of socialist voting and the buying of soap.' (Lazarsfeld 1969:279)

The Forschungsstelle and new forms of Knowledge

New forms of knowledge require new institutional settings. By the late 1920s in America the rise of quantification within empirical investigation led to concern over the institutional organisation of such knowledge. Frederick Ogg, for example, reported to the American Council for Learned Societies on the changing nature of research and the situation facing American scholarship. One passage reads:

> ... to an astonishing extent this newly organised research finds its habitat outside the traditional centres of productive scholarship, that is the universities, and the problem is suggested of what this means in the future, both for the university and for the quality and effectiveness of research itself. (Ogg 1928:156)

The precursor of the habitat of social research outside of the university, or of research institutes only loosely attached to universities, is that of Lazarsfeld's Viennese *Forschungsstelle*. With his keen interest in the history of knowledge, Lazarsfeld in his *Memoir* writes: 'It [the *Forschungsstelle*] antedates, as far as I know, all such university institutions in this country [America] except the one at the University of North Carolina created by Howard Odum'. (Lazarsfeld 1969:758) Odum was a dedicated Southerner who established his institute to help the South, but it does not pre-date Lazarsfeld's *Forschungsstelle*. According to Siegfried Kracauer (date unknown) who once worked at the Bureau of Applied Social Research, Odum's institute was established in 1925, the same year as Lazarsfeld established the *Forschungsstelle*. The reason for Lazarsfeld thinking that Odum's institute may pre-date the *Forschungsstelle* is that he mis-dates the founding of his own institute. In his *Memoir* (Lazarsfeld 1969:274) Lazarsfeld states that it was established in 1927, when it would appear more likely that it was 1925. Hans Zeisel, one of the key figures of the *Forschungsstelle*, places its founding in 1925. (Zeisel 1968:8)

Unlike the Bureau of Applied Social Research that Lazarsfeld established at Columbia, there are no archival records for the *Forschungsstelle;* those that did exist were destroyed by the National Socialists. Zeisel's date, however, is likely to be correct – he was renowned for his keeping of personal records. Marie Jahoda informed me that although she was 'not quite sure about the formal date of establishing the *Forschungsstelle*' that the difference 'between 1925 and 1927 may well be the difference between the original idea and some preliminary work on the one hand and the formal incorporation on the other'. She added, 'I am, however, quite certain that some survey work was already in progress in 1926'.[18] (Correspondence with Jahoda 19.5.75) If the actual date of the founding of the Forschungsstelle is somewhat shrouded in uncertainty, its legal position is even more uncertain. Lazarsfeld himself was unsure as to its formal status:

18 Some of the early sampling for their survey work that the *Forschungsstelle* did was very crude indeed - questionnaires would simply be left at street tobacco kiosks for customers to fill in if they so wished.

The situation was that in order to do empirical studies, you needed machinery and you needed money, and so I obtained permission and there was really no resistance to the idea. I obtained permission from the professor to create this kind of unofficial little *Forschungsstelle* which was not part of the university. I don't know what its legal position was. But Bühler, who was head of the psychology department, was also head of this little *Forschungsstelle*.[19] (Lazarsfeld 25.5.73)

This confusion concerning the legal position of the *Forschungsstelle* is indicative of its innovative nature. One of the difficulties faced by Lazarsfeld, both in Vienna and New York, was that both of his institutes derived part of their funds from private commercial contracts, a situation which generated not only legal problems so far as financial arrangements were concerned, but also resistance from traditional university academics over the question of 'correct' procedures for scholarly activity. The *Forschungsstelle*, as Lazarsfeld recalled:

...was a sequence of improvisations, and the basic elements of a research organisation developed only slowly. In spite of a number of external formalities, it never fused into a stable organisation. It was only when I came to the University of Newark that the different components, all concurrently in my mind, could be integrated into some kind of an institutional plan. (Lazarsfeld 1969:287)

There may well have been no 'institutional plan', but there was a research plan. The *Forschungsstelle*, by its very novelty, and through the university's conservatism, was left to struggle as best it could, driven by the enthusiasm of those who worked there, and Lazarsfeld's own energy. It was never, and could not have been, locked into the existing structure of the university. The whole question of location of the *Forschungsstelle* and its relationship to the University of Vienna was raised with Jahoda:

D Morrison: The empirical side of the social sciences obviously requires more money for its operations than it did during its pre-empirical days. Was that one of the reasons why the *Forschungsstelle* was never really integrated into the university...because it could never afford such a heavy financial burden, or was it more that the university was just so conservative?

---

19 Karl and Charlotte Bühler moved to Vienna in 1922 and remained there until 1938 when Hitler moved into Austria. Their Institut became world famous during its existence. Karl Bühler was a major influence on Lazarsfeld. Born in 1879, he had worked with Oswald Kuelpe who was a leading figure of the Wuerzburg School of Psychology. Charlotte Bühler had studied under Georg Simmel, Henrich Rickert and Edmund Husserl. The Institut in Vienna became famous for its study of children and developmental psychology. Lazarsfeld even worked on the child psychology programme himself using his own child as a subject of observation.

M Jahoda: Yes, I think it was. It was both. You see the market research studies were in principle meant to be profit-making, not for an individual but the institution. The university in those days felt that really it was quite shocking. You know, that we could do work that one gets paid for and use the money for something else. It was, I think, the conservatism of the university. There was a liaison with the university, but it definitely was not part of the university and I think it was the market research that led to the impossibility of making it an integral part of the university.

DM: What was the reaction of certain academics to it... I'm thinking particularly of the psychologists?

MJ: Well, there was two professors, Karl and Charlotte Bühler. Now Charlotte Bühler really got an enormous benefit for all her work from Paul. You know, he was the only mathematically sophisticated person... She did a lot of interesting work on children and young people and began to see that numeracy in psychology was really important, but she hadn't been trained that way. So Paul did really an enormous amount of work for her and I'm quite sure she appreciated it and if she could have established him in a tenure position, which didn't exist for anybody apart from a professor, she would have done it, but she was quite an arrogant person. She exploited Paul as much as he let himself be exploited.[20] She was very good for him and his general career, but I think in the end it suited her to have him available at the University as a Dozent and do his, quote, 'his dirty business' not quite close to her. (Jahoda 26.9.73)

In reflecting on the history of the *Forchungsstelle*, Hans Zeisel considers that 'one of the permanent achievements of the *Forschungsstelle* was to make the act of buying academically "acceptable"', and to have raised market research to an academic discipline.[21] Such work raised the status of market research, and in doing so forced a distance between the *Forschungsstelle* and its own academic acceptance, but it never really provided the hoped-for revenue, and the ideal of returning a profit from market research to subsidise more academic projects

---

20 It is interesting that Lazarsfeld in his 'memoir' should also raise the question of Charlotte Bühler's exploitative nature: 'She had a Prussian ability to organise the work activities of many people at many places. Some felt exploited by her, but I always appreciated her training and help'. (Lazarsfeld 1969:296)

21 As evidence for this, Zeisel presents Lazarsfeld's 'The Psychological Aspect of Market Research', which appeared in the *Harvard Business Review* of 1934, and a number of chapters which appeared in 1937 in 'The Techniques of Marketing Research', American Marketing Society.

never materialised fully. The financial state of the *Forschungsstelle* was always precarious. Jahoda:

> You know, the *Forschungsstelle* was every day in danger of bankruptcy, and Paul was not a good administrator. He was absolutely shocking. You know he paid for an old study with the money from a new study and of course the books didn't add up. He was a very messy administrator. (Jahoda 26.9.73)

Years later the same 'method' of operation tended to characterise his running of the Bureau of Applied Social Research at Columbia University. Although the Bureau was a much more powerful and well organised operation than the *Forschungsstelle*, the university, when it finally accepted responsibility for it, had to absorb a small amount of debt that Lazarsfeld had managed to accrue. Perhaps as befitting an innovator Lazarsfeld was never an orderly worker, but it was his energy and talent for organisation that kept the *Forschungsstelle* going. The true extent of the debts that afflicted the *Forschungsstelle* only truly emerged after Lazarsfeld had departed to America. Gertrud Wagner recalled the situation the staff faced in the absence of Lazarsfeld: 'We tried to keep the *Forschungsstelle* going when Paul left. I tell you it was full of debt. We had a terrific amount of debt when he left. So [Karl] Bühler came along and was very worried indeed, as he was connected with it'. (Wagner 9.10.73) Lazarsfeld, in reflecting on this period of institution building, mentions that when he was in America he received numerous letters from the Bühlers, 'cursing me for the financial embarrassments I had created for them'. (Lazarsfeld 1969:310)

Although it was always the hope of Lazarsfeld to use market research moneys for other studies it must be recognised that the selling of marketing research, an activity hardly known at that time, and in a bankrupt Austria, was an audacious plan and never likely to succeed in its entirety. Nevertheless, such tactics did allow support not just for 'other work', but provided some, no matter how little, financial support to numerous unemployed students of his acquaintance. Wagner describe conditions as follows:

> The money was never really there for what we wanted to do. I don't think Paul calculated very well the cost of things. In order to get contracts he took the money he could get. It fulfilled the purpose that people were paid for their manual work, and it paid for paper, etc... but it never really brought any money in. It never paid him a decent salary and also this Marienthal - there was never enough money. The money that there was never served to pay Lazarsfeld but to pay his taxis, because he had hundreds of visits to make, and he always took a taxi. People used to laugh at that. (Wagner 9.10.73)

The study of the unemployed community of Marienthal at least had the benefit of a grant from the Rockefeller Foundation, but it was only small, as was the subsidy given for expenses provided by the Central Trades Council of Vienna. The whole precarious nature of the *Forschungsstelle* enterprise is amusingly captured by Zeisel in a talk he gave many years later describing the financial situation that he and his co-workers faced:

> Before leaving America [to give the paper] I asked Mrs Ullman, who today works for Marplan in the United States, what memories she had of those years gone by. She answered me: 'I remember coming to see you once to tell you I had not received my pay for four weeks'. To which I apparently replied... 'Ah yes, four weeks isn't such a long time after all'. I fear that the only thing we paid regularly was the coffee of our collaborators who worked on their labours in the depths of a Viennese coffee cellar. I'm sure we never gave them any more than this because at the end of the month those among us that had a second job (for example, I was under instruction as a lawyer in my father's firm) had to put in a part of their salary. (Zeisel 1968:9)

Despite this rather 'loose' organisational structure, the work that the Forschungsstelle conducted, but mainly through *Die Arbeitslosen von Marienthal*, gave the outside world the appearance of a well-organised operation. Leopold von Wiese, editor of the *Kölner Vierteljahrshefte für Soziologie*, the leading German sociology journal at that time, reviewed the study in its last issue before it was banned by the National Socialists in 1934.[22] Von Wiese, clearly impressed by the Marienthal study, presumed a much more complex and solid research institute than actually existed must have been responsible. After mentioning the shortcomings of his own field trips, Von Wiese noted of the Marienthal study:

> The Vienna enterprise had a different structure where more advanced and theoretically better trained observers could devote themselves to their task for a longer period (the participation of medical doctors was helpful) so that scientifically valuable results were achieved, which went well beyond the mere purpose of training students. (Quoted in Lazarsfeld 1969:284)

The reality of the enterprise was far from Von Wiese's impression of it. The 'amateurish' founding of the *Forschungsstelle* was described to me by Wagner:

> Well, the *Forschungsstelle* was set up in 1925[23] in some rooms and Paul started to get orders from firms and we started the market research. We started with nothing. Just two rooms in the flat of a friend and people made the questionnaires and we tried them out – actually quite good they were. Paul got a few co-workers to help – actually we were friends of his. (Wagner 10:73)

Although the *Forschungsstelle* did move to larger premises later, the continued sense of 'muddling through' is well captured by Jahoda's description of her first contact with social research:

---

22 The journal ran to twelve volumes before it ceased publication, but was started again in May 1948 with Von Wiese once more as editor, appearing under the new title *Kölner Zeitschrift für Soziologie.*

23 This supports Zeisel's dating of it and not that given by Lazarsfeld as 1927.

I remember – in the early days I still had to go to school. I was not even then at university and was therefore in the very early years just an occasional visitor, but I remember very clearly... this might have been some time in 1926... how I got to do my first bit of empirical social psychological writing. I came just as a visitor one day to the Forschungsstelle and found Paul and Zeisel and everybody in a terrible mess because they had done a market research project which had been due two weeks ago. There I was, I came in wanting to gossip, but no. Hans Zeisel took five papers which I remember distinctly. It was about men's clothing, and Zeisel said, 'Sit down and write a chapter on this'. So I sat myself down, not knowing anything about it, you know, apart from being familiar with the general idea. I took the tables and interpreted them. You know, this research production – never having quite enough money, never being quite able to do everything one wanted and using every opportunity. That was how it was. That was the kind of atmosphere that prevailed in the *Forschungsstelle*. (Jahoda 26.9.73)

The atmosphere may well have been one of informality and muddling from crisis to crisis, but it would be wrong to see the *Forschungsstelle* as simply an informal collection of individuals who were friends of each other. Although Lazarsfeld did, as already noted, confess that he did not know 'what its legal position was', it was nevertheless a formally constituted organisation in the sense of having members, and distinguished members at that. According to Zeisel the legal position of the *Forschungsstelle* was that of a 'club under the leadership of Karl Bühler and the auspices of prominent personalities of the city'. (Zeisel 1969:45) These 'prominent personalities' were drawn from the chambers of commerce and agriculture as well as labour unions. A large group of university professors were also on the board. For example, the economists Ludwig Mises and Richard Strigl were members, although they did leave after a brief term of service. Otto Potzl, the distinguished psychiatrist, was also a member. Commerce and industry were represented by Hugo Gunseler, the president of Bally, Kurt Schechner, president of Julius Meinl, and Manfred Mauntner-Markhof, who belonged to a renowned family of Austrian industrialists.[24] In all the board had around twenty members. Karl Bühler, however, had particular responsibility for the *Forschungsstelle* since not only was he head of the Board, but was also the link connecting it, no matter how tenuously, with the university. It was not surprising therefore that he should be concerned to discover, on Lazarsfeld's departure, the debt-ridden nature of the enterprise, and be relieved when a rich industrialist was found who took over all the debts on being made head of the *Forschungsstelle*. Wagner remarked:

We found a man, a fairly rich man. I think his name was Gold. Yes, I'm nearly sure a Mr Gold. He came along and he was fascinated by Lazarsfeld. I don't know where they met, but he was fascinated by the

24 See Zeisel 1968 for a list of members.

idea of market research. He had made a lot of money in some business. He live in a hotel in Zurich – one of the famous ones, I forget which. When Lazarsfeld left he said he would become the head and in order to do so he had to pay all the debts. So everybody was very happy. But problems arose because Lazarsfeld had always written the reports himself and therefore when he left there were really difficulties. I know I was suddenly obliged to write reports and I certainly couldn't do it. Of course, Gold was very disappointed because we were left to him as the people who could do it and so he was disappointed that he had paid the debts. (Wagner 9.10.73)

Wagner's difficulties were due not simply to personal failings, but were indicative of the extent to which traditional forms of intellectual training failed to prepare people for the kind of tasks generated within a research organisation such as the *Forschungsstelle*. Indeed, when Lazarsfeld was in charge of the Princeton Radio Research Project at Newark, the inappropriateness of traditional training became apparent. A new set of skills had to be learnt by the staff, which meant that in the meantime Lazarsfeld shouldered the bulk of the work, particularly the writing, using the pseudonym Elias Smith:

So far as the pseudonym goes, well, I became director of the Princeton Project and had to establish again a staff of young people. They didn't know how to write and I wanted to give the impression what a big group we were, so I wrote most of the things. But I didn't want to have all to my name so I just invented the pseudonym to hide how much of it was a one-man operation. (Lazarsfeld 25.5.73)

Thus a new type of research organisation, with the division of labour, group work and hierarchical structuring of relations which is now a familiar part of academia, grew out of the application of empirical knowledge to social science. New forms of knowledge generated new organisational forms, which in turn required the establishment of new roles within scholarship. The advantage that Lazarsfeld had in creating the new role of managerial scholar, and in establishing research institutes geared to collective enterprise, both in Vienna and during his early years in America, was a ready pool of young researchers without prospects of employment. Certainly during the depression years of his early time in America, and before the days of computers, ready work, even though repetitive, could be found for unemployed young people manually tabulating data. Such job creation slotted well into the ethos of the New Deal, and Lazarsfeld's own socialist background. In fact, the idea of providing work for his young colleagues and friends was ever present in the idea of establishing a commercially funded research operation. As Jahoda said:

I should say, however, that there was another reason that made the idea of the *Forschungsstelle* such a great success, and this was the terrible unemployment and poverty among students and graduates from the university. You know, we were all very active in the socialist youth movement and we knew hundreds, literally, of gifted young people who had a contribution to make but nobody paid them a penny for it. So I'm sure that in Paul's thinking the possibility of providing some income for this large group of gifted young people also played a major role in not wanting to give up. We had a predominantly left membership. You see the interviewers ...we had a pool of maybe 30 interviewers. Of course they didn't have regular employment. They were paid by the amount of work, and when we went to Marienthal we deliberately recruited people who could go and talk to the Nazi Party members. But you know... unemployment was so high among young intellectuals... it was such a desperate tragedy that we did what we could to help our friends. So most of the people were good straightforward socialists. (Jahoda 29.9.73)

The Twilight of Research

The last days of the 'good straightforward socialists' who made up the staff of the *Forschungsstelle* were played out amidst the final act of the Republic, and the rising tide of European Fascism. Yet, the Fascists' progress in Austria was delayed longer than in either Germany or Italy due to the persistence into the 1930s of an organised working class. Although inroads had been made into that class by the far right, its political organisation and support was still basically intact. But the Party fought its fight too late. Had it fought earlier, when its power was more intact, the outcome would not have been significantly different – a Socialist Austria could not have withstood the powers outside its borders that were arranged against it. Even so, the end of the Republic was brutal, and the crushing defeat of the *Schutzbund* more complete than if the Party had fought when many of its members wished it to. Elizabeth Schilder related the feeling of impending doom that many Party workers felt after 1932 when in March of that year Dollfuss abolished representative government, and following the example set by Mussolini collected most of the important ministries into his own hands:

> I was convinced the fight was coming. After 1932 I knew the fight had to be fought. I had been in Berlin – I had contact with the Germans – I was a member of a left group. We knew the fight was coming and we thought we could do something, but we wanted to fight earlier. We always asked Otto Bauer to fight, to fight. (Schilder 28.6.74)

Indeed, the failure to take action when Julius Dollfuss staged his coup saw the Party's grip on sections of the working class falter. As Braunthal, a Party activist, noted, the rank and file members became increasingly disheartened with the Party's refusal to take a stand against Dollfuss, and watched in despair as its power was eroded. (Braunthal 1945:280) The crux of the problem was that the Social Democratic Party, radical as it was in its tradition, spirit and structure, was no instrument for insurrection. Viktor Serge[25] in his memoirs movingly captures the nature of the Social

---

25 Serge first adopted the pen name Viktor Serge for an article he wrote defending Friedrich Adler after his assassination of the Prime Minister.

Democratic Party, its lack of daring in making the psychological and physical leap to armed revolution:

> If only a Red Austria had joined with the Hungarian Soviet, would not a troubled Bohemia, and then Germany have followed their example? Revolution was maturing in Italy during this period. But perhaps it was already too late. If only after 1918.... If only the commission on the nationalisation of the main industries, established by the socialist government, had not been such a farce. If only the Social Democrats of Austria had had a little of the impassioned energy of the Bolsheviks of Russia... Its opportunities lost, its hours of daring past, little Austria found herself jammed in the middle of the expanding counter-revolutions of Hungary, Italy and Germany; at home Socialist Vienna found itself menaced by the countryside and the Catholic bourgeoisie.[26] Prince Starhenberg was recruiting his peasant bands against it. I attended meetings of the Social Democrat Party activists; they were middle-aged men, few of them fit, who drank their beer as they listened to the speakers. The Schutzbund would march past the town hall with 30,000 bicycles garlanded with flowers. Otto Bauer, who was greeted on all sides by affectionate glances, watched the parade of this working-class force, so confident, so deserving of a glorious future. If only it had been a matter of just deserving. (Serge 1963:189)

Even at the time of the Dollfuss putsch Bauer considered, 'We still believed we could come to a peaceful solution through negotiation',[27] but tragically, the Party in defeat, following the failed uprising in February 1934, became more radical and revolutionary than it had ever been when it was legal. For a time it even changed its name to the Revolutionary Socialists, and turned its back upon its former democratic traditions. Its power, however, was spent. The splintering into groups, the growth of suspicion and hostility, by-products of its new underground role, were problems, but none so great as the distancing from the masses, where the real power had lain. It had been a Party based on openness, a Party used to running the live of thousands of members, but now its gigantic structure was shattered, leaving the mass of its followers, so used to taking directives, without either leaders or an organisation through which directives could be received. Although valiant underground work was carried out, the Party was effectively finished, especially after the National Socialists assumed power. They routed out the activists in the socialist underground with far greater thoroughness than the Austrian Fascists had ever done. As part of the underground network, the *Forschungsstelle* fell victim:

> Late in November 1936 the police raided the so-called Office of Economic and Statistical Research; besides the Director, Mitzi Marie Jahoda, and part of her staff, they caught Fritz Jahnel, the Information Chief who was in contact with Mitzi Jahoda. (Buttinger 1953:375)

---

26 The Fascism that emerged in Austria was a Clerico-Fascism.
27 Otto Bauer quoted in Gulick (1948, Vol. 2:1351).

Jahoda, as a well known socialist, was a natural candidate for suspicion as an underground activist. She had, after all, along with Lazarsfeld, given the Socialist High School Students a powerful reputation among young intellectuals,[28] and still lived in the Karl Marx-Hof[29] at the time of the uprising. She was affected by her experience during those February days:

> I still lived where I had lived with Paul in the Karl Marx-Hof, in a community building. The cannons of the government were directed against this. Life changed in its total quality fantastically. Also, I became immediately quite active in the underground and I was arrested in the *Forschungesstelle* in 1936. The whole atmosphere was terrifyingly changed. (Jahoda 26.9.73)

Wagner, who left for England in the early part of 1936 owing to the impossible position that her husband now found himself in, given that he had been a journalist on the *Arbeiter-Zeitung*, the main newspaper of the Social Democrats, commented on the atmosphere at this time:

> Mitzi [Marie] Jahoda, who was always a very ardent socialist and very politically minded, used the Forschungesstelle as a cover for the underground movement and all letters... many of the letters which came to it... well, she used it for that purpose. I think people there knew about it and agreed with it too. I wasn't there any more but our friends were, and the socialist movement was a hundred times more important than the *Forschungesstelle*. (Wagner 9.8.73)

Lazarsfeld had by this time left Austria for America, supported by a one-year Rockefeller Scholarship. It had always been Lazarsfeld's intention to return to Austria, but after his fellowship was extended for another year due to the deterioration in the political climate of Austria, his sabbatical became a permanent residency. He did, however, return to Austria in 1935 to obtain an immigration visa for America, and according to Schilder was extremely worried by Jahoda's political activities. His concern must have been obvious to all concerned since Stacey May, an officer of the Rockefeller Foundation, wrote a note for inclusion in Lazarsfeld's docket: 'has done excellent work despite worry entailed in his family situation'. (Rockefeller Fellowship Docket 32.4.34 - writers files) Indeed, one of the reasons for Lazarsfeld accepting the offer of a Rockefeller Fellowship was that even by 1933 unfettered social research in Austria was becoming increasingly difficult. After commenting that by the

---

28   See Buttinger (1953:82-83) for a discussion of the political career of the worker Joseph Simon and his move from the Socialist Labour Youth to the Socialist High School Students attracted to it by its reputation forged by Jahoda and Lazarsfeld.

29   The Karl Marx-Hof was a huge round building with a massive archway leading through to an enormous courtyard, which was not only the pride of the Social Democrats building programme but came to be admired by other countries and copied. For example, the Quarry Hill Housing Project in the centre of Leeds that was built in 1930 was modelled on the Karl Marx-Hof and was only demolished in 1978. Quarry Hill was the largest and most modern housing project in Europe when it was built, housing 3,000 people.

time Lazarsfeld accepted the Fellowship, 'our marriage didn't really function properly' so the break seemed understandable from that point of view, Jahoda gave the reasons for his leaving as:

> He had the *Forschungesstelle*, as you rightly say, but you can't imagine what a struggle it was to keep it going, and here was this chance - it was like a sabbatical which was undreamed of then, and also the chance not to worry — can I pay the interviewers, and where do I get the next study? It was a chance of breaking out. So I think the great prestige of the Rockefeller fellowship, the personal problems and the fantastic effort of running the *Forschungesstelle*... It was that sort of situation where a break which was originally planned for one year seemed from every conceivable point of view the right thing to do and also by 1933, the political situation in Austria had very much deteriorated. Paul didn't want to avoid this as a person, but it seemed already to spell the end of the institute and unfettered social research. (Jahoda 26.9.73)

The political climate was such that even by 1932, upon Dollfuss's seizure of power and the subsequent outlawing of the Socialist Party in 1934, Lazarsfeld's position at the *Gymnasium* (High School), where he taught physics and mathematics to supplement his meagre salary at the Psychology Institut, was terminated. His vague position at the university was left unaffected by the changed political situation, but by 1933 the future of the *Forschungesstelle* looked uncertain, and in personal communication with Zeisel, it was his view that the *Forschungesstelle* began to die as early as 1934, some two years before the arrest of Jahoda. (Letter from Zeisel 8.3.73)

Following the police raid on the *Forschungesstelle*, and the imprisonment of Jahoda, only released after ten months on the condition that she leave the country immediately, political suspicion hung over the organisation, making life increasingly difficult. Although many other members were also in danger after the jailing of Jahoda, Hans Zeisel managed to keep the *Forschungesstelle* going with the aid of a Mr Fallowday, whom the financial backer, Gold, had drafted in as 'adviser'. However, not only was unfettered social research no longer welcome in Austria, but market research became increasingly redundant as the business world itself began to suffer from shortage of money with which to fund marketing studies. Nevertheless, the *Forschungesstelle*, although a shadow of its former self, kept afloat until as late as 1938, when the National Socialists finally closed it down.

The idea of a *Forschungesstelle* had been born out of Austrian Socialism and it was inevitable that it should finally be forced under by those very forces which its members had always stood out against. However, the rationale of the *Forschungesstelle*, the establishment of social research as an empirical activity collectively organised, was not to be so easily killed. Indeed, the *Forschungesstelle* forms an important episode in the history of social research not just at the institutional level of organisational innovation in higher learning, but in terms of the operating logic of research. This 'logic', developed by Lazarsfeld, of combining industry money with academic expertise became central to the early development of mass communication research, particularly at the methodological level. Not for Lazarsfeld the addressing of issues from within the sanctuary of the academy, but rather the engagement in applied social research. Indeed, Lazarsfeld engaged in the development of focus groups as a method of social enquiry in America while working on the concrete issue of propaganda for the Office of War Information.

Three

Lazarsfeld in America: The Institutionalisation of Knowledge

T here is a romantic notion that the state of exile and its associated insecurity favours creativity but, as Henry Patcher rightly notes, 'The myth that exile produces Dantes, Marxes, Bartoks is not justified in the mass. More often exile destroys talent, or it means the loss of the environment that nourished talent morally, socially and physically'. (Patcher 1970:17) Successful scholarly transition depends on a variety of factors: age, established international reputation, the discipline or subject area of the individual, but not least the nature of the host culture – its openness to foreigners, employment levels and the particularities of the discipline to be entered.

Franz Neumann, viewing his situation in the face of the rising tide of National Socialism, commented on his decision to leave Europe for the safety of America:

> Thus a clean break – psychologically, social and economic – had to be made and a new life started. But England was not the country in which to do it. Much as I (and all the others) loved England, her society was too homogeneous and too solid, her opportunities (particularly under conditions of unemployment) too narrow, her politics not too agreeable. One could I felt never quite become an Englishman. Thus the United States appeared as the sole country where, perhaps, an attempt would be successful to carry out a threefold transition: as a human being, an intellectual and a political scholar. (Neumann 1953:17-18)

For Lazarsfeld, the choice of the United States of America as his new home was not the conscious decision that it evidently was for Neumann, but rather stemmed from a variety of factors, not least the fact that he was already resident in the United States when the change in the Austrian political situation made return inadvisable. (Morrison 1998)

Lazarsfeld arrived in America in 1933 on what was then a prestigious Rockefeller Fellowship. His Marienthal study had brought him to the attention of the Rockefeller Foundation's representative in Paris, but it was Karl Bühler who appears to have promoted his application, out of a sense of loyalty to Lazarsfeld and regret that he could not do anything for Lazarsfeld within his own Institut. Indeed, what drove Lazarsfeld out of Austria were the political and cultural facts that had plagued his advancement within the established university system.

When it came to promoting Lazarsfeld in 1933, Karl Bühler, whose wife, along with his two main assistants, was Jewish, felt that even though he wanted to he could not make him a Dozent; instead he appointed the gentile Egon Brunswik, but by way of consolation he put Lazarsfeld forward for the Rockefeller Fellowship. Thus the anti-semitism which had hung over Lazarsfeld, blocking both his academic and political careers, was in a way instrumental in obtaining the fellowship; but it was not as if in America the facts of his biography no longer mattered, or were turned into attractive qualities loved by his host culture. Lazarsfeld was aware that anti-semitism in America might also be a restricting factor in the advancement of his career, but his Marxism was no block to acceptance.

When he had not been long in America, he described himself at one lecture as a Marxist on leave, to which Cuthbert Daniel shouted, 'And who gave you permission?' Liking a smart comment, Lazarsfeld employed Daniel on the spot. Bernard Berelson commented, 'Well, it was certainly a long leave'. He continued:

> [Lazarsfeld] was substantially interested in the voting studies. He could pretend that it was a political topic of importance – how do people make decisions in a capitalist democracy? – which gave him some bona fide link with his socialist history, but he never was socialist and Hans Zeisel neither. Hans Zeisel worked for one of the major advertising companies (McCann - Erickson) for most of his career here, and you don't do that against a genuine solid background in European socialism. (Berelson 12.7.73)

This, however, is to miss the point about Lazarsfeld and Austrian socialism. Despite its hold over its members, the Austrian socialist movement had none of the theoretical and disciplinary severity associated with the Communist Party. Unlike a communist, one did not need to break faith with a hard body of doctrine in order to be rid of the Party, since even the doctrine had the flexibility of the various strands of thought that created it. One did not have to break with the Party cell since it never had any cells, only clubs; and one did not have to abandon future dreams, since the dream was already extant in embryonic form. Lazarsfeld was, therefore, an Austro-Marxist on leave, in the sense that in America he had left the social world he had known, but his new world was close enough for him to feel comfortable. As he said: 'You know as an old Viennese socialist I really felt completely at home with the New Deal – with the Roosevelt administration, and really as long Roosevelt lived there was, so to say, nothing to criticise from my point of view. I was just completely in agreement with the whole of the New Deal line'. (Lazarsfeld 2.6.73)

If American politics were to his taste, his Jewishness was another matter, creating a distinct awareness of his delicate position as 'outsider':

> You know, when I first came here there was still a certain amount of genteel anti-semitism. And my accent... as a matter of fact, I was less affected because my being a foreigner over-shadowed my being Jewish. No one thought of me as Jew because of my foreignness – the accent saved my life.

To anyone who knew Lazarsfeld the idea that his Jewishness would not present itself as a most obvious and unmistakable feature is preposterous. Yet is rather characteristic of the man to believe in his ability to hoodwink the world in such a way, but in reality simply fool himself about his escape. His 'foreignness' fed a basic insecurity, one which Bernfeld had probably detected in his analysis of Lazarsfeld's fondness for statistics. According to Marie Jahoda, Lazarsfeld 'was always sensitive about his Jewishness – he had the most idiotic, but persistent inferiority feeling'. (Jahoda 26.9.73) Even when established at Columbia, Lazarsfeld felt it necessary for some time to 'apologise' for his presence:

> You know for years I had a collection of jokes that I used in public about my accent, because I know people were shocked, especially when I talked as some official representative at Columbia. The first minute I would make a joke about I didn't come with the Mayflower or something like that.

The 'problem' of acceptance was common to most émigrés, as John Marshall, in his official capacity as a senior foundation official dealing with many émigré scholars, was well placed to observe. He commented: ' I think Paul won't hold it against me if I said that at times he was a highly manipulative person.... He was after all – he was typical of a refugee – they felt they had to manipulate the people around them in a way they could secure their position'. (Marshall 1973) Indeed, Robert Lynd wrote to John Marshal in the early part of 1939 that: 'He [Lazarsfeld] and I differ temperamentally as to the wisdom of being candid rather than mildly evasive, but I have no question at all as to his basic integrity.... I find him open-minded and co-operative'. (Lynd letter to Marshall 16.3.39)

To a great extent Lazarsfeld was at home in America at the level of personality, intellectual orientation and political orientation. Noting the difficulty of 'adjustment' faced by many European exiles, Neumann observed:

> On the whole, the German exile, bred in the veneration of theory and history and a contempt for empiricism and pragmatism, entered a diametrically opposed intellectual climate: optimistic, empirically orientated, a-historical, but also self-righteous. (Neumann 1953:17)

Lazarsfeld was certainly not 'diametrically opposed' to the American intellectual climate when he arrived in 1933. He was sufficiently close to feel 'at home', yet sufficiently removed by his insistence upon qualitative work as a necessary accompaniment to quantitative research to form a link with older, more humanistic traditions of scholarship. After he had worked with Samuel Stouffer on the Depression and the Family study,[1] for example, Stouffer wrote to Lazarsfeld praising his interpretative abilities: 'Your personality is present everywhere and... you know as well as I what a temptation it would have been to have kept the study down to a rather dull level too close to facts.'(Letter Stouffer to Lazarsfeld, 19.3.37)

Although when his fellowship expired in 1935 Lazarsfeld, in the early stages of his academic career, was relatively unknown, and did not belong to any particular school of thought that might have made integration easier, he was advantageously placed to gain recognition. He had all the legitimacy of the quantifier, yet extracted himself from the sterility of pure quantification by his insistence upon the need to transcend any single approach to arrive at a broad conceptual integration. He could, furthermore (a lesson well learnt during his Forschungsstelle days in Vienna), bridge the academic and lay worlds. Charles Siepmann, in a letter to John Marshall, contrasted Adorno's presentation of himself and his work to that of Lazarsfeld:

> Many thanks for your letter of December 11th. I know what you mean about Adorno. You know him, of course, much better that I, but I should judge on slight acquaintance that he isn't likely to become acclimatised in the way you hope. I do however believe that his criticisms and approach in its present form has real significance and that there are those whose reactions to it would be sympathetic. He is, I fear, essentially an intellectual and not like Lazarsfeld either capable of or concerned to communicate at a popular level of interpretation. (Siepmann to Marshall: 12.12.40)

Yet, the ability of Lazarsfeld to cordially associate with others outside a tightly drawn circle of academics, particularly with people in commerce, drew criticism. As Berelson said:

> Well, the academics didn't really trust him. He was – well you know how it is with academics – he was too pushy, he was foreign, he was too bright, and he was too self-confident, arrogant sometimes to them, and too tied in with the business and commercial world. And he was supporting this personal institute of his which attracted all sorts of bright young people around Columbia, and this was a source of resentment. With commercial contracts he was always wheeling as he was doing it – as indeed he was – with a kind of sleight of hand. You know the joke around the Bureau was that you paid the deficit of the last study with the grant from the next study, and that's how people lived around there. But it wasn't a political criticism, and in many ways it wasn't even – I think it's fair to say – a scientific or

---

1   See a shortened version in Stouffer (1962), chapter 6.

academic criticism, it was a little of that... that it wasn't theoretical enough, it was all dirty empiricism, fact grubbing and so on. It was a little unfair, but a large part of it was sort of personal on a grand scale.[2] (Berelson 12.7.73)

Berelson himself, through Lazarsfeld's 'sponsorship', became the Director of the Bureau, and had been around in the early days of its establishment, thus in a good position to observe Lazarsfeld's manoeuvres and the antagonism they created. He recalled the attacks made by C Wright Mills on Lazarsfeld for his close association with commerce:

> I can still hear Wright Mills saying, 'Why, Paul Lazarsfeld works for *True Story* magazine' as though no self-respecting academic of any persuasion would do that. Paul always felt, 'I don't understand what Wright is complaining about. These people are generous with the research funds, they allow me to raise questions... we have the opportunity to do the Decatur Study. (Katz and Lazarsfeld *Personal Influences* 1955)

As if almost to defend Lazarsfeld, Berelson then added the piquant observation: 'After all, it was Wright who went out there to do the magazine survey on women in a small middle western town... interesting the way all the convolution's worked their way out'. (Berelson 12.7.73)

Robert Lynd, a senior figure at Columbia University, and possibly the most important contact Lazarsfeld made during his first years in America, was a key supporter of Lazarsfeld, but according to Berelson, whilst Lynd was always sympathetic and helpful, he had reservations of a political nature concerning the Bureau. Lynd never really understood what was going on in the Bureau, but nevertheless considered that important methodological advances were being made for the betterment of American sociology. He was, however, slightly concerned over the question of academic freedom. This, presumably, stemmed from the Bureau's close relationship with the world of commerce, and it is certainly the case that such financial links prejudiced the Bureau's position *vis à vis* the University. It was, however, the location of the Bureau on the periphery of the University in its early days which drove it into such commercial relationships. At one point Lynd even wondered whether or not Lazarsfeld might opt for a career in market research and abandon his academic ambitions altogether. Marshall and Lynd had a conversation concerning Lazarsfeld's true feelings towards an academic life:

> In short, the acceptance of any consultancy such as is outlined will make it necessary for Lazarsfeld to decide which of the two alternatives confronting him he is to take. If he chooses the academic course he must do so with a clear recognition of the fact that he is giving up the other

---

2   Writing on Lazarsfeld's influence, James Coleman says '...here, too, is the key to the hostility that some sociologists felt towards him (in particular, those sociologists engaged in scholarly, non-empirical, social philosophy in the European tradition). They saw a discipline being captured, taken away from them, moved in directions they neither liked nor had the skills to pursue'. (Coleman 1982:1)

alternative where with his present interest in polling and marketing research, he could undoubtedly earn a considerable larger salary. Lazarsfeld has always said he preferred academic research but he must now decide. (Marshall's summary of conversation with Lynd 21.4.41)

At this time Lazarsfeld had been made associate professor at Columbia, and the Bureau, whilst not fully integrated into the university, was nonetheless established, even if it had been a long battle. Yet, Marshall and Lynd need not have worried about Lazarsfeld opting for a career in market research. He was not about to give up what he had so consistently striven for, a research institute that would ensure his academic standing. Indeed, the early history of mass communications research and its methodological development, including focus group research, owes much to the biographical imperatives of Lazarsfeld, the key to which can be found in a few lines of his own memoir relating to his early days in America: '... it never occurred to me to aspire to a major university job. I took it for granted that I would have to make some move similar to the creation of the Vienna Research Centre if I wanted to find a place for myself in the United States'. (Lazarsfeld 1969:301)

Institutional Establishment

Lazarsfeld's establishment in America is a twin story covering his own development and the development of mass communications research: the career of one is the career of another. In discussing the innovative nature of the Princeton Radio research project and the search by the Rockerfeller Foundation to find a director to run the study, Lazarsfeld said 'you see it was a completely new field. I remember one day a friend of mine, in 1937 or so, introduced me to a group of colleagues and said, "this is a European colleague who is an utmost authority on communication research", and, on seeing that no one was especially impressed, he went on to say 'as a matter of fact he is the only one who works in this field'. (Lazarsfeld 25.5.73)

Mass communications research developed from the Rockefeller Foundation's interest in the place of radio in people's lives, dating from 1934, and in particular the enthusiasm of John Marshall at the Foundation. Marshall was reading as widely as possible in the area, and was particularly struck by *The Psychology of Radio* by Handley Cantril and Gordon Allport. (Cantril and Allport 1935) He remembered the impact of one particular sentence:

> Towards the end of that book there is a statement to the effect 'of course we really don't know whether or not what we are saying is true, but we shan't know until we have done some research'. I went up to see Cantril and in the course of the talk said, 'well, why don't you get some research going?' He said, 'I would very much like to.' That was the beginning – as simple as that. I don't think I had any interest in that field until I read that sentence.[3] (Marshall conversation 6.7.73)

3   The statement Marshall is probably referring to occurs on p271 of Cantril and Allport (1935), where such an appeal is made.

The opportunity to create a research centre came with an offer to analyse some data collected under the auspices of the National Youth Administration which was housed at the University of Newark. Lynd had recommended Lazarsfeld for the job to Frank Kingdon, the recently appointed President of Newark University, and it was Kingdon's idea that in addition to analysing the NYA data Lazarsfeld should teach a research course at the university. The possibility of establishing an institute modelled along the lines of the *Forschungsstelle* was not lost on Lazarsfeld, and he suggested to Kingdon that the NYA project be extended to enable the formation of a research centre. Kindon agreed to this suggestion and work was started towards the end of 1935, although the Center was not officially recognised until 21 May 1936.[4] It was during this period that Max Horkheimer so generously helped Lazarsfeld out with much needed funds. This led to Lazarsfeld's later repayment of the debt by employing Adorno on the Princeton Radio Research Project.

Frank Kingdon had high ambitions for the development of Newark University, but they never materialised.[5] At the time, however, Lazarsfeld believed that Kingdon would develop Newark into a successful academic centre, and was thus reluctant to accept the Directorship of the Rockerfeller-funded Princeton Radio Research Project when it was offered him, if it meant abandoning the start he had made on establishing his research centre at Newark. He wrote to Hadley Cantril of Princeton University, where the Rockefeller grant had been placed, in an effort to have the grant transferred to Newark. It was a 'pushy' suggestion, but shows Lazarsfeld's hand. He wrote, and the letter is worth quoting at length:

> I invented the Research Centre [Newark] for two reasons. I wanted to direct a rather great variety of studies, so that I was sure that from year to year my methodological experience would increase and that is, as you know, my main interest in research. And I tried to build up groups of younger students to be educated just in the kind of research procedures I tried to develop. Now as to the first point I think your project would do splendidly. Radio is a topic around which actually any kind of research method can be tried out and can be applied satisfactorily. But I am somewhat worried in regard to the second point. I don't know if you are aware that by now there are each term graduate students from other universities coming to Newark to work with me on different studies and that is one of the main features of the Research Centre from my point of view. The question is therefore would it be possible to set up at least part of your project in such a way that it could be used as a sort of training

---

4   The Newark Center quickly established a reputation for itself, sufficiently so that in 1936 both Everett Hughes and Robert Park were interested enough in its activities to visit it, and George Lundberg of Benington College and John Jenkins of Cornell sent graduate students there for special training.

5   Kingdon began to neglect Newark as his energies began to be channelled in the direction of a career in politics.

institution? There are many forms possible, but as a matter of principle we should see eye to eye in regard to this point because it is so important for me.

This leads to another question. I am not worried about the limited duration of your project – it seems as if it were always possible to find a job in America. But it is probably not always possible to set up a Research Centre. The University of Newark is certainly not an important place at this moment but I feel rather certain that its Research Centre can become important in ten years from now. I would hate to see it collapse and I am sure it will if I drop it now. You have to understand me in the right way: the Research Centre does not need my work for the next year – what it needs is that I identify whatever I do in some way with its name....

You see all comes back to an European attitude which might be not so easy to understand from your point of view. I feel strongly that I don't want to go ahead alone, that I want to stand for an institution and try to build up an institution which is able and willing to stand for me. Of course, I will have to do very different things, less glorious but about the same way as you are professor in Harvard, then in Columbia, then in Princeton. But as my poise and my post and my name cannot compare with yours, I try to identify whatever I do with an institution which might after some time acquire the dignity which I myself for reasons of destiny and maybe personality can hardly aspire to. Of course in spite of this European attitude I am now American enough to see the great advantage which your offer implies and I would love to accept it. So this whole letter is an effort to get your help in my effort to co-ordinate the actual situation brought about by your project and the long-range plans which I have tried to explain in this letter. (Lazarsfeld to Cantril 8.8.37)

Lazarsfeld's 'European attitude' was discussed with John Marshall:

D Morrison: I always got the impression that Lazarsfeld was very aware that if he was going to make it he had to make it attached to an institute rather than particularly as an individual. This seems to be a great motivating force with him – that is, it was his institute and he rose or fell depending on the institute.

J Marshall: Yes, well this is of course a typical central European attitude. Any scholar worth his salt in Germany or Austria would have his own 'Institute'. He brought that attitude over to this country with him.

This explanation of Lazarsfeld's 'European attitude' further helps to explain why his career followed a path of institutional innovation. He came from an academic culture where professors were much more closely identified with their departments than their English or American counterparts, and where the pinnacle of success was to have a successful 'Institute' associated with one's name. As Lazarsfeld recognised, the chance of him fulfilling this ambition by becoming head of a major American university department were however extremely restricted. Hence he was obliged to establish his own institute.

At one point, along with Robert Merton (although Merton was never as keen on the undertaking) Lazarsfeld attempted to establish a centralised training school at Columbia for the whole of American social sciences. This effort at institutional innovation failed. There was no way that American social scientists were going to hand their students over to Lazarsfeld for training. The planned professional training school was intellectual colonisation on a grand scale, and as Berelson, who was privy to the manoeuvres, informed me: '...they [other academics] would no more have sent one of their students over to him than they would have dropped them out of the window'. (Berelson 12.7.73)

In terms of institutional innovation, of having a centre that 'will stand for me', Lazarsfeld had to content himself with the Bureau of Applied Social Research. But matters were not easy. Cantril had responded to Lazarsfeld's plea for a tie-up between Princeton and Newark: 'Your suggestion about a tie-up with the Newark Research Centre is, I fear, out. I'm sorry you didn't get the money there but it is one of these somewhat absurd American grants to an "institution" and it would be impossible to have the work carried out elsewhere'. (Cantril 9.8.37) Impossible or not, that is just what happened – Lazarsfeld did operate the project from Newark and not Princeton. All the letter heads of the project had to carry Princeton University's name and not Newark's, but the only real sign of the project residing at Princeton was a single office and one secretary:

> I made it one of my conditions that the headquarters of the Princeton Project would be at Newark. I mean, I never spent a night in Princeton or anything. I went down there every few weeks for one day or so, and that lasted for about one year when the Princeton Project was in Newark. Then the university began to decline, and I mean it became clear it had no future. Then we moved the Princeton Project from Newark to New York.(Lazarsfeld 1973)

The reason why Lazarsfeld got his own way, and could make it a condition that the project be housed at Newark, was that Cantril's heart was not in the study. The directorship of the project was first offered to Frank Stanton, but he had just been promoted at CBS and considered the whole project, in terms of its career potential, a somewhat risky venture. To Lazarsfeld, the émigré, no such reservations existed. This was security indeed – two years guaranteed salary, with a likely extension to four years. The salary itself was attractive – seven thousand dollars per year. Following the non-acceptance of the job by Stanton, Cantril wrote Lazarsfeld: 'With Stanton not taking the directorship I am stuck and will refuse to carry on myself; as you know, my heart is not in this type of research as much as yours. Furthermore I am not too good at it. Lord but I'd be

71

relieved and happy if you would accept'. This put Lazarsfeld in a very strong bargaining position to drive what conditions he wanted, and he did, ensuring that the basis for 'his institute' was protected.

Interestingly, in his letter to Lazarsfeld Cantril remarks: '...I asked [George] Gallup and [Frank] Stanton about the line-up for you as objectively as I could and they both thought it would be a good move. Gallup thinks very highly of you, as does Frank [Stanton] and both thought that you could readily land something you liked when this was up'. (Cantril 9.8.37) Such connections with the world of commerce, represented here by Gallup and Stanton, created suspicion towards Lazarsfeld within academic circles. Even as early as 1935, when his Rockefeller Fellowship had expired, he had taken a temporary job at the University of Pittsburgh's Research Bureau of Retail Trading, working on studies such as 'How Pittsburgh Women Decide Where to Buy their Dresses', and 'How Pittsburgh Drivers Chose Their Gasoline'. While engaged in the former, he had been the house guest of Edgar Kaufman, a wealthy local business magnate, and during the latter project had repeated contact with Paul Mellon. The Mellon family, along with the Rockefellers and Du Ponts, constituted one of the three great dynasties of wealth in America. Lazarsfeld's status as an academic 'outsider' was not helped by the ease with which he moved in business circles. Yet this was essential in allowing him access to the funds necessary, in the absence of firm university support, to develop the institute that would come to stand for him.

The arrangement that Lazarsfeld made with Cantril to protect his emerging 'institute' meant in principle that the Radio Project simply became one more study which the Newark Centre was to conduct, but in practice the sheer size of the Rockefeller grant, which amounted to three times the total operating budget of the Centre, meant that the two became more or less synonymous. However, the growth of Lazarsfeld's new Centre created strains with the parent university, especially as the university began to decline. Lazarsfeld's Centre was in danger of being isolated, which was not something he cared for. He was only too willing, therefore, to remove his Centre when the suggestion was made by the President of the university that it should look for a new home. That new home was to be at Columbia University in New York. It did not return to its ostensible home at Princeton, to which the original Radio Grant had been given, for the reason that Princeton by this time was not too keen on retaining ownership. Lazarsfeld in his *Memoir* rather dramatises the Project's release by Princeton:

> Meanwhile, internal difficulties had developed between Cantril and me. During the negotiations with the Rockefeller Foundation for a renewal of the grant it became clear that an administrative decision had to be made. Either the project would stay at Princeton with Cantril as the main figure but with a new director, or, if I were to remain, the project would have to look for another institutional base. The Foundation naturally turned to Stanton as a third insider to arbitrate the situation; from the outcome I gather that Stanton put his weight on my side.

Lynd prevailed on President Dodds of Princeton to release the project. In the fall of 1939, the Office of Radio Research was turned over to Columbia University, and at the same time I was appointed lecturer there. (Lazarsfeld 1969:329)

In fact there appeared to be very little opposition either to Lazarsfeld remaining as Director, or to the Project going to Columbia; it would seem that Princeton University wished to rid itself of both the Project and Lazarsfeld. Certainly there was mounting friction between Lazarsfeld and Cantril, something which Lazarsfeld hints at in the above extract from his memoir.

On 13 January 1939 an article appeared in the *Princeton Alumni Weekly* entitled, 'Psychologists to Study Martian Hysteria'. This referred to a study of the panic reaction to Orson Welles's broadcast 'The War of the Worlds'.[6] A passage reads:

Dr Cantril's study will seek two objectives: first, determination of the general extent and nature of the public reaction to the broadcast; second, the social-psychological reasons for this reaction in various types of individuals. This novel research undertaking will be greatly aided by work already performed at Princeton by Dr Cantril in the Princeton Radio Project.

Lazarsfeld must have written a complaining letter to Cantril very shortly after the article appeared, for on 26 January Cantril wrote to Lazarsfeld expressing his disappointment, anger and bewilderment over his reaction. From the content and tone of Cantril's letter it would seem that Lazarsfeld must have objected to the emphasis given to Cantril's role in the project by the newspaper reporter. The relevant parts of Cantril's letter reads:

I am glad you expressed yourself on the release, but I must say that the reaction seems a bit infantile. Perhaps we should all have directors' uniforms with differential insignia. It is hard to image that people like Frank, Gallup, Allport, Katz, Stouffer would maintain petty jealousies, and I should like to think that you, too, would have sufficient perspective in things not to let such trivia bother you.

As soon as I got your letter I went over to the office of the *Alumni Weekly* to see what the fuss was all about. No one had mentioned the piece to me, and I seldom see the sheet. I must say that the report seemed quite harmless.

Cantril makes his own lack of enthusiasm for the project clear:

If the project could go on completely without me I should honestly be much happier. But apparently I am a strategic link in the chain. I am willing to play the role only for two reasons: (1) [President] Dodds feels that we should not tell the Foundation outright that we do not want a

---

6   The study was published as *Invasion from Mars* under the authorship of Cantril, Gaudet and Herzog (1940).

renewal; (2) I am anxious to help you make a reputation and attain some sort of eventual security in these highly insecure days. Please believe me that these are my only motives. Since they are my only motives, I frequently feel that I should drop the whole thing and concentrate my time more on two books: *Mass Psychology* and *Public Opinion and Propaganda*. If I have to become involved in many emotional reactions, I may reconsider my whole position.

You will know that I do not like to write this way. Yesterday I dictated a gentle answer but last night I began to wonder why in hell I was letting myself in for more years of minor interruption to the work that interests me most. Few people would go on with this when they were so anxious to focus spare energies on other things. Hence from a purely logical point of view, your reaction was untimely. (Cantril 26.1.39)

The *Alumni* article now seems rather innocuous, and clearly Cantril found Lazarsfeld's attitude somewhat mystifying. Lazarsfeld's reaction is intelligible, however, when viewed in terms of his self-image as Director, and his awareness that identifying himself with an institute presented him with his best chance of making his way in American academic life. It is difficult to believe that Lazarsfeld really considered that Cantril had designs on the Project, but it must be remembered that the project had been the basis of Larzarsfeld's 'Institute', and it is therefore understandable that he should have reacted strongly over his name not being sufficiently linked with it. After all, at that time Lazarsfeld was still in a state of considerable uncertainty with regard to his future position, and the recognition that had been forthcoming had been largely due to his building up a research centre on the basis of Rockefeller funds and the commercial contract that he had obtained.

Whilst Cantril had originally been pleased to have Lazarsfeld rid him of the responsibility for running the project, it would seem that by this time he wished to be rid of it altogether, and President Dodds was not committed to it. Reviewing the situation in January 1939 Marshall recorded '...Dodds fears that work of this kind may not only get little from the faculty, but in making demands on them may detract them from other interests worth developing.' (Marshall 18.1.39)

Marshall seems to have grown weary with having the radio research project located within a university. He worried lest the fact that it did not fit easily with existing university social science work might mean that it would be 'definitely harmful to... have a university influence its direction'. (Marshall memo 18.1.39) Marshall was seriously thinking of alternative locations for the study, in particular handing the Project over to the radio industry itself, or rather to the Joint Committee on Research which it had recently established.[7]

---

7   It must be noted, however, that he also considered giving it to the New School for Social Research in New York which of course is a university, but he was going to do so on the grounds that it had been suggested that training in broadcasting should be undertaken there, and not so much for its research expertise.

The blunt fact was, however, that Lazarsfeld was by now indispensable to the project. He had stamped his presence on it so strongly that any consideration of its future had to take account of him as its leading figure. Not only had he cultivated the necessary contacts and drawn together the research team, but his methodological expertise could not be replaced. Even so, Marshall was concerned about Lazarsfeld's style of operating, and called Stanton and Cantril to his office to discuss matters on 2 March 1939. Both men assured Marshall that they would act to 'check and balance' Lazarsfeld, but could not engage actively themselves as researchers on the Project. The very next day Lazarsfeld called at Marshall's office to present his views on the situation. Marshall recorded:

> Lazarsfeld is evidently not too happy at the prospect of having the project continue under Princeton auspices, preferring to see it located in some university like Columbia, where it would gain advantages of being a real university enterprise. (Marshall 3.3.39)

It is not suggested that Lazarsfeld was operating some kind of machiavellian strategy, but simply that he appreciated the problematic situation within which the Project found itself. Lazarfeld's views had to be taken into account in any decision on what was to be done, and in that sense power rested very much with him. Given that the Project was now operating out of New York it made good sense to sever the connections with Princeton and transfer it to Columbia, especially since Lynd was enthusiastic about having it housed there. In his appraisal of the Project's history, Marshall summed up the situation thus:

> Another outcome is worth noting, particularly in view of the transfer of the Project from Princeton to Columbia. At Princeton, as President Dodd's comments imply, it never really found a home; there was not at Princeton other work in progress closely enough related to the work of the project to provide an adequate background with which it could articulate and from which it could draw personnel guidance. At Columbia, the Project found sympathetic and hearty sponsorship through Prof RS Lynd. As a result, in June 1940 [sic] Dr Lazarsfeld was given a permanent appointment to the faculty of sociology with the rank as an Associate Professor, the university taking over the major portion of his salary. At Columbia the Project has close relations with the School of Journalism, with the graduate department in the Social Sciences and the Teachers College. (Marshall 31.8.41)

It is certainly true that the Project 'never really found a home' at Princeton, nor was it likely that it would have done so had it remained. From the point of view of the future prospects of both the Project itself and Lazarsfeld's own career, Columbia was a much more suitable location. Yet it would seem that even had Lazarsfeld wished the Project to remain at Princeton matters would have been far from easy. Quite apart from the fact that at Princeton the Project could not attach itself to existing intellectual interests which would have fed into and given support to it, there was also the fact that Lazarsfeld appears not to have been personally acceptable to the faculty members:

> According to Cantril there will be no difficulty in the project
> continuing under the nominal sponsorship of Princeton, but Cantril
> believes its office must be in New York City. He doubts if it would be
> advantageous to Lazarsfeld or the project to have Lazarsfeld working in
> Princeton, particularly on the grounds that Lazarsfeld would not be
> personally very acceptable to the members of the Princeton faculty he
> would come into contact with. (Marshall 2.3.39)

There can be no certainty as to why Lazarsfeld should have been unacceptable.
He was undeniably 'foreign', and Princeton was renowned for its Ivy League
sense of superiority. And despite his Viennese charm, Lazarsfeld could be
rather forceful. Samuel Stouffer, writing to Frederick Mills of Columbia
concerning Lazarsfeld's proposed appointment as professor, obviously felt it
necessary to inform him of Lazarsfeld's personal characteristics:

> Paul has his defects. He is not an orderly worker, and if he gets a bright
> idea he is likely to pursue it to the detriment of orderly routines. I
> rather admire that kind of guy myself. In spite of the fact that he has
> lived in this country for seven years or more, he has a distinct foreign
> appearance and speaks with a strong accent. This prejudices some
> people against him, and I think some are further prejudiced because
> they feel that there is an occasional arrogance in his manner. Actually,
> Paul is one of the most modest of men, but he does have a rather heavy
> Germanic way of presenting a topic which tends to make some people
> feel that there is not as much in the topic as the difficulty in following
> would suggest. I think such critics would be occasionally right, but I
> can testify from experience that there is plenty of pure gold in them
> thar hills. (Stouffer 17.2.41)

Clearly Stouffer felt the necessity to protect Lazarsfeld by mentioning his
'foreign appearance' and his occasional appearance of arrogance. Factors such
as these could well have led to difficulties in assimilating into the world of
Princeton. In addition, all those who knew Lazarsfeld appear to have been
particularly impressed by the power of his intellect. Lynd, for example, wrote
to Marshall in 1939 describing Lazarsfeld as 'the ablest combination of great
technical training and ability and of imagination and energy to carry through
work that I know of in this social-psychological field.... He has far more
imagination than Stouffer of Chicago'. (Lynd 16.3.39) Given his position as an
'outsider', his easy mastery of intellectual matters, exhibiting itself as
confidence or at times arrogance, may well have provoked hostility in certain
quarters. And then there was always his association with commerce. At a place
such as Princeton, with its feeling of social superiority, it was hardly surprising
that Lazarsfeld, as the 'clever foreign outsider' culturally distanced from other
faculty members, should prove, in Cantril's words, to be 'not acceptable'.
However this may be, on moving to Columbia University the Princeton Radio
Research Project was re-named, on the suggestion of Lynd, the Columbia
Office of Radio Research 'so as not to identify it further with Princeton

University'. (Lynd letter to President Dodds 5.12.39) It was later renamed in 1944 the Bureau of Applied Social Research, evidently on the suggestion of Robert Merton, to signify that the organisation had moved beyond media research in its scope of operation.

A Benevolent Foundation and an Unenlightened Industry

Bernard Berelson states that the 'modern version of communication research' can be traced to the 'development of both academic and commercial interests', with the 'former largely co-ordinated, if not stimulated by the Rockefeller Foundation seminar of the late 1930s'. (Berelson 1959:1) Despite the various traditions that now make up the field, this is basically correct. However, in so far as commercial research was concerned, it hardly rose above the level of head-counting and contributed very little to the initial academic development of the field. The radio industry in the late 1930s was more or less exclusively concerned with the listener as a prospective purchaser. The research divisions of the radio companies, almost without exception, were organised to promote the sale of time, and engaged in little direct research themselves. Most of their energy was devoted to the interpretation of the data obtained from outside agencies such as the Co-operative Analysis of Broadcasting (CAB) or Crosley Survey, and the Clark-Hooper Survey. Such commercial agencies served not only the radio industry itself, but advertising agencies as well; consequently their studies were mainly concerned with identifying which members of the radio audience were likely to buy the products advertised on the radio. In addition, given that most of the agency enquiries were conducted by telephone it meant that even in establishing the size of the audience such research was deficient - many radio listeners did not possess a telephone. However, crude as this data was, it did provide a certain basis for broadcast planning. It served the interests of the advertisers, but it was the 'needs' of the audience which was missing, something which the Rockefeller Foundation was most concerned about.

The closely interlocked interests of the radio and advertising industries troubled those at the Foundation who were interested in the qualitative improvement of radio broadcasting, and the development of a radio network servicing the nation. The Foundation's concern can be gauged from the following abstract of a memorandum, probably the summary of a conversation between John Marshall and Frank Stanton, then of the Research Division of CBS:

> More important still in this respect is the relation which has grown up between the industry and the advertising agencies on the one hand, and between the agencies and buyers of time on the other hand. It is a fact that one of the national chains felt obliged deliberately to curtail its research to maintain good relations with the advertising agencies who acted as intermediaries of sponsors in the purchase of time. Data which the chain was collecting proved contrary to some of the contentions on

which agencies were selling time. To maintain its profitable relations with the agencies, the chain's only choice was to give up the research. (Memorandum, May 1937:6)

The suspicion which the industry harboured towards more penetrating research and its unwillingness to experiment led John Marshal to describe the industry's position as operating from 'unenlightened self-interest'. (Marshall 6.7.73) The situation that confronted Frank Stanton at CBS provides an excellent illustration of this attitude. In 1936 Stanton had been given the responsibility of presenting CBS's evidence before the Federal Communication Committee's hearings on the allocation of radio facilities. During the course of his preparatory work he discovered that the industry's assumption that listener interests were directly related to signal strength was incorrect. In fact, a majority of listeners indicated as their favourite programmes those which were third or even fourth in the order of reception quality. Consequently he urged CBS to conduct a study to discover the basis of listeners' liking for various programmes. The proposed study was turned down on the grounds that it would have 'no immediate commercial value'. (Recorded interview between Frank Stanton and John Marshall 6.11.36)

It is a characteristic feature of foundations to support an area of research only so long as foundation money is essential to its success. Once other finances begin to flow into an area they tend to disengage themselves from support, and search for other areas of work where their moneys can have greater proportional effectiveness. In the case of radio research, however, not only was the field virtually unmapped; there was also little possibility of other agencies channelling funds in that direction. George Gallup, for example, wrote to John Marshall in relation to Hadley Cantril's proposed study of radio, the proposal that was to become the Princeton Radio Research Project:

> Most of the research in the field of radio has been concerned with the measurement of the size of audience listening to various programmes. We know virtually nothing about the influence of radio on listeners, the reasons why persons listen to certain programmes and not others.
>
> The organisations which are now engaged in radio research are not in a position to do research of this character largely because research procedures are required. Since the results have no immediate commercial value it is extremely unlikely that such a project would be undertaken by industrial concerns.
>
> Again, let me say that I am most enthusiastic about this plan and hope that your committee will pass favourably upon it. (Gallup 19.5.37)

Although Cantril was offered the Directorship of the Radio Research Project, and wished to be involved, he did not want to carry the full burden of running such a programme of research, and hence persuaded Lazarsfeld to accept the position of Director. What Cantril wanted, as did the Foundation, was someone who would advance not just the empirical understanding of the audience, but (of equal importance in understanding why focus group research developed within mass communications research and not some other branch of the social sciences) the development of an appropriate methodology for the task. The whole enterprise was new. There was no specific methodology for communications research. There is a note in the Rockefeller archives which Marshall wrote to the Trustees of the Foundation outlining what he saw as the plan for the Radio Research Project. It reads: 'Of the four years the proposed study will require, the first will be devoted to developing and testing techniques by which evidence needed to answer these questions can be secured'. (Marshall, considerations presented to the Trustees, Rockerfeller Foundation Archives (RFA), 21 May 1937)

There was therefore an urgent drive for conceptual clarification of the field and for the development of the methodological tools that would allow empirical statements to be made about the role of radio in peoples lives. Out of this framework for enquiry, which laid the foundation of the field of communications research in the early days, came a type of operating logic that directly resulted in the development of focus groups in the hands of Merton. Right from the beginning of the Radio Research Project there was an insistence on the audience as people to be investigated rather than talked about. Thus, the statement by Gallup that 'research procedures are required' is interesting in light of the Rockefeller Foundation's brief to Lazarsfeld to developed a methodology suitable for examining the audience as part of the overall strategy of the Foundation's research programme. In some ways this instruction played into Lazarsfeld's 'over keen' interest in methodology at the expense of substance, although it is worth noting at this point that he had brought Adorno on board because, as he informed me, 'I felt it would be just wonderful to relate Adorno to empirical research'.

However, even though stress had been placed on methodological development by the Foundation, the programme of research was still expected to deliver results, and by the spring of 1939 Lazarsfeld had produced little by way of articles or monographs to satisfy the Foundation. Questions began to be asked within the Foundation about the wisdom of continuing to support the Radio Research Project. A review committee concluded: 'In the next phase of the project time and money should be provided for the detailed analysis and interpretation of some of the material collected to date.' (Review Committee 10.3.39) Yet six days later Lazarsfeld, whilst in Chicago, received the following Western Union cable from John Marshall in New York:

> DISCUSSIONS IN OFFICE INDICATE RELUCTANCE TO INVEST IN NEW RESEARCH PENDING FORMULATION OF PRESENT FINDINGS STOP FEELING HERE THAT NEED IS FOR BREATHING SPELL TO SAVE PROJECT FROM BEING VICTIM OF ITS OWN SUCCESS STOP RESULT DECISION TO MAKE NO RECOMMENDATION TO TRUSTEES NOW STOP READY TO REVIEW SITUATION IN JUNE IF FORMULATION IS SUFFICIENTLY ADVANCED BY THEN TO PROVIDE BASIS (Marshall 16.3.39)

Both the reviewing committee and John Marshall were correct that the Project was in danger of becoming a 'victim of its own success'. A vast amount of data had been gathered, but there was a distinct lack of any overall theme running through the work, and after two years of operation this absence, not surprisingly, gave rise to alarm. Whilst there were no reservations about Lazarsfeld's intellectual capacity, since that had been demonstrated clearly enough, there were doubts as to whether, or when, he would produce anything substantive. Lazarsfeld was well aware of which way the wind was blowing, and in a letter he wrote to Cantril and Stanton in the winter of 1938 he specifically mentioned that he was: '...much worried about the fact that the prolongation of the project will come up with Marshall and the Foundation at a time when no major unit of the project will be finished'. (Lazarsfeld 18.11.38)

Ithiel de Sola Pool, who was the Director of the School of Public and International Affairs at Princeton University where the project was then based, before moving to Columbia University, wrote to Hadly Cantril making his recommendations clear: 'a least a book manuscript should be in presentable shape by June 1st.' If that was forthcoming, then Pool felt, 'the Foundation as well as the university will be highly appreciative and proposals for further research would then receive all the sympathetic consideration they deserve – meantime anything like the opening up of new research must be sedulously avoided'. (Pool 18.3.39)

By working night and day Lazarsfeld and his team did produce a report sufficient to satisfy Marshall, which was delivered on the morning of the deadline. Lazarsfeld quickly followed this up by finding a publisher. Lazarfeld wished for a commercial publisher and not, as had happened with the project's first book, *Invasion from Mars*, (Cantril *et al* 1946) Princeton University's own press. *Radio and the Printed Page* (Lazarsfeld 1940) did find a commercial publisher, after great difficulty, in Duel Sloan and Pearce. Within a few months, according to records in the Rockefeller Foundation Archives, it had sold over one thousand two hundred copies, and thus began what was to be a short but fruitful period of collaboration between Lazarsfeld, and Duel Sloan and Pearce, who published not only the two subsequent volumes of radio research, but also *The People's Choice*. (Lazarsfeld *et al* 1944)

The relationship between the academic and the foundation official has within it many of the stresses and strains generally associated with patronage: the academic grateful for the money which allows him to work, yet resentful at having to submit his work to someone whom Lazarsfeld described as, 'A little fellow, who you can't be quite sure whether he could get a professorship, and suddenly he has an enormous amount of power to give money away'. (Lazarsfeld 2.6.73). But such 'interference' can be productive. After all, it was the Rockefeller Foundation that initiated the study of radio, not Cantril or Stanton, and certainly not Lazarsfeld. Indeed, at the substantive level Lazarsfeld had little or no interest in communication research. For him the project was simply 'a rather spectacular job' and of interest only because of its methodological challenge.

Whether or not outside 'interference' is productive depends on the nature of the intellectual enterprise itself, the personality of the producer, and the character of the external agency officer, along with the intellectual ethos of the funding agency. A crucial question, however, is how far the external agency's 'concerns', or interests, should be accepted by the academic community as worthy of attention, particularly if such 'concerns' do not fit ethically with those of the staff to be engaged on the research, or fall outside their intellectual interests. In times of economic stringency values are often relaxed so that work which would have been refused in more prosperous times is accepted as a financial necessity. If universities, however, wish their associated research institutes to engage in 'pure' research then alternative sources of funds must be provided. To live by contract work is a precarious existence. The other fact is that research institutes are expensive to maintain, and there is little point in holding up university departments as a yardstick of procedure since it was the departmental structure's very inability to handle large-scale empirical work that led to the establishment of the Lazarsfeld-type research institute in the first place.

In the case of Lazarsfeld his own manipulative skills allowed him to survive by satisfying the external agency's demands whilst at the same time not letting it interfere with what he considered the central task of his work. Lazarsfeld was constantly acting like a businessman in looking for new avenues of revenue to support the Bureau and his research operations[8] but it is worth noting that the more applied the research of an institute, the less destructive such 'interference' is likely to be. Adorno, for example, was working at such a high level of abstraction that any 'interference' necessarily went to the core of his ideas. But taken as a whole the Radio Project was very open to suggestions of a practical and procedural nature. Indeed the Project's success depended in part on co-operation and suggestions from a variety of interested parties. Given the administrative nature of large parts of the work then, it can be argued, that 'interference' had positive benefits. Adorno, on the other hand, was still working in the European tradition of the lone scholar where only 'pure' intellectual criticism could be of benefit and thus could only be provided by scholars of equal intellectual standing to himself. To a person of Adorno's persuasion, that was a very limited circle indeed and it certainly did not include foundation officers or other 'lay' individuals who were asked to comment on his

---

8   There can be no better example of this than him having the whole of the Bureau learn Spanish. I discovered in the Rockefeller archives a note to the effect that Lazarsfeld and his co-workers had employed an instructor to teach them Spanish. When Lazarsfeld was asked about this he said: 'I remember that now. I can remember it very vividly - we paid an instructor... Look, that was just a complete political misjudgement.' This was during the War... I was sure somehow that the building up of South America would be the main...post-war task of the United States. I didn't know the main task would be to build up Germany and Japan. I didn't foresee the cold war. You see if it hadn't been for the cold war I still think that would have been very important. I was absolutely sure there lay the cultural international future of the United States – I still think if it hadn't been for the cold war – it was not a stupid exercise.' (Lazarsfeld 15.6.73)

work. (Morrison 1978a) According to Marshall, Adorno had commented that the Radio Project was 'subject to the whim of a young ignoramus', meaning Marshall in his capacity as the controlling foundation officer.

The decision by the Foundation not to extend the music side of the Project, simply to have 'Adorno's research papers... filed with the Project materials and so kept available for possible future development' (Marshall, inter-office memorandum 1.5.40) was part and parcel of the questioning of the lack of output of the Project, added to which, of course, the Foundation could not see the benefits of what Adorno was doing. In this sense, the Foundation was operating in a manner not too distinct from that adopted by the industry. Both demanded that the research be practically useful; the industry wished to protect its commercial interests, and the Foundation wished to correct what it saw as shortcomings in the performance of radio as a cultural force. To Adorno, this was administrative thinking in action and a corollary of engaging in administrative research.

Although Marshall by the 'threat' of refusing to recommend a further release of funds had temporality 'disciplined' Lazarsfeld into selecting a theme which then formed the basis for a report, and subsequently *Radio and the Printed Page*, his main desire was to get Lazarsfeld to confront his own work, and to clarify his aims. James Rowland Angell of the NBC wrote to Marshall: 'I am still quite unconvinced that Dr Lazarsfeld will in fact focus his shotgun upon a few central problems. His mind is abnormally prolific of ideas and these do not seem to me to fall naturally into significant co-ordinated patterns'. (Angell 28.2.39)

Marshall raised his worries about Lazarsfeld and the overall state of the Project with Robert Lynd, a member of the guiding committee and Lazarsfeld's main sponsor at Columbia. In fact Lynd had been a major supporter of Lazarsfeld from his very first arrival in America.[9] Lynd wrote to Marshall, first reassuring him as to Lazarsfeld's great intellectual capacity, and spelling out where the basis of the problem lay, and how it might possibly be corrected:

> I think what he needs is a stronger hand (you, a committee or?) holding him to a *defined* program. I don't believe he had a clear-cut set of definitions and of criteria as to priority in undertaking this job. This was in large part due to the situation: the Foundation did not know what it wanted but wanted a field of alternative possibilities opened up. This played into Paul's over-wide field of interest and aided and abetted him in following his curiosity than narrowing a program.
>
> I believe Paul will produce an amazing amount of valuable material on the work done to date. I have no question about that. The money has been well spent. But if you go on – and my judgement would be to do so, tho' in June – I believe you must set up a situation that will help

---

9   Lynd was one of the first people Lazarsfeld made contact with in American because of Lynd's *Middletown* study, which Lazarsfeld paid credit to in *Die Arbeitslose von Marienthal*.

Paul to explore *selected* problems. He is so darned able that there is no point in throwing out baby and bath. Every researcher has an Achilles heal. His is his intellectual curiosity and everything interesting. He *can* be channelled. ...The need, therefore, is to use his great strength, but to see that his sailing orders are more explicit. (Lynd 16.3.39)

Marshall was clearly influenced by Lynd's advice; he wrote a letter in the summer of 1939 to Professor Richards of Magdalene College, Cambridge, laying out his concerns about the development of mass communications research, and suggesting how problems might be resolved:

In the past couple of years it has been increasingly clear that most of my work has been in a field which for lack of a better name I have to call mass communication. It has also been increasingly clear to me that work in that field is hampered for lack of a systematic and disciplined approach. Talks during the last year have convinced me that it is possible to work out some such approach and further that can best be done by a small group of people who in themselves represent different possible approaches to the subject. (Marshall 16.8.39)

The outcome of such deliberations was that Marshall instituted the seminars which Berelson saw as forming the beginnings of mass communication research as a co-ordinated field of enquiry. They began in June 1939 and continued until June 1940. In addition to Lazarsfeld and Marshall, the regular seminar participants were Charles Siepmann, Lyman Bryson, Lloyd Free, Geoffrey Gorer, Harold Lasswell, Donald Slesinger and Douglas Warples. (Morrison 1978b)

It was not just methodologically that the field urgently needed to advance, but conceptually. At one of the seminars Lasswell first introduced his now famous model of the communication process: who says what, to whom, in what channel, with what effect. This model of the communication process may not be one that many contemporary media researchers would hold to, considering it a distorting influence on the field in giving rise to the effects paradigm, but in discussing the seminars Marshall captured the pioneering spirit of the enterprise and the difficulties they were faced with: 'It seems platitudinous today, but that concept of Lasswell's of mass communication had not arrived at that point. Imagine if you can, research in mass communication that wasn't guided by those thought considerations and you have a picture of much of what Lazarsfeld was attempting in 1939'. (Marshall conversation 6.7.73)

The number of participants was deliberately restricted, making the meetings more like a working party than seminars in the full sense. In total ten memoranda were produced. All survive apart from number eight, which is missing from the Rockefeller Archives. The memoranda are extremely thoughtful documents, intended to influence thinking within academia and government, and were sent out to a large number of distinguished academics drawn from a variety of disciplines. Thus, whilst ostensibly the seminars were initiated to 'control' Lazarfeld, they came to have much greater importance for, as Berelson rightly noted, they aided the co-ordination and stimulation of mass communications research in general. They were also important in an indirect way to the development of focus group research.

The war in Europe had already begun before the first seminar was held. The gathering momentum of the struggle in Europe signalled America's likely future involvement, and in term of the establishment of focus group research it is of interest that a report on the seminars written in July 1940, and signed by the above mentioned participants, reads:

> This report is a statement of belief, belief in the significance of three facts. We believe first, that in the exacting times which lie ahead, public opinion will be a decisive factor. If America is to meet the necessity of adapting to a changing world, and at the same time preserve the ways of life that Americans hold dear, the adaptation must be achieved with public consent. In securing consent, public opinion and the influences affecting it will be crucial. We believe, second, that for leadership to secure that consent will require unprecedented knowledge of the public mind and of the means by which leadership can secure consent. To secure it, public policy, as never before, will have to take account of public needs and predispositions. We believe, third, that we have available today methods of research which can reliably inform us about the public mind and about how it can be influenced in relation to public affairs. (Seminar Memorandum July 1940)

The question was, how to introduce the emerging field of communications research into government thinking, or at least, how to introduce the work of the Columbia 'school'. Throughout the seminar memoranda, which include detailed discussion on methodology, concept formation and the organisation of research, there appear frequent references to the possibility of America entering the war, and the changes that such involvement would mean in terms of altering prevailing attitudes, and organisational practices. Success was held to depend very much on the free flow and use of communications by government. In light of such references I presumed in my initial, and at first partial reading of the Rockefeller files, that the seminars had originally been convened to consider such matters. It was only in conversation with John Marshall that the actual history and significance of the seminars came into view:

> *D Morrison:* Perhaps I could ask you about the main impetus behind the setting up of the seminars of 1939 to 1940. There seems to be two main thrusts to me. One was the idea of co-ordinating. That is, the idea that mass communication research must be co-ordinated into some kind of body in any useful advancement was to be made. And the second, seems to be the difficulties that America faced if she entered the war, and it seems to me, that the first part, that is the co-ordinating factor, gets swamped by the

actual difficulties which America would face and you thought you should address yourself to that.

J Marshall: I wouldn't read the record that way. No.

DM: You wouldn't?

JM: No. Well my interest in those seminars... I guess my interest was the basic one... I got the money and I organised it... to arrive at a concept of what research in mass communication should be undertaken. Now let me go back a little bit. There was a prior episode. At a date when maybe you can ascertain, when the question of further support for the Bureau came up. There was a feeling among a number of us who were concerned... not necessarily in the Foundation... on the part of Bob Lynd and probably on the part of Charles Siepman who was by that time in the picture, and others. We felt that Lazarsfeld's research had been admirable for the first period, but that it was scattered and unfocused. With Lazarsfeld's agreement we therefore subjected him to a day's examination. My recollection is – I can't be sure of this, that the meeting was held at the Century Club.

DM: I think maybe it was the Graduate Club.

JM: No... It may have been, it may have been...Yes, the Graduate club, yes it would have been down there. Yes that's where it was. We had a group and we sort of cross-examined Lazarsfeld all that day, trying to get him to define some focus for his work – in the next period of his work. While we did get Lazarsfeld to agree to certain foresight on what he would go on to do, the work was still in a conceptual muddle. There was no sharpness to it what-so-ever. So we came to agree in the spring of 1939 that we would hold this series of meetings at monthly intervals through the coming academic year. That is September 1939 until June...[1940]. Well, as the first meeting took place the war had broken out. Someone said, 'of course our discussions will have a much firmer orientation if we regard the War as a "theatre". Public attention will be predominantly focused upon the war, and it gives us a kind of laboratory situation in which we can perhaps really sharpen our thinking.' Now I would therefore strongly correct the idea that the initiating force here was the needs of the country. It was rather that we saw in this rather disastrous situation of the war an unhappy opportunity to conceptualise this whole field of research. The war as it were put all the factors into sharp focus.... To round that up... it was only as we completed... only as we contemplated mass communication research in wartime that it became clear to us that perhaps this did have some practical outcome. Do you know what happened then?

DM: No.

JM: Well Harold Lasswell of course was a member of that group. Lasswell had just achieved some attention in Washington by utilising his developing method of content analysis in a trial in which the government was prosecuting someone for alleged subversive activities. This meant that Lasswell had established a good many contacts in Washington. We all said that if this can be made use of in the wartime situation then we wanted it to be made use of. I suppose I got some specific release from the Foundation for this document. It was a private document and supposedly not for publication. Lasswell had the bright idea of introducing this to government thinking at the level of the secretaries to secretaries of various departments. So Lasswell organised a group of secretaries to secretaries who turned out to be rather extraordinary men. We went down to Washington, Lasswell and I and one or two others, for a day's discussion of how the implications of this report could be realised in government research. Lasswell was perfectly right, and in this way these secretaries to the secretaries made their principals immediately aware of how research such as this could be used for the advantages of government and I think from then on a very considerable part of the research went over into government offices. (Marshall 6.7.73)

Enter Merton: The Joining of Forces

At Columbia, Lazarsfeld had a powerful backer in Robert Lynd, yet there was still a question hanging over the style of work that Lazarfeld had come to represent. To some extent the opposition to Lazarsfeld's advancement was focused on Lazarsfeld himself, but the battlefront over his appointment was much larger than that. The basic question was what the shape of sociology should be, and what was the purpose of social enquiry. This was an epistemological struggle as well as a methodological one, turning sociology at Columbia into a political question – one that was stalking American sociology in general. Paul Lazarsfeld and Robert Merton became the appointed captains of two warring armies, although neither assented to their allotted rank. Lazarsfeld represented the empirical quantitative wing of sociology, and Merton the theoretical wing.

While still an instructor at Harvard University, Merton had already established himself as one of the leading young theorists in his field with the publication in 1938 of his seminal paper, 'Social Structure and Anomie'. (Merton 1958) Within two years of the paper's appearance he had become a professor at Tulane University and Chairman of the Sociology Department. He accepted the invitation to go to Columbia as an assistant professor, but as Morton Hunt points out:

> Not until some time after his arrival at Morningside Heights [the area of New York where the university is located] did Merton learn that he had been hired almost as much for his symbolic value as for his ability. The sharpest fight in modern sociology – a field where there is even more sectarian bickering than there is in psychiatry – between the mathematically orientated opinion-sampling empiricists and the pontificating concept-making theorists. The Sociology Department at Columbia was so badly split between these factions that for several years it had been impossible to hire a new man simply because the two sides could not agree on one. At last a compromise was arranged and each side would make one appointment. The empiricists chose Lazarsfeld, who had created his 'Office of Radio Research', and the theorists chose Merton, at that time an excellent specimen of a concept maker. (Hunt 1961:59,60)

Professor Chaddock, who held the post of full professor, had committed suicide a few years earlier, and the Department had not been able to agree on the type of scholar to fill the vacant post. Columbia at that time had one of the most active and prestigious sociology departments in the country, but was completely divided between the empirical sociologists represented by Robert Lynd, and the more theoretically speculative sociologists represented by Robert MacIver. Intellectual differences were overlaid with personal bitterness when MacIver wrote a particularly critical review of Lynd's *Knowledge for What* (1939), in which he emphasised the utilitarian conception of elucidation to which MacIver was so trenchantly opposed. The rift within the department was a microcosm of the world of sociology outside Columbia. The situation led the patriarchal President of the University, Nicholas William Butler, to go to the unprecedented lengths of establishing an outside committee to resolve the deadlock. MacIver and Lynd could each name their own candidate and whoever was the older got the associate professorship, and the younger would be appointed as assistant professor. The splitting of the full professorship in this way resulted in Lynd choosing Lazarsfeld, who being older was rewarded with the associate professorship, and MacIver choosing Merton. This arrangement was supposed to perpetuate the split in sociology. It did nothing of the sort.

Asked about the situation surrounding his appointment to professor, Lazarsfeld memory was still vivid:

> I remember even now. I remember the figures exactly. Chaddock had US$ 8,000, and that was split into US$ 4,500 associate professorship

and US$ 3,500 for the assistant professorship. MacIver and Lynd would each name their candidate and whoever was older got the associate professorship and MacIver picked Merton, and Lynd picked me.[10] And we were supposed to perpetuate the MacIver split – it never turned out that way. But it was as simple as that. It was a judgement of an ad hoc committee which forced this solution on the department, and you see MacIver and Lynd could not interfere with the department.

All was not plain sailing as Lazarsfeld recounted:

> MacIver was chairman of the department and so his agreement was necessary by the constitution. Lynd wasn't chairman. Lynd became chairman later, and MacIver still retained a certain power. He could have vetoed Lynd I suppose. He knew me vaguely. He knew Lynd would make an empiricist a professor, and MacIver couldn't change that, but he could have objected against this particular man. But MacIver was extremely – he was a Scot – and extremely restrained, a very great gentleman. In a way an extremely mean person, but extremely civilised, and so one day I got invited – several times in fact – to play bridge with MacIver and a friend of his. And that was MacIver's way to size me up. How do I behave at bridge, because he could not object against an empiricist, but he could say the man wouldn't fit or wouldn't be appropriate for Columbia. If he had said that, then probably Lynd would have had to choose another man. But he never talked to me at that time about any substantive matter – he just wanted to know am I acceptable, so to say. And I knew exactly why I was invited to play bridge. (Lazarsfeld 15.6.73)

Any professional advancement, be it academic or otherwise, usually involves a social component, and MacIver may well have been looking for an opportunity to dish Lynd by refusing his choice on extra-academic grounds. Had he been particularly ruthless he could no doubt have found some aspect of Lazarsfeld's social behaviour to object to. It is in this context that Stouffer's letter in support of Lazarsfeld's professorial appointment, referring to Lazarsfeld's 'foreign appearance', ought to be read.

The appointment of Merton, supposed to perpetuate the divide in sociology, in effect assisted the development of the Bureau's place within American sociology by affording it theoretical respectability. The influence of Merton on Lazarsfeld has, according to James Coleman, not been given due regard. (Coleman 1980) The judgement of Everett Rogers, although perhaps somewhat over-stated, is that 'Merton was so important to the Bureau of Applied Social Research's program in communication research that perhaps we ought to refer to 'Lazarsfeld-Merton' as the most important creators of the field of mass communication research in the United States'. (Rogers 1994:304) The simple fact is, however, that had Lazarsfeld been the narrow empirical

---

10　See MacIver (1968:141) for a brief account of Merton and Lazarfeld's selection.

researcher his critics cast him as, there would have been little intellectual basis for the friendship both men developed towards each other, nor could they have collaborated so well over the proposal for 'A Professional School for Training in Social Research'.[11] This proposal represents a good statement of Lazarsfeld's (and Merton's) thinking on the methods of social enquiry. Written in 1950, nearly a decade after the establishment of focus groups as a method, what the 'Proposal' shows is a framework of thought that is manifest in the strictures Merton believed ought to inform the practice of focus group research.

In many ways the proposal to establish a training centre at Columbia for the whole of American social science was the logical conclusion of Lazarsfeld's career to that date. The establishment of the Bureau as a 'laboratory for field research in the social sciences' was a pioneering enterprise, but by the mid 1950s the idea of such institutions had 'now become institutionalised' and is 'no longer sufficient reason for existence'. The Bureau was no longer unique. Lazarsfeld had his research institute that would 'stand for me', as he termed it in his letter to Cantril of 8.8.1937, and now it was opportune to increase his influence further as an educator.[12] (Hanover Report of the Bureau 1956) The training that was to be provided by the proposed 'expanded' Bureau was in all aspects of social research, and not just quantification, for which the Bureau and Lazarsfeld in particular had been so severely criticised. Training was to be given in qualitative research.

In discussion Lazarsfeld agreed that it was perhaps easier to 'pass on' quantitative techniques than it was qualitative skills. The recognition of this is present in the 'Proposal'. After praising the Lynds for their Middletown study (1929), and Thomas and Zaniecki for their monumental work on the Polish Peasant (1927), Lazarsfeld and Merton wrote: 'The graduate student of social research has received little training in the collection of field materials such as these. In effect, he is told only that perceptiveness or ingenuity is a precious

---

11 A much abbreviated form of this proposal can be found in Lazarsfeld (1972) entitled 'A Professional School for Training in Social Research'.

12 The Hanover Report was the result of a staff conference of Bureau members held at Hanover, New Hampshire on June 28/29th 1956 to discuss and plan what ought to be the future operations of the Bureau. Reading the report and the comments of contributors to the conference then what emerges is a picture of uncertainty within the Bureau. It was suffering somewhat from a crisis of identity. Although there was by no means uniformity of opinion among the staff, Clara Shapiro's information to the Policy Committee is noteworthy: 'From the point of view of the Bureau's status in the Profession: It would be easier to recruit competent personnel if the Bureau enjoyed a clearer position and an enhanced status in the profession.' She further noted, that from the point of view of self-esteem, a staff member 'could be made happier in his job if he felt more certain of the status of the Bureau'. The picture that emerges is of an institute which to a certain degree had exhausted its initial innovative capital of excitement and purpose. At the organisational level as the Bureau developed and expanded, the response had been to simply add new research divisions. Consequently the original sense of belonging resulting from intense interpersonal contact had been severely weakened. Social intercourse where it existed took place within the Divisions, rather than across the Bureau as a whole.

asset for the field worker'. No easy solution was posited. But, whilst accepting that students vary in their capacity for qualitative work, and that such differences could not in all likelihood be erased through formal training, nevertheless though 'perceptiveness cannot be induced by training, it can be enhanced'.

As always on Lazarsfeld's part there is a refusal to mystify procedures either by submerging them in obtuse and vague writing or by not being explicit. His insistence that clear and direct articulation is the basic precondition for progress in social research and theory was the source of some of his annoyance with the Frankfurt School. His refusal to mystify is evident:

> All too widely it is assumed that qualitative procedures must remain an elusive, private, and incommunicable art. Yet it is plain that there are recurrent situations and problems in field work which can be met successfully by communicable and transmissible procedures. The basic aspect of training must not be allowed to go by default. (Lazarsfeld and Merton 1950:71)

As we shall see, Merton's 'manual' on focus group research is true to the above insistence; it is a clear guide in how to handle 'recurrent situations'. In terms of the 'Proposal', the lacking of training in qualitative analysis was to be rectified by collecting case materials drawn from 'the literature of previously unstandardised kinds of qualitative field observations', and identifying the common observational procedures. The premise was that the repeated working through of such case materials would provide not only more standardised modes of observation, but would also 'sensitise the student to a wider range of strategic data than is ordinarily recognised by students schooled only in the more routine techniques of collecting field data'.

It is, however, in the area of 'Case Materials Centred on the Translation of Social Science Classics into terms of Contemporary Social Research' that Larzarsfeld, along with Merton, most forcefully exhibits an appreciation of the pitfalls of over-specialisation:

> The graduate student of social sciences tends towards one or the other of two opposed, and equally indefensible positions, in regard to social research. He is, at one extreme, forever subject to the dangers of intellectual parochialism. Taught to place great store by precision of research, he may come to limit his studies to those narrowly constrained problems which have little importance for advancement of the discipline.
>
> At the other extreme, some students, not infrequently the more capable among them, may rebel against what they take to be the excessively confining nature of research aimed primarily at precision (even at the expense of the intellectual significant problem). These students are tempted to abandon systematic empirical research altogether. Over-reacting against the threat of parochialism, they turn

exclusively on the 'largest' problems of the time, after the fashion of the social philosopher. They confuse the abstract importance of a problem with the prospect of advancing knowledge about the problem. (Lazarsfeld and Merton 1950:73,74)

Few statements by Lazarsfeld show so keenly his insistence on a judicious balance. For him, and Merton, the object of professional training in the social sciences was 'to provide for that combination of skills and scholarship which exhibit the distinctive merits of both the distinctive limitations of neither... it must produce neither mere social technicians nor mere social philosophers'.

Another concern exhibited in the 'Proposal' was that the student often emerged from his or her training equipped to conduct social research, but not 'schooled in a range of problems to which he might most favourably apply his research skills'. They proposed to overcome this through the *explication de texte*, a process that Lazarsfeld held in high esteem. The 'classics' of sociological writing, such as Simmel, Durkheim, Weber or Spencer, were to be 'converted into intensively examined rather than superficially scanned texts':

> A single page may be the occasion for an extended reformation. The student is brought to see that behind each significant statement in such a text, there lies a problem, more implied than stated. For in the period antedating systematic research, these authors characteristically set forth 'answers' to a problem without stating the problem itself in strict terms. Seemingly simple conceptions – the concepts of 'common will' implied by Rousseau, or the concept of social class implied by Marx, for example – are found, upon due scrutiny, to involve multiple meanings in different contexts. (Lazarsfeld and Merton 1950:76)

By following such a method the student was supposed not only to broaden his or her own conceptual vista, but to convert aspects of the work into operational research terms. However, as a protection against abstracting concepts and thus destroying the meaning they had for the original author, the student was also required to return 'them to their contexts in the original source, with the intention of uncovering the central intellectual concerns of the "classical" author'.

Through such procedure the student would see his or her own work in a more historical setting. In addition, the careful and detailed examination of the 'classics' was intended to inject a degree of humanism into the student's training. Indeed, it would seem that in viewing the development of social research within America Lazarsfeld and Merton were somewhat concerned at the over-emphasis on technical virtuosity at the expense of deep understanding. Commenting on the need for humanism, they stated it 'would curb the inadvertent tendency for a new barbarism in the social sciences. Above all, it would save the would-be technician from himself'.

Presumably what Lazarsfeld and Merton are describing in their proposal for training in the social sciences is their concept of the ideal social scientist, in other words, themselves to a certain extent. But of special importance is the commitment to a systematic approach to knowledge. It is not surprising, therefore, that simply because focus groups are a qualitative technique Merton never abandoned the practice to non-systematic procedure, nor wished for them to act as a single method in social enquiry even within a single study, let alone act as 'the method' of collecting data on the audience. What Peter Lunt and Sonia Livingstone (1996) detected in Merton's approach to focus group research is better seen not as the product of the effects tradition of communication research, but a product of a profound conception of social scientific knowledge.

As we can see, Lazarsfeld's was not a narrow view of sociology, nor did he himself engage in the abstracted empiricism of which, for example, C Wright Mills accuses him. Nor from a reading of his philosophical papers can it be concluded that he ever advocated such a style of work.[13] From his early days in Vienna there is a clear insistence upon a variety of approaches to social scientific enquiry coupled with the wish to erode the restricted disciplinary frontiers of social science to establish a more totally integrated whole. Neither was his insistence on rigorous methodology, something that we also see in Merton's demands for the practice of focus group research, intended to deny the importance of structural analysis within sociology. His perfecting of polling methods was intended to rid them, by way of contextual analysis, of their atomistic and individual character.[14] As Boudon notes:

> In contextual analysis, the respondent is defined not only by a number of individual characteristics (age, sex, opinion on various questions, educational level, occupation, etc) but also by variables that describe the milieu from which he comes. In this way, the investigation loses its atomistic character and can, by means of adequate analysis, regain the macrosociological tradition typical of Durkheim.
>
> Thus, it is wrong to say that Lazarsfeld's methodology leads to a restrictive notion of research unsuited to the preoccupations of macrosociology. On the level of intentions he always tried hard to refine this methodology to the point where empirical sociology could meet the classical requirements that sociology take into account 'social structure' and the situation 'as a whole'. (Boudon 1972:425)

Thus although it might have been expected from Lazarsfeld's reputation that the arrival of Merton would continue the split that existed in the sociology department at Columbia, with a greater understanding of Lazarsfeld's thinking on sociology, one can see how the two men would not have great differences. With the two in 'double harness'[15] the Institute that Lazarfeld always hoped he would have, and that would 'stand for him', was assured.

13 See for example his article 'The Obligation of the 1950 Pollster to the 1984 Historian'. (Lazarsfeld 1964)
14 In this context see Herbert Blumer's attack on polling in his article 'Public Opinion and Public Opinion Polling' (1948).
15 See Stein (1964: 214,215) for this comment and his experiences of working at the Bureau as a graduate student.

Organisation, Training and Influence

Edward Shils, observing the institutionalisation of sociology within American, notes the early dominance of the University of Chicago, and attributes its pre-eminence not only to the 'intellectual power' of some of its staff, but also to its superior institutionalisation when compared to other universities.[16] However, 'although Chicago sociology was embedded in a more ramified co-operative network, its institutionalisation was in one important respect like that of Durkheim's school. It depended very much on one important intellectual personality at a time.' (Shils 1970:793) Consequently, after Park and Thomas left, its dominance declined. But, as Shils also notes, 'not only internal developments reduced the centrality of Chicago. New centres were emerging in the East, places which had never been sub-centres of Chicago.' (Shils 1970:794) Among those new centres, the most important were undoubtedly Harvard and Columbia. At Harvard, under the triumvirate of Talcott Parsons, Henry Murray and Clyde Kluckhohn, 'a deliberate attempt was made to integrate the theories of social structure, culture and personality'. Although the teaching programme was adapted to such a conception of the subject, the research training programme did not move forward at the same intellectual pace. Harvard's Laboratory of Social Relations, furthermore, 'never became the intellectual drill ground which the Bureau of Applied Social Research became shortly after the end of the Second World War'. Whilst the 'Laboratory' did become the home of a number of studies, it never developed the identity which the Bureau achieved, and as a result lacked the solidarity among its intellectual mentors which characterised the Bureau. As Shils notes:

> ...it was in fact a centre consisting internally of several non-communicating segments — and this reduced its capacity to impose itself effectively on the subject as a whole. At the same time, it should be stressed that each of the major segments was a powerful intellectual personality — Parsons, Murray, Kluckhohn, Bruner, Stouffer, and Homans — each of them in one way or another a forceful generator of ideas and works. A high degree of consensus among them might have swept the field — It did pretty well as it was! (Shils 1970:795)

In no way should the impact of Harvard sociology be underestimated. Both by way of 'free-floating ideas', and through the placement of students in key university positions, its influence was enormous. But it lacked the more formal organisation of Columbia, and furthermore it had such a distinguished number of staff[17] that the domination of an individual was unimaginable, unlike at Columbia where Merton and Lazarsfeld acted as one. Berelson:

16 Chicago University was the first University anywhere in the world to establish a department of sociology. This it did in 1892. Its instruction programme was based on an adapted form of the German university seminar, but with closer supervision of doctoral students.

17 See Parsons (1956:23) for the Institute's list of members.

In the early days – the days when I was a staff member... back around the forties... Paul was so imaginative, innovative, sparking off all sorts of ideas that there wasn't much room for anyone else. Then, added to that, Merton was such a distinguished figure. He and Paul were so closely married, and each of such stature, that there just wasn't any room around. I remember at one point... a few of us raised a question about some issue, and so it went to a sort of staff meeting. I don't think they discussed it beforehand, but Paul and Bob so thought alike, or they got such signals from each other, or... if you said it's grey today then I quickly put the tone of grey on it... They just took it over in such a way that a few of us as a matter of fact just left the meeting... what's the use, why try this, they were running the thing. (Berelson 12.7.73)

Viewed historically, Columbia had a greater and probably more lasting impact than Harvard. The source of this success lay in the marrying of ideas to an institutional setting capable of transmitting them in practice. Merton, for example, came out of Harvard having studied under Parsons, and although he drew support from large-scale thinking in the mode of Parsons, his own more limited theories of the middle range were more articulate and manageable. His celebrated paper on theories of the middle range, although later given further expression,[18] was originally produced as a discussion paper four years after he had joined the Bureau and intended as a reply to Parsons's address to the American Sociological Society on 'The Position of Sociological Theory'. Although Merton was not at total variance with Parsons, he did object to his suggestion that the chief task was to deal with 'theory' rather than with 'theories'. Merton states his position on sociology very clearly:

Sociology will advance in the degree that the major concern is with developing theories adequate to limited ranges of phenomena and it will be hampered if attention is centred on theory in the large. I am confident that this is not in basic disagreement with Mr. Parsons; that it is a difference in emphasis rather than substance; indeed, later passages in his paper suggest as much. But I think it important to supply just that emphasis. I believe that our major task *today* is to develop special theories applicable to limited ranges of data.... I am suggesting that the road to an effective conceptual scheme will be more effectively built through work on special theories, and that it will remain a largely unfulfilled plan, if one seeks to build it directly at this time. (Merton 1948c:165,166)

Merton was suspicious of attempts to evolve total systems of theory 'adequate to the entire range of problems encompassed by the discipline', preferring the

---

18 Paper presented by Parsons to the Annual Meeting of the American Sociological Society, 28-30 December 1947, which appeared in the *American Sociological Review*, 1948.

model of the 'older' sciences with their emphasis on theories of specific types of phenomena. Such theoretical goals fitted well with the operational framework of the Bureau.

The relationship between Merton and Lazarsfeld was of great significance not only for the Bureau, but also for their respective academic reputations, which in turn fed back and helped legitimate and strengthen the Bureau. Two committees, the Mills, which reported in 1944, and the Cheatham, which reported in 1945, examined the operation, running and rationale of the Bureau of Applied Social Research within a university setting. Lynd, as Chairman of the Sociology Department, adamantly defended the Bureau to the Cheatham committee, stressing the contribution that such an organisation could make to sociology as a discipline:

> The sheer difficulty of gathering data of a new sort has meant that in the past sociology has stressed overmuch theory and generalisation by data. This has given the discipline a bad name at a time when economics has been forging ahead as an empirical science supported by far more ample government and business collected statistics. History likewise tends to look down its nose at sociology from the peak of its complacent confinement of its own efforts to presented library materials.
>
> It is precisely in order to get away from this kind of different situation in a new and sprawled field that we have stressed in our department the Bureau of Applied Social Research. If sociologists are to use empirical data they simply have to go out and dig them up. And that is precisely what the Bureau is doing. (Lynd 31.1.45)

Whilst Lynd supported the Bureau in face of the inquiry, his general attitude was a good deal more ambivalent. Patricia Kendall (Lazarsfeld's third wife) captures very well the schismatic attitude towards the Bureau that existed within the Sociology Department among both staff and students, and indeed, probably reflected the outside world's view as well:

> *P Kendall:*   Well, [the schism] was at two levels. Some of the faculty in the department didn't see anything particularly useful about the Bureau. Robert Lynd for example, [though] he was a great friend and sponsor of Paul's, he felt the Bureau was a trivial enterprise and discouraged people from working in the Bureau. I had a university fellowship at one point, and Lynd got quite excited. I was working at the Bureau in addition to having the university fellowship, because the fellowship stipulated that I could not do any paid work for any organisation. So he was very much on the look-out, watching what the Bureau was doing, and some of the students felt the same way. They did not want to work at the Bureau.

> *D Morrison:* What was the reaction of your peer group about going into such an innovative field?
>
> *PK:* Well, as I say there was a schism between the students who were theoreticians and didn't want anything to do with the Bureau[19] and those of us who were more empirical, and wanted to work on these kinds of studies; even though we were doing the most menial kind of tasks. Seymour Martin Lipset for example never worked at the Bureau. Much later in 1957 he did his union democracy study through the Bureau but when he was a student – he was a contemporary of mine – he did not work at the Bureau and didn't want to. Some of us were very pleased to work there. I'm sure I started publishing much earlier than my class mates. I started to publish with Paul and Bob Merton at the centre. (Kendall 9.6.73)

Kendall worked with Merton, as the junior author, to produced the Bureau's detailed manual of focus groups, which possibly to this day remains without rival. It is essential, if the development of focus groups is to be fully grasped, to understand the operating background from which the technique arose. Although criticisms were made against the Bureau for being too quantitative, the question is much more complex than that. Certainly the more theoretical elements within the Sociology Department could find ready criticism of the Bureau's emphasis on empirical work, but it would be wrong to see the criticism polarising simply around the theoretical/empirical divide. For example, although it would seem that Lynd had reservations concerning the Bureau, he nevertheless had sponsored Lazarsfeld's place at Columbia in opposition to the more speculative sociologists proposed by McIver. It would seem, quite apart from the overt intellectual dislike of empirical work in some quarters, an important objection to the Bureau was the manner in which it proceeded; that even where members of the Sociology Department could not object to empirical sociology there existed a disquiet about the nature of the empirical work undertaken, and its framework of operations.

Lazarsfeld himself recognised, and even accepted, the criticism of triviality of some of the Bureau's work, and was well aware that some of its studies might appear to be insufficiently academic. He knew that if the Bureau was going to legitimate itself in the eyes of the university its work had to be seen as intellectually respectable. A former Bureau staff member informed Leiba Brown:

---

19 Commenting on the Bureau and Lazarsfeld's managerial style, Lewis Coser states: '...he (Lazarsfeld) always wanted his research organisations to be much more than a place of work – namely, collaboratively *Gemeinschaften* rather than tightly organised bureaucratic machines.' (Coser 1984:114) Coser goes on to observe, however '...those who worked in the organised chaos did not always find it the happy *gemeinschaft* that Lazarsfeld dreamed of. Some graduate students complained that they were not really being trained by learning through doing, but were in fact exploited as drudges'. (Coser 1982:115)

> There was a continued pressure to keep academic. We all looked down
> our noses at our bread and butter. Lazarsfeld would say, 'make
> something out of this'. We tried to pull our market research into an
> academic context. The university questioned the commercialisation of
> the Bureau, yet forced us into it. There was an effort all the time to
> academise it. (Brown undated :7)

Lazarsfeld did believe that seemingly trivial studies could produce important
generalisations and could be used for the development of concepts.
Nevertheless, such a position also acted as a rationalisation which put a
convenient gloss on the Bureau's financial dependence on market research work.
Some studies just *were* trivial and could not be 'academised', at least not in the
hands of those other than Lazarsfeld. Patricia Kendall commented:

> Some of us disapproved, no not disapproved, felt reluctant about some
> of the studies that were taken on. The first study that I ever did on my
> own was Sloan's Linament. I felt it was a pity... it was a good experience
> for me. I did everything from beginning to end. I felt it was a pity, it
> was a good study. A pity that it had to be on something so trivial as
> that. But I knew if I was to stay at the Bureau my salary had to be paid.

DM: You couldn't see it generating generalisations?

PK: It was a very trivial study, a very small study. Besides the
        fact that it gave me experience and brought in a small
        amount of money to the Bureau it was very hard to make
        any generalisations.

Lazarsfeld would not have claimed that higher level generalisations could be
developed from a single 'trivial' study. He saw generalisation emerging through
the development of integrating constructs from a number of such studies.
However, there is no evidence that such a practice was pursued in any
systematic fashion at the Bureau, although such studies did allow good student
training in research methods.

The Influence of Theory

The arrival of Merton in 1941 was thus of undoubted help to the reputation of
the Bureau in the theoretical camp. According to Peter Blau, a doctoral student
at the Bureau in the late 1940s, having the theoretically sophisticated Merton
engage in empirical work 'tended to destroy the preconceptions, which most of
us students initially shared, that a social theorist is not concerned with
systematic empirical investigations. My new interest in the integration of
theory and research motivated me to take all the courses and seminars on
research methods Lazarsfeld offered, and to decide to do an empirical
investigation'. (Blau 1964:20 in Rogers 1994:305) Although the presence of
Merton helped to dilute the criticism of 'fact grubbing' levelled at the Bureau,
it was never to throw off its empirical mantle. Why should it have? Indeed, it
says much about the veneration of theory within sociology that the Bureau,

and Lazarsfeld in particular, should have drawn such scathing criticism. But we will see later in discussing the modern day use of focus groups how the continuing lack of respect for rigorous empirical work has served to limit the benefits of the methodology.

Despite the fact that Merton was seen as the theorist and Lazarsfeld as the empirical researcher, it would be wrong to see Columbia's appointments as reflecting the intellectual position of the two men. Whilst not wishing to cast them both in the same mould, the differences between them were neither so great as to inhibit meaningful collaboration, nor so great as their present reputations would suggest. For example, the paper which Merton gave to the American Sociological Society in 1948, 'The Bearing of Empirical Research Upon The Development of Social Theory', could easily, for the most part, have been written by Lazarsfeld. To quote just one pertinent section:

> In general, the clarification of concepts, commonly considered a province peculiar to the theorist, is a frequent result of empirical research. Research sensitive to its own needs cannot avoid this pressure for conceptual clarification. For a basic requirement of research is that the concepts, the variables, be defined with sufficient clarity to enable the research to *proceed*, a requirement easily and unwittingly not met in the kind of discursive exposition which is often called 'sociological theory'. (Merton 1948a: 514)

The closeness and respect that Merton and Lazarfeld had for each other make it wrong to see influence as a one-way trade. Both were locked into a genuine exchange of ideas. But Merton did more empirical work than he might otherwise have done had he not associated with Lazarsfeld. Marie Jahoda, who went to the Bureau in the late 1940s at Merton's insistence to help on a housing study, and knew both Lazarsfeld and Merton very well indeed, was particularly well placed to appreciate their relationship:

> It [housing study] was a brilliant study, a wonderful unpublished study.[20] He really is an old criminal for never having published it. When I see Merton these days I still tell him he is a criminal...You know, under Paul's influence Merton did much more empirical work than he would otherwise ever have done. You see, I wrote these two volumes of this first-rate empirical study which was under Merton's overall direction. And he didn't publish it because it didn't make a contribution to a theory of the intermediate range. So you see Merton has his complexities and difficulties. (Jahoda 12.7.73)

---

20 The study was funded by the Lavanburg Foundation. The intended book was to be entitled *Patterns of Social Life: Explorations in the Sociology and Social Psychology of Housing*. Although never published, substantial references to it can be found in Merton's part of a joint article which he wrote with Lazarsfeld entitled 'Friendship as a Social Process: A Substantive and Methodological Analysis'. Lazarsfeld and Merton (1954). See also *The Social Psychology of Housing*, Merton (1948).

Berelson commented:

> Bob [Merton] could present an image of his relationship with the new
> empirical world of Stouffer and Lazarsfeld. Even though the empirical
> work he did, the big housing study never got home – never came off,
> and the Kate Smith study[21] is really a puny little thing. That is about
> as much empirical work as Bob did in those days, although he was
> always around and so on. In addition, in later years I always felt - I don't
> mean to say there was any motive on Bob's part, but the
> consequences... Merton got a positive rub off... when you look at
> Columbia for a distinguished sociologist, Lazarsfeld was impossible,
> and that made Merton stand a little higher relative to him. Bob got the
> first honorary degree. They couldn't give it to Talcott Parsons because
> no one could understand what the hell he was talking about and so
> forth. Lazarsfeld was still quote 'not one of us' unquote, and so there
> was Bob Merton, and he got a lot from both of them. He was heir
> apparent and he, quote, 'united the traditions' unquote. Parsonian
> Grand Theory and Lazarsfeld empiricism, and there stood Bob at that
> historical juncture being the man who was going to unite them –
> middle level theories and so forth. It was just a kind of... everybody got
> something out of it. (Berelson 12.7.73)

If both Merton and Lazarsfeld gained from their association, their close
collaboration was even more decisive for the overall intellectual impact that the
Bureau made upon American sociology. As Shils noted, Harvard suffered from
the lack of consensus among its leading figures and this dissipated some of its
strength, but in the case of Merton and Lazarsfeld an unusual degree of
empathy existed, which made not only for a reduction of intellectual conflict,
but also for cohesion and direction at an administrative level. This cohesion,
plus the rigorous research training provided by 'on the job' learning which, as
Shils notes:

> ... increased the proliferation of the Columbia Center, at a relatively
> high level of technical competence, and encouraged the diffusion of its
> procedures and mode of thought to many non-academic institutions
> which sociology had not penetrated before. It also made Columbia a
> national and international centre for sociology. (Partial sub-centres
> were formed at Chicago and Berkeley – wherever, in fact, a 'research
> facility' was created. The survey Research Centre at the University of
> Michigan was an exception to this; it did not derive from Columbia.)
> (Shils 1970:794)

Merton was deeply enmeshed in the ethos of empirical work; even on joining
the Bureau in 1941 his theoretical work on the development of science was
deeply empirical in the historical mould of social enquiry – it shows an

---

21 The Kate Smith study is a reference to *Mass Persuasion: The Social Psychology of a
War Bond Drive* Merton (1946).

absolute attention to factual detail. It must also be noted that he engaged in focus group research almost from day one of joining the Bureau, and that he developed the 'training manual' laying out and describing the method that he originated. Methods in the social sciences do not change very much over time, and to have created a new method and approach to social enquiry is not the mark of a 'removed' theoretical scholar. What is interesting is the role that the Bureau played under the governorship of Merton and Lazarsfeld in, as Shils says, the 'diffusion of its procedures and mode of thought to many non-academic institutions which sociology had not penetrated before'. The establishment of academic sub-centres of the Bureau is clear enough, but it was mainly its survey research procedures that were transported and not focus group research. Though such a method has only recently re-emerged within academia as a valuable tool for social exploration, it has been popular for a long period within market research. Thus Shils's almost casual observation concerning the Bureau's penetration of non-academic institutions is significant in understanding the career of a method.

The Importance of Contacts

Lazarsfeld's network of contacts criss-crossed a wide variety of domains: academia, marketing, media, commerce, foundations and other granting bodies, and government. Apart from Lynd, amongst his academic contacts in his early days the key figure was Samuel Stouffer. Lazarsfeld recounted his first meeting with him:

> I was then at Newark – I would say 1936 and the Social Science Research Council commissioned a series of studies on the depression. Stouffer was made the Research Director and laid out the programme – the effect on religion, on reading, on education and so. They were not original studies but only used available material. And Stouffer consulted with Lynd who he should invite and Lynd mentioned my name, and Stouffer invited me to Chicago. Anyhow Stouffer and I met in 1936 in Chicago to... see if he could use me and at that time I had done work on unemployment in Austria. That was a very strange meeting because Stouffer and I hadn't known each other. I had never met him or read his work or he mine, but we immediately got on extremely well. I remember very vividly something which was meant to be a kind of lunch to feel each other out – we stayed for hours and hours and then Stouffer immediately asked me to work with him on one of those monographs[22] and I met repeatedly on those monographs and I acquired a tremendous respect for him, and I think he rather liked me. And then when I wrote *Radio and the Printed Page* I asked him to write in it. So we became very close friends and there was hardly anyone I respected as much. He bought a little farm near Dartmouth College – New Hampshire – and I spent a summer in Dartmouth. We were together at the outbreak of the Second World War. I remember we were at

---

22   The study referred to is 'Depression and the Family'. (Stouffer 1937) See chapter 6 of Stouffer (1962) for a shortened version of this.

his farm and listened to it on the car radio. So that was probably the most important personal contact I had. (Lazarsfeld 2.6.73)

The personal contact was to prove important to Lazarsfeld, especially following Stouffer's appointment as the director of the professional staff at the Research Branch, Information and Education Division, of the War Department. Stouffer channelled some of the work of the War Department through the Bureau. This not only provided a valuable source of finance, but in addition helped confer official recognition and status on the Bureau. Years later Lazarsfeld recognised his debt to Stouffer by dedicating one of the Bureau's major works, *The People's Choice*, to him.

Lazarsfeld became a consultant to the Office of War Information on survey work. As part of that consultancy he gave a great deal of time and energy to Stouffer's *The American Soldier*. For example, a sizeable part of the third volume, which Carl Hovaland was largely responsible for, was taken up with the Bureau's contribution, and after the war Lazarsfeld spent a full term at Harvard helping Stouffer with the measurement procedure for the first volume. Merton also became a consultant to the Office of War Information working on *The American Soldier*[23] but mainly tracing the qualitative material. Merton, according to Lazarsfeld, felt that Stouffer's work 'was too dry'. The intense respect that Lazarsfeld had for Stouffer was not there on Merton's part: 'I don't know what Merton missed in Stouffer, but they never had the intensity of respect for each other which I had for both of them. It [*The American Soldier*] was a spectacular event, and Stouffer's ability to work, he was just perfectly unbelievable'. (Lazarsfeld 26.6.73)

The American Soldier was an enormous organisational research feat; an exemplary exercise in the collection and management of data. Lazarsfeld, in the longest review ever given to any book at that time by *Public Opinion Quarterly*, wrote with an air of deep regret, 'Why was a war necessary to give us the first systematic analysis of life as it is really experienced by a large sector of the population?', and then finished his review finished by wondering where such large-scale work in sociology would come from in the future. (Lazarsfeld 1949:404) *The American Soldier* did not meet with universal acclaim, especially from the more humanistic tradition of social enquiry. AM Schlesinger, for example, mockingly refereed to it as *The Statistical Soldier*. (Schlesinger 1949) But Lazarsfeld appreciated the collection of facts. He used its findings to show that common-sense views about the world, such as that black soldiers did not suffer the effects of heat as much as white soldiers, were often mistaken. In his work on the study, Merton produced some very sophisticated analysis of discontent among soldiers through the concept of reference group and relative deprivation. But, according to Lazarsfeld, 'Stouffer always felt that Merton overdoes' the interpretation of data. Not surprisingly 'Merton and Stouffer never clicked', (Lazarsfeld 2.6.73) but Lazarsfeld had no difficulty in bridging both the particular worlds that Merton and Stouffer represented.

---

23 Stouffer, Samuel A *et al* (1949) *Studies in Social Psychology in World War II* Vol 1-4 Princeton NJ Princeton University Press.

The appreciation for the Bureau's work by the War Department can be gathered from the fact that through the intervention of Stouffer's help Lazarsfeld gained American citizenship, a rare occurrence. Although Lazarsfeld had arrived in American in 1933 he had never bothered to acquire American citizenship; thus, when the war broke out, 'I was, so to speak, an enemy alien, and during the war no enemy alien could become a citizen'. Not having American citizenship he could not engage in military research:

> By lucky coincidence we had – as resident aliens – to fill out papers. Austria was occupied in 1938 and most Austrians began to call themselves Germans, but I just out of spite kept calling myself Austrian. That was the legal loophole by which I could then get citizenship during the war – because the fact that I kept calling myself an Austrian while legally America had accepted Austria as part of Germany – you see? Somehow Stouffer managed all that, because he wanted me as a consultant. I was one of the very few people who got citizenship during the war – because [without it] Stouffer couldn't have used me or the Bureau. (Lazarsfeld 2.6.73)

Having gained American citizenship through the intervention of Stouffer, Lazarsfeld and the Bureau were in a position to accept research commissions from the War Department. It was this contact that Lazarfeld had with Stouffer, and through him to War Department, that led directly to the invention of focus groups.

In the opening pages to *The Focused Interview* (which incidentally, and much to Merton's dismay, was spelt with a single 's', not a double), a brief account is given of the early development of the technique:

> The focused interview was initially developed to meet certain problems growing out of communications research and propaganda analysis. The outlines of such problems appear in detailed case studies by Dr Herta Herzog [Lazarsfeld's second wife], dealing with the gratifications found by listeners to various types of radio programmes. With the sharpening of objectives, research interest centred on the analysis of responses to particular pamphlets, radio programs and motion pictures. During the War Dr Herzog and the senior author [Merton] of this manual were assigned by several war agencies to study the social and psychological effects of specific efforts to build morale.[24] In the course of this work, the focused interview was progressively developed to a relatively standardised form. (Merton, Fiske and Kendall 1956:5)

In November 1941 Merton and his wife were invited to the Lazarsfelds for dinner. Lazarsfeld had just received a request from the Office of Facts and Figures in Washington to conduct tests on responses to several morale-boosting

24   See the Kate Smith War Bond Study in RK Merton, M Fiske and A Curtis, *Mass Persuasion* (New York: Harper, 1946).

radio programmes. On arrival for dinner Merton was hurried out of the Lazarsfelds' apartment to the studio to see how he and his team tested audiences responses. This type of enthusiastic activity was rather typical of Lazarsfeld, but radio research was an unknown world to Merton, as indeed it was to most social scientists at that time. The story is best taken up by Merton himself:

> So off we went and then it was that I saw a strange spectacle... I enter a radio studio for the first time, and there I see a smallish group – a dozen, or were there twenty? – seated in two or three rows. Paul and I take our places as observers at the side of the room as unobtrusively as we can; there was no one-way mirror or anything of that sort. These people are being asked to press a red button on their chairs when anything they hear on the recorded radio program evokes a negative response – irritation, anger, disbelief, boredom – and to press a green button when they have a positive response. For the rest, no button at all. I soon learn that their cumulative responses are being registered on a primitive polygraph consisting of a number of fountain pens connected by sealing wax and string, as it were to produce cumulative curves of likes and dislikes. The primitive instrument became known as the Lazarsfeld-Stanton program analyser. Thereafter, we observe one of Paul's assistants questioning the test-group – the audience – about their 'reasons' for their recorded likes and dislikes. I began passing notes to Paul about what I take to be great deficiencies in the interviewers' tactics and procedures. He was not focusing sufficiently on *specifically* indicated reactions, both individual and aggregated. He was inadvertently guiding responses; he was not eliciting spontaneous expressions of earlier responses when segments of the radio program was being played back to the group. And so on and so forth.... At any rate, after the interview is over, Paul asks me: 'Well, what did you think of it?' I proceeded to express my interest in the general format and to reiterate, at some length, my critique of the interviewing procedure. That of course, is all Paul has to hear... 'Well, Bob, it happens that we have another group coming in for a test. Will you show us how the interview should be done?' I allow as how I will try my hand at it – and thus began my life with what would eventuate as the focused group interview. (Merton 1987:553)

This account offers insight into the creativity of methodological development by the addressing of concrete problems. But before examining focus groups as such, and Merton's strictures on how they should be conducted, it is useful to explore the administrative setting that framed the development of them, through the experiences of Adorno, or more precisely Lazarsfeld's experience of Adorno when he worked on the Rockefeller Radio Research Project. Adorno had nothing but disdain for examining the audience through use of the Programme Analyser, 'that machine' as he referred to it.

Enter Adorno: The Clash of Forces

The study of the unemployed of Marienthal was the most significant work to be produced by the *Forschungsstelle*, but it was the emphasis on the unemployed community, and not the unemployed individual, which gives the work its sociological stamp. Yet Lazarsfeld himself was always somewhat 'uncomfortable' with the description 'sociologist': 'I was defined as a sociologist which really didn't mean anything. I mean, I always did the same work. In Vienna it was called psychology and here it was called sociology'. (Lazarsfeld 25.5.73) This suggests, as Raymond Boudon notes: 'a refusal to become enclosed in one discipline, sociology, in which, nevertheless, the limits and specific nature are more difficult to define than is the case in all other social sciences'. When Lazarsfeld was given the distinction by Columbia University of allowing him to chose a name for his chair he adopted the title, 'Quételet Professor of Social Science'.[25] As Boudon comments: 'One of Lazarsfeld's main intuitions is that methodological similarities bring together, not only socialist voting behaviour and the consumption of soap, but also theory or conceptualisation and research, psychology and sociology, economics and sociology, history and sociology'. (Boudon 1972:418)

The wide-ranging nature of Lazarsfeld's interests help us understand his appreciation of someone such as Theodor Adorno, who on the surface would appear to be a strange choice of intellectual bedfellow. Given that the empirical audience has increasingly come to be explored through focus groups by media and cultural studies, it is worth examine Adorno's relationship to empirical communications research, since although the writings of the Frankfurt School do not form the key texts of cultural studies they are nevertheless influential in a way that the more empirical writings of Lazarsfeld are not. Focus group research itself owes more to quantification than qualitative research, at least historically, and indeed, as I will argue, as a logic of procedure. Thus those within media and cultural studies who revere Adormo's type of theoretical reasoning, and at the same time use focus groups to advance their understanding of the audience, ignore at their peril the more 'hard nosed' empirical tradition from which they emanated.

The recruitment of Adorno to the Rockefeller-funded Radio Research Project resulted from a methodological desire by Lazarsfeld to marry critical theory

---

25 By taking this title Lazarsfeld cleverly avoided being trapped into a narrow definition of himself. It was Robert Merton who suggested to administrative officers of Columbia University that Lazarsfeld be named Quételet Professor of Social Science. The choosing of this title emerged from Lazarsfeld's historical research on the history of quantification and his recognition that the Belgian Adolphe Quételet ought to be considered the founder of empirical social research. (see Kendall 1982) Quételet (Adolphe) was Belgian and began his life as a natural scientist, but became attracted to social science during the period of unrest that culminated in the French-Belgian revolution of 1830. He was an astronomer dedicated to uncovering for the social world eternal laws similar to that of astronomy. He concerned himself almost exclusively with the interpretation of large scale statistics. See Lazarsfeld, 1961 for a concise, but exceptionally researched history of quantification.

with empirical social research, and to do so in the first instance by understanding the appeal of music. Adorno may have scorned the Stanton-Lazarsfeld program analyser as a tool of naïve American empiricism, but as a mechanism for understanding the audience's response to programme material, when allied with focus groups, it was not to be dismissed. One could not have the development of a field of social enquiry into the operations of the media that failed to take into account the audience, and out of that necessity came focus group research. Lazarsfeld had this to say about the music side of the Radio Research Project:

> Look, you have to understand how that came about. I have always been interested in music, and already in Vienna I wanted to study popular songs. I invented this machine – this programme analyser. In Vienna I even had student dissertations. I wanted to find out for some reason why... what is it in the musical structure which makes songs popular. I had this idea that people would just push buttons, and say that I like it or dislike it, and then a musicologist would analyse the musical structure and would relate musical structure to action somehow.

Action (*handlung*) was the conceptual territory of jurists drawing upon the philosophy of law. Lazarsfeld, and we can see this in his interest in how people made up their mind to vote or decided to make a purchase, was interested in the empirical study of action. The fact that the 'programme analyser' was supposed to assist in understanding the popularity of popular music left Adorno mystified.

Adorno was not really known to Lazarsfeld before he appointed him to run the music study: 'I had heard about Adorno but hadn't known him... I had read, he had written under a pseudonym one to two papers on Jazz'. This is probably a reference to Adorno's article 'Uber Jazz', which appeared in the *Zeitschrift für Sozialforschung* in 1936 under the pseudonym Hektor Rottweiler (a not inappropriate name given Adorno's uncompromising personality). Lazarsfeld had hired a young psychologist, Wiebe, who was also a professional jazz player, to assist Adorno in translating critical theory into an operational instrument for empirical enquiry. Gerhart Wiebe later became Dean of the School of Communication at the University of Boston, but at the time had just graduated:

> I had this idea that the combination between such an esteemed theorist abstract man like Adorno, and such a typical American Middle Westerner like Wiebe... I wanted music... I wanted a European, and then an American Empiricist together, and it worked miserably. First Adorno was very intolerant – he held the view that Wiebe was just the lowest kind of human being. (Lazarsfeld 2.6.73)

Even accepting the fact that Adorno was never an easy person to collaborate with, his relationship with Wiebe would appear to have been an absolute disaster. How far this can be attributed to differences in intellectual background is hard to say. Adorno commented, some thirty years after, that 'I once had an assistant of Mennonite lineage whose ancestors had come from Germany long before.' Although not mentioning Wiebe by name, Adorno said:

> He hardly grasped what I was after. A certain resentment in him was unmistakable: the type of culture that I brought with me and about which I was genuinely unconceited, critical of society as I already was, appeared to him to be unjustifiable arrogance. He cherished a mistrust of Europeans such as the bourgeoisie of the Eighteenth Century must have entertained towards émigré French aristocrats. However little I, destitute of all influence, had to do with social privilege, I appeared to him to be a kind of usurper. (Adorno 1969: 348,349)

The reference to eighteenth-century émigré French aristocrats is typical of Adorno, larding his writing with unnecessary displays of erudition which were out of place in his new host culture; but then, to be out of joint with the 'times' was a mark of distinction so far as he was concerned, and formed part of the 'critical' spirit. As he himself said: 'I consider myself European through and through, considered myself as such from the first to the last days abroad, and never denied it.' (Adorno 1964:338)

To Adorno, 'adjusting' involved the danger of accommodating to that which his critical stance ought to separate him from. So far as he was concerned, integration into American culture with its commercial monoliths was a denial of everything he stood for, both in his personal and intellectual life. This imperviousness and insistence on keeping his past life intact drove the more pragmatic Lazarsfeld to the brink of despair: 'When we talked about the project then I got desperate because he wouldn't produce anything I could use or send to the Foundation. I mean he would write very long memoranda which were so unintelligible that I couldn't use them, or what was much worse he embarrassed me when talking to people'.

Worse, much worse, was Adorno's social performance. What particularly upset Lazarsfeld was that he would send Adorno to talk with musicians 'who felt that they distributed culture to American high school children' and who, according to Lazarsfeld, 'were furious talking to Adorno. Instead of him trying to understand them... when they opened their mouths Adorno would tell them what idiots they were.' In private Lazarsfeld admitted that 'Adorno was absolutely right' but then added, 'that's not the way to conduct an investigation, a study... you have to listen'. Adorno upset so many people that to some extent he became a liability. Lazarsfeld said that Frank Stanton, using his connections from his position within CBS, would arrange for Adorno to meet various people only to have them phone Stanton complaining, 'why do you waste my time talking to this madman?'. (Lazarsfeld 2.6.73)

Yet there was no doubt of Lazarsfeld's respect for Adorno's intellect. Indeed, shortly after Adorno was appointed to the Radio Research Project, Lazarsfeld wrote his co-directors, Frank Stanton and Handly Cantril: 'My summary impression is very favourable and I think it was good luck for us when we took him on. I am, at this moment, inclined to consider him our most valuable staff member in spite of the technical difficulties which might come up from time to time in view of his un-American personality'. (Lazarsfeld 7.3.38) Not only did Adorno possess the type of European theoretical background that Lazarsfeld considered the Project needed, but Adorno was also a noted musicologist, and a musician of some note – of concert pianist standard, according to Lazarsfeld.

Employing Adorno was also the repayment to Horkheimer of the debt he owed him for providing Lazarsfeld with a small subsidy when in 1936 Lazarsfeld needed financial help to establish his research centre at the University of Newark. During the initial months of the Centre, no money was forthcoming from the university, and Horkheimer had generously helped finance a study on authority in relief families[26] and subsidised a study on job hunting, as well as donating two thousand dollars to the general running of the Centre, half of which was to be considered a debt to be later repaid. The early months of the Centre were precarious ones for Lazarsfeld, and not surprisingly he felt he owed Horkheimer more than just a financial debt.

Horkheimer wanted Adorno to join the 'School' from Oxford. Knowing this, Lazarsfeld had the Project pay half his salary, with Horkheimer making up the rest. Adorno accepted Lazarsfeld's offer to join the Radio Research Project, feeling that Horkheimer would not have recommended him to take the post unless, 'I, a philosopher by calling, could handle the job'. (Adorno 1969:340) However, on arrival at the offices of the Project, housed in an unoccupied brewery, Adorno was taken aback on being confronted with 'administrative research'. He notes in his memoir his 'astonishment at a practically orientated kind of science, so entirely unknown to me'. (Adorno 1969:343) His lack of familiarity with this form of research is abundantly clear from his own admission that he did not really know what a research project was: 'the American use of the word 'Project', which is now translated in German by *Forschungsvorhaben*, was unknown to me.' He understood 'the word "method" more in its European sense of epistemology than in its American sense, in which methodology virtually signifies practical techniques for research'. (Adorno 1969:340 and 343)

Such misunderstanding on Adorno's part cannot be attributed to any lack of command of English, since Lazarsfeld, after first meeting him, wrote to Stanton and Cantril that 'he worked in Oxford for the last few years and speaks a better English than I do'. (Lazarsfeld 7.3.1938). But to speak a foreign language does not mean the absorption of the culture which the language expresses. Adorno's 'un-American personality', to use Lazarsfeld's description, was a polite way of saying that Adorno lacked the social skills necessary to operate successfully in a research world that was closely tied into the media industry, where cleverness might be admired, but abrasiveness was not. At the intellectual level, however, Adorno did not consider that

26 See M Komarovsky, *The Unemployed Man and his Family* (1940). This study was Mirra Komarovsky's thesis, but the whole project was supervised by Lazarsfeld. He also wrote the introduction to the book.

one could measure culture, and was vehemently against the Lazarsfeld-Stanton programme analyser that Merton, who was hardly theoretically unsophisticated, developed into a new tool for understanding the audience response to culture, namely, focus groups. To Adorno the programme analyser captured for him the naïveté of American empirical social research. As he expressed himself in his Memoir, he was:

> ...particularly disturbed by the danger of a methodological circle: that in order to grasp the phenomenon of cultural reification according to the prevalent norms of empirical sociology one would have to use reified methods as they stood so threateningly before my eyes in the form of that machine, the program analyser. (Adorno 1969:347)

As far as Adorno was concerned, the statistical average of respondents' opinion about the stimulus remained, despite the seeming objectivity of the data, at the level of subjectivity. However, despite his criticisms of American empirical methods, following his move from New York to Berkeley Adorno produced through the use of elaborate scaling techniques his study of the Authoritarian Personality. As Martin Jay cleverly comments, 'culture might not be measurable, but it seems as if bias more easily could'. (Jay 1973:224)

Adorno's gift for misunderstanding the world around him was truly remarkable. Some of this may be put down to cultural confusion, but not all. His arrogance, especially when meeting senior figures from the radio industry, drove Lazarsfeld to despair. But then, as Donald MacRea notes in his review of Adorno's *Negative Dialectics*: 'I thought Adorno on our one meeting, the most arrogant, self-indulgent (intellectually and culturally) man I had ever met. Some twenty years later, I can think of additional claimants for that position, but I doubt if they are serious rivals. *Negative Dialectics*, one of his last works, bears out my opinion'. (MacRea 1974:786) John Marshall, who as the foundation official in financial control of the Radio programme was one person that Adorno should have cultivated, found Adorno difficult:

> Adorno would have been an embarrassment to anybody, he was an embarrassment subsequently to his colleagues in Frankfurt. I was visiting Frankfurt in 1959 and one of my very congenial contacts there said I probably ought to see Adorno. I said I just don't want to and he said, 'I don't blame you, I don't want to either'. He said, 'as a matter of fact although he is a colleague of mine I see as little of him as possible.' He was a highly abrasive and cock-sure little man. (Marshall 6.7.73)

Lazarsfeld had to reprimand Adorno for his deliberate display of intellectual superiority. In exasperation he wrote: 'Don't you think it is a perfect fetishism the way you use Latin words all through your text? There is no doubt that the words 'necessary condition' express everything which the corresponding Latin words express, but you evidently feel magically more secure if you use words which symbolise your education'. (Lazarsfeld letter to Adorno undated)

Reading the material in the Rockefeller Foundation archives and Lazarsfeld's own papers of the period, one cannot help but feel a certain sympathy, even pity for Adorno at his own self-image as the exile whose duty it was not only to safeguard the best of German *Kultur* from the jackboots of barbarism, but also from the ignorance of the plimsolled democratic masses of America. Under Horkheimer's authoritarian rule the Frankfurt School was always removed from the real world of politics, not just in America but Germany too before they fled the rising tide of the very National Socialism their work had tried to explain. To have continued to publish the *Zeitschrift für Socialforschung* in German for so long, rather than in the language of their new host country, struck Lazarsfeld as suicidal madness. There was an absolute refusal to engage, in the way that Lazarsfeld did, with the world around them.

Adorno and Audience Research

To separate out the social and intellectual elements of Adorno's make-up is to render a disservice to his obvious cleverness, but it was a cleverness dashed through with ignorance, and an arrogant ignorance at that. He was dismissive of ideas contrary to his own, and rejected much simply because he did not understand. Lazarsfeld, for example, upbraided him for his ill-considered dismissal of other people's verification techniques and pointed out in the same letter as quoted above, that his 'text leads to the suspicion that you don't even know how an empirical check upon a hypothetical assumption is to be made.' Of course, the clever dialectical footwork of which Adorno was a master has a charm of its own, leading the reader through a labyrinth of arguing to a suspicion of all 'appearances' and a distrust of one's own sense experience; the world is as Adorno spins it. Lazarsfeld was not impressed at the intellectual sleight of hand practised by Adorno. For example, after discovering that, contrary to his expectations, people remembered news better when transmitted via radio than by print, Adorno labelled such a situation as paradoxical, simply, as Lazarsfeld noted, 'because the fact does not correspond to your assumptions'. Further, Lazarsfeld complained, 'You make statements about what people do "in America", although you have had personally hardly any experience, and even if you had, you could neither prove or disprove such kind of generalities in which nowadays not even travelling journalists write anymore'. (Lazarsfeld letter to Adorno undated)

Adorno's reference to the Lazarsfeld-Stanton programme analyser as 'that machine' cannot hide some fundamental difficulties between the two men. Yet despite such dissatisfactions on Lazarsfeld's part, he never wished to undermine Adorno's theoretical position, adding 'You know that I agree with you that empirical research should be guided by theoretical considerations'. It was far from the case that Lazarsfeld did not respect Adorno intellectually; at one point he wrote to his co-directors of the Radio Research Project, Hadley Cantril and Frank Stanton, that it was 'a great relief to me to have someone around whose problem is that he has too many ideas and not too few'. (Lazarsfeld letter to Cantril and Stanton 7.3.38).

On Adorno's part, however, there was a great reluctance to study the empirical audience, and certainly not by that machine. His concentration was on the text, and not the audience. At one point he was sent to interview key figures in the radio industry. From an examination of Lazarsfeld's files it would appear that questions were put and Adorno duly received his answers. Adorno, however, then re-arranged the answers so that they were not necessarily placed against the original question, but against a completely different question if Adorno thought it better. One can imagine that Lazarsfeld, the rigorous methodologist, was mystified by Adorno's behaviour. Lazarsfeld made excuses on Adorno's behalf, wondering whether he just had an odd way of behaving, or whether he was engaged in some kind of theory-building exercise. Even so, it seems an odd way to build theory.

This criticism of Adorno, based around his objection to empirical method, is not meant to diminish the very real intellectual difficulty that he faced at a particular historical period of capitalist development and consciousness. Frederic Jameson writing on the difficulty of Adorno's work, after commenting on Adorno's 'Hegelian spirit', observes:

> How to analyse the part as a part when the whole is not only no longer visible, but even inconceivable? How to continue to use the terms subject and object as opposites requiring a synthesis to be meaningful, when there is no synthesis even imaginable, let alone present anywhere in concrete experience? What language to use to describe an alienated language, what system of reference to appeal to when all systems of reference have been assimilated into the dominant system itself? How to see phenomena in the light of history, when that direction seems to have disappeared? (Jameson 1967:40)

With the triumph of National Socialism the lights may have gone out all over Europe, but it left the Frankfurt School in the miserable gloom of their own pessimism, and in Adorno it involved a refusal to accommodate to what was a twisted world both in its thinking and in its practice. Part of that practice was of course the embracing by social enquiry of empirical methods.[27] Adorno even

---

27 The philosopher, Gillian Rose, in her work on Adorno, *The Melancholy Science*, states: 'Adorno insists that empirical research and the techniques listed, must be distinguished from 'theory', reserving 'theory' to mean a commitment to a view of the production of value in exchange as the underlying process in society in relation to which all other phenomena are to be understood. He deplores the use of empirical research apart from such theory. However, he lists techniques for ascertaining beliefs, attitudes and behaviour, including those which he used himself, in isolation from theory. In some of his other discussions of sociology and empirical research, he persists in presenting empirical sociology as hostile to theory, and as confining itself to ascertaining opinions. He tends not to discuss sociology which has used empirical methods to investigate theories, for example, the sociology of class or the sociology of organisations, although he was well informed about such work.'(Rose 1978:97) Rose goes onto comment: 'One of the origins of Adorno's argument is his experience on Paul Lazarsfeld's Princeton Radio Research Project' and quotes Adorno comments relating to the fact that all that was expected from him was the collection of data of use to the music industry. Clearly, as Cantril's letter of 7.3.39 shows, this is a gross over-simplification of his perceived role in the project – one must presume, that it 'suited' Adorno's epistemological position, to deny the critical role that he was allotted in what was a very empirical project when viewed in its entirety.

refers to the music project of the radio research programme as 'the so-called Music Study', (Adorno 1969:347) almost as if he cannot bring himself to accord it the respect of using the correct title. He was unconvinced that empirical methods could illuminate the basic structure of society, and refused to accept that one could proceed from the opinions of individuals to the social structure and the 'social essence'. One might agree with that, but not with the statement in his Memoir covering the period with Lazarsfeld (Adorno 1969), that some of his confusion arose from the fact that only later, after having left the project, did he realise that: 'Insights into the relationship between music and society were not expected of me, but rather information.' Nothing could have been further from the truth. It was precisely these insights that were wanted, and why music as a relatively non-controversial aspect of content was selected for the study of such relationships, rather than other aspects of radio. Hadley Cantril wrote to the Rockefeller Foundation:

> The general work of the Office would not be well balanced if the effects of radio upon social groups alone is studied. It is reasonable to assume that the social system determines what radio does and can do. This leads to rather precarious questions, but at least they should be opened to discussion. The Directors, aware of their responsibilities (for reasons of tact as well as scientific integrity) have selected the field of music for the investigation of the influence of the social system upon today's broadcasting. (Cantril 7.3.39)

The above is an extract from a proposal to continue the Princeton Radio Research Project; a few months later Lazarsfeld wrote a somewhat similar continuation proposal, and once more expressed the need for a more total approach to radio, but again showed recognition of the likely controversy he considered could be mitigated by focusing on music:

> I am quite aware that the entire approach to the music study is unorthodox and, as it were, a gamble. I have, however, become more and more optimistic about it as work progressed. It is a process of increasing returns. This is one of the reasons, I feel, that the study should not be dropped now. With a relatively small additional investment, a great deal of wealth of information and ideas will be made available.... But there are two strong reasons that the entire effort had to be undertaken. One is that music covers more than half the available radio time. The other is a sort of moral responsibility. I feel that one just should not study so important a tool as radio without looking into its setting in the whole framework of our culture. Since I am aware that such analysis might lead to somewhat controversial results it seemed best to make the experiment in the field of music, which is least exposed to public distrust. Besides the great intellectual expectations I attach to Dr Adorno's work, I should feel that the project had failed its major task if nowhere in its work were a social critique attempted.

To further support his request for funds for the continuation of the music study Lazarsfeld sought to give a fulsome picture of the progress that had been made by mentioning that a book was in the offing, but also sought to remind Marshall why music had been selected for a social critique:

> The second and final project exhausting the material of the past two years of the Radio Research Project is the carrying to completion as a published book of the study made under the Music Project. This study has been a bold but difficult attempt to formulate the impact of American socio-economic institutions upon the upward of fifty percent of radio time devoted to music. It is obviously undesirable to omit entirely from a study of a privately owned medium of communications in a democracy the pervasive factor of what such private control does to radio broadcasting and listening. Since this is a delicate matter, the first section of the Radio Research Project selected music as the mildest and least explosive area of broadcasting. The general theoretical approach has been formulated and five specific aspects have been studied and are in tentatively final form. The joining of the segments and the final preparation of the book as a coherent whole remains to be done. (Lazarsfeld 27.12.39)

There is evidence to suggest that this book was to be written by Adorno in collaboration with George Simpson, but owing to the non-continuation of the Music Project it was never forthcoming.[28] Marshall was not without sympathy to the exercise that Adorno was engaged in,[29] but the studies had run on past the deadline for completion. Lazarsfeld, with seeming diplomatic skill, expressed his regret to Marshall at his decision not to find further funds for Adorno and asked Marshall to review the situation 'on the grounds that Lazarsfeld's belief in the value of Adorno's work might justify retreating from what Lazarsfeld agreed to be a perfectly justifiable position'. Marshall did review the situation, and as part of that review read all of Adorno's material that had been produced whilst working on the Music Project, but:

> This review left JM still much engaged by the originality of Adorno's approach. Certainly this approach has many novel features, and in many respects promises a view of the social significance of broadcasting beyond anything JM has seen. But JM's final decision may be summarised as follows: The real issue is the utility of the study, and

---

28 Between 1938 and 1940 Adorno, with the aid of Simpson, produced four music papers but not all were published. These four papers were 'A Social Critique of Radio Music', which appeared in *The Kenyon Review* 1945, 'On Popular Music', printed *in Studies in Philosophy and Social Science* 1941, 'The Radio Symphony', published in *Radio Research* 1941, and finally an unpublished paper, 'A Study of NCB's *Music Appreciation Hour*'.

29 In conversation with Marshall he mentioned that he found the music side of the Radio Project exciting work which fell broadly within a humanistic tradition to which he was favourably disposed. He informed me:: 'Paul felt that the enquiry so far had been basically too sociological and it should also be humane and artistic. And I said I couldn't agree more. He brought Adorno into the picture and I was impressed. (Marshall 56.7.73)

that utility must be measured by the effects which can be anticipated for it in remedying the present deficiencies of broadcast music.

Marshall had certain reservations about the style of Adorno's writing, to the extent of questioning the mainspring of his motivations:

> Adorno's present critique, just as it undoubtedly is in many of its adverse comments, is written in a tone which stresses the present deficiencies of music broadcasting to a degree that would be bound to put all those responsible for it definitely on the defensive, with the probable result that they would be left more inclined to rationalise those deficiencies than attempt any remedy of them...

At one point in his memorandum, Marshall wonders whether Adorno ought not to be given the assistance of a collaborator:

> ...someone representative of the present system, but tolerant enough of Adorno's position to see what was useful in it and interpret that for people certain to be less tolerant. Finally, the tone of Adorno's paper leaves room for doubt that Adorno would be able at present to collaborate in such a way. He seems psychologically engaged at the moment by his ability to recognise deficiencies in the broadcasting of music to an extent that makes questionable his own drive to find ways of remedying them. (Marshall 5.1.40)

On the one hand there was an appreciation for Adorno's critical spirit, although not total clarity with regard to what Adorno was saying, but on the other Adorno was not helping his own case by his approach to people. Lazarsfeld had repeatedly asked Adorno to moderate his language and to write in a less insulting style. Following a long paper Adorno had produced for Lazarsfeld, Lazarsfeld found himself having to engage in one of his periodic vituperations:

> You seem to confound the independence of the critical mind with the readiness to be insulting. So if you find a juicy insult you feel satisfied without considering other insulting possibilities. On page 111 you state that the radio networks are interested in catering to the preferences of their listeners because of their fear of losing their licences. Could it not be that they are at least as interested to sell time to advertisers by providing the big audience and therefore cater, etc? On pages 107 and 109 you express a theory that the broadcasting officials who decide on programs pick out so low grade programs because they have as bad taste as the broad markets have. Could it not be that these officials are not morons but scoundrels who corrupt the masses against their better knowledge? (How many radio officials listen to their own programs in private life?) You see at this point of my argument I don't try to keep you from being insulting, I just try to show you how illogical and without foundation you are when you select one insult rather than another. And if insults are necessary in a critical study – I don't want to argue about

that now – don't you think they should be based on orderly procedure? (Lazarsfeld undated)

The Foundation's advisers had difficulty in extending any more sympathetic understanding than they had already given. In such a situation, Lazarsfeld could do little to extend Adorno's contract beyond that which had been formally agreed. There is sufficient evidence in the Rockefeller archives, plus conversations with Marshall himself, to consider that Marshall, despite being called a 'young ignoramus' by Adorno, was impressed by the originality of Adorno's thinking. But the problem was that there was an absence in his work of what the foundation officials defined as 'evidence'. For Adorno to be dependent for the continuation of his work on an institution such as the Rockefeller Foundation, to have them pass judgement on his work when their humanistic naïveté precluded understanding the present historical position of American culture, must have appeared a cruel joke. To be sure the operating assumptions of the Foundation, with their belief in bringing 'good music to the masses', as if the problem was one of mere communication, made it part of the same crushing corporate mentality that was mass culture. For Adorno the fostering of research to find facts, as if facts were knowable in themselves, was the very spirit that denied reflective thought. But then critical theory was never sociology. For Adorno it was not simply a question of transmitting 'good' music, that is music considered good by social convention, but of making available music that possessed the capacity to break down rigid and preconceived ways of experiencing the world. Hence his disappointment in America with Jazz, which he thought musicologically would have possessed a freer, more spontaneous form than he considered it did. Adorno complained that '…music under present radio auspices serves to keep the listener from criticising social realities'. (Adorno 1945:212)

The Answer is in the Text

Although Adorno clearly knew 'what monopolistic capitalism and the great trusts were' (Adorno 1969:340) he had not, before his arrival in America, appreciated how far rationalisation and standardisation had permeated certain cultural forms, specifically popular music. This was important since man's self-realisation had to be approached through cultural activity as well as work. But it appeared to him that the harmonising of the individual with technological society had reached such proportions that most people thought in rigid preconceived categories so that they were no longer capable of spontaneous experience. In the case of popular music he saw the general tendency of society, its thrust towards uniformity, as having robbed many individuals of their ability to invest such music with their own feelings. While he recognised that such a situation was not universal and that young people were still capable of investing popular music with meaning, the radio industry, with its monotonous and repetitive 'plugging', fitted the rhythms of the industrial process and undermined the possibility of such 'meaning'. That is, the boredom produced by the work situation – the young were not fully as yet lashed to the industrial machine – resulted in a craving for excitement during non-working hours, the time which was the only area remaining for freedom, and erected a machinery for distraction based upon intermittent attention.

Although popular music was not the opiate of the masses, as Marx had characterised religion, the borrowed thought is obvious. There is a seriousness attached to the role of culture and social change in Adorno's work that is missing in 'traditional' Marxism. It was essential, therefore, so far as Adorno was concerned, to alter musical content so that the heavy hand of a repressive culture could be lifted from the mass of its audience, allowing them the possibility of viewing reality differently. Self-realisation was a cultural as well as an economic activity. The whole question was one of making available music that possessed the capacity to break down rigid and preconceived ways of experiencing the world; but then culture did not exist in a vacuum independent of larger social relationships. Adorno was critical not only of American musical culture, but the structural features that underpinned such expressions.

The relationship between substructure and superstructure had occupied Marxists at all times. Although giving greater independence to the superstructure than common in 'traditional' Marxism, and more importance to culture, Adorno was nevertheless extremely critical of administrative research for treating the two spheres as unrelated and therefore unproblematic. The question remained, however, as to how exactly to alter arrangements. This seems to be a fundamental difficulty with critical theory: synthesising theory with praxis, and handling praxis in any other than a theoretical manner. (see Slater 1974:177) Adorno's position was made quite clear in an attack on administrative research, a phrase coined by Lazarsfeld:[30]

> One should not study the attitudes of listeners, without considering how far these attitudes reflect broader social behaviour patterns, and even more, how far they are conditioned by the structure of society as a whole. This leads directly to the problem of a social critique of radio music, that of discovering its social position and function. (Adorno 1945:210)

In an earlier paper, 'On Popular Music', Adorno made his position quite clear with respect to the function of modern popular music. Yet what is noteworthy about the style of analysis engaged in by Adorno in this paper is the way in which textual analysis operates as a substitute for empirical examination of actual functioning:

> Listening to popular music is manipulated not only by its promoters, but as it were, by the adherents of this music itself, into a system of response mechanisms wholly antagonistic to the ideal of individuality in a free, liberal society. This has nothing to do with simplicity and complexity. In

30   The term 'Administrative Research' is often credited to Adorno, but it is more likely to have been Lazarsfeld who coined the term to describe the work he was doing during his radio research period with the Rockefeller Foundation – see Lazarsfeld (1941) for this uncertainty.

serious music, each musical element, even the simplest one, is 'itself', and the more highly organised the work is, the less possibility there is of substitution among the details. In hit music, however, the structure underlying the piece is abstract, existing independent of the specific source of the music. This is basic to the illusion that certain complex harmonies are more easily understandable in popular music than the same harmonies in serious music. For the complicated in popular music never functions as 'itself' but only as a disguise or embellishment behind which the scheme can always be perceived....

Popular music, however, is composed in such a way that the process of translation of the unique into the norm is already planned and to a certain extent achieved within the composition itself. The composition hears for the listener. This is how popular music divests the listener of his spontaneity and promotes conditioned reflexes. Not only does it not require his effort to follow its concrete stream; it actually gives him the model under which anything concrete still remaining may be subsumed. The schematic build-up dictates the way in which he must listen while at the same time, it makes any effort in listening unnecessary. Popular music is 'pre-digested' in a way strongly resembling the fad of 'digests' of printed material.(Adorno 1941a:21,22)

Adorno's position was that as far as 'serious music' is concerned, or rather 'good serious music', the listener cannot supply the framework automatically, since 'every detail derives its musical sense from the concrete totality of the piece, which, in turn, consists of the life relationship of the details and never of a mere enforcement of musical scheme'. (Adorno 1941:19) Consequently, the music is not 'pre-digested'; 'no such mechanical substitution by stereotyped patterns is possible in serious music. Here even the simplest event necessitates an effort to grasp it immediately instead of summarising it vaguely according to institutionalised effects. Otherwise the music is not "understood"'.(Adorno 1941:22) One must ask the question, however, which seems unproblematic for Adorno, what happens if the music is not understood? It is this type of 'textual' analysis that makes it possible for Adorno to take the objective musical structure and say something about its receptivity in the past, and its receptivity in the present, without necessarily 'knowing' anything about listeners' responses.

Adorno was a fine professional musician, and noted musicologist. He had trained under Alan Berg in Vienna, and taken piano instruction from Edward Steuermann, as well as being editor of *Anbruch*, a Viennese periodical of modern music. Martin Jay comments that even as a young man Berg 'found Adorno's uncompromising intellectuality a bit disconcerting'. (Jay 1973:23) While in Vienna Adorno moved in radical cultural circles, and attended readings by Karl Kraus, 'that most unrelenting upholder of cultural standards', which along with his participation in 'arcane musical discussions of the Viennese avant-garde' reinforced existing predispositions: 'Never during the remainder of his life would Adorno abandon his cultural elitism'. (Jay 1973:23). Thus one can well imagine the cultural shock on his arrival in America, confronting a popular music industry 'that constantly renewed [its] efforts to sweep the market with new products, to hound them to their graves; then repeat the infanticide manoeuvre again and again'. (Adorno 1941:39) The shock given him by the music industry was matched only by that of being confronted by empirical social research.

Quite a few leading academics acted as 'consultants' at various times to the main radio research project. One such figure was Geoffrey Gorer, the British anthropologist. Gorer was asked to comment on one paper that Adorno had written in collaboration with George Simpson. The paper was read by Adorno at a Radio Research Project Seminar on 26 October 1939, and not as Adorno notes in 1940 (a mistake which now appears to be gathering historical momentum).[31] This paper, entitled 'On a Social Critique of Radio Music', or a derivative of it, subsequently appeared as a published article in 1945 in the *Kenyon Review* under practically the same title. (Adorno 1945) Gorer's long commentary on Adorno's paper is both thoughtful and constructive, and relates directly to points concerning the collecting of responses to stimuli, and why the development of focus group research came out of media research, and not some other field.

Gorer began his review by commenting that Adorno's paper 'really falls into two categories: (1) the reaction of an extremely sensitive person to the sound of transmitted music, and (2) the hypothesis about how an appreciative public reacts to this radio music.' Gorer claimed that he was not competent to judge on the first part, and was willing to 'believe that Dr Adorno's statements about the deformation produced by the technique of radio are justified'. He then follows this, however, with a fairly damning comment about the lack of evidence in Adorno's work for the statements that he makes. For Gorer, Adorno's critique of the performance of music consists of assertions, which in the absence of evidence are not supported by sufficient reasoning to make them convincing:

> All the way through he [Adorno] assumes that... other undesirable forms of listening are a strictly modern phenomenon dependent on radio transmission, with the underlying assumption that up until recent years all listeners of music listened with the intensity and comprehension which he considers desirable. Beyond that, that up until the middle of the 19th century composers were subsidised by aristocrats as a means of obtaining prestige. I see no evidence to presume that sympathetic listening was statistically more intense then than now, although fewer people were exposed to the experience.... Consequently, all the arguments about the degeneration of listening seem to be founded on the unproven hypothesis that earlier listening was of a more intensive character. I do not know of any evidence of this....

If this lack of evidence bothered Gorer, it paled against his concerns about Adorno ignoring the empirical fact of reception:

---

31 See Adorno (1969:352) for the original mistake and Jay (1973:191) for reproducing it, as well as Pauling (1974:214).

> To sum up, I think Dr Adorno has presented some very interesting hypotheses which might be verified by future research. I do not think he has succeeded in proving anything or in justifying his interpretative method of social critique. I have frequently maintained that in any social situation it is necessary to know both the stimulus and responses. As a corrective to the bias of the Princeton Radio Research, it is useful to have some analysis on the stimuli, but this only becomes meaningful when and if it is collated with specific responses. (Gorer 2.1.40 – Rockefeller Archives)

There is no direct documentary evidence of Adorno's response to Gorer's insistence that the audience must be studied and not assumed from the text, but the correspondence surrounding the music side of the Radio Research Project does show, though not on Lazarsfeld's part, deep dissatisfaction with the way the research was being handled. Lazarsfeld's attempt to have the music side and Adorno's contract extended resulted in failure, even though, ever the optimist, Lazarsfeld felt further intellectual effort would produce valuable results.

Years later, in his memoir relating his experiences as an émigré, Adorno returned to the criticism he faced while working for Lazarsfeld on the music project, and takes up directly some of the points Gorer raised concerning the need to study the audience:

> It is an open question, to be answered only empirically, whether and to what extent the social implications observed in the content analysis of music are understood by listeners themselves, and how they react to them. It would be naïve to take for granted an identity between the social implications to be discerned in the stimuli and those embodied in the 'responses'. It would certainly be no less naïve to consider the two things as totally uncorrelated with each other in the absence of conclusive research on the reactions. If in fact, as was deduced in the study 'On Popular Music', the standards and rules of the popular music industry are the congealed results of public preferences in a society not yet fully standardised and technologically organised, one can still conclude that the implications of the objective contents do not completely diverge from the conscious and unconscious awareness of those to whom they appeal – otherwise the popular would hardly be popular. (Adorno 1969:353)

The intervening years would appear to have produced a shift in Adorno's thinking, but as Martin Jay comments in discussing Adorno and the Authoritarian Personality study, 'His stress on grasping the objective spirit rather than measuring reactions to it had diminished by the end of the decade'. (Jay 1974:224) Even so, although the above may appear to be a concession to some of Gorer's basic points, especially his opening lines referring to the need to study how music is 'understood by the listeners themselves', the statement as a whole is only a nod in the direction of a full-blown empirical examination of experiences. For example, the concluding part of his statement that 'the objective contents do not completely diverge from the conscious and unconscious awareness of those to whom they appeal – otherwise the popular would hardly be popular' may be clever, but is it correct? Or perhaps more precisely, what Adorno has done is recognise the need to study the audience, but then propose it is not really all that necessary since his musicological argument is that the structure of one is reflected in reception by the popularity with the other. One still does not know how the music is received, only that it is received by large numbers of people with sufficient frequency to make it popular. Nor does one know the meanings that it has for the listener, only that it is liked.

What the development of focus groups as a research technique points to (hence the attention given to Adorno) is that to remain locked on the text, or to focus on theorising about the role of music in the reproduction of consciousness, is a cul-de-sac in understanding the reception of text. A textual or purely theoretical approach cannot grasp the meaning that texts occupy in people's lives, how they are incorporated and 'transmitted' through the individuals' own interactions with the surrounding world, both material and symbolic. This does not mean taking the responses of individuals as the prime source of sociological knowledge, as Adorno would have it, but understanding the messages themselves in conjunction with individuals, as indeed Merton insisted upon.

Nor does it mean that such work cannot be critical of wider social structures. Invariably we bump up against general cultural factors when individuals account for their responses. In so doing one is drawn into the participants' world, and by extension the world at large, even though the wider social factors that structure the participants' accounts are not necessarily perceived by the individuals themselves. It is this entry into the wider world through the accounts of the participants in focus groups which makes it difficult at times not to take a critical perspective, in a somewhat similar way to Herta Herzog's very early interview work with women listeners to radio soap operas. Her work, although usually seen as forming the beginnings of uses and gratification studies, can also be seen as falling within a 'critical theory' camp. In fact, her wonderfully titled article, 'On Borrowed Experience', first appeared in the Frankfurt School's own journal, *Studies in Philosophy and Social Science*. (Herzog 1941) Although not written in the language of modern day feminists, it is a damning account of the position of women in society, where their restricted experiences led them to 'borrow experiences' from soap operas, or at least that is a message that one can read from the work. There is nothing, in other words, about the empirical examination of audience response to messages that necessarily interferes with a critical stance, even one might say, a critical theory perspective.

Adorno's work in communication research during this period of the establishment, not just of focus group research, but mass communication research in general, did not really prosper. The failure to marry critical theory with empirical social research bothered Lazarsfeld:

> The defeat of this hope in the Princeton Project has left a troublesome question in my mind. After the war Adorno was an active member of

119

the Berkeley group that produced *The Authoritarian Personality*. Their basic concept of the Fascistic character was developed by Adorno and was no less speculative than what he wrote for us; nevertheless, his colleagues in California were able to convert his ideas into the famous F-scale. (Lazarsfeld 1969:325)

Lazarsfeld generously blamed himself, considering that his 'duties in the various divisions of the Princeton Project may have prevented me from devoting the necessary time and attention to achieve the purposes for which I engaged Adorno originally'. But Adorno's Californian situation was entirely different from that experienced while working in New York with Lazarsfeld. No doubt he felt more comfortable and familiar with the Marxist-Freudian atmosphere of the set-up at Berkeley. Why Adorno should have been empirically more successful while working on the Authoritarian Personality Studies is an interesting area of enquiry which must remain outside the scope of this book. However, the lack of success at a procedural level while working with Lazarsfeld was because Adorno did not confront the audience as an empirical subject. Talk about 'encoding and decoding' as in Stuart Hall's seminal paper of that title,[32] while much more empirically suggestive than Adorno's writing on music, nevertheless still fails to engage with the audience in the concrete real terms of their own lives and lived expressions. It is those 'lived expressions' that demands investigation if we are to understand how decoding actually occurs among various populations and with what resources.

Because of this insistence by the Rockefeller Foundation on understanding the empirical audience, one shared by the key researchers in the programme, with the stress on the methodological development of the field, which focus group research can be seen as growing out of, it is not surprising that it was difficult to know how to handle Adorno's work. However, one feels that many of the researchers, particularly from what one can label the humanistic tradition of communications research (who are now gathering the method of focus group research to them as a way at long last of approaching the audience as people rather than through the text) would probably feel more sympathy to the theoretical traditions swirling around Adorno than the tradition of hard-core empirical work associated with Lazarsfeld and Merton. The modern users of focus group research, unknown possibly to themselves, are, as I have attempted to show, heirs to a tradition of empirical work that they may feel uncomfortable with, even wish to dissociate themselves from. But as I will show in the next chapter, focus group research has been torn from its original anchorage and is, as practised, not only incapable of fulfilling its original promise, but incapable of promising much at all.

---

32   See Stuart Hall, 'Encoding and Decoding', Stencilled Paper 7, Birmingham CCCS 1973.

Four

The Rise of Focus Groups: The Missing Years

R obert Merton has suggested that it might be possible to carry out a case study of the diffusion of the method of focus groups. One feels that to do so would unveil a very tortuous path indeed. But, as Merton says:

> ...utilising the now available resources of citation analysis coupled with interviews or questionnaire enquiries among representative samples of different populations of social researchers would provide some understanding of the extent and directions of that diffusion or a modest, delimited and readily identifiable innovation as well as the kinds and determinants of diverse kinds of changes in it as it spread to one or another research sector. (Merton 1987:562)

This would form a suitable 'strategic research site for investigation of the diffusion of intellectual innovations'. My own investigation is of a more limited kind. I have sought to document the role of Paul Lazarsfeld in creating the framework surrounding the development of focus group research and his contribution to sets of ideas, and the historical situation surrounding the entry of the method into audience research. My intention now is to examine the part that media research played in the genesis of the method, and then account for the reasons why the method virtually vanished from the academic language of research, but formed a central part of the language of market research.

In the opening pages to *The Focused Interview*, Merton gives a brief account of the early career of the technique:

> The focused interview was initially developed to meet certain problems growing out of communications research and propaganda analysis. The outlines of such problems appear in detailed case studies by Dr Herta Herzog, dealing with the gratification's found by listeners

to various types of radio programmes.[1] With the sharpening of objectives, research interest centred on the analysis of responses to particular pamphlets, radio programs and motion pictures. During the War Dr Herzog and the senior author [Merton] of this manual were assigned by several war agencies to study the social and psychological effects of specific efforts to build morale.[2] In the course of this work, the focused interview was progressively developed to a relatively standardised form. (Merton, Fiske and Kendall 1956:5)

I have already discussed the research setting within which focus groups as a type of enquiry into the audience found acceptance, indeed, 'forced' their development. The politics of the situation, the gathering clouds of war, demanded that the audience be studied and understood in a rigorous empirical manner. Of course Adorno, and the Frankfurt School in general, had for years set as a central task the understanding, through a combination of Marx and Freud, of the nature of authority and the development of personality structures that gave rise to the acceptance of domination. But the brute fact of the situation faced by the Allies was one where the fox was in the hen-coop and mobilisation of all available resources, including the social sciences, in particular the emerging field of mass communication research, had to be put at the service of government. This strengthened and legitimated the quantitative empirical wing of the social sciences, indeed, saw it emerge with increased confidence after the war, with Foundation moneys pouring into the 'new science', and this is despite the attacks made on empirical sociology during the McCarthy years for gathering facts at the expense of extolling 'American values', and on the Foundations for supporting such a wayward child. (See Morrison, forthcoming)

Reading today the research manual on focus groups, which Merton developed out of his and his colleagues' experiences working with 'several war agencies', one can see just how developed the technique had become even then. Yet it is interesting that the authors mention the 'Group Interview' by Emory Bogardus which appeared in the *Journal of Applied Sociology* in 1926. Bogardus is sometimes credited with founding the use of focus groups, (Kitzinger 1994), but his work is best seen as the pre-cursor of the focus group interview, and not as the beginning of it. His use of group interviews has a more experimental feel than what we now associate with the conducting of focus group research. Furthermore, although Bogardus does recognise something of group dynamics at work that might generate richer material than had the interview been conducted with a single individual, the material collected is really individual data. In fact, it appears that Bogardus's decision to use group interviews was based on cost, and not because of any methodological advantage that they might offer. He writes:

---

1   See 'What Do We Really Know About Daytime Serial Listeners?' in Paul F Lazarsfeld and Frank N Stanton (eds), *Radio Research 1942-3* (New York: Duell, Sloan and Pearce, 1944).

2   See the Kate Smith War Bond Study in RK Merton, M Fiske and A Curtis, *Mass Persuasion* (New York: Harper, 1946).

In the newer fields of social research, the personal interview is achieving a place of increasing scientific importance. Its role in bringing fundamental attitudes to the surface of scientific scrutiny is secure. But the deeper it penetrates social attitudes the slower and more expensive it becomes as a method of research.

Hence, as the individual intelligence tests are being supplemented by group tests, so the individual interview is being supplemented by the group interview. The latter is developing not so much as a complete substitute for the former, but as a substitute for the less personal part. Large amounts of valuable work in connection with personal interviews can be accomplished by the group interview, leaving to personal interviews only the most vital phases. (Bogardus 1926:372)

Like any technique the development of focus groups was part of a general intellectual movement. The work of Lazarsfeld and his colleagues in their study of Marienthal, and prior to that the ethnography of the Chicago school, can all be seen as leading to the development of the focus group. Bogardus' use of group interviews, coming not out of ethnography but psychology, can be understood at the technical level as feeding into the development of focus groups, but not as the originator.

Despite the fact that the origin of focus group research was part of the early enterprise of establishing communication research as a distinct field of intellectual endeavour, what is strange is that although focus groups had their beginning in the pioneering days of communication research in the 1940s, and showed much promise for academic workers, they were lost sight of in the academic world until they re-emerged as a tool of exploration in the late 1970s, and only gained legitimacy as a method in the 1980s. This was not the fate of focus groups within the realm of market research, where the technique was embraced with vigour. Indeed, one of the reasons for their non-adoption by academics was the attention paid to them as a method of social enquiry by commercial researchers. The reputation of focus group research suffered in the same way that the research reputation of Lazarsfeld did, in that both had too close an association with commerce. As we shall see, the association of focus groups with the commercial enterprise of market research made the technique look 'grubby', and not appealing to respectable scholars. This, however, does not account for the original non-uptake of the method after its promising beginnings at the hands of Robert Merton and his colleagues.

I have already noted the attraction of qualitative research for many modern day communication researchers, most particularly for those from the humanistic or cultural studies side of the field who feel uncomfortable with quantification. Thomas Lindhof comments that 'the turn to qualitative research among those who are curious about its utility comes partly from a recognition that much quantitatively based research takes for granted the very empirical "facts" that require fundamental examination'. (Lindhof 1987) If this is so, then history has been forgotten. Early communications researchers such as Lazarsfeld and

Merton insisted on the marriage of techniques, indeed, the development of focus group research by Merton was accompanied by proclamations of their benefit as a method of 'explaining' data collected by quantitative methods. Conversely, Merton never thought that focus groups should be used as a stand-alone technique, but always in conjunction with other methods. As James Curran's observed concerning the over-dependency by some researchers on focus groups, or discussion groups as he calls them, too large a claim is made for their benefit, and by extension for the generation of data from a single method - a method, furthermore, that cannot generate data capable of being generalised to the population as a whole. Not that one always needs to generalise to populations as a whole, but I would argue, and I take it that this is Curran's concern also, that it is not beneficial to an intellectual field to have its audience data overwhelmingly drawn from limited populations.

According to Lindhof, it was the 1970s that saw qualitative work in communications gain in respectability and popularity:

> Conference papers arguing for consideration of qualitative research methods in mass communication began to be presented at the International Communications Association, the Speech Communication Association and other meetings in the late 1970s. Book chapters and journal articles detailing such arguments soon followed. The scepticism that greeted the idea that the study of communication through the perspectives and observed natural behaviours of social actors is particularly valuable has largely subsided. (Lindhof 1987:XI)

Qualitative research consists of more than focus group research, and in Britain at least there has been a strong tradition of qualitative work in the realm of production studies.[3] Yet it is the case that focus groups, as a qualitative technique, has only of lately come in from the cold, being associated in most academic researchers' eyes with the 'quick fix' approach to knowledge of the market researcher.

In 1988 Sage Publications, a publishing house with a keen eye for the market, published two handbooks on focus group research, *Focus Groups as Qualitative Research* by David Morgan, and *Focus Groups: A Practical Guide for Applied Research* by Richard Krueger. Margrit Hugentobler reviewed these two works for *Health Education Quarterly* (the field of medicine is a heavy user of focus groups). Hugentobler posed the question: 'Does the fact that Sage is publishing two books on the same topic mean that the sciences are getting about ready to reclaim a valuable research tool that for too long has largely been left to the domain of the marketing researcher?' Hugentobler considers that focus group research has suffered from a lack of respectability through its association with market research:

---

3   See Burns (1977), Tracey, (1977), Schlesinger (1978), Golding and Elliot (1979), Elliot (1971); and Turnstall's (1971) pioneering work on national journalists as an occupation, although using survey research, was driven by his extensive interviews with journalists, as was Chibnall's (1974) work on the local press.

Is it that as social scientists and practitioners we have associated focus groups with the image of the slick consultant moderator asking a group of carefully selected housewives about how baking makes them feel, only to look for themes in these experiences that can be translated into the next cake-mix advertising campaign? Though not a very appealing idea, the extensive use of focus groups in marketing research should tell us something about the power of this method – given the millions of dollars spent each year in attempts to convince us of the superiority of a specific product or service.(Hugentobler 1991:253)

The Hijacking of a Method

It should not be assumed, as Hugentobler does, that because market researchers use focus groups extensively that focus groups must therefore be a powerful method, no more than it is the case that because market researchers use survey research extensively that survey research also must be a powerful method. Whether or not a method is powerful is not a dependent of the groups that use the method, but on the qualities it is deemed to possess for establishing certain kinds of truths. If a client will buy a particular technique then market researchers will sell it to them, and use it irrespective of its power to deliver the claims that are made for it. However, in the case of focus groups their benefit has time and again been demonstrated; they certainly beat guessing what people might think of products. But focus groups are not wholeheartedly embraced by commerce, certainly not by the media industry. As often as not focus groups are used by the media industry as intelligence-gathering, with the results placed along side other intelligence which is often intuitive rather than empirically based: one does not base expensive campaigns and policy on the findings of a few group discussions. Nor do commercial clients trust the market research moderator to have 'got the story right'. The story, in my experience, is much more likely to be trusted the closer it fits in with the existing views of the client, who after all has usually had years of experience of operating in the field that is being researched. The results of focus groups, as often as not, are used to increase confidence that the decisions to be undertaken are the right ones.

What is particularly interesting about Hugentobler's comment, however, is the suggestion that academics have steered clear of focus group research because of its close association with market research. There may well be some truth in this. In the nervous world of the academic, a product of the perpetual peer examination of each other's intellectual capacity, status is derived from respectability, and respectability is dependent on correctness, on mastering the procedures and practices that are held as the canons of scholarship. Heightened status is awarded to those who imaginatively extend the frame of scholarly practices.

Status is also derived from membership of the academy itself. Indeed, in creative occupations that are not particularly well rewarded financially, it is to be expected that compensation for lack of remuneration will be sought by jealous attachment to standing. No one is more disdainful than academics towards members of other institutions that are considered inferior to their own. The heightened sensitivity to both individual and collective status of by academics, that transforms at a personality level to an over-representation of brittle egos, may well have downgraded focus groups as an acceptable method of intellectual practice because of its close association with market research, an activity held in low esteem by academics. Why this should be so is not too hard to figure.

The reference by Hugentobler to the marker researcher as the 'slick consultant' speaks of an antagonism commonly found among university researchers towards their commercial counterparts. Of course there are basic differences between the operations of market research and university based research. Yet the differences in approach to knowledge could not alone account for the dismissiveness of many academics towards market researchers. Indeed most academics do not understand what market researchers do, tending to focus only on the clip-board interviewer in the shopping precinct asking about holiday intentions.

A classic example of this misunderstanding is evident in Martin Shaw's and Roy Carr-Hill's study of responses to the coverage of the Gulf War. They opted for a postal random sample of a district of Hull and Beverley, which provided a response rate of only 40 per cent. Shaw and Carr-Hill defend their sampling decision[4] by attacking market researchers for approaching people in the street, claiming that such a method skews the responses on the grounds that interviewers have a tendency to approach those who look respectable: 'Because of our concern to avoid the trap of quota sampling, wherein only nice-looking people are approached in the street (Survey Methods Centre 1991), we decided to draw a sample from the electoral register'. (Shaw and Carr-Hill 1991) Street quota interviewing which Shaw and Carr-Hill seem to think captures market researchers' approach to sampling is mainly reserved for product research, and as such serves the purpose for which it is designed – it does not need the precision or depth of enquiry of the social research that market research also engages in, often for government departments, and universities. Furthermore, quota interviewing, usually inter-locked quotas, are the most common survey approach used by market researchers, but they are not used exclusively as Shaw and Carr-Hill seem to believe: 'Our selection of a random sample from the electoral register avoided the recognised dangers of quota samples, on which all national UK opinion polls are based'. (Shaw and Carr-Hill 1992:147)

This is no place to debate the merits of quota sampling over random sampling. All samples have their strengths and weakness, but it is just not the case that

---

4   Admittedly they also use Moser and Kalton (1979) as a defence for their 40 per cent response rate as a level of return that can be expected from a postal survey to a non-special interest group, but it does not take a careful reading of Moser and Kalton to realise that a 40 per cent expected response offers its own cautionary tale when selecting the method of data collection.

'all national UK opinion polls' use quota sampling — even if they did there is nothing in general wrong with that — nor is it the case that quota sampling in social research is conducted in the street, as Shaw and Carr-Hill believe. In fact, no serious market research social survey company would dream of using street interviews for any complex and in-depth social research survey; they are always conducted in the home.

Such ignorance can have the benefit of providing self-esteem, in this case a feeling of superiority that other researchers engage in practices that 'proper' researchers would not consider, and 'proper' researchers here is taken to mean those confined to a university. In fact, the methodologies used by market researchers are the very same as those used by university-based researchers; although it must be admitted that some of the techniques used within the shared methodological framework are, at least within the qualitative domain of market research (especially with the use of projective techniques) little more than social alchemy. Market research, however, is a very competitive business, and to stay one step ahead of rivals the offering of 'difference' through the adoption of new techniques is a powerful tool for the selling of research services.

This 'social alchemy' does not occur on the survey or quantification side of market research, where the canons of performance have a tightly drawn disciplinary boundary. This is not to say that the analysis and presentation of data, the reporting only of specific breaks, is not used to convey a particular story, but then, this is also the case with academic presentation of survey data, and whether it is wrong or not depends not on what the 'story' is one wishes to tell, but on the reasons for wishing to tell that story rather than some other story. As with all story-telling, selectivity must occur in deciding what to include and exclude from the narrative.

It would be an overstatement to say that the methodological discipline associated with survey research keeps the researcher honest, but it is the case that the ground upon which the practice stands is much more firm than the shifting sands of qualitative research. Survey research is open to greater rigorous canonical inspection than that which is possible with focus groups. One may have, in the case of survey research, the partial presentation of data and one may have the obviously 'contrived question', but the fact is that inspection is possible and reputations suffer from what is considered poor performance. Yet it would be foolish to ignore that 'pressure' is not from time to time applied by clients on market researchers so that 'friendly' surveys are produced. The 'pressure' will variously depend on the nature and area of enquiry, but the public misrepresentation of data, or perhaps more accurately the delivery of 'friendly data', is invariably a client practice and not the practice of the market research company. The company can if it wishes object to how the data is handled, and even dissociate itself from its own service by refusing to have the company's name attached to the results, thus undermining the legitimacy of the study.

As an industry, market research is a complex enterprise, connected to the studious research of the academy, yet closely tied to the business practices of commerce. One suspects that it is this association with commerce that prejudices the practice of market research in the eyes of the academic community, and as often as not, as with the nature of all prejudice, a single characteristic is taken as a universal condition. The resentment that academics have towards their own low pay finds ready focus on a group of similar researchers who receive significantly higher remuneration, as well as an expense-account life style unknown to even the most senior academics. In an industry where presentation is important, both of research and of the self, it is not surprising that even the most junior market researcher quickly develops the public persona of the confident individual, and the social skills necessary for transient social exchange not found in the average academic steeped in a code of pride where esteem is having a place on the backlist of a reputable publishing house. Thus to the outsider, that which Hugentobler classifies as the 'slick moderator' is to the insider no more than professional performance, a performance often enacted in front of the client. Indeed, some of the techniques, or performances, are for the benefit of the client as much as for the pursuit of enlightenment. But then, methodologically speaking, qualitative research is a much more come-as-you-are party than quantitative research. If it works, it works; the problem is being not quite sure what is being worked or at work. Such epistemological questions, however, can be left for later discussion.

To remain in existence a market research company must return a profit. This brutal fact colours the whole research operation. The senior researcher is a salesperson and business manager as well as a researcher. By its very nature market research is not an activity that lends itself to the critical inspection of social arrangements or the structural formations of society. Market researchers may on ethical grounds refuse to handle certain accounts – often those of the tobacco industry – but such ethical positions are more affordable if business is good, not so easy to hold if profit targets have not been met, nor to be lightly struck in an industry where the reward for a good year is usually that of an increased target for the next year. The industrialisation of knowledge is a treadmill of performance. The refusal to handle an account is thus almost invariably based on an incapacity to carry out the research due to a lack of resources, or the profit margin is too low, or the client is known to be exceptionally demanding and difficult. Within a market research company one could not expect radical research of the type that might mark university production.

Whether or not the university scholar's role is to act as the moral conscience of society it is certainly a role with a long and respected tradition, made possible only by the special arrangement of a separation of the university from the state, and the separation of the university from commerce. In Britain the distance on both counts is closing. The consequences for scholarship of this closure we have yet to see but one can make out shadow being cast over independence. Accountability is management-speak for control, be that control by the market or control by direct state intervention.

A Tainted Method

Although the independence of the universities is now in a process of re-negotiation, past independence should not be over-played. Discussing his work with Wagner Theilens, *The Academic Mind* (1958), and the effect of McCarthyism on thinking in American academia, Lazarsfeld confessed that his chief finding that the political climate of the period showed little impact on critical thought was probably the result of poor sampling on his part; namely, that he should not have included in the frame institutions that never had any thought to begin with. However, whatever the contemporary encroachment on independence within British universities, or the actual manifest level of critical thought, historically the ethos is one in which the scholarly researcher is free from political or commercial constraints. It is ethos, rather than practice, that has schooled generations of scholars, especially in the humanities and social sciences, to keep a distance from industry or commerce. It is this very distance, perhaps best captured symbolically by the description of universities as 'ivory towers', that has now led to an increased demand for university research to have commercial applicability or usefulness.

However, the university researcher in the humanities and social sciences, and especially so in communications, is likely to be of a political and intellectual persuasion that does not find the value structure of the world of commerce and industry appealing, and in not a few cases would find the political economy of society in need of radical re-arrangement. This might be especially true of cultural studies. As John Storey writes:

> All the basic assumptions of British Cultural Studies are Marxist. This is not to say that all practitioners of cultural studies are Marxist, but that cultural studies is itself grounded in Marxism. All its major texts are informed, one way or another, by Marxism: whether or not their authors regard themselves as Marxist, post-Marxist, or Marxisant (using the rhetoric, vocabulary, models, etc, without necessarily a commitment to the politics). (Storey 1994: viii)

The attractiveness of a university setting for such individuals is precisely its removal from the heartland of commercial and industrial production, indeed, a common defence in the acceptance of low salaries is that poor remuneration is the price paid for such a privileged work setting, bitterness arising, of course, when the low level of the salaries are now matched by the importation of commercial practices and routines into the university. Thus, one now has commerce, and the commercial practice of performance indicators, but without any of the associated salary benefits.

It is not surprising, therefore, that university-based researchers should look dismissively on those researchers who service the engine of commerce at salaries considerably higher than their own. The preservation of the gap between themselves and market researchers in terms of definitions of performance is essential in maintaining status when status cannot be achieved

129

through material reward. Within the arena of status politics the market researcher cannot be awarded the right of intellectual respect since by doing so the university researcher devalues that which promotes his or her sense of well being. Status is as precious to them as it was to the new *Mittlestand* of Weimar Germany who in a similar market position to many other groups lived by selling their labour and fiercely held onto, by various protective devices, their feelings of class superiority (*standesdenken*) amidst an increasingly threatening world. If this comparison seems fanciful then one only has to reflect on the disparaging remarks made by staff in the established universities towards the new universities that were formally polytechnics. This disparagement, furthermore, is not restricted to personnel, but subject areas also, most notably media studies, but also communication studies, which owe their origin, certainly as mass courses, to the polytechnics and not to the established universities. Media and communication studies, tainted from the beginning by their perceived humble origins, has been riven by the conflict of status and a resentment by established disciplines at the newcomers presumption in joining the halls of serious knowledge.

The behaviour of the market research community, its often glossy and expensive performances, especially at conferences, damns them in the eyes of the university researcher – although the mumbled ramblings from over-long and under-rehearsed papers given by university researchers ought to shame anyone whose intent it is to communicate. There is a difference in style, especially in qualitative research, and a difference in the approach to knowledge, between the academic and the market researcher, but worse, so far as the academic is concerned, market researchers borrow from university research and make money out of doing so.

In the realm of quantitative research then the relationship between the academy and market research is one of reasonably respectful exchange; although one still finds market researchers' quantitative work referred to by academics as opinion polling, which carries the connotation of superficiality, rather than survey research, which carries the connotation of depth. The qualitative researchers raid the academy for ideas and concepts, in particular psychology. The robbers are usually psychology graduates who enter market research as trainees and then move upwards to occupy senior positions. Talent is rewarded within market research by a rapidity of promotion unknown in the university world. The outcome of this is often the transforming of complex concepts into a garbled operation of buzz words. These 'buzz words' undoubtedly pass for knowledge to clients, but bear little relationship to that which the original authors intended. Yet market research is inventive, and the cutting edge of focus groups research is undoubtedly in that domain, and not in the domain of the university. However, it is because focus group research has no real formal set of procedures, unlike quantitative work, that some outlandishness can take place. But it is this lack of formal procedures that has led to their being embraced by media studies scholars untrained in, and unappreciative of, quantitative techniques. It is at this point, therefore, that we return to the other central question concerning the place of focus groups in the history of communication research.

One reason for the failure to adopt focus groups by university researchers stems from the fact that it was an area of methodology that was heavily colonised by market research, and market research, for the reasons already advanced, has always been regarded with suspicion by academics. The basis of that suspicion is ignorance (but not total ignorance since market research does have a fairly high level of visibility), and on a keen regard for status by academics wishing to separate themselves from perceived inferior intellectual groups. The method, in short, has been contaminated through close association with market research, and to have adopted the method would not have bestowed either methodological or social respectability upon the university researcher. Yet this can only explain why the method was not adopted once market researchers had seized upon it. It cannot explain why it was never adopted in the first place, why it was left to the market research industry to exploit the full potential of focus groups.

If one looks at Lazarsfeld's career, his interest in methodology, and the state of communications research in the early 1940s, especially the desire under Lazarsfeld's tutorship for communication research to address the empirical audience, then it is clear why focus group research emerged in communication research and not some other field of intellectual enquiry. It was imperative to know empirically how the audience received messages, a fact that was given added impetus by the war and the need to know how propaganda was received, understood and interpreted. Radio as a medium, furthermore, was the ideal focus for group discussions. Later we will see that for a focus group to work effectively it is necessary to have it focus on some particular topic or issue, and that one of the technical skills needed for such research is to be able to focus the group effectively and not have it wander from the subject of enquiry. Media material, be it radio programmes, newspaper stories, films, or television programmes is ideal for such purposes: often it can form the subject of the enquiry itself as well as acting as an aid to focus the thinking of the participants.

In terms of the history of the development of a method, then, communication research, especially under the guidance of Lazarsfeld, was a more likely terrain for the invention of focus group research than possibly any other area of research. What the development of the technique points to (hence the attention given to Adorno), is that to remain locked on the text is a cul-de-sac in understanding the reception of the text. A textual or purely theoretical approach cannot grasp the meaning that texts occupy in peoples lives, how they are incorporated and 'transmitted' through the individuals' own interactions with the surrounding world, both material and symbolic. This does not mean taking the responses of individuals as the prime source of sociological knowledge, as Adorno would have it, but understanding the messages themselves in conjunction with individuals, as indeed, Merton insisted upon.

In search for explanations of the process of communications that are not solely focused on the text, media researchers had to turn to the audience. One could never read from the text what readings people might construct for themselves. Textual analysis, and content analysis for that matter, is but one step in uncovering the circulation of meanings. In the important content analysis work of the Glasgow University Media Group one sees a shift in their later work to include the audience through the use of focus groups, and they have done so in a very inventive way. (Philo 1990) After their experience of empirical work it was perhaps understandable that the Glasgow group should turn to the empirical understanding of reception, which was in any case always close to the surface in their *Bad News* studies. (1976, 1980) While including the audience as a rightful object of study in their more recent work, the Glasgow University Media Group always addressed their subject matter as sociologists, and not as cultural theorists. There was always in their work a firm grasp of the power relationships behind the messages on offer that is missing in much textural analysis engaged in by those working within the tradition of cultural studies.

Focus group research has now been taken back from market researchers and dusted off to serve as the new tool of understanding by academics. This adoption of a technique so heavily exploited by market researchers, and now in danger of being taken up with messianic zeal by academic researchers, does not signal a shift in respect by academics for market researchers. Far from it; the social grounds for their disdain remain as strong as ever. It was the necessity to get to grips with the audience that has driven the acceptance of focus group research. The recent uptake of the method may also have something to do with the increased presence of feminists within the ranks of the communications research community, and their injection of an often personalised language of politics as a challenge on all fronts. Given that their driving concern is the explication of the subjugation of women in society, it is perhaps not surprising, although it does not necessarily follow, that they should place weight upon the experiences of ordinary women and wish to give voice to those experiences in their research efforts. The focus group can do just that. Furthermore, qualitative research of the focus group variety is seen by some feminists, unlike survey research, to be feminist methodology. In other words, focus groups have been appropriated as a politically correct methodology. As we shall see, focus group research in the hands of some feminist scholars does not look like research as it is conventionally understood in the tradition of western scientific rationality, but rather a process of understanding and awareness of the self through the collective activity of research; in other words, a political activity in a strict sense.

The emphasis that feminist scholars have placed on people is to be welcomed, both academically and politically. After all it is not women in the abstract that suffer domination, but women in the concrete exigencies of their everyday lives. Theoretical discussions of exploitation cannot fruitfully go on without empirical examination of the experiential aspect of what domination actually means, both in terms of description, and in terms of understanding the incorporation into thinking of forms that assist the dominating process. Within 'cultural studies', and media studies, it was the very abstractness of much of the writing that produced the charge of irrelevance, (Cashmore 1994: Chapter 4) that the understanding it gave was only relevant to initiates. For cultural studies to save itself, the examination of text had to include the audience if it was to escape the charge of obscurantism. The inclusion of the audience through focus group research offered one way out of the mire of its own making.

A Struggle for Meaning

The concept of *Verstehen* – understanding the meanings individuals attribute to their acts and to the acts of others in order to gain empathetic understanding – has almost from the beginning of sociology formed an important part of its operations, and has certainly been fundamental to qualitative interpretative research. Indeed, the qualitative tradition in social enquiry is much older than the quantitative tradition, as Nicholas Jankowski and Fred Wester (1991) note: 'During the last years of the nineteenth century and the first decades of this century, as social issues became topics of academic study, virtually all research was of a qualitative nature'. Jankowski and Wester note the foundational position of qualitative research in the early classic works of Weber, Durkheim, Simmel and others, and continue:

> As academic specialisations were defined and university departments created, qualitative methods gained a solid foothold. Several factors may explain this emphasis. First, there was still a strong affiliation of social science with the mode of investigation utilised in philosophy and the humanities. Second, the social sciences were young and searching for global, overall perspectives; the essay format was more suitable to this task than that of the contemporary research article. Finally, what eventually became known as 'the scientific method' had yet to be fully developed and applied to the social sciences. (Jankowski and Wester 1991:46)

Yet quantification is not an American export. In fact practically all the modern empirical techniques were developed in Europe. Sampling techniques were derived as a sequence to William Booth's (1903) massive survey of life and labour in London, and factor analysis invented by the Englishman Charles Spearman. Family research with its emphasis on quantification owes itself to the Frenchman Frédéric Le Play, and Gabriel Tarde proclaimed the necessity of attitude measurement along with communications research. The notion of applying mathematical models to voting was carefully worked out by the Marquis de Condorcet during the French Revolution. Condorcet's contemporaries, Pierre La place and Antoine Lavoisier, both undertook social surveys for the Revolutionary Government, and their student, the Belgian, Lambert Quételet, according to Lazarsfeld, 'finally and firmly established empirical social research under the title *physique sociale*, a term that Comte claimed he had invented'. To his regret, he was forced to create the much more linguistically ugly term, sociology, to signify his claim to the area. As Lazarsfeld also points out, 'Max Weber was periodically enthusiastic about quantification, making many computations himself' and 'Toennies invented a correlation coefficient of his own'. Yet, it is true that, 'before 1933, nowhere in Europe did empirical research acquire the prestige, a home in universities, financial support, text books, or enough devotees to form...a critical mass: the number of people sufficient to maintain each other's interest by providing a reciprocal reference group'. (Lazarsfeld 1972:328)[5]

The rise of the quantification wing of sociology does not mean that interpretative sociology was somehow fallow; we have seen Lazarsfeld's own annoyance at being viewed merely as an advocate of quantification, as if an interpretative appreciation of social life formed no part of his thinking. But it was with the ascent of quantification within sociology, fed and bolstered by the Lazarsfeld group at Columbia University, that the focus group entered the academy. The insistence by the founders of focus group research that it was only truly valuable when combined with other methods restricted its uptake by university researchers in the quantitative realm of social enquiry, and at the same time it was ignored by the very group of researchers who now so heavily favour it – those working within the interpretative tradition of sociology. Within media research the reclamation of focus groups from market research was due to those who in the cultural studies tradition, facing the pressing intellectual problem inflicted by a text-based approach to the audience which could not really say anything concrete about the empirical audience. Cultural, or media studies, had nowhere to go, if it was to have any voice of authority, other than to the empirical audience and via a method that did not do violence to their interpretative approach to knowledge. Briefly then, to understand the domain of the non-acceptance of focus groups, we must look at the world of ideas itself.

Jankowski and Wester (1991) in their thorough overview of the qualitative tradition and its contribution to mass communication research split the history of social enquiry into three periods: the early period, 1890-1930, the middle period, 1930-60, and the late period, 1960 to the present. They note that social enquiry in the early period developed almost entirely along qualitative lines, although not absolutely. In America it is the founding in 1892 of the Sociology Department at the University of Chicago that sees the firm establishment not just of sociology, but through the extensive use of the case study, qualitative research. Reference has already been made to Lazarsfeld's comments concerning the lack of a firm institutional foundation that would have extended the influence of the Chicago School's leaders longer than in actual fact was managed. It was not as if the influence of the Chicago School and their style of work was lost from sight to social enquiry, but the 'middle period' saw a fierce methodological debate that had its roots in the rise of 'positivism', which assisted the displacement of the type of qualitative work the School had

5   The above potted history of empirical social research is also taken from Lazarsfeld 1972.

become famous for. Even by the 1930s Chicago sociology itself was infected by the methodological debates that were afflicting the rest of the social science community, and a 'separate division with a quantitative orientation had developed at Chicago'. (Jankowski and Wester 1991:48) This 'middle period' is the period of Lazarsfeld, in which the dominant paradigm[6] of mass communication research was defined. To quote Jankowski and Wester on their classification of the 'middle period':

> In the course of the 1930s, then, proponents of quantitative methods gained an upper hand in the methodological struggle. The Chicago-style case study had all but disappeared as a mode of social science by the 1950s. Survey research had become *the* method in the social sciences; as Benny and Hughes (1956:137) remarked, modern sociology had become 'the science of the interview'. As the influence of positivist theory and quantitative methodology reached its peak in the 1950s qualitative research came to be seen as a preliminary activity which could, at best, lay the groundwork for 'real science'. (1991:49)

It is in the third period ('1960s to the present') of Janowoski's and Wester's divisions that we see the disenchantment with quantification, especially survey research, coming to the fore, or, as I would prefer, a reassertion of the lost ground of social enquiry to be found in Weber's interpretative sociology, but which during this period takes many glorious forms, symbolic interactionism, ethnomethodolgy and ethnography. Of the interpretative strains of sociology it is ethnography, developing from anthropology, within which focus group research sits. However, for the sake of intellectual tidiness the focus cannot be held to be ethnography, but only a technique that an ethnographer might use as a part of an ethnographic study: the type of information gathered in the focus group is too flimsy for a full or rounded account of the cultural world of the participants.

There is no space here to go into the dismantling of the domination of quantification that began in the 1960s, or the critical attacks that were launched on functionalism and grand theory. But from a point where sociology appeared confident of its own knowledge, assisted by a professionalisation through quantification, intellectual life for the sociologist was not to be as confident again. If one was an ethnomethodologist, how could one be certain about anything, except that counting could not give meaning?

What marks out the 'late period', at least in empirical terms, and also at the theoretical level as critique of grand theory, is a demand to include people in the frame of study; people as people, and not people as variables. If in the late 1960s and 1970s the world was changing, it did not seem that sociology could account for those changes; worse, quantification had removed it, both politically and emotionally, from the very lives of those it sought to study.

---

6   See Gitlin 1978 for his criticism of the dominant paradigm and discussion of Lazarsfeld's procedures.

Without doubt the long tradition of interpretative sociology during this period continued. Although the approaches employed were often very diverse and underpinned by a variety of philosophical thought, qualitative research gained a respectability long since absent: the technician had given way to the artist, or at least the art of interpretation as opposed to demonstration through figures and 'proofs' was now a solid part of the agenda of a humanistic sociology.

The re-seeding of the social sciences and the humanities that began in the 1960s, that saw research activity begin, if not to bury survey research then muffle its voice, opened up the possibility within mass communication research for a re-thinking of its own procedures. Throughout the social sciences a space was created for the emergence of a more qualitative understanding of social performance. This is not to say that the quantitative arm of enquiry took a backstage position. For example, Faulkner and Spector (Faulker 1982), quoted in Jankowski and Wester (1991:71), examined the publication policy of five major sociology journals between 1973 and 1978. In two of the most prestigious journals, *The American Sociological Review* and *The American Journal of Sociology*, less than ten per cent of the articles published scored as qualitative research. However, commenting on this state of affairs Jankowski and Wester, after noting quantitative research has 'remained predominant to this day', conclude that matters 'may be under transformation'. To support this statement they cite the introduction of new journals such as *Urban Life*, *Symbolic Interactionism* and *Qualitative Sociology*, where the stress is on interpretative sociology. They also note in the area of mass communications the space given to qualitative studies in the established journals, such as *The Journal of Communication*, *Media Culture and Society*, and *Critical Studies in Mass Communication*. And indeed, attention was drawn at the beginning of this chapter to the spate of handbooks on focus group research methods.

So far as journal publishing is concerned, it is easier for editors, and the readers that articles are sent to for their professional judgement, to judge quantitative work than it is to judge qualitative work. An article based on quantitative methodology, with its clearly laid out rules of procedure, is more likely to generate consensus agreement as to merit than an article based on qualitative methodology. By its very nature the qualitative article is more interpretative and thus prone to greater vagaries of judgement. Thus one can have a publication bias which does not necessarily reflect existing levels of interest in types of work. On the other hand book publishing is an industry whose prime purpose is not necessarily to advance knowledge, further a particular approach, or even to reflect the actual state of a discipline or field, but to make a profit, or at the very least not to make a loss. Book publishing is not therefore always a good indicator of the condition of a discipline, but more the conditions upon which a profit can be made. The two do not necessary coincide, but will bear some resemblance to each other. By and large publishers do not want empirically based quantitative studies, indeed they tend not to want studies at all, but text books, views of the field, books on methodology, and theory books. In short, books that can be produced relatively inexpensively, that will have a large readership, and, in the case of UK publishers, an American sale, something not easily achieved by an empirical study of British life. Research monographs, which empirical quantitative studies tends to produce, are not favoured by publishers. It is the more discursive book, often featuring material from qualitative studies, that is preferred.

Thus one ought to be somewhat cautious in deducing actual levels of interest in research approaches purely from publication records. However, Jankowski and Wester possibly do offer some reflection of the increased attention given to qualitative work based on the actual fermentation of approaches taking place in the social sciences. As they argue in documenting the rise of qualitative research within mass communication, especially as they call it, 'cutting edge' research: 'Most of this work originates from academic researchers who have been influenced by the methodological upheavals in the humanities and social sciences':

> However, practitioners coming from another institutional context have also contributed to qualitative methodology: marketing research makes extensive use of open and group interviews, and other exploratory techniques. Indeed, one of the major marketing-research organisations in the field – the European Society for Opinion and Marketing Research (ESOMAR) – has for many years organised seminars on qualitative methods and published on their application. (Jankowski and Wester: 1991:72)

It is certainly true that ESOMAR has been very active in promoting qualitative research. After all, qualitative research, focus group research in particular, forms a central part of market research operations, and it is not surprising therefore that the industry's seminars, workshops and conferences should give considerable attention to the publication of the latest work in the area using such a method. But university-based researchers hardly ever attend such gatherings. There are good financial reasons, let alone intellectual ones, why academics should be absent. The high conference registration fees – although sometimes reduced rates can be negotiated by academics – are prohibitive to most university-based researchers, as are the accommodation charges of the plush venues that market and industry media researchers favour. Furthermore, the presentation costs involved in the delivery of some papers, with their dizzying display of specially shot video material, would make most academics gasp, not to mention the amount of time that is spent on preparation, often running into weeks. Research in the market research environment is knowledge plus style, and at times it is difficult to distinguish where one ends and the other begins.

This is not to downgrade the substantive methodological contribution that market research has made, but to illustrate that the academy and the commercial research industry are different worlds, and to stress the central point that the popularity of focus group research within market research has in no way been responsible for its present popularity within university mass communication research. Its present popularity owes itself to the long process of intellectual history wherein quantification has loosened its grip as a method of procedure, amidst a general repositioning of thought that has increasingly valued an interpretative approach to social questions, social problems and the generation of meaning.

The Bridging of Worlds

Lazarsfeld is a crucial figure in the genesis of the method. His contribution is a fundamental part of the intellectual developments that led to their creation, rather than the moment of their establishment. Even so, it must remembered that it was Lazarsfeld who hurriedly took Merton to the CBS studios to observe the reception study in operation, and of which Merton began to 'focus' the proceedings. Thus, at many levels Lazarsfeld is crucial to the origins of focus group research. David Morgan credits Lazarsfeld with the transfer of the method to market research.

> Outside of the social sciences, this work [focus groups developed by Merton] was transplanted into marketing research by Paul Lazarsfeld and others. Although his fellow sociologists have emphasised Lazarsfeld's quantitative contributions, marketers have always given time to his qualitative work – a balance that was important to Lazarsfeld himself, as was his dual involvement in academia and marketing. (Morgan 1988:11)

The origination of focus group methodology within academic social science, and the subsequent take-up by market research, prompts Morgan to ponder why this was so:

> One likely reason is that Merton and his colleagues published very little research that used the method they had proposed. For example, in The Student Physician (1957) Merton *et al* made widespread use of tabulations from survey data and quotations from diaries that the students kept, but only mentioned in passing the fact that they also used focus groups.
>
> … Meanwhile, work with groups had become closely associated with social psychology, and most of the development of qualitative methods centred on participant observation and individual interviewing. Neglect thus appears to be the basic reason why focus groups never took hold, both by the techniques creators who turned to other pursuits and by its potential users who concentrated on other methods. (Morgan 1988:11,12)

It is highly likely that Lazarsfeld's close contact with the world of commerce, a world that moves around lunches and informal meetings, did, at the individual level, make many market researchers aware of the 'Columbia technique'. But it is not as if the technique could not have been known to the academic world. After all Lazarsfeld and Merton, even in 1941, were not insubstantial figures in the social sciences, and were certainly not locked away on Morningside Heights. The operation of the technique, furthermore, was published in some detail, first published as a methodology report in the highly prestigious *American Journal of Sociology* in 1946 under the title 'The Focused Interview' (Merton and Kendall 1946), and in book form by the Free Press in 1956 as *The Focused Interview.*[7] *A Report of the Bureau of Applied Social Research, Columbia University. A Manual of Problems and Procedures.* (Merton, Fiske and Kendall 1956) It was very much a manual of how to do focus groups, and remains one of the finest exposition of the method. The report was first drafted for the Research Branch of the Information and Education Division of the War Department, of which the head of the professional staff was Samuel Stouffer and the head of the experimental section Carl Hovland. According to Merton (1987:556) two editions of this manual were published in mimeograph form by the Bureau of Applied Social Research before the Free Press adopted the work. It is unclear from Merton when the mimeograph was first produced, or at least I cannot discern when, but more than likely it was around 1942-3. Although not a publishing house, The Bureau of Applied Social Research was well known for its mimeographed work, and thus the technique of focus groups could not have been without an academic public; in short, the method was not hidden from sight.

It is certainly true, however, as Morgan has pointed out, and his reference to the Student Physician is a good example, that the technique did not feature heavily in the publication of the Bureau's substantive studies, and it may be therefore that social scientists failed to grasp the full power of the technique, whereas market researchers could see its profitability. They were disposed to embracing the technique as part of a panoply of methods for the generation of revenue. Even so, the adoption of the method by market research was a 'slow burn' and did not become a standard part of research practice until the 1970s.

There is no single explanation as to why focus groups, although originating within the academic sphere of operations, were left to be developed by market researchers. One can place their non-adoption by the academic world within the social movement of ideas, and see their 'defeat' as part of a struggle to define the correct operating practices of sociology and the triumph within that struggle of quantification, or one can see non-adoption in terms of more individual manoeuvres: that for idiosyncratic reasons insufficient publicity was given to their presence. What is required for as complete an explanation as

7   The term 'focused interview' sometimes causes confusion. In many methodology books the focused interview is used to refer to a single interview and is unconnected to focus groups. To clarify the situation: Merton and Kendall in their 1946 article 'The Focused Interview' say '...for several years, the Bureau of Applied Social Research has conducted individual and group interviews in studies of the social and psychological effects of mass communication, print and film. A type of research interview grew out of this experience, which is characteristic enough to merit as distinctive label - "The Focused Interview"' .(Merton and Kendall 1946: 541) The focused interview is thus a procedure to be used with a single interviewee, with groups and, in the former use, differs from a depth interview in the manner in which it proceeds.

possible is the examination of how various factors combined together to restrict the technique's entry into mainstream social science.

Morgan's observation, as a satisfactory explanation for their 'hidden' status, that little reference to focus groups was given in the Bureau of Applied Social Research's substantive work, whilst correct, overlooks the methodological position of the Bureau, Lazarsfeld's own methodological enthusiasms, and Merton's own position on how to conduct focus groups. Sufficient has already been said about Lazarsfeld's belief that a variety of methods was often required to establish social facts, and that what methods were to be adopted was dependent on the social question to be addressed – it was the question that called forth the methods to be adopted, and not the other way around. There was no question of one method existing suitable for all questions. In so far as Lazarsfeld was concerned, any phenomena to be properly explained needed diverse sorts of data, and had to be approached from a variety of angles; all part of his wider insistence on clarification of the language of research and his desire for explication. Focus groups were just one part of this process. If Lazarsfeld were alive today then no doubt he would be alarmed at the weight placed on focus groups as a single method of explanation of social process that some social scientists now place on them. Merton himself is alarmed at what he sees as a misuse of focus groups by the market research community as a single source of explanation. The following comments were given in an address to public opinion and market researchers, but could easily be applied to much current academic use of focus groups. Merton drew on his experiences gained with Carl Hovland in conducting focused interviews for the Research Branch of the War Department, which formed part of the 'American Soldier' studies:

> Our qualitative adjuncts to the experimental design soon convinced that brilliant designer of experiments Carl Hovland that both kinds of data were required for sound conclusions: the rigor of the controlled experiment had its costs since it meant giving up access to the phenomenological aspects of the real-life experience and invited mistaken inferences about the source of that experienced response; the qualitative detail provided by the focused group-interview in turn had its cost since it could lead only to new hypotheses about the sources and character of the responses which in turn required further quantitative, or in this case, further experimental research to test the hypotheses.

Having delivered his description of his work with Hovland, Merton then turned on what he saw as the folly of current applications of the technique:

> From what I have read and heard, I gather that much of focus-group research today as a growing type of market research does not involve this composite of both qualitative and quantitative inquiry. One gains the impression that focus-group research is being mercilessly misused as quick-and-easy claims for the validity of the research are not subjected to further, quantitative test. Perhaps the pressure of the marketplace for

quick-and-easy — possibly, quick and relatively inexpensive — research make for this misuse of focus groups. That misuse — the term seems a smidgen less harsh than 'abuse' — consists in taking merely plausible interpretations deriving from qualitative group interviews and treating them as though they had been shown to be reliably valid for gauging the *distributions* of response. (Merton 1987:557)

This is a pretty damming critique of the current use of focus groups by market researchers. One feels, however, that it would be nothing like the critique he would make of academics who use them as a stand alone method without bothering to validate the claims made from them by other procedural checks. Merton at least recognises the commercial pressures that might lead to such practices by market researchers, but where is the excuse that academics have for such 'abuse'? Whatever the excuse, in so far as Merton is concerned the crime is against understanding, committed through a violation of methodological procedure. He does not exactly say it, although he is pretty tough in the context of the audience he is addressing, that he does not consider the findings from stand-alone focus groups the basis for anything other than as a start for further exploration, or as a check on data collected by other methods.

Peter Lunt and Sonia Livingstone, although to an extent appreciating Merton's position, comment directly:

> Although this quotation gives significant weight to qualitative methods, we suggest that Merton, nonetheless, subordinated them to quantitative methods. He expressed concern about current practices in market research that made isolated use of focus group interviews to draw conclusions about the prevalence and distribution of ideas and attitudes. As this usage is customary in contemporary focus groups, some justification for current research practice is required.
>
> ... In contrast, contemporary theories of the audience are more concerned with the way that active audiences contribute to the negotiation and construction of meanings. (Livingstone 1990) The audience is seen, not as an aggregate of atomized opinions or attitudes, but as individuals located in concrete social groups who construct meaningful social actions partly through the discursive interrogation of texts. In this context, the focus group is used to identify the dimensions of complex stimuli that may have causal power in diffusion, but to examine the everyday ways in which audiences make sense of television. (Lunt and Livingstone 1996:82-5)

True, as Lund and Livingstone say, 'Merton and Lazarsfeld, and others studied audience response to mass media in order to understand the mass diffusion processes that lead to attitude and opinion formation' (p84) and the origination of focus groups grew out of this attempt to understand the persuasive power of messages. However, Lunt and Livingstone's criticism of Merton and the defence of modern practices of understanding the 'active audience' through focus groups that do not use additional method to validate the findings, is description of a practice given as an augmented case for the practice. This will not do. The problem of knowing the distribution of the 'everyday ways in which audiences make sense of television' remains. The findings that certain people may 'construct meaningful social action through the discursive interrogation of texts' does not give any certainty about whether people in general construct such meanings. Furthermore, to say that Lazarsfeld and Merton treat the audience 'as an aggregate of atomised opinions or attitudes' is false and part of the revisionist version of history so strongly attacked by James Curran. As Raymond Boudon takes pains to point out when discussing Lazarsfeld's methodology:

> In contextual analysis, the respondent is defined not only by a number of individual characteristics (age, sex, opinion on various questions, educational level, occupation etc) but also by variables that describe the milieu from which he comes. In this way, the investigation loses its atomistic character and can, by means of adequate analysis, regain the macrosociological tradition typical of Durkheim. (Boudon 1972:425)

It is wrong, therefore, of the 'new practitioners' of focus groups to 'invent' faults in the past as a way of excusing or legitimating existing bad practice. Mass communications research should be very cautious about building its understanding of the audience on focus group research; indeed, one might be better off sticking with textual analysis and theory, for at least then there is no claim to be studying the empirical audience and confusing our understanding of the audience by unsubstantiated data.

However, if one can see the dangers in too ready an adoption of the technique by mass communication researchers, one can also, from the above, glean some understanding of why the method did not gain automatic entry into the social sciences, yet why it flourished in market research. The survey, or quantification side, of market research has all the rigor, the insistence on correct sampling and so on, that academic survey research possesses. Both market research and academic research cannot in the realm of survey research ignore knowledge drawn from the statistical sciences. In practice, as already noted, there is hardly any such thing as the perfect sample, be it a survey conducted under the auspices of a university department, a research institute, government department or a market research agency. 'Accommodations' must be made not only in such matters as drawing the sample, but in deciding what type of sampling procedure to adopt; for example, a loosely structured quota sample, inter-locked quota sample, random sample, random walk sample and so on. The sample to be drawn will be theoretically driven, that is, it will depend on what it is one is attempting to achieve in terms of goals set for the project, which will of necessity be impregnated by theory, even though the theory may be of a low-order variety. Thus heated debates may take place over whether or not the 'correct' procedure was followed, and correct here means the adoption of the most appropriate forms for the task in hand. Simple pragmatic factors will also enter, not least of which is the available money to spend, and that is the case for almost any survey. Even if one had unlimited funds it does not follow that one would opt for a census. Using sampling, estimates of population parameters can be made with known degrees of precision. For any required degree of precision of estimate the sample size required is a function of the variation with regard to that characteristic in the population (usually estimated from the sample standard deviation). These calculations are based on statistical theory, in particular the Central Limit Theorum and the Law of Large Numbers.

The above discussion of survey methodology is not meant in any way to be instructive in a practical sense of conducting survey research, but to establish the point, as firmly as possible, that in undertaking survey research one cannot escape from sets of principles and rules upon which the method is based, in particular the principles of sampling and statistical analysis. It is not possible to create a mode of operation that fundamentally breaks with the accepted practices of procedure without at best calling into question the validity of the activity, and at worse having the work totally dismissed. Every researcher worries about the correctness of the sampling procedure adopted, the nature of the sample itself, and how the data once collected and run has been interrogated. Interpretation of the data is another matter. For most work in the social sciences interpretation involves going beyond the data. Unless one is engaged in pure description the data will not, so to speak, make sense of themselves, but even if one is engaged simply in 'pure' description the description is still infused with the theory-informed questions of the survey itself.

Distorting Research

Market researchers, no more than university-based researchers engaged in quantitative survey research, cannot depart from the principles that underpin such work without incurring charges of incompetence and a dismissal of their results. This does not of course make the results of survey research 'correct'. One might have epistemological reasons for challenging the method itself, as indeed was the basis of some of Adorno's disquiet while working with Lazarsfeld; however, leaving aside such objections to survey methodology as a way of providing 'correct' understanding, what cannot be escaped is that there is a correct way of doing such research, and it is the delineation of the procedure that allows judgement to be made about the correctness of the results in a way that is not open to most qualitative work. What this means is that market researchers could 'hi-jack' the focus group for their own ends, and leave behind the rather rigorous instructions that Merton laid down for their use. Hence Merton's characterisation of the market researcher's use of focus groups as a stand-alone method as one of 'misuse'.

There was no way that market researchers, or anyone else for that matter, could 'distort' survey research in the way that Merton believes market researchers did with focus group research. It is true that for certain types of market research projects some rather loose sampling does takes place as well as the adoption of some rather unsatisfactory interviewing procedures. Nevertheless principles exist by which such activities can be judged as loose or unsatisfactory, and if the judgement is made that the survey has strayed too far from the principles it is totally discredited. It was easier, in other words, for market researchers to 'bend' focus group research to their own ends; namely, the selling of the technique to clients with insufficient regard give to the status of the findings, in a way that was not possible or even desirable in the selling of survey research. In short, focus groups as a method readily lends itself to corruption.

Having said that, Merton is rather harsh on market researchers, because as ever his operational framework is that of the rigorous sociologist. For Merton, to use a method in a way that cannot substantiate the results claimed from the method must have a whiff of the fraudulent. However, in the practice of science the fact that something works does not mean one always needs to know, or indeed does know, how it works. Thus while agreeing with Merton that the use of focus groups as a stand-alone method without any other checks on the validity of the findings does create problems, one might want to consider that focus groups do work; but here we come to the problem of what 'work' means. The problem of reliability will not go away. In the realm of focus groups one cannot operate with the principle of 'if it works it's good', since without the types of checks Merton suggests – the bringing into play of other methods to check the findings, and in particular the creating of hypotheses which can then be tested by other methods – then the knowledge generated from stand-alone focus groups remains very suppositional indeed.

As I have already noted, Merton's criticism of focus group research should really be directed at the academic use of focus groups, and not so much at their use by market researchers, who are not too concerned about the actual knowledge status of the findings from focus groups. Their concern is to provide for the clients insight into the question the client is interested in, be it a product, the response to a programme, or the presence of an attitude. It is a different knowledge game to the one played by Merton the social scientist. Thus, what is taken as 'working' has a different set of rules in the qualitative branch of market research than what those within the social sciences, and that is why Merton's attack is valid for academia but not so valid for market research.

One might reason that even if the function of the focus group in the hands of the market researcher is merely to provide insight, then if one cannot trust those insights it follows that they are valueless, indeed even dangerous if acted upon. Yet the focus group is often used by the clients of market research companies to test whether or not they are right in their own reasoning on some aspect of their operations. In this sense the focus group is used as a check on their existing knowledge and not as a primary source of knowledge that then requires verification. Indeed, if it is primary or new knowledge that is being gathered then it is the client and not the market research company that will follow up the findings by further research to verify or substantiate the findings, possibly by survey research, especially if the client needs to know the distribution of the responses discovered in the focus groups.

In defence of market researchers' use of focus groups it must also be pointed out that quite a lot of the focus group studies conducted are undertaken on very small and tightly defined target groups so that focus group research in such instances, depending on how many groups are conducted, reproduces, to a reasonable degree, the conditions of generalisability associated with survey research. This, of course, is not the case with the use of focus groups in most academic communication research, where small populations are supposed to say something about the audience in general.

On the principle that 'if it works it is good' what market research was allowed to do because of the lack of principles or strict procedures that characterises survey research, was to simply slice off from Merton's more rigorous programme that which it wanted and jettison the more cumbersome aspects of the method. Unfortunately, it would appear that academia is doing the same. The difference is that social sciences, because of the type of knowledge wished for, cannot afford to go down the same loose path as their market research cousin. Or if they do then the researchers need to be very circumspect indeed about the findings derived by such a method. Once focus groups were unencumbered by the scaffolding of verification that Merton had erected, then for market researchers focus groups were a gift to profits and their popularity assured. The social sciences cannot adopt the focus group methodology in such a cavalier way. If it wishes to use it they have to do so in the more rigorous manner laid out by Merton. Committed to a disciplined approach to knowledge, academics cannot 'float off' one part of the method; it is all or nothing.

It must be remembered that in terms of intellectual history the development of the method in 1941 occurred at a time when the quantification wing of the social sciences was rapidly growing in strength, thus it was highly unlikely that only the qualitative part of the technique would have been adopted by the new and rising breed of researchers. In addition, but this must be no more than conjecture, those in the humanistic or qualitative tradition of social research are likely to have associated the method with the Bureau of Applied Social Research. If this was the case then such scholars are not likely to have been attracted to a method that came out of the Lazarsfeld stable, with its emphasis on measurement. And indeed, if one examines the Merton, Fiske and Kendall report to the Bureau (their manual on focus groups) there is nothing 'soft' about it. It is clearly in the tradition of the type of rigorous methodology associated with quantification that was the hallmark of the Bureau, and would not be appealing to qualitative researchers.

If the method did not appeal with any great force to the qualitative researcher then why it never struck home with quantitative researchers either must be an open question. Merton certainly had high hopes for the method. As he stated in addressing the American Association for Public Opinion Research: 'Speaking for myself, I thought of the focused interview as a generic research technique, one that could be and would be applied in every sphere of human behaviour and experience, rather than one largely confined to matters of interest in market research.'(Merton 1987:562) Perhaps the combination of the quantitative and the qualitative that the original method demanded allowed it to fall between two stools; the qualitative researcher on the one hand and the quantification researcher on the other. As laid out by Merton the focus group method is not an easy technique to use; although one must agree with Merton that as originally advanced focus group research opened up a depth of understanding to the social sciences that is most unusual. Strictly speaking it is a combined method. Only in current day practice, both in the hands of academic researchers and market researchers, has it become a single practice. And it is that single practice that has robbed it of its power of explication. The fact that it was a combined activity may well have limited its attractiveness, or perhaps robbed the technique of a visibility sufficient to be taken serious notice by the academic community. For example, as Morgan has already noted, although Merton used focus groups along with survey data and diary reports in his study of the student physician, he only mentions focus groups in passing. Thus important as focus groups may have been in developing the research, they are not given recognition in the overall scheme of the study. Indeed, unless used as a stand-alone method, focus groups tend in general to be overshadowed by other methodological practices, certainly in citation. It is, however, through the use of them as a stand-alone method, as a single source of knowledge, that they have now come to be so well known, and, I would claim, mistakenly applauded.

Five

Focusing on the Focus Group

The Focus Group and Cultural Studies

The focus group method grew out of a tradition of empirical social research that many of those now using focus groups as a way of understanding the audience would wish to dissociate themselves from. But this disassociation would appear to be more of a political than a methodological quarrel. Of course given that the subject area of the social sciences is social life then the question of how best to understand social arrangements and social movements is political in the sense that the methods one chooses structure the representations that are made of the social world. But there is no correct method for the social sciences. One of the strengths of western scientific rationality has been its refusal to accept anything as given, to subject everything to scrutiny and challenge, and that includes the foundations of its own procedures.

To separate off quantitative work from qualitative work is not good procedure, but to turn one against the other, as a political divide, is destructive to the life of the mind. Robert Merton, (theorist and empirical researcher), and Patricia Kendall, (statistician and empirical researcher), in their conclusion to one of the first articles on focus group methodology in 1946, write:

> Social scientists have come to abandon the spurious choice between qualitative and quantitative data; they are concerned with that combination of both which make use of the most valuable features of each. The problem becomes one of determining 'at which points he should adopt the one, and at which the other, approach. (Merton and Kendall 1946:556,557)

Not wishing for a separation of approaches themselves, nor believing that such a separation, intellectually at least, existed in the social science, Merton and

Kendall saw the advantage of focus group research as integrating both qualitative and quantitative approaches in a single practice. The division between quantification and qualitative work did exist in the social sciences, and indeed still does, but to make use of one method it is not necessary to denounce other methods. Yet Stuart Hall writes in *Culture, Media, Language*, 'From its inception, then, Cultural Studies was an "engaged" set of disciplines, addressing awkward but relevant issues about contemporary society and culture'. (Hall 1980:17) Much later in the book, in a chapter titled 'Introduction to Media Studies at the Centre', Hall states: 'Audience-based survey research, based on the large statistical sample using fixed-choice questionnaires, has at last reached the terminal point it has long deserved – at least as a serious sociological enterprise'. (Hall 1980:120) Hall mentions with approval David Morley's more differentiated approach to the audience, but if one looks at Morley's interview work, especially his *Family Television. Cultural Power and Domestic Leisure* (Morley 1986), then in his Foreword one finds the statement:

> In particular it must be borne in mind that this research was based on a sample of respondents who were quite deliberately selected as belonging to one specific type of household – the traditional nuclear family living together with their dependent children. Moreover, all the families were white and all lived in one area of inner London.

He warns, quite rightly, that one cannot use the findings of his interviews to generalise to the population as a whole, but only to families of a similar type, which in effect is the white working class and lower middle class in London. I am not, however, so sure one can even do that from his sample. His unemployed men in one section of his sample appear to be suffering mild clinical depression. If so, it was their depression which was the key variable in understanding their heavy use of television and video film, not family structure; their reduction in interest in an outside world that they had once been interested in before unemployment bares all the hallmarks of depression.

Yet it is not always necessary to generalise to populations as a whole, and Morley's study does provide keen insights into cultural power within the family, something that is normally hidden from sight and would certainly be difficult to get at through survey research. Morley is well aware of the limits to his study, and refers to the work as a pilot project. In his section on methodology he draws attention to the role of focus groups in allowing 'insights into the terms within which our respondents themselves defined their viewing activities', but says, 'this pilot project aimed to pursue the problems facing broadcasters in relation to the questions outlined above, and thus clarify the problems which will need to be resolved in later survey research'. (Morley 1986:51)

One cannot have social enquiry based on a single method or approach, or rather if one does, the limits of that enquiry are likely to be small indeed. Thus to say that survey research has come to the 'terminal point that it has long deserved' in serious sociological work is as wrong as it is damaging to media research as an investigative activity, and to deride quantification as positivism has a righteous certainty often not found outside of religious or political movements. (see Willis 1980) Indeed, reading Fred Inglis' account of cultural studies one does wonder what the nature of the activity is. In his account cultural studies is a kind of spiritual activity:

> The moral of this deliberate excursus into moral theory is that as a temporary convenience, Cultural Studies should take biography (or life histories) as their canonical subject matter, and the narrative as the circumscribing form of all their enquiries, whether into pop, sex, civil war or just the spectacular life of the shopping mall. My contention has been that in the absence of more convincing grand narratives of history and politics, we shall do best by way of holding together our academic and our citizens' lives if we seek out those stories which indicated how best to live in the present.... I will risk declaring that *this is the way the best and the brightest of present-day students in the human sciences want to learn to think and feel.* And having learned to think and feel thus, this is how they want to act and live. There is, as always, a story hidden in these assertions. It is the story of how Cultural Studies will make you good. (Inglis 1993:214)

It is the claim to a single method, or approach to knowledge, that is wrong, and at times quite frightening in the way in which the claims are cast. Such statements certainly have the feel of cultishness. Yet in what way, for example, could cultural studies, without drawing on data from survey research, or the electronic recovery equivalents, have an understanding of the distribution of popular taste for programmes? Such understanding could certainly not be achieved from focus group discussions, interviews, or participant observation. One may, from such methods, get an interpretative understanding of what makes a programme popular, what the structures and meaning of it are in terms of the symbolic universe of the individual, but not the reach of its popularity. And that often needs to be known even for those who wish to study a particular cultural phenomenon. Of course it might be agreed that such data would be useful to cultural studies, but the work itself, the actual collection of the data, is not considered, to use Hall's phrase, a 'serious sociological enterprise'.

The use of the word 'serious' in this manner is a classic way of discrediting without argument. A 'serious sociological enterprise' comes to mean no more than what the writer considers to be good, but is given the force of a canonical judgement that leaves the writer as the definer of a field of research. Now, the technical collection of BARB data, from which the rating figures are produced, may not be a 'serious' sociological enterprise in its collection of pure information, but the data thus collected are a very important source for the development of sociological knowledge, once subjected to sophisticated longitudinal analysis. Is the suggestion really that we do not need survey data on the audience, or is it that if one collects data on the audience by survey methodology then one is not engaged in a 'serious sociological enterprise'? One might concede that audience rating data is more a commercial inventory than sociological activity, but that could not apply to actual studies that used survey methodology to enquire into attitudes to, say, the coverage of war, and used complex questioning about the limits of state violence as a legitimate means of resolving conflict in relation to sets of issues. If it does mean that such activity falls outside serious sociological enterprise, then what it suggests is that the sociological enterprise is a very limited project indeed.

Knowledge is built from a variety of sources and by a variety of methods. Why it should be that cultural studies have an antagonism to quantification cannot be explained by ignorance, but by the roots of its own activity. As Inglis correctly states, 'English is first parent of Cultural Studies.' (Inglis 1993:30)[1] The literary approach to culture does of course come from a different tradition of observation than the attempt to 'measure' it associated with survey research. Indeed, the whole qualitative approach to cultural examination, the examination of texts, participant observation, case studies, life histories, oral history and so on, has been the most successful approach. But that is not a reason for damning other methods. It is noteworthy, for example, that Hall traces the pedigree of cultural studies back to key texts, most notably Richard Hoggart's, *The Uses of Literacy* (1961), Raymond Williams's *Culture and Society* (1958) and *The Long Revolution* (1961) and EP Thompson's, *The Making of the English Working Class* (1963). These works, to a greater or lesser degree, expose the hidden history and culture of ordinary people. It is this unearthing of the hidden through the method of analysis adopted by cultural studies that has been its solid contribution to communication research. Yet the keen observations that one finds in Hoggart's work can also be discovered in George Orwell's documentation of working-class life, poverty and unemployment in *The Road to Wigan Pier* (1937). Orwell, forsaking at times a literary mode of 'disclosure', attempts household budgetary analysis, a tradition of analysis

---

1   Richard Hoggart's *The Uses of Literacy* is referred to as one of the 'sacred texts' (p47) of cultural studies, giving it, in Inglis' hands, a cultish feel. Hoggart was for a time in the 1980s chairman of the board of the Broadcasting Research Unit. Certainly Hoggart's preference for the 'lived experience' rather than the type of empirical work the Broadcasting Research Unit actually did, is identified by Inglis as the central method of Cultural Studies. 'The key term in all this, as it is for everything that might be included under the head of Cultural Studies, is *'experience'*. (p51) After discussing the nature of 'experience', Inglis goes on to say: 'But however it is, it is a consequence of the intellectual history sketched in these first two chapters, as it is an axiom of Cultural Studies, that live experience is an absolute value in itself, as well as being the moral measure of historical and political meaning. It is the conceptual term which ties together the individual and the great arc of history. As we shall see in later chapters, it takes a pasting from philosophers of representation as well as from more traditional sceptics. But it remains at the centre of the vocabulary of Cultural Studies, and one of the key honorifics.' (Inglis 1993:52) Michael Tracey, the first head of the Unit, commented after one of his innumerable battles to have survey research accepted by the 'father of British cultural studies', that like W H Auden, Hoggart believed that 'no objective measurement can ever compete with the single intuitive glance'. The research staff were simply shocked, even unnerved, by the presence of such single-minded belief in a literary approach to knowledge.

firmly established as far back as the 1850s in the monumental painstaking work of Frederic Le Play in France.[2]

'Surveys' have had an important part to play in descriptively bringing to the surface hidden culture. Henry Mayhew's huge study,[3] *London Labour and the London Poor* published in 1851, and the eight volumes of Charles Booth's *Life and Labour of the People in London*, published serially 1889-1897, as well as Benjamin Seebohm Rowntree's study of poverty in York, *Poverty, A Study in Town Life* published in 1901 and his later enormous systematic study, with Bruno Lasker, of unemployment in York, *Unemployment, a Social Study*, produced in 1911.[4]

The surveys referred to are by no means cultural studies; they were fact-finding missions, mainly concerned with the objective facts of particular cultures, although in the case of Rowntree's first York study the subjective elements, culturally generated individual traits that created secondary poverty, were examined. They were mapping exercises rather than deep cultural cartography, although in Rowntree's and Lasker's study of unemployment in York sixty research teams visited every worker's house and in the following months short

---

2   Chris Jenks in a chapter titled 'Cultural Studies: What Is It?', does mention as 'old lines of thought', contributions or starting points for Cultural Studies, George Orwell, 'a near contemporary of the triumvirate of Hoggart, Williams, and Thompson who are held as the key moving figures of Cultural Studies.' (Jenks 1993:155); but interestingly it is Orwell's observations on popular fiction 'in relation to a sense of 'dominant ideology, his analysis of the absence of a working-class presence in nineteenth-century fiction (other than through the representation of a 'mob'), his falsely prophetic 1984 views on mass culture/mass audience through the ever increasing power of the mass media' (p155) that is mentioned, and not the Le Play type of social accountancy mentioned.

3   Jenks (1993) does mention Henry Mayhew's *London Labour and the London Poor* and Charles Booth's *Life and Labour of People in London* as examples of the lineage of cultural studies. He also includes Jack London's *People of the Abyss*, Walter Besant's *East End*, James Greenwood's *Low Life Deeps* and the novels of Charles Dickens and Arthur Morrison, and the writings of Henry James, Mearns, Sims, Engles and as he says 'many, many more'.

4   See the 'Afterword' to Jahoda, Lazarsfeld and Zeisel's *Marienthal. The Sociography of an Unemployed Community* (1972) for a good review of sociographic literature. The afterward was written for the original study *Die Arbeitstlosen von Marienthal* in 1933 to document the 'spiritual and methodological ancestors' of the study. At the time it was the first effort to write such a history, attempting to serve the development of three centuries. It is not only an impressive achievement, but shows the breath of knowledge of Lazarsfeld – although he may not have been actually responsible for this section of the book, more likely Zeisel judging by the fact that he pens a brief note at the beginning of the 1972 afterward explaining its origins. Boudon commenting on Lazarsfeld's philosophical papers gives special mention to Lazarsfeld's breadth of reading: 'The historical task that Lazarsfeld sets for himself is so close to his heart that he does not try to avoid the phase which is thankless, yet indispensable, to the work of the historian – namely, to uncover, assemble and read critically works that are relatively unknown or difficult to obtain. Few sociologists, or even historians of sociology, can claim to have studied Hermann Conring, Sussmilch or Petty. Few books on Max Weber mention the fact that he himself was directly involved in large-scale empirical inquiries. Few sociologists have made it their business to analyse in detail the significance of the objections levelled by Halbwachs against the 'average man' of Quételet'. (Boudon 1972:417,48)

life histories were gathered on every unemployed man and woman. Despite Arthur Bowley's pioneering sampling work in the social sciences, Rowntree did not trust sampling even in the second social survey of York. (1935) By 1941, however, when his report *Poverty and Progress: A Second Social Survey of York* appeared he did include a supplementary chapter, 'An Examination of the Reliability of Social Statistics Based on the Sampling Method', to ward off criticisms that he had not sampled.[5]

Had such work been combined with the type of close participant observation often favoured by cultural studies then it would have been immensely enriched, of that there is no doubt. But one might equally argue that the more tightly delineated areas for study favoured by cultural studies could well benefit from a widening of vision to include the broader terrain of operation allowed by quantification, but still using key understandings gained from the original approach. To do so would certainly make such studies much more powerful politically. Such an effort would require great intellectual imagination, and it might be that to do so would collapse its intellectual task of establishing its own procedural forms, of capturing 'authentic experiences'.

What the early survey work on poverty shows is that one cannot hem in areas of research activity by absolute commitment to any one single method, nor denounce methodologies designed for different activities to that which oneself is engaged in. It may be that the intellectual questions one is interested in can only be approached by a particular procedure or method, but, to turn on other methods as something not to be entertained in any study, reduces the world to only that which can be studied by the chosen single method. Nor does a strong position on a single appropriate method allow the exchange of knowledge between studies operating on different operational principles. The outcome can only be an impoverishment to knowledge in its widest sense. It would certainly limit cross disciplinary fertilisation of ideas and co-operation between disciplines.

Factors of personality, as well as the intellectual establishment of some epistemological position, ought to be taken into account when considering why researchers select the method of approach that they do. Qualitative work, and none more so than participant observation, tends to involve a fiercer commitment to a research project than does quantification. Indeed, one sees people in the qualitative field 'taken over' by the research, so that differences between the subjects of the research and the researcher be collapsed in the common enterprise of understanding. Such involvement is highly likely to raise claims for the superiority of the technique or method one is using, since in a sense the very immersion of the self in the method means that one is talking about ones own life, and not just the life of others.

---

5   See Madge (1962: 363, 1972 ed) for this explanation and for Rowntree's concerns about sampling.

Qualitative work of the participant observation kind is very demanding indeed, intellectually, sometimes physically, and always mentally. Furthermore, such involvement with a particular world means that other worlds do not exist, or at least only as shadows of the 'real' world one is in. The likelihood is that the world under study is celebrated. And indeed there is a great deal of celebration of working class culture within cultural studies, an appreciation for the 'authenticity' of the culture that goes back to the rationale of the original 'descriptors' of the area.[6] The danger is, however, that the celebration of a culture also means that the method used for study becomes celebrated; a celebration moreover that corrals the area off to those not working within it.

If viewed in terms of the sociology of an intellectual movement, then the distinction drawn between quantitative and qualitative work by those within culture studies becomes easier to understand, especially their objection to quantification. To view the development of cultural studies in this way also affords linkage with my earlier observations about its cultish position within communication research, where the liturgy of methods of the broader church are, indeed must be, denied legitimacy. A more simple explanation, which would still not deny the above argument, is that cultural studies'recent existence as a branch of communication studies, an existence which Lawrence Grossberg highlights as significantly damaging to cultural studies (Grossberg 1973), has meant that it has had to fight hard for its recognition as a legitimate activity, often in the face of hostile objections from the established church, as it attempted to go beyond existing understandings or beliefs. A certain zealousness is understandable in the circumstances, and characteristic in the development of any school of thought.

Cultural studies, which as its title suggests embraces a terrain wider than the position and role of the media in social life, has had an enormous influence on the framing of the language of research adopted by media studies, first in England and more recently in America. One thing that characterise both cultural studies and media studies is their opposition to the methods of quantification. Not surprisingly, therefore, for those wishing to study the audience directly the focus group could be expected to have a ready appeal.

The focus group is not participant observation, and nor should it strictly speaking be seen as ethnography, but as a constituent element of ethnographic methodology. The danger, and David Morley is already guilty of this, is to turn an aspect of a methodological procedure into a full and complete methodological process. This is not meant as a criticism of Morley's work with group discussions since in his study of *Family Television* (Morley 1986) he certainly points out that survey research could profitably be used on a number of the problems that his research helped clarify. There is no question, however, that Morley has been one of the most visible media researchers using focus group methodology. The real problem is that other researchers, having liked what they have seen in Morley's

---

6   Jenks (1993:154) even notes the romanticisation of working-class life in writers such as Hoggart, going so far as to call it a 'romanticism bordering on sentimentality'.

work, have adopted the method as a full programme of research. My concern is, that having found a method suitable to their intellectual and ideological needs in studying the audience, media studies researchers will feel even more righteous in their dismissal of quantification. Having acquired an empirical method by which to protect themselves against the charge of being overly theoretical, locked into textual analysis, media studies can get on with their business undisturbed by thoughts from other shores. The question is, however, what is the nature of the planking that will keep the raft afloat?

The Rules of Focus Group Research

Klaus Bruhn Jensen in his provocatively titled paper, 'The Past in the Future: Problems and Potentials of Historical Reception Studies' neatly encapsulates reception analysis:

> Reception analysis may be defined as a qualitative form of audience-cum-content analysis, comparing the discourses of media contents and the discourses of the audience – as recovered through interviewing, observation, and textual analysis – in order to interpret and explain the process of their interaction in specific social contexts at a particular historical juncture. Media and audiences thus contribute to the production and circulation of meaning in society. History may be read as a discourse, which is articulated increasingly through the mass media, and rearticulated in part by their audiences. (Jensen 1993:21)

Jensen then goes on to trace the intellectual roots of reception studies that draw on several theoretical traditions: Chicago School sociology, symbolic interactionism, ethnomethodology, oral history, life histories and 'various so-called ethnographic approaches, deriving from an anthropological tradition', the latter giving 'what Geertz calls 'a thick description' of media in everyday life, combining observation, interviewing, diaries, family photographs, and other evidence.' All is not good, however. Jensen offers the warning: 'It is perhaps a weakness of contemporary audience research that a particular method may assume the status of a fetish'. Powers are attached to that method that it simply does not possess. Edward McQuarie, in reviewing Richard Krueger's, *Focus Groups: A Practical Guide for Applied Research*, (Kreuger 1988) argues that the inherent weaknesses 'of the book are due primarily to the author's enthusiasm for the technique. It is surely not the case that "Focus groups place people in natural, real life situations". (p44) McQuarie then states: 'Participation in a focus group is just as unnatural and constrained an activity as participation in any other social science research endeavour'. (McQuarie 1989:372) Because participants in focus groups appear to enjoy themselves, and because the groups themselves are often conducted in convivial surroundings, it does look as if focus groups are natural. Yet viewers do not in their everyday lives sit around and discuss programmes in the guided fashion of a focus group, nor are they asked to sit and watch a programme in the manner of some pedagogical exercise. Falseness, as a lack of true social setting, is thus structured into the methodology. But then all methodology interferes, to a greater or lesser extent, with the 'natural' situation it is designed to study or understand, and in many cases it is only with quite strong, even deliberately designed 'interference', such as raising arousal levels, that 'normal' states can be observed. In the case of focus groups, they are actually less normal to most people than the completion of a questionnaire: most people are only too familiar with completing forms requesting information about themselves, be it for tax purposes, or making insurance claims.[7]

However, the central point to extract from McQuarie's review of Krueger is that he considers the mistake about naturalness to have arisen from the author's 'enthusiasm for the technique' It is from such enthusiasms that the fetishisation of a method noted by Jensen can arise, especially in the case of media studies with its discovery of a 'safe' empirical way for entering the 'real' world of the audience. As Birgitta Höijer points out in her discussion of theoretical and methodological considerations in studying viewers: 'Any single study cannot grasp the dynamics and all the complexities of the reception of mass media products'. She therefore stresses the need, 'to choose a perspective and be aware of that choice and its underlying assumptions.' (Höijer 1990:32) One might add, it is not just that any single study cannot grasp the dynamics and complexities of reception, but that a single method cannot either. 'Anything,' as David Morgan says in his book *Focus Groups as Qualitative Research*, 'that a technique does notably well is done, at least partially, at the expense of other things that can only be done poorly'. (Morgan 1988:20) This point is close to one that David Stewart and Prem Shamdasini make in their book *Focus Groups, Theory, Practice*. Their concern is with those researchers who steadfastly claim the superiority of a certain type of data over another as a way of organising knowledge. They draw on Klaus Krippendorf's (1980) distinction between *emic* and *etic* to support their argument. Emic data is that which 'arises in a natural or indigenous form' and 'they are only minimally imposed by the research or the research setting', while etic data 'represent the researcher's imposed view of the situation'. As Stewart and Shamdani observe, hardly any actual research is of the pure etic or emic type, and it is better to 'think of a continuum of research, with some methods lying closer to the emic side of the continuum and some techniques lying closer to the etic side'.

Clearly focus group research with its insistence on the participants speaking for themselves in an open dialogue is closer to the emic side of the continuum than survey research, where the more closed dialogue and 'forced' responses place it on the etic side of the continuum. Stewart and Shamdani state:

> Neither emic nor etic data are better or worse than the other; they simply differ. Each has its place in social science research; each complements and serves to compensate for the limitations of the other. Indeed, one way to view social science research is as a process that

---

moves from the emic to the etic and back, in a cycle. Phenomena that are not understood well often are studied first with tools that yield more emic data. As a particular phenomenon is understood better and greater theoretical and empirical structure is built around it, tools that yield more etic types of data tend to predominate. As knowledge accumulates, it often becomes apparent that the explanatory structure surrounding a given phenomenon is incomplete. This frequently leads to the need for data that are more emic, and the process continues.

The distinction made between etic and emic data may have 'its place in the social sciences research' but the reasoning given by Stewart and Shamdasani for why this should be so is not quite the one I had in mind when raising the spectre of an over-concentration on one approach (emic), nor part of my plea that focus group methodology is not the holy grail for studying the audience. The mistake that Stewart and Shamdasani make is to take knowledge in the social sciences as a system which adjusts in line with some self-awareness of imbalance, but where imbalance is seen as non-problematic. First it moves one way and then it moves another way, as if it were a computerised flight director following a set course for progress to some definable point. Knowledge in the social sciences is not cumulative in the way suggested; as often as not it is in a process of continuous dismantlement, revising and restructuring, so that the social sciences have said very little of a solid lasting nature, appearing more as contemporary history always struggling with itself to reflexively keep on top of the moment.

The idea that etic data comes in to play when emic data has out-stripped its own understanding and then etic data runs ahead of itself and emic data comes into bat is fanciful not only for the above reasons, but because most of the players are not watching the total game, or indeed, posses a shared understanding of the nature of the game to allow such strategic entries. In fact, it is the very difficulty of agreeing about the rules of the game – the methodology as such – that produces not different definitions of the game, but different games each with their own rules. It is better to look therefore for internal validity of the games at play set against some external judgement of the value of the game, than it is to talk about etic and emic data being better or worse than each other – the games at play are simply different. This allows one to judge the appropriateness of the type of data collected in terms that make sense to the activity itself, and come to agreements about what that type of data can do in a way that is not dismissive of the activity – or if dismissiveness is felt to be in order when judged by some external criteria of value allows one to examine how the rules have been played may have contributed further to the considered lack of value.

Games and Rules

If we hold with the idea of the development of knowledge as involving 'games' and not as suggested by Stewart and Shamdasini a 'game' that at certain historical points moves types of data across to 'compensate for the limitations of each', then we avoid the type of statement made by Hall that survey research applied to the audience has no place 'as a serious sociological enterprise'. What Hall is doing is defining the subject by the method, indeed, creating the subject in terms of the method; rightly so, since I am suggesting that is unavoidable. He has a particular understanding of sociology drawn from the method, and indicated by the prefixing of sociology with 'serious'. In fact, this is what the general public and politicians do all the time. They define the subject by the method – the subject is created by the method – and it is the method that they do not like. Were sociology merely statistical, with all that implies in terms of description, then the general public, as likely as not, instead of having a low opinion of sociology would have a high opinion. They would do so because sociology itself would be different in that its subject, due to the methods adopted, would be different.

By holding to the idea of games and not a game, each being determined by sets of rules – the methods – then it can be shown that the statement made by Hall is mistaken in that the examination of the rules, his preferred rules which determine the game, turn out to be faulty – the game cannot be conducted by those rules because the rules themselves expose in the course of their application that they are incapable of completing the game. Of wider significance is that this misapplication of rules, which means by extension that the subject has been drawn wrongly, has rather large consequences for cultural studies, or does so when one discovers a persistent misapplication of rules, that is, that through constant misapplication the game engaged in by cultural studies cannot be completed.

Graham Murdock's criticism of cultural studies for ignoring political economy, and its refusal to attribute adequate reference to the role of the material in the generation of meaning, provides a perfect case for what I have been saying about rules exposing their own faults as a guidance to the game or subject. What Murdock is saying, in my understanding, is that the rules – the method – followed by cultural studies does not complete the game, and because it does not it leaves cultural studies open to the charge of being a structurally incomplete activity from which certain consequences follow, not the least of which is the production of the inconsequential, the inconsequential here defined as a limitation of reference. Expressed more bluntly, cultural studies does not go anywhere. (Murdock 1989) That is, the 'story' is incomplete, and is so because of the refusal to carry on in the face of what the rules demand, or rather have exposed. This is certainly the case in many areas of social enquiry through cultural studies' stubborn resistance to quantification.

If we now carry the idea of the limitation of reference, an incompleteness as a consequence of the rules, over to the area of focus group research the fault lines of cultural studies begin to appear as cracks. To do this we must stay with the notion of a method not being able to complete what the rules of that method expose; in the case of focus groups, the need to discover the distribution of responses found within the focus group setting.

Qualitative work cannot be used as a substitute for quantitative work, and neither can quantification be used to do the work of qualitative research. The rules of the game are different. It is true that survey work can collect subjective data, but it is not its strength. Qualitative work cannot collect the statistical distributions of responses of large populations. Yet the rules – the method – of focus group research although interpretative in nature have a logic which exposes those rules to the rule of quantitative research. To know how some people incorporate television into their lives remains at the level of the inconsequential unless it is known whether they speak for more than themselves – the story is incomplete and because it is incomplete loses its power of narration. It is not, however, that all focus groups need the rules of other games to make them valuable, and thus the rules in such cases do not expose an incompleteness, the rules can 'finish' what they began. But often, and most usually, the language of the rules leads to quantification statements. It cannot be otherwise. And indeed, the very disclaimer that the findings from a particular focus group study cannot be generalised to the population as a whole exposes that for the story to be complete the findings must be able to be generalised to a population outside of the sample population. Furthermore, the disclaimer does not stop the findings being read 'as if' they can be generalised to a wider population than the small number of people that were exposed to the research questions.

For example, to conduct 12 focus groups, which is a quite a lot, recruiting ten respondents to achieve eight arrivals we can realistically assume 100 respondents overall. If we then split for gender we have 50 men and 50 women in our sample. If we then make a three way split for age we have roughly 17 women aged say, 18-30, 17 women aged 30-45 and 17 women aged 45 and over. The numbers would also be the same for men. If we now wished to split by another variable, say socio-economic status and only made a two-way split by combining groupings, it would leave us with roughly only 9 working-class women in each age cell and 9 middle-class women in each age cell. We might wish to put in geographic breaks, but clearly the number of groups simply would not carry such portioning. If the subject of enquiry was viewers response to the television image of the Gulf War, then one might finish with statements such as older men (45+) were less upset by images of death and injury of Iraqi soldiers than were younger women, (18-30), and provide the explanation that this was so because the younger women were less convinced of the justice of the war than were the older men. However, this finding that younger women tended to support the war less than older men and thus were more upset by images of enemy death is drawn from only 17 people, but then if one found that it was the middle-class women aged 18-30 who were the most upset by such images and that they were so because of all those in the sample they objected to the war the most strongly then the findings would be drawn only on nine people. Furthermore, given that within a single group opinions would not be held evenly nor responses to the images shown held with equal emotion – some may even have held diametrical views to the majority – what would such findings tell us? Very little at one level and a lot at other levels. We would certainly be in possession of knowledge about the possible range of responses to the images of war, and how sentiments to images are formed.

The story, however, would be incomplete because of the limitation of reference and thus, to keep with the earlier descriptive categories, inconsequential. And this is the danger faced by cultural studies, the crux of which is embedded in Hall's denunciation of survey research, that in refusing to acknowledge quantification the studies are inconsequential. The rules demand that the findings from the groups are bedded in some wider significance. It is not that interesting to find out the attitudes of a mere nine women to war. It only becomes interesting if these women are representative of more than just themselves. Quantification, by survey methodology, cannot be escaped in such a situation, and this is not because the example taken is really illustrative of engaging in quantification by a qualitative method, but that the rule of the method entails the question, 'I wonder how many people feel as they do'? Furthermore, rather than go straight to quantification, the focus group with its ability to explore meaning helps to dilute the imposition of meaning in the questions asked in the survey, or if the survey occurred before the focus group were conducted, it assists in the explanation of findings by taking the statistical responses for examination of what might be going on 'behind' the figures.

The inability to say what the responses in focus groups signify in terms of a wider audience robs such work of its full meaning. In the given example of the Gulf War, even though the researcher may openly state that the findings cannot be generalised to other people, if such generalisation is not given then the results become so meaningless that the reader is 'forced' to given meaning to them by making the generalisation themselves through an assumed general applicability to wider populations. Without this assumption the research makes little sense, or is so trivial as not to be worthy of serious reading. Why bother reading the accounts of a few people drawn from the general population, if there is nothing special about them? They are not, for example, special witness to great events, or key players in some unfolding drama, but ordinary people who derive their status of interest by what they may tell us about people generally.

This relates to my earlier point. It is necessary to judge research operations in terms that are internal to the activity itself, and thus connect with those involved with the research by judging it through the rules of that game and not through the rules of some other game. Indeed, it is the misapplication of rules that characterises the quantification/qualitative divide. Focus group research, on the whole, conducted as a stand alone technique exposes by its own rules the poverty of its narrative power. There are exceptions which will be dealt with later, but the method, or rule, forces upon itself the very question of representationality. For example, it is common to be given some comment or statement in the course of a focus group that excites because it is unexpected, and because it seems to offer a very good insight into the matters under enquiry. One feels that one is 'on to something', only to have the excitement dissipate by finding no other person in any group approximating such thinking, and thus the area, or lead, is dropped. This may be referred to as the exploration of meaning, but the process of 'dropping' is quantification by another name. Indeed, the dropping of a line of enquiry because it is not reflected elsewhere, is quantification by any name. What one is doing, and this is the logic of the rule governing the method, is having a finding supported by being supported by others within the sample of enquiry. Repeated confirmation gives confidence that there is something 'there' which leads inexorably to the question, is it elsewhere? But the elsewhere is never examined. Having played the quantification game, because that in fact is what the rule entails even in the confines of the focus group research, the game is refused further play by the refusal to extend the enquiry and seek confirmation of the findings, or more accurately, to seek to confirm whether the confirmed findings of the focus group research would be found if wider groupings of people were used. It is at this point that the rule is broken and the game being played by that rule shambles to inconclusion, or what I have referred to before as inconsequentiality. This refusal to attempt to gauge how far the findings from focus groups are representative of wider sentiments robs the technique of political power.

To get over this problem by qualitative work one has to engage a considerable number of focus groups. To make generalisations one needs, in addition to a large number of focus groups, a carefully drawn sample from a clearly defined, and preferable small, target population. Only then might one be confident of the generalisibility of the findings. Given the number of groups required to achieve such a task it is likely one will require some technique of quantification for handling the mass of information collected. The danger here is that this procedure can easily lead to a structuring of questioning to facilitate ease of quantification which then runs the risk of robbing the focus group of its full potential for generating the type of interpretative data that they are so suited for. All of which raises the question of whether it might not be better to have employed survey research techniques in the first place, or if one would not wish to abandon the types of understandings offered by focus group methods, follow up the focus groups with a survey that will allow the findings to be generalised. Of course, it may be that a survey will show that the views held by the participants to the focus groups are not supported by a larger population, but then, that is the very point of the survey exercise, namely, to discover the distribution of the responses.

Jenny Kitzinger, in a very thoughtful article on the importance of interaction between research participants, concludes from a review of over forty published reports of focus group studies that focus group work 'has not been sophisticatedly developed as a research technique within social science in general'. (Kitzinger 1994:104) It is difficult, however, in the realm of qualitative work to develop a sophistication of method such as that allowed in the realm of quantitative work. Nevertheless, Merton and his co-workers were quite explicit in their characterisation of the focused interview. Writing with Paticia Kendall in 1946, Merton comments on the work of the Bureau of Applied Social Research undertaken over several years with individual and group interviews into the 'social and psychological effects of mass communications' in the areas of radio, print and film. They argue that a specific type of interview emerged which 'might appear superficially similar' to other type of research interviews, but in fact differs in several respects. Merton and Kendal document, in broad outline, the characteristics of the focused interview:

1. Persons interviewed are known to have been involved in a *'particular concrete situation'*: they have seen a film; heard a radio program; read a pamphlet, article or book; or have participated in a psychological experiment or in an uncontrolled, but observed, social situation.

2. The hypothetically significant elements, patterns, and total structure of this situation have been previously analysed by the investigator. Through this *'content analysis'* he has arrived at a set of hypotheses concerning the meaning and effects of determinate aspects of the situation.

3. On the basis of this analysis, the investigator has fashioned an *'interview guide'*, setting forth the major areas of inquiry and the hypotheses which locate the pertinence of data to be obtained in the interview.

4. The interview itself is focused on the 'subjective experiences' of persons exposed to the pre-analysed situation. The array of their reported responses to this situation enables the investigator (a) To test the validity of hypotheses derived from content analysis and social psychological theory, and (b) To ascertain unanticipated responses to the situation, thus giving rise to fresh hypotheses. (Merton and Kendall 1946:541)

They continue: 'From this synopsis it will be seen that a distinctive prerequisite of the focused interview is a prior analysis of a situation in which subjects have been involved'. It can also be seen from the synopsis that detailed foreknowledge of the situation is considered necessary so that the moderator 'need not be devoted to discovering the objective nature of the situation' and that equipped 'in advance with a content analysis, the interviewer can readily distinguish the objective facts of the case from the subjective definitions of the situation'. (Merton and Kendall 1946:541)

There is no disguising the fact that the focus group research developed by Merton and his colleagues at the Bureau was part and parcel of the effects tradition of research. Although this tradition may not now be popular with many contemporary communication researchers, it must be remembered that the effects tradition is a broad one. The effects measured by Merton included the effect on understanding of messages and images which could now well be called reception analysis, an altogether more acceptable title among those who might decry the effects tradition. But above all Merton would have insisted, whatever one cares to call the activity, that the greatest endeavour be made to determine that what we say is true. But then, Merton and his associates were working with focus group methodology to help the war effort, where to have wrong results could lead to disaster, not just on the home front but on the battlefront.

The work completed by Merton and his associates was done not just to understand the processes necessary for building morale among civilians, with the aim of contributing to the war effort through bond buying and so on, but to help understand how combat soldiers perceived the enemy and their own role in the war. Whereas Kurt Lewin was fond of saying that there was nothing like a good theory for solving a problem, Lazarsfeld, in reflecting on that thought, and the circumstances of much of his research career at the Bureau, said in conversation that 'there is nothing like a good problem for giving you a good theory', and in this case, one might add, a good technique. Merton's work with focus groups was initiated for sound practical reasons, and hence there was an insistence on making them as rigorous as possible so that the findings could be applied with some confidence to real problems.

Writing in 1988, David Morgan, in reassessing Merton's early use of focus groups, comments that 'there is now almost no recognition of the potential value of focus groups in experiments'. Morgan considers this unfortunate, because as he later comments, the use of preliminary groups to define 'manipulations of independent variables and measures of dependent variables is analogous to developing questions in interviewing techniques'. By 'exploring the topic of interest with the targeted subjects of the research, it is possible to operationalise the theory in a way that is meaningful to the participants'. That is, to help give the study external validity, a benefit also for their use with survey research. Indeed, the manipulation of variables that forms a central part of survey research meant that surveys were often referred to, as Lazarsfeld himself did on occasion, as experiments. However, focus groups can, something not generally appreciated according to Morgan, increase 'the chance of designing a successful experiment' by assisting in the selection 'of a more powerful manipulation for the independent variable and more sensitive measures for the response variables'. What Morgan is particularly critical of is the armchair speculation that is often engaged in by experimenters in analysing why and where an experiment produced anomalous results, because 'the experimental researchers feel qualified to explain their own failed predictions stems in part from their assumed familiarity with the population they typically study: students'. As he says, 'there is no substitute for exploring the research outcomes with the participants who in fact generated them'. (Morgan 1988:37) In other words, instead of assuming to know why the subjects of an experiment do as they did, it is better to explore their responses with them and one way to do so is through focus groups.

However, much as Morgan supports the use of focus groups for the benefit of experimental research, and much as he appreciates the instructions provided by Merton on how they should be used, he envisages a much larger role for them than described above. He notes that focus groups had 'their origins in sociology, although nearly all current applications are in marketing research…. From a social science point of view, focus groups are useful as a self-contained means of collecting data or as a supplement to both quantitative and other qualitative methods'. (1988:10) Despite this recognition, and in opposition to Merton's position, that focus groups can be used as a self-contained means of collecting data, he nevertheless places their lack of development within the social science at the door of the original users and at the door of mass communication as a field of research:

> In searching for reasons why focus groups have received a more positive reception in marketing, one factor that stands out is that most of the original work was done in the field of communications research and relied heavily on the use of films and story boards as 'stimulus material'. Merton and his co-workers argued that this was necessary because it was the discussion of these materials that in fact 'focused' the discussion. In reading their manual, (Merton *et al* 1956) it is often difficult for a social scientist to make the leap to projects that do not revolve around such stimulus materials. This is not the case for marketing researchers, who use a variety of prepared materials in their assessment of how consumers respond to different 'concepts' in marketing strategy. (Morgan 1988:12)

In the absence of film as a stimulus market researchers created their own stimuli by which to focus the group on the topic or object under investigation, and under the influence of motivation research imported psychodynamic techniques aimed at unearthing 'preconscious' (unaware) or unconscious (repressed) states. Early moderators within market research using techniques to facilitate the examination of the unobservable – language here taken as observable – tended to come from clinical psychology: 'like group therapy, group interviewing was supposed to provide the clinically trained observer with new keys to underlying, but fundamentally observed, motivations'. (Morgan 1988:13)

My own feeling on this, having observed some of the techniques, is that the payment of money for performance can result in ridiculous display. Some of the techniques used appear to have no relationship to anything, preconscious, unconscious, or any other state except the need to do something. To present a 'feely-board' consisting of surfaces varying in their degrees of softness – fur, wool, carpet, sandpaper etc – and have respondents relate the feelings of the material on the 'feely board' to the product, is one way to fill in time, but it is questionable if it is time well spent.

Morgan is right in his assertion that market researchers had little difficulty in adopting focus group research to their own needs, and in finding stimuli removed from the original domain of communication research. They also, but not always, dropped a substantial element of the rigour insisted on by Merton; most especially in their adoption of the focus group as a self-contained method of collecting data. Whether the fact that the rest of the social sciences could not see where the stimulus material was to come from to allow them to incorporate focus groups into their research tool kit in the manner of Merton working in communication research, is difficult to say, but it is true that the use of them, in a similar fashion to much of their use in market research, as a self-contained method of gathering data has probably now given a spur to their current popularity.

The adoption of focus groups as a stand-alone method transforms them into a tool that can be used for practically any kind of research; indeed, my concern is that they will become the first and final call of research for many academics wishing to 'get some research underway', especially in Britain under the increased pressures to be seen as actively engaged in research. Talking to people is hardly novel, but to then surround this basic form of communication with the aura of a named research method is to have pulled off a rather clever intellectual trick, namely, the assumption of expertise.

Focus Groups and Survey Research

I have argued at some length that focus group research used as a stand-alone technique breaks the rules of its own logic, that focus group research, on the whole, demands that the findings be quantified. Indeed, I argued that the investigative technique itself is premised, whether the researcher admits it or even recognises it, by a low-grade quantification approach to knowledge. The method is practically always faced with the question, how may people think that, or how many people would share such interpretations of happenings? This, of course, only applies to the use of focus groups, most usually in the social sciences, when they are utilised as a totally enclosed method of investigation, and not as an aid to some other aspect of research. I am not suggesting that all qualitative work should be quantified; often it would be pointless or impossible. All I am saying is that focus group research, as an aspect of qualitative work, has a special relationship to quantification.

My literature search on focus groups used in academic research suggested that the field of health research is the heaviest user of them. Victoria Ward, Janet Betrand and Lisanne Brown, all working in the area of medical or health research, writing in 1991, state:

> In recent years, focus groups have gained increasing acceptance as a research methodology in the field of health and family planning. Whereas a decade ago, focus groups were often passed over because the information obtained in this manner was considered 'too soft', many applied researchers now consider them a highly appropriate means to obtain an in-depth look at motivations of human behaviour. (Ward *et al* 1991:226)

These writers illustrate the way in which focus groups have been used in health research; focus groups 'were originally used in health and population primarily as a complement to survey research, not as a stand-alone methodology.'

164

Although increasingly used in such a manner 'the conventional sample survey of the target population continues to be the most commonly used method for assessing attitudes and behaviours', for the reason that surveys 'have the important advantage that they yield quantitative results that (if the sampling is probabilistic) can be generalised to a larger population'. (Ward *et al* 1991: 267) The title of their paper is 'The Comparability of Focus Group and Survey Results', and this ready acceptance of the benefits of the generalisabilty of results generated by survey research prompts the question to Ward and her colleagues of whether or not the results gained from stand-alone focus groups can in terms of prediction to a larger population compare favourably with survey research. In attempting to answer this question they note that there 'are relatively few examples of empirical research comparing qualitative and quantitative techniques, and they have not provided conclusive results'. (Ward *et al* 1991:268) However, reporting on three case studies of their own, they conclude that, although they do not wish to advocate a 'universal replacement of surveys with focus groups', the results from their analysis 'do indicate that focus groups yielded results similar to those obtained from surveys in the three studies reported herein.' (Ward *et al* 1991:269) The areas covered by the three case studies were that of attitudes towards vasectomy, and acceptors to tubal ligation, and the countries in which the studies took place were Zaire, Guatemala and Honduras. They conclude their paper on the comparability of the results of the survey research and the results of focus group research into the above topics by saying:

> The research indicates that on those variables that can be examined through focus group methods the results from the focus groups are highly consistent with those from surveys. This suggests that in situations where time, funds, and personnel capable of computerised data analysis are in limited supply, focus groups represent a viable alternative for obtaining information on attitudes, beliefs and behaviours of a given population.... This method is *not* appropriate where the findings need to be generalisable with precision to the large population, but in many situations it may be appropriate in guiding program efforts. (Ward *et al* 1991:282)

The data obtained from the focus groups according to Ward and her colleagues 'would have led program planners to the same conclusions regarding program design as would the results from the survey'. However, to find a case where something works is not to say that it will work in all cases. Without a survey one could not know if the findings were capable of being generalised to the target population as a whole. Findings, furthermore, were not consistent on all the variables; discrepancies did occur. However, Ward and her colleagues working in countries where research resources may be limited are perfectly correct to consider the absolute value of focus group research in such situations and to use the results as if they had the certainty of generalisability.

The point to underscore, in light of my comments on rules, is the fact that researchers should wish to have evidence that the results from focus group research are comparable to the results gained from survey research using bigger populations. That is, implicit in most focus group research is generalisability. This implicitness is not there in all qualitative research, for example ethnography, where generalisation to populations as a whole is not sought, or more importantly, desired – ethnographers are much more likely to wish to seek out what is common to cases of a particular type.

Focus group research, used as a stand-alone method, is not ethnography and therefore the defence of it on the grounds that ethnographers would wish to mount in defence of their absence of quantification and the ability to generalise to populations as a whole is forfeited. Adeline Nyamathi and Pam Schuler argue that the focus group interview 'is a qualitative research method for gathering information which, when performed in a permissive non-threatening group environment, allows the investigation of a multitude of perceptions on a defined area of interest'. They comment:

> As a qualitative method which bears similarities to enthnography, grounded theory, phenomenology and participant observation, the major goal of data gathering is the generation of detailed narrative data as opposed to numerical data. As such, it is a systematic study of the world of everyday experience. (Nyamathi and Schuler 1990:1282)

Whilst true that the collection of data in focus group research is narrative and not numerical, it is not the case, as Nyamathi and Schuler state, that focus group research is the 'systematic study of the world of everyday experience'. The topic under enquiry might be very distant indeed from that of everyday experience, but nevertheless one wishes to know what people think and feel about it. Such a case would be a project designed to understand attitudes to, say, genetic engineering, or a conflict in some distant part of the world, or a European trade agreement. The subject of the focus group might be so far removed from their everyday world of experience that the participants to the group have never even thought about the topic before attending the session. Furthermore, focus groups might be conducted among very specific and specialist groups in the population, for example, investment bankers or neuro-surgeons, to determine attitudes to proposed legislation affecting their area of professional operations, which is not quite the mundane 'world of everyday experience' that the phrase normally suggests in its ethnographic usage. The danger is, and this is the mistake that Nyamathi and Schuler make, that because focus group research uses the interview technique in informal settings that it has a naturalism to it associated with more genuinely ethnographic approaches to social life. As already pointed out, this is wrong. The technique is not natural, but a deliberately constructed exchange between the moderator and the members of the focus group, and a constructed exchange between the members of the focus group themselves orchestrated by the moderator and often stimulated and focused by the deliberate introduction of stimuli. There is no element of participant observation; although with the relaxed exchange of information a feeling is often generated that provokes a sense that one is observing the participants lives. In fact it is only their lives as recounted by them, not as actually lived.

False Understanding

The very real danger of focus group research is that by associating it with other deeper interrogatory methods for understanding social life the researcher believes that he or she has more 'material' than they actually have. It is false understanding, because focus groups provide a limited understanding of the factors involved in the responses which if not carefully monitored are then used as an authoritative narrative of the object and subjects under investigation. In the same way that a warning was given that focus groups cannot be used to provide generalisablity, a warning must also be given that focus groups provide 'limited reference', to use my previous terminology. Just as they provided limited reference to a population as a whole, since they cannot with certainty provide data on the general distribution of the responses found in the sample, they also provide only limited reference to the life world of the individual – what you see is what you are told!

Linda Lederman in talking about the popularity of focus groups in market research says that the technique owns much of its prescience as a 'reaction to the limitations found in the use of large-sample polling techniques':

> Although the polling techniques were providing market researchers with numbers, the surveys generated little insight into what was really going on in the market place, the 'why' behind the numbers. To address that shortcoming, the focus group interview technique was embraced to explore people's thoughts, feelings and behaviour. Thus the emphasis in the use of group interviews on their ability to generate data about the 'why' behind the behaviour; the ability to ask the kinds of questions that surveys don't ask and that individual interviews, too, miss. (Lederman 1990:117)

Borgardus's very early use of the group interview was developed in part as a response to the cost of conducting individual interviews: in a sense, he got lots of interviews for the price of one, and even now one comes across this as a reason for their adoption. For example, Kerth O'Brien in his work with focus groups examining social relationships and Aids-preventative behaviour states that: 'Group interviews are an effective and relatively inexpensive means of interviewing several people at once'. (O'Brien 1993:361) That is not, however, how focus group researchers would see the bringing together of individuals as a group to discuss some topic or issue; as Linderman observed, the development of focus groups was not just to get at the 'why' questions missed by opinion polling, but to trawl areas of thought that can be missed in a one-to-one interview:

> In focus group interviews, the group rather than the individual is interviewed. The group potentially provides a safe atmosphere, a context in which the synergy can generate more than the sum of the individual inputs. Interactions take place among the interviewees themselves as well as between group members and the interviewer. These multiple interactions lead to the synergy inherent in small groups. The result is an incremental increase in output. The data generated by focus group interviews are often richer and deeper than data elicited in the one-on-one interview situation. (Lederman 1991:119)

It is the dynamic exchange between the individuals in the group that gives focus groups their special characteristic and strength as a research method. As David Morgan says: 'The hallmark of focus groups is the explicit use of the group interaction to produce data and insights that would be less accessible without the interaction found in the groups'. (Morgan 1988:12) So central is the interplay between participants in generating information that would otherwise remain hidden, that Jenny Kitzinger even rounds on researchers for the stultified way that they report their findings:

> Reading some such reports it is hard to believe that there was ever more than one person in the room at the same time. This criticism even applies to many studies which explicitly identify their methodology as 'focus group discussion' – in spite of the fact that the distinguishing feature of focus groups is supposed to be the use of interaction as part of the research data. (Kitzinger 1994:105)

One is sympathetic to Kitzinger's position, but it is not always necessary in reporting findings to capture what actually went on in the groups. Her point, however, about interaction between participants is vital in understanding how focus groups can claim a special methodological distinction. In her own work, true to the insistence for reporting more than one voice at a time, she shows how the dynamics of the group encourages participants to open up and explore avenues of enquiry that may have remained closed had the single interview been used:

> ... it should not be assumed that groups, by definition, are inhibiting relative to the supposed 'privacy' of an interview situation. In fact, depending on their composition groups can sometimes actively facilitate the discussion of otherwise 'taboo' topics because the less inhibited members of the group 'break the ice' for shyer participants or one person's revelation of 'discrediting' information encourages others to disclose. For example, when one group member revealed that needles were often left lying around her block of flats another women said that she experienced the same problem. She added that she would not usually volunteer such information because: 'you don't want folk to know it goes on in your bit' and it is not the sort of information you reveal to an 'outsider'. (Kitzinger 1994:111)

This is a classic case of group members taking comfort and courage from the supportive presence of others so that information is delivered that otherwise would not have been volunteered. However, Kitzinger's groups, like much of the focus research of the Glasgow University Media Group, of which she is a member, uses pre-existing friendship or occupational groups and not group situations where the members do not know each other before coming together for the research exercise.

Market research companies are strict in insisting that members of the group must not know each other. Their concern is that the findings from the groups will be 'contaminated' through the expression of similar thoughts as a consequence of friendship or that similarity of thinking formed the basis of the friendship, so that the existence of friends in a group lowers the range of thought present. However, a claim can be made in the type of work which the Glasgow University Media Group undertake that constructing the groups out of pre-existing social, residency, or occupational groups helps to provide an approximation of naturally occurring data such as that which might be collected in the course of participant observation research. The pre-existence of the group means that they bring that existing 'world' with them when attending the focus group session, or at least the communicative element of it. But Kitzinger, as well as showing how membership of a group can produce information that might have remained hidden to the researcher had she elected for a one-to-one interview approach, provides a very good illustration of how the dynamics of a group actually work to generate visibility of feelings and articulations of thinking. Kitzinger argues in the course of an aids media research project she was 'unable to persuade one women to explain what she was thinking, and it was only the timely intervention of her friends that helped to clarify what was going through her mind'. Kitzinger then produces an extract from the focus group transcript, doing exactly what she has critiqued other researchers for not doing, producing accounts that show the dynamic exchange that takes place among participants.

Kitzinger showed the group an image from a particular advertisement. One participant, Gail, 'had immediate association with the image', associations which Kitzinger, as the researcher, was 'at a loss to understand'. Two of Gail's friends, Tessa and Brenda, evidently 'caught on very quickly to what she was thinking and helped her to articulate it':

JK:	Can any of you imagine what this means? What the slogan underneath might be?
Gail:	(Gail bursts out laughing, hides head in hands, suddenly Tessa joins in) I'll say nothing! Oh, Brenda don't make me laugh.
JK:	Are you making up fantasy slogans for it in your head?
Gail:	No, no no! (Pause)
JK:	Can you imagine what it might say?

	(Laughter followed by silence)
JK:	Gail, please tell me!
Gail:	No, no, no (laughter) don't make me laugh.
JK:	Please!
Gail:	I don't know.
JK:	Would you be happier writing in down?
Gail:	No! (all laugh) It just makes me think of things...
Tessa:	What, are you thinking of? Oral sex?
Gail:	Yes, that's right!

Commenting on the above exchange Kitzinger says:

> Not only do co-participants help each other to overcome embarrassment but they can also provide mutual support in expressing feelings which are common to their group but which they might consider deviant from mainstream culture (or the assumed culture of the researcher). This may be particularly important when working with those who are oppressed or marginalised such as, in our case, drug users, and male prostitutes. (Kitzinger 1994:111)

The type of studies mentioned by Kitzinger, drug users and male prostitutes, and the use of focus groups to approach them, are areas where the technique can be used as a stand-alone method. It would be nigh on impossible to generalise to the identified populations in such 'deviant' cases. To begin with one would not know the universe, nor would it be possible to establish it. Furthermore, the chance of getting a high response rate, even if one could find the population, is highly unlikely. In the absence of such a possibility then the results from focus group research can stand in for quantification. Indeed, the result gained from the sample is very likely, given the contained world of the respondents, to contain the elements of the larger world or population from which the sample was drawn. The results from such focus group research, in other words, is likely to be representative of more than that provided by the participants, and allows the calculation of the distribution of attributes and behaviours in wider populations if the researcher wished to do so. The career and behaviour of the drug user, or the male prostitute, could be examined through such a method, although better in the case of the male prostitute than the drug user since this latter group are likely to form a less enclosed world than the former, and thus more careful attention would have to be paid to the sample. However, even then one presumes that the research is examining a certain type of drug user, that is, a drug taker located in a specific set of circumstances. A 'self-enclosed world', by which generalisation is made possible from focus groups, refers to behaviours structured by the 'deviancy itself': that it would be unlikely that anyone engaging in that behaviour fell outside the repertoire of behaviour associated with the deviancy.

To go back to the earlier point concerning survey research and sample size being determined in part by the size of the standard deviation, then in the case of deviant groups the size of the standard deviation would be so small that a very small sample would probably suffice in collecting data. If one wished to get inside the world of the deviant, to understand it from the inside, survey research on its own would be a totally inappropriate method; for such truly ethnographic work, participant observation would probably be the most appropriate method. But the focus group in such a situation, if quite a number were conducted, would furnish some of the advantages of survey research in terms of generalisability.

A Natural Language?

Although focus groups are by no means natural, and are a structured response to a research need, they nevertheless contain features of 'naturalness' not found in survey research, in particular the 'naturalistic' expression of language. The language of research, the methodology used, structures the conversation between the respondent and the researcher, and one of the great advantages of the focus group as a research setting is that the respondent or participant controls the manner in which they wish to express themselves. With middle-class participants this tends to be the studied expression of the 'official meeting', whereas with working-class members, not so used to the 'official meeting', the expressive form tends to more closely approximate the informality of the 'leisure meeting'. How expression is given depends to a certain degree on the skill of the moderator in encouraging a relaxed atmosphere within the group. It is not always the case that the focus group benefits by having the meeting run on a very informal relaxed line. But generally it does, hence the provision of alcohol.[8]

Commenting on the advantage of focus groups over survey research, Stewart and Shamdasani, after noting that while focus groups 'can produce quantitative data', comment that 'focus groups almost always are conducted with the collection of qualitative data as their primary purpose':

> This is their advantage, because focus groups produce a very rich body of data expressed in the respondents' own words and context. There is a minimum of artificiality or response, unlike survey questionnaires that ask for responses expressed on five-point rating scales or other constrained response categories. Participants can qualify their responses or identify important contingencies associated with their answers. Thus responses have a certain ecological validity not found in traditional survey research. (Stewart and Shamdasani 1990:12)

---

8 The tradition within market research in Britain is to provide alcohol for participants to focus groups, but this is not universal, for example, it is rarely if ever provided by market research companies in the United States. As rule, the focus groups conducted by the ICS at Leeds follow the practice of market research companies and do provide participants with alcoholic refreshment.

They also comment, however, that such 'freedom' of expression makes the data provided by focus groups idiosyncratic', and that this makes 'the results of focus groups more difficult and challenging to summarise'. One of the very real strengths of focus group research is that people are talking for themselves much more than is the case with survey research, where to a greater extent they are talking through the researcher. Furthermore, because the situation is 'focused' then unlike participant observation there is not the difficulty of the researcher always having to catch the sense of what is being said through the context of the utterances, indeed, one knows the context of the statements in a way not so possible in the more fluid situation of participant observation. In the 'hidden world' of participant observation the researcher may not always grasp at any particular point the meaning of what is being said, since one of the objects of the method is to understand the 'hidden world' on the basis of the unfolding of meanings, hence the necessity of the researcher to 'live' with the subject(s) of the investigation.

The focus group method is not participant observation, but the 'natural' use of language in the focus groups make them a powerful tool for the examination of issues, and in particular the development of survey instruments. Although in certain circumstances focus groups can effectively be used as a stand-alone technique, it is quite clear from what has been said previously that to do so gives them, in the main, a 'restricted reference'. The benefit of focus groups for the survey researcher is that not only is one in possession of data to assist triangulation, but that they provide the opportunity to understand how people address the world, and by extension, how they understand it. Thus not only do focus groups allow the incorporation of 'natural language' into the survey instrument which, once 'officialised' in the survey questionnaire, will make sense to respondents, but they allow insights into the social world in which the questionnaire is to be delivered. For example, Kerth O'Brien in his study on social relationships and AIDS preventative behaviour specifically used focus groups to develop health surveys.

The language of the clinician is not the language of ordinary people and to have questions that used correct clinical terms but which meant little to the respondent, or more likely, meant different things to the respondent, would have spelt disaster in using the results to plan a health campaign. The focus groups conducted by O'Brien were part of a long-term program of research that explored the features of social relationships among gay and bisexual men at risk from AIDS. O'Brien says:

> Focus groups inherently allow an investigator to learn the phraseology that participants used to describe their own experiences. With this information, the investigator can design a questionnaire using words and phrases to enhance respondents' understanding and, hence, to enhance data quality.

O'Brien then goes on to show this process in practice:

> For example, when we began conducting our groups, we referred to the human immuno-deficiency virus as 'HIV' – the name used by most health researchers working in this area. The focus group participants were more likely to refer to HIV as 'the AIDS virus' and to the epidemic as the 'AIDS epidemic'. Had the questionnaire used the HIV wording some respondents might have been confused. By using the population's own wording, the questionnaire presumably obtained more useful information. (O'Brien 1993:366)

The value of anchoring knowledge about social and psychological processes in the norms, values and experiences of those studied gives a particular power to focus group research, especially when the experiences of the groups studied may be at a distance from those of the researcher. Diane Hughes and Kimberly Dumont, for example, in their study of dual-earner African-American families used focus groups in the planning stage of their research. Not only, and as to be expected, did focus groups provide valuable material in their own right, but they were crucial in assisting the researchers to design a questionnaire that meant something to the target population – dual earner African-American families. However, to say that the focus groups provided valuable material in their own right, is not to say that such material could stand alone as evidence about such families, just that focus group research is a good way of exploring an area where prior knowledge is limited and as a base for further exploration guided by the initial understanding. Indeed, for any entry into a new field of research, focus groups are indispensable. Hughes and Dumont:

> Focus groups are in-depth group interviews employing relatively homogeneous groups to provide information around topics specified by researchers. They have real strengths that make them particularly useful for facilitating research that reflects the social realities of a cultural group. Focus groups provide researchers with direct access to the language and concepts participants use to structure their experiences and to think and talk about a designated topic. Within-group homogeneity prompts focus group participants to elaborate stories and themes that help researchers understand how participants structure and organise their social world. In their reliance on social interaction, focus groups can also help researchers identify cultural knowledge that is shared among group members as well as to appreciate the range of different experiences individuals within a group may have. Each of these brings researchers closer to a phenomenological understanding of a cultural group. Such understanding can help investigators ask better research questions and develop the measures needed to study them. (Hughes and Dumont 1993:776)

What Hughes and Dumont wanted, among other things, was to develop items 'to assess race relations at work and racial socialisation' in a situation where such items were not available in the research literature by which to measure such constructs. Thus the focus groups helped generate the items, but also greatly assisted item wording. As they say, 'by listening to the words participants use and the way they speak, researchers may be better able to bridge the gap between their own language and that used by the population of interest'. What they discovered was that 'participants used much simpler language than that contained in the original item pools.' They then give examples: 'For instance, they [participants] referred to African-Americans as blacks rather than as African-Americans'. In their revision of the questionnaire all items were changed to reflect the actual usage of language rather than the 'politically correct' use of language common to American academia. After all language reflects worlds, indeed, language is how we come to know the world and create it, thus, unless one had some political axiom to grind – the imposition of one view of the world on another view of the world – then as researchers the substitution of terms was essential if the subjects of the enquiry were to be allowed a voice that accurately reflected how they determined racial operations. Hughes and Dumont show how the focus groups in their study not only allowed them to adapt existing items to produce more culturally sensitive research, but helped the structure of the questions themselves:

> Participants also used simple words and spoke in short sentences. We revised many questionnaire items to reduce the number of words and syllables it contained in them. As an example, the item 'Have you ever done something to prepare your child for the possibility that s/he might experience racism or discrimination in his/her childhood' was changed to read 'Have you ever told your child that some people might treat him/her badly because she/he is black'. (Hughes and Dumont 1993: 800]

They conclude by saying: 'Thus, the focus group highlighted differences in the language commonly used by the focus group participants and that typically used by academic scholars'.

Administrative Rationality

Whilst agreeing with Hughes and Dumont that focus groups can help the wording of questions at a general level by providing access to how the participants talk about issues and the terms and words used to describe areas of interest, focus groups are an uneconomic means of pre-testing questionnaires – although it does not appear that that is what Hughes and Dumont actually did. They seem to have been made aware that the participants used more simple words than the researchers themselves did, and spoke in shorter sentences than they did. Based on this information they then adjusted the items in their questionnaire. In general, however, the focus group is likely to be too unwieldy for the precision needed for questionnaire construction and alteration. That is better done by pre-testing the questionnaire with a variety of respondents on a one-to-one basis. A good hybrid method of pre-testing questionnaires is that of dynamic piloting. This has elements of the focus group combined with one to one testing. It is, however, exhausting and expensive.

Several copies of the finalised questionnaire along with the questionnaire stored on computer are taken to a central location. Field interviewers then recruit respondents from outside the hall and these are invited in to complete the questionnaire. This is usually done in batches of about seven respondents with instructions given by the research executives to the field interviewers stating what characteristics they want from each batch of respondents – old, working class, female, unemployed and on. Sat at a table each respondent completes the questionnaire supervised by the field worker, but in the presence of a researcher. Any stumbling over questions, hesitations or puzzlement by the respondent prompts the researcher to investigate the difficulty that the respondent is facing in answering the question. The respondents' view on how the question ought to be worded will also be sought. At the end of each session the researchers, plus the field workers, guided by the senior researcher acting as moderator, form a 'focus group' to examine the results of the exercise. When agreement is reached about the nature of the difficulty and what words ought to be used, questions dropped and so on, alterations are made to the computer-stored questionnaire and new questionnaires run off for the next set of respondents to be invited into the hall. The whole process is repeated and new questionnaires run off for the next session. The questionnaire is dismantled and rebuilt in close contact with people who will form the subject of the eventual enquiry. It may be, for example, that a very old person is not familiar with a term, or is embarrassed by some term and a more suitable one is sought, but the substituted term must also be tested to see if it works with other age groups. During the course of a whole day about five different sets of respondents can be taken through the dynamic pilot. The final questionnaire is then taken back to the office, worked on and produced anew (the alterations made with speed in the course of the dynamic pilot tend to produce a rather ragged questionnaire). The new questionnaire is then taken back to the hall to be tested the following day, and the same procedure is gone through again until it is considered that no more changes are required. The final questionnaire produced by the dynamic pilot is, however, still required to be piloted in the normal way, that is, by taking it into the field and tested at various sample points.

The dynamic pilot, a method that is rarely used due to the sheer intensity and expense of the process, is a good example of a specialist use of focus groups to assist the design stage of questionnaire development – the focus group consisting of the field workers and the researchers focusing on a specific problem, namely, the construction of a questionnaire through examining the responses to a text. The use of a dynamic pilot is best retained only for the most complex and difficult questionnaires. Most questionnaire design does not demand that type of attention, but it is important to realise that to test questionnaires by a traditional focus group method is not the best use to which focus groups can be put. Their advantage is at a prior stage of development, namely, in gaining familiarity with the area to be investigated; helping to assist concept formation; to develop a hypothesis; and in the creation of the language to be used in the questionnaire.

Although focus groups are good for sensitising the survey researcher to the language that participants use before constructing the actual questionnaire, Hugentobler suggests that they can, and indeed should, be used as a substitute for survey research in certain circumstances. She points to the high rate of illiteracy in many developing countries, and for this reason focus group 'interviews are quite extensively used by health educators involved in program development, planning and evaluation in developing counties'. Hugentobler also considers that the 'alarming figures about the high percentage of at least functional illiteracy in this country [America] raise questions about the validity of commonly used survey data gathered from such population groups' and adds, 'the focus group technique can fill a gap here in increasing our understanding of the behaviours and perceptions of persons who have difficulty understanding and filling out lengthy questionnaires but may be most in need of health educational programs'. (Hugentobler 1991:254)

On the surface this seems to offer a good argument for the benefit of focus groups in many parts of the world, and not just developing countries. But this only holds good for postal surveys where the respondent must read and complete the questionnaire unaided by a field worker, not for questionnaires using face to face interviews where the questions are read out to the respondent and the questionnaire filled in by the interviewer. Of course it does mean that in such a situation where literacy is restricted, the use of show cards and other interviewing aids is also restricted. In advanced industrial countries face to face interviewing is one of the most common methods for social research, although telephone interviewing often using computerised routing of responses to questions and the direct feeding of data into the computer is also common. In fact, telephone interviewing in America is the most common method of interviewing. The sheer expense of shipping interviewers to places where a field force may not exist in a country as large as America makes face to face interviewing impractical, plus the fact that many run-down areas of America's inner cities risk the lives of interviewers sent into such areas, especially at night. This problem is not unknown in Britain, with some field workers simply refusing to go to certain areas, or if they do the expense involved is high since they may have to be accompanied by a 'minder'.

Even in a country as small as Britain geographical factors play a part in who is interviewed and by what method. Very few companies wish to sample above the Caledonian Canal in Scotland. Indeed, if sample points are drawn randomly it is not unusual to first take out the Hebrides from the sample frame. To ship interviewers to the Islands is expensive, indeed, anywhere becomes expensive if the field work company does not have interviewers based in or near the area. People living in the Isle of Wight, for that reason, are hardly ever consulted by survey researchers. Yet the use of telephone interviewing skews the sample since the effectiveness of the sample depends on the degree of telephone penetration, which in certain of the poorest quarters and tenement buildings of inner cities is not high.

It is not so much illiteracy, one suspects, that makes the focus group a favoured method of collecting data in developing countries, but the cost and difficulty of drawing a sample to give reliability to the numerical data collected. To sample effectively one must have existing data on the population; only advanced industrial countries possess such data. One needs to know the location of households. For example, the absence of addresses and the floating population of the townships of South Africa make collecting of basic data on such populations by survey research a methodological nightmare. Thus the reason why focus groups are so heavily used in developing countries is not one of illiteracy, since as stated, face to face interviewing requires no literacy on behalf on the respondent, but one of access, sampling and expense especially in situations where money is likely to be scarce, or where what money does exist is likely to be considered better spent on the non-research parts of an aid program.

Survey research methodology grows out of administrative thinking and the rationality associated with advanced industrial societies and the bureaucratic management of resources. The type of responses demanded by questionnaires may make little sense to cultural groups not affected by industrialisation. Oral cultures, where a high emphasis is placed on 'story telling' and the non-literal expression of meaning, would find it perplexing to answer in pre-fixed categories of response. To complete a questionnaire is to be part of the logic of the world from which that questionnaire comes, indeed, one has to be locked into the grammar of the rationality so that thoughts can be organised in a way demanded by the questionnaire. In other words, the respondent must be able to summarise experience in an arithmetic or quantifiable manner. The use of scaling in survey research only makes sense if one can think in terms of scales, that is, to separate out thoughts and allocate strength to the parts that have been separated. In survey research one is being asked to compartmentalise experiences for the sake of quantification, but with the recognition that such compartmentalisation is not an unfamiliar process for the respondent. The ability to be able to do this occurs because the administrative form of thinking which permeates survey research rests on structures of thought that are an integral part of the structure of modern advanced industrial society.

Of course survey research, for these very reasons, has its limitations even in advanced industrial societies. Not all thought can be captured by the language of survey research, but sufficient can be captured for a story to be told that has a sense recognised by both the teller and the listener. It is the limitation of the story, or the type of story, that survey research tells that prohibits the method from claims to be 'the' method for the social sciences. The 'story' must be added to by other stories created out of other methods that reach into non-quantifiable meanings. But it would seem doubtful that in certain cultures the questionnaire survey, and the demand that it makes for a certain type of thinking, could proceed to create a narrative that reflected the narrative of the lives it refers to. And this is not a matter of the technical completion of the questionnaire, but a question of the rationality of the methodology where the connecting sides in the story construction fail to touch each other.

Thus in those cultures where the type of rationality required for successful questionnaire completion is absent or in question, focus group research is likely to be highly preferable to survey research as a method of gathering data. One of the areas where focus group research does come into its own, especially when used with survey research, is that of cross-cultural analysis, when the cultures examined possess the type of rationality within which the type of questioning posed by survey research readily fits. Lynne Millward, after commenting that 'the survey method is not designed to investigate phenomena in any great depth', notes 'yet its design must be built on some assumptions about the meaning of certain things for a particular population of people'. In the focus group such assumptions can be tested as well as providing a forum in which issues are raised that might 'never have been considered in relation to the topic at hand'. Focus groups can also 'establish the variety of opinions concerning a topic, establish relevant dimensions of attitudes and identify relevant indicators for the constructs being measured' which when carried over to cross-cultural comparative survey research, have the added advantage that 'they can clarify the relevance of certain concepts and redefine them using common vernacular. They can be used to test various questionnaire items for readability, comprehension, wording, order effects and response variation'. (Millward 1994:278)

Six

Problems and Procedures in the Conduct of Focus Groups

ocus group research is, as Mary Brotherson and Beth Goldstein say, 'essentially an act of interpretation, one that attempts to convey the meanings people construct from shared or individual experiences'. (Brotherson and Goldstein 1992:335) This is something that all focus group researchers would more or less agree with. The freedom of participants to construct their own meanings is one of the strengths and advantages of this form of research over survey research. However, Janet Bertrand, Judith Brown and Victoria Ward consider that they have the added advantage over survey research in that 'they allow the members of the target population to express their ideas in a spontaneous manner that is not structured according to the researcher's prejudices... participants are free to volunteer information on points that are important to them, but that the researcher may not have anticipated'. (Bertrand *et al* 1992:198, 199) This last point is certainly the case, but to suggest, as they do, that survey research proceeds on the 'prejudices' of the researchers is a baffling comment, especially when focus group research may have been undertaken to ground the items used through collecting the thoughts and meanings generated by people. If by prejudice they mean that survey research is not free from theory, then it would be an odd way to view theory and an even odder use of the term prejudice; but the real concern is the implied view that focus groups are somehow 'natural events'.

What should not be overlooked is that the moderator is a further disrupter to what might be considered 'naturally' occurring conversation. As Morgan says: 'because the discussion in focus groups are controlled by the researcher, we can never be sure of how natural the interactions are'. (Morgan 1988:16) Furthermore, the topic under discussion may not be one that participants to the groups might entertain as part of their everyday world of conversation. Morgan: 'The frequent goal of focus groups is to conduct a group discussion that resembles a lively conversation among friends or neighbours, and most of the problems come from topics that fail to meet that goal'. (Morgan 1988:22)

Fortunately in mass media research the usual subject of enquiry, the media, form a central part of people's daily diet of conversation; thus, there seems nothing 'unnatural' about having people talk to researchers about such matters. Focus group research around media issues does indeed take on the appearance of a lively conversation between friends or neighbours, and it is unusual for a respondent in a group to have nothing to add to the exchange of information. Many discussants are extremely knowledgeable about the media in a localised sense and will frequently correct the researcher on small matters of detail relating to some program. Nevertheless, the fact that the media form part of people's everyday conversation, and thus provide focus groups with an air of naturalness, does not prevent them being highly structured events, not least because of the presence and role that the moderator plays in directing the conversation to issues the researcher is interested in. As Jill Swenson, William Griswold and Pamela Kleiber state: 'There is a growing consciousness among scholars that the very act of conducting qualitative research alters the naturalistic conditions of the social phenomenon. The presence and probing of a moderator in focus groups produce dynamic group processes that might not otherwise occur'. (Swenson *et al* 1992:459)

In Swenson's own study using focus groups consisting of community leaders and news professionals to examine the role of journalism in rural development he found that not only did the intervention of the moderator influence the dynamic of what was discussed but repeat focus groups a few months later showed that some participants had become not just more conscious of the need for rural development but had become more involved in promoting it. Indeed in the Institute of Communication Studies panel study on the 1992 General Election (Morrison 1992), when participants were asked where they got most of their information from about the election, they named the focus group itself. The information they had gained was not simply acquired through the act of showing television coverage of the election, but through the probing of issues by the moderator and by the generation of political discussion among the participants. Indeed, members in some groups of youths confessed that they had never discussed the election or politics with their friends because to do so was 'uncool'. Yet in the privileged setting of the focus group they were quite happy to give thought to political issues and exchange views with each other. There was no doubt that the questioning by the moderator (independent of the dynamic which is supposed to be one of the key benefits of focus group research in generating information) produced conversations that would not naturally have taken place. There is no reason to consider this as 'wrong', we cannot consider focus group discussions as consisting of naturally occurring meetings which just happened to be organised by the researcher or sites of natural conversation. The presence of the moderator reduces even further the naturalness of the exchanges that occur.

Terry Bristol and Edward Fern, using group process theories, offer an insight into the dynamics of exchange within a group, and cast doubt on their usefulness as a predictor of individual behaviour. Although both Bristol and Fern are academics the paper was written for the journal *Advances in Consumer Research*, and deals specifically with consumer behaviour, where a test of the effectiveness of focus group research, or at least in some research, is the ability to understand consumer spend. Bristol and Fern's concern is that what is often witnessed are group attitudes and not the individual expression of an attitude:

> One authority on focus groups cited a case where a respondent declared that he would not buy a prestige car because it was ostentatious. After one hour and thirty minutes of focus group discussion, the same respondent declared that he was fickle and that he would buy a prestige car and show it off to his friends. Presumably, this revelation provides insight into the respondent's 'true' attitude about prestige cars. However, it also indicates that people change their minds during group discussion. At best, professional judgement by the moderator is necessary to make these types of determinations. (Bristol and Fern 1993:444)

The above example is taken from research on automobile purchasing intention, and may to academic communication researchers, because of the subject matter, not appear relevant to the type of focus groups that they conduct. However, if we refer back to the discussion of Paul Lazarsfeld's research activities, for example his studies on voting behaviour – *The People's Choice* (Lazarsfeld *et al* 1944) – and his studies of consumer choice, and the lesson that any research no matter the subject can throw up general methodological issues and aid the formation of concepts applicable to behaviour in general, the results from such realms of study ought not to be ignored. If we relate Bristol and Fern's comments on automobile research to the voting study by the Institute of Communication Studies, then one is faced with the possibility that the responses given concerning how the individuals said they would vote were shaped by the group but did not necessarily, once away from the group, reflect their actual intention, or more precisely, offer a reliable indication of how they would vote come the point of decision-making.

Bristol and Fern's concern with the data collected in focus groups stems from the simple problem of ignorance, that there is no empirical work to show the effects that the group has on the individual. Yet evidence is not missing entirely:

> Although the effects of using qualitative techniques on the quality of attitudinal output has not been empirically examined, some work has proceeded in social psychology that applies to this problem. Many studies have found that initial tendencies of individual group members intensify or sometimes change with group discussions. (Kaplan 1987, Whitney and Smith 1983) Several theories have been suggested to explain this phenomenon, several of which apply to the use of qualitative techniques to measure consumer attitudes.

Bristol and Fern then go on to list and examine the various theories. They begin with social facilitation and social impact theory:

181

Social facilitation is perhaps the simplest theory from which predictions can be posited about measuring attitudes across social and non-social settings. This theory suggests that mere presence of others is a sufficient explanation of behaviour in groups. (Allport 1924) The presence of observers or co-actors has been found to result in greater individual performance. (Markus 1978; Zajonc 1980) However, we are interested in the effects of others on individual attitudes. Ideas from self-awareness theory (Duval and Wickland 1972) apply here. The presence of others leads individuals to focus attention on themselves and increase self-awareness and thought about one's own attitudes and feelings. (Carver 1979) Increased self-awareness has been found to lead to polarised attitudes and evaluations. (Ickes, Wickland and Ferris 1973; Scheier and Carver 1977)

Attitude polarisation does not mean that attitudes are created which never previously existed, but that the existing attitudes become more extreme – it is 'a shift or change in degree but not in direction':

We expect individuals attitudes to become more polarised when others are present during the thought-eliciting procedure. Therefore, we expect that the interviewer-directed thought-eliciting methods (ie focus groups, nominal groups and individual interviews) will produce more polarised attitudes than using open-ended, self-administered questionnaires. (Bristol and Fern 1993:445)

Social impact theory, however, goes further than facilitation theory in that it posits that it is not just the presence of others that influences thought, but that the 'impact of others on individuals' beliefs, cognitions, values, and emotions is some power function of the number of people present'. Lalane and Nida (1980) would also predict that the status of group members would impact on attitude polarisation – higher status individuals would cause greater attitude shift than lower status individuals. (Bristol and Fern 1993:445)

Most usually focus groups are recruited on the basis of the status similarity of the participants, thus polarisation through status is not likely to be a strong factor in attitude formation, but that does not rule out normative influence through social comparison. Bristol and Fern:

Social comparison theory was originally formulated by Festinger (1954) to explain the effects of social communication on opinion change in groups. One derivation of this theory has been used to go beyond mere presence theories to explain polarisation of group members attitudes that result from group discussion. Simply, group members' desires to be favourably evaluated leads them to adopt an attitude that is more extreme than the group norm, to the extent that they are aware of this normative position. (Goethals and Zanna 1979)

This is not to say that such a factor will be at work in any particular group since even within the theory's own terms three necessary conditions must be satisfied before such an effect is to occur: participants must desire to be favourably evaluated, the setting must be such that it provides a standard of comparison, and finally, the situation or setting must make it possible for the evaluation of others to take place.

The final theory brought into play by Bristol and Fern to suggest attitude change due to the act of participation in a group scenario is that of informational influence through persuasive argument:

> An alternative explanation of attitude polarisation or change in groups is information influence or persuasive-arguments theory. (Kaplan 1987; Vinokur and Burnstein 1974) This theory posits that the exchange of information in groups lead members to consider facts that they had not previously considered when initially forming their attitudes. (Allison and Messick 1987 This new information could not only lead to attitude polarisation, but to attitude change or depolarisation. (Vinokur and Burnstein 1978) Weakly held attitudes may be more easily changed because the individual is more influenced given contradictory information provided by others. (Bristol and Fern 1993:446)

Bristol and Fern argue that 'evidence for both polarisation and depolarisation given group discussions has been reported'. (Vinokur and Burnstein 1978; Whitney and Smith 1983) However, the important fact to register in terms of the above discussion on 'naturalness' is not so much the validity of the theories of the effect of group formation on individual thought, or the strength of the evidence to support such theories, but that focus groups, and the presence and role taken by the moderator, are likely in some way to 'distort' and 'interfere' with naturally occurring conversations.

One can see why polarisation of thought is of particular concern to the clients of market researchers since if what is being measured is an effect of group membership then it is not a good predictor of attitudes and behaviour in the natural setting of everyday life outside the parameters of the focus group. Such considerations reduce confidence in market findings drawn from focus group research.

Although social scientists have different concerns from clients of market research companies involved in product research, methodologically the concern is the same, namely, that the method itself, although appearing natural, affects the material that is gathered. Since all methods, to some extent, effect the data gathered, this might not appear to be much of a problem, but it is if the method claims naturalness, or more precisely, limited interference.

The fact that 'influences' are at work in focus group research, not least the influence of the moderator since it is he or she who directs proceedings, should not detract from their value as a qualitative method. All that is being said is that they are not as 'free' as some researchers would imagine, and that the very group dynamics that are its main strength over single interviews also entail influences that ought to be taken into account in deciding the nature of the material collected. It can be argued that the influences leading to polarisation of views are 'washed out' in the power of information generation and insight gained by the discourse that takes place. Yet there is one factor that will not 'wash out' in the general mix of benefits offered by focus group research but which remains as a stubborn stain to fundamentally undermine the data collected, and that is, where the participants 'feed' the moderator the information which they think the moderator would like to hear.

Moderated Demand

The phenomenon of experimenter demand is well known to experimental psychologists, although care is not always taken to guard against it. Basically, experimenter demand refers to the situation where the respondent or subject guesses what is going on, realising what is expected of him or her and 'helping' the experiment along by performing in ways that they think the experimenter would like. This can work at more than one level. For example, in a case reported by Grant Noble, although it is so 'pure' it almost seems apocryphal, a four-year-old girl was brought to the laboratory by her mother to take part in a Bandura-style experiment into imitative aggression. Although such studies differ in execution the basic format is the splitting of subjects into groups for the purpose of control. Some see an aggressive film of someone hitting a Bobo doll, while others see a non-aggressive film. All subjects are then taken to a room which features, among other toys, a Bobo doll. The little girl in question, walking into the laboratory prior to the experiment, was heard to say, 'look mummy there's the doll we have to hit'. (Noble 1975:134) In such a situation, where the subject has spotted what is supposed to happen, the data collected from the experiment is valueless. Experimenter demand can, however, work in more subtle ways, as David Gauntlett, reviewing all the main effects studies, reports:

> Subjects who are treated to the quite bizarre and unusual experiences common to laboratory experiments are likely to realise that *something* is 'going on', and although the researchers should be well aware of the possible effect of experimenter demand their methods show a surprising ignorance or indifference to it…. A study by Borden (1975) found that subjects significantly increased their displays of aggression in the laboratory when being observed by a man, or by someone of either sex who appeared to be a karate enthusiast; when the observer left the aggression declined in both instances. The presence of a female observer, or an observer of either sex who appeared to be a member of a pacifist organisation, led to much lower levels of aggression being displayed, which did not change when the subject was left alone. (Gauntlett 1995:18)

Gauntlett rightly concludes: 'These results suggest that the subject's behaviour was directly influenced by their assumptions or knowledge about the kind of responses which the observer would want or expect to see'. Gauntlett goes on, however, utilising Freedman's (1986) argument in his overview of effects studies, to say, 'a major reason why laboratory experiments find larger effects than field studies is simply the relative absence of experimenter demands in field studies'.

What was at work was not just that the subjects gave the responses that the observer wanted or expected to see (this has great relevance to focus group activity), but that the subjects adjusted their behaviour in line with what they thought appropriate to the values and personality of the experimenter or observer. For example, they made judgements about the difference in the attraction of violence between men and women, and believing women to enjoy such activity less than men calmed their own response. A similar process was at work with the karate and pacifist observers, in one case judging violence as valued behaviour, in the other non-violence as valued behaviour.

Most researchers, I would think, would consider focus group research to be part of the tradition of field studies, in which, as Freedman and Gauntlett point out, do not suffer experimenter demand in the manner of experimental studies. If it is correct that much of the failure to find effects in the field is due to the absence of experimenter demand – although other factors are involved – it must be reassuring that the focus group is free of experimenter demand. Nevertheless, while agreeing that focus group research patterns itself on field studies – 'natural' contact with people – in actual fact, they have by their 'falseness' – the deliberately constructed contact with people – much more in common with the experimental situation of the laboratory than is usually acknowledged. Of course, as currently conducted, they do not begin to even approximate the central feature and rationale of the experiment, that of controlling and manipulating variables. However, it is worth reflecting back on the origins of focus group research in the hands of Robert Merton, where they were seen as an 'experiment', and indeed through the checks and devices he employed have claim to be seen so.

Thus while not arguing that focus groups share the central feature of the experimental method, they nevertheless share features of the experimental situation, and do so much more closely than they share the features of the field situation. As such one does get experimenter demand, or as I shall now refer to it, moderator demand. This 'demand' is twofold. One 'demand' is relatively easy to detect, the other not so easy and probably causes greater damage to the data collected than is ever realised by focus group researchers. In some cases of 'moderator demand' there is even the danger that the data collected is valueless because it is little more than the reflections back by the participants to the group of the moderator's own values and sensibilities. To be more circumspect; the data is heavily infused with the values and sensibilities of the moderator through the operation of the demand forces.

As stated, 'moderator demand' works at two levels. Level one is where the participants recognise the aim of the research and consider the type of response to questions that they think the moderator will appreciate. For example, if the moderator is wishing to find out feelings about a new household labour-saving device, such as a microwave oven, the moderator may well wish to know the domestic circumstances of the individual, their work routines, attitudes to technology and so on before focusing the discussion on the microwave oven itself. It should be quite clear before too long that the researcher is collecting this material in the direct interest of a manufacturer. As a result distinct lies might be told by the participants to facilitate the smooth functioning of the focus group, or agreement given to statements which are not accepted as true, to carry the conversation along a route which is helpful to the moderator.

Such first-level 'moderator demand', although not always easy to detect, really tends to affect market research and not academic social science research. But first-level 'moderator demand' is not necessarily always absent. One might, for example, be examining attitudes towards violence on television, and respondents believe, even though one might say one is from the University of Leeds conducting research into people's attitudes to violence, that you are working for a television company, regulatory body or government department. Respondents will enquire who you are working for, and despite assurances that the work is 'academic' one is never quite sure that the explanation is accepted. I have certainly experienced such situations where answers have been given that the respondent has imagined would suit the client. People like to be helpful, at least if they have been asked along to be a member of a group specifically set up to help with some research. To repeat: focus groups are not naturally occurring events, but it is 'natural' to help by providing considered helpful answers to questions if one has been asked to help with some research.

The first level of 'moderator demand' is not, I would consider, as great a worry for academics as the second-level 'moderator demand'. This second level is pernicious and difficult to detect; namely, that the participants to the group are sensitive to the values and sensibilities of the moderator and adjust their responses in light of their perceptions. It matters little that the perceptions of the values and sensibilities of the moderator are mistaken; in such a situation what is believed is what is true.

The problem that academics face, especially with working-class participants, is that they are seen not just to be intellectuals, but liberal too. In my experience this becomes apparent in almost every focus group when discussing newspaper readership. Asking what papers they read, one invariably gets some embarrassment 'over-confessing' to reading the *Sun*. Groups differ even within the same socio-economic groupings, but if embarrassment does surface, it infects others. There is a tendency when faced by an intellectual not to expose what they themselves know to be their popular taste in news literature. If the *Sun* is nominated as their preferred reading material it will often be accompanied by comments to disassociate themselves intellectually from appreciation of the paper. Others will add another more 'respectable' title to their reading list, often producing bizarre combinations, such as the *Guardian* and the *Sun*, or *Sun* and the *Telegraph*.

This 'embarrassment' can be overcome by gaining their confidence as the focus group progresses, but it is through small tests such as this that one is aware of the possibility of second-level moderator demand taking place. It must be said, however, that in a setting of strangers where each does not know the occupation of the other, and hence the status conferred by different jobs within the same overall socio-economic grouping has not been established, a reshuffling of readership from the actual to the status functional is to be expected, and does go on. But, such 'shuffling', although always to be expected, is a much more marked feature of the groups that I now conduct as an academic than ever it was when I conducted them as a market researcher. The market researcher is seen as a 'professional' just doing his or her job in a non-judgmental fashion, whereas the academic comes from the world of learning whose very core is that of judgement. It is also true that the academic represents the past world of the participants, the testing and tested world of the schoolteacher.

The full force, however, of the second-level moderator demand, and one difficult to detect in operation, is in the area of substantive social topics, such as race, gender, punishment, violence, sex and politics; indeed, many of the very areas that the communication researcher may wish to examine in terms of response to media representation. The fact that the academic is perceived as the educated liberal presents the difficulty of knowing when the participants to the group are moderating their views in a kind of conspiracy of silence to meet with the approval of the moderator. Even in the area of party political discussion the belief that the academic may be a Labour voter offers the danger of not bringing to the fore Tory statements from the discussants, or, and more likely, produces a much more 'reasonable' discourse than would otherwise be the case were they discussing political issues with someone else.

It is easier for respondents to 'place' the academic on a whole host of socially sensitive topics than it would be for them to place other occupations. The popular view is that those working in the social sciences, humanities and related areas are liberals, marked out by tolerance to differences. In such cases the moderator demand effect could be very large indeed. Although not always easy to detect, the second-level moderator demand effect must be born in mind by the moderator at all times and constant checks made to ensure the discussion is as 'relaxed', as possible so that participants 'forget' the status of the moderator or the original projections that they made concerning the values, sensibilities and beliefs of the moderator. The very demeanour and style of address of most academics stands, certainly to working-class participants of focus groups, in stark contrast to their own presentation of themselves, both in demeanour and language.

Race is one particular area which even the racist knows is circled by judgements that are not evenly distributed, whereas gender is a much more unclear area of approved and disapproved address. Indeed, in male working-class focus groups commentary about women which would be considered sexist to the liberal academic is presented as shared discourse. Only at the extremes does one detect an awareness that there might be limitations placed on the reference that is permissible to make towards women; the rest is just seen as general banter to which it is presumed the whole world, including that of the moderator, could not find exception. The problem is, however, of knowing what part moderator demand is playing in keeping the boundaries of discourse in place. In the area of race, the academic moderator, with all the projected assumptions poured onto that position by participants, will influence the boundary of discourse, if not exactly to liberalise conversation, at least to cage the conversation to some degree.

Participants in focus groups, especially working-class participants, will test the moderator to discover the grounds of the permissible. What is at work here is the determining of the extent to which moderator demand is going to influence proceedings. It goes on in all areas, but some areas more than others. The term 'slag' might be used to refer to a promiscuous woman, and in the subtle interplay of conversational response judgement made as to the type of moderator/person they are talking to. However, as stated, sexist comments are so common amongst the male working class that there is a presumption, within limits, that all share them. Even so, any expression that might be taken as discomfort or unfamiliarity with such terms then brings moderator demand in with full force: it is not the 'pub conversation' anymore but the talk of the doctor's surgery. Race is quite another matter, where the presumption of the academic moderator as liberal intellectual brings moderator demand into more clear and observable operation.

Because race is clearly attached to political parties and historically has formed part of the politics of extermination in a way that gender has not, then even the acknowledged racist is aware that 'rules' exist governing public expression of racist sentiments. There is not the assumption that all will share or approve expressions that are used to describe non-white people. A degree of caution can therefore exist when participants recount their feelings and experiences which involve questions of race. Again, the moderator is on test, not for approval of racist sentiments, but as a guide to determine the ground rules of the discussion. Any detection of the 'liberal' will increase the effect of moderator demand. Many British working-class men are racist in their use of language so if one finds no racist comments in the course of such a grouping, even of a restricted as opposed to elaborated form, then one can postulate that moderator demand is occurring. That is, that the participants have formed a perception of the moderator as a type of person that would not like such areas discussed in the terms that the participant would like to, or normally does discuss them. Racist feelings are so pervasive within the British working class, or at least as manifested in their language, that even when conducting focus groups on topics totally removed from what one would have thought would allow the introduction of racist sentiments they are worked into the conversation. One would not, for example, have thought that focus groups organised to examine television signal overlaps and viewers' preferences for one television station's regional news output rather than another's would produce racist comments, but one such project I conducted managed to do just that. One would have expected viewers to express a preference for one station over another based on some information criteria when applied to the news, or even total apathy, but not an indifference about which channel was received 'so long as it didn't have any more darkies on'. What I am saying, is that racist sentiments among the British working class are so deeply rooted that they manifest themselves in the most unexpected quarters of enquiry. Race forms a permanent view of the world for them and thus if racist statements are rarely encountered, one can guarantee that moderator effect is at work.

Perhaps it is due to the simple statistical fact that because market researchers conduct many more focus groups than academic researchers that conversations with them frequently result in tales of the appalling sentiments that people hold, but yet one rarely hears this in conversation with academic focus group researchers. A market researcher specialising in conducting focus groups, working for a successful medium-size company, could well do two hundred focus groups a year. Consequently, the researcher is likely to be exposed to such sentiments more than the academic researcher conducting only a few groups for the occasional research project. Of course, it might be that the academic in conversation with other academics is not so ready to relay such stories, either on the ground that to do so is to increase the circulation of such sentiments, and perhaps inadvertently reinforce them, or a desire for political reasons to hide the racism of a group they feel compelled in other ways to support. Or it may be that the liberal academic social scientist feels uncomfortable uttering racial remarks even to make some illustrative point. It might also be that they never received such comments in the course of their work; but if so then one can be pretty sure that moderator demand has taken place, that the participants to the group have detected a liberal sympathy that has then fed the nature of the responses received

Although experimenter demand is recognised within experimental psychology as something to be guarded against, as a feature of focus group research moderator demand is overlooked, one suspects because focus groups are viewed as naturalistic data collection rather than experimental data collection. It is the 'natural element', or as I have argued the appearance of naturalness, that has led to a dismissal of this aspect of interference with the subject. However, it should be noted that even in that most natural of field work situations, namely participant observation, moderator or observer demand can be present. The classic work of William Foote Whyte, *Street Corner Society* (Whyte:1943) illustrates a classic case of observer demand.

Cornerville was an Italian community in a run-down part of Boston, and Whyte 'joined' the Norton Street Gang, led by Doc, who like other gang members engaged in a variety of illegal activities. Doc knew the purpose of Whyte's presence in Cornerville. Although Whyte was accepted into the gang, at one point even engaging in a voting racket, one day Doc complained to Whyte: 'You've slowed me up plenty since you've been down here. Now, when I do something, I have to think what Bill Whyte would want to know about it and how can I explain it. Before I used to do things by instinct.' (Whyte 1942:301) Whyte, the researcher, was clearly altering how Doc operated, at least in the sense of making him reflect on actions rather than behaving 'instinctively'. Of particular importance in the context of moderator demand in focus groups is the fact that Doc at the very point of acting was considering how he would report the activity to Whyte on the basis of what he considered Whyte might wish to know.

Certainly this is a case of observer demand, and may be somewhat unusual to participant observation studies. And by and large observer demand in participant observation work is not the problem that moderator demand is in focus group research. In fact, at a reasonably early stage in Whyte's study Doc tells him to stop asking so many questions of people since it made them uneasy, especially given the racketeering that was going on in the community, and argues that all Whyte had to do was 'hang around' and he would get the answers to what he wanted to know – there was no need to ask any questions at all.

A Matter of Resources

As part of the collection of essays edited by Morgan (1993) to advance focus group research, Morgan and Kreuger (1993), in their contribution 'When to Use Focus Groups and Why' attempt to collapse myths about focus groups. The first myth that they attack is that they form a cheap way of doing research. They are not cheap, or rather, they only appear to be so because, as they say, 'the research team donates a large amount of labor' or they only appear to be cheap if 'the labor is paid for from another source'. Focus group work is labour intensive, and the skill to do it may not be available within the research team. Morgan and Kreuger comment that if it is found necessary to hire professionals then the costs in America, at the time of their writing, could for the total project 'easily exceed US$1000 per group and may even fall into the range of US$3000 to US$4000 per group'. US$1000 would seem remarkably cheap to run a group even by 1993 prices, unless Morgan and Kreuger are simply referring to hiring a moderator for his or her time spent with the actual group, and not a full professional service – recruitment of participants, conducting the group, payment of incentives to participants, provision of refreshments, hiring the hall, transcription charges, report writing and presentation of the results. To have a full service provided by a market research company in Britain a cheap deal would be a £1000 per group rising to a high of £1700 per group. Some companies are just more expensive than others and may charge a top rate of around £1700 if the subject area is likely to be difficult, and the sample to be recruited not easy to find. Most companies would charge around £1200 per group.

The above costs of focus group research for a professional company is clearly out of the range of most academic research projects. For example, the health study of the Glasgow University Media Research Group reported on by

Kitzinger would easily have cost them more than £50,000. Admittedly, in focus group terms, theirs was a massive study with some 52 groups conducted in total. Even allowing for the purchasing power of bulk buying it is doubtful that they would have got the rate down to below a £1000 per group, especially given that the wide geographic dispersal of their groups would have meant considerable travelling expenses incurred by the market research company, whose personnel tend not to favour bed and breakfast accommodation.

Cost apart, it is not likely, nor is it to be recommended, for academic researchers to use professional companies for focus group research, except in special circumstances. It may be that one knows a past academic whose reputation was established in the area you are interested in and has left academia for the higher financial rewards of market research, and would be suitable to run the focus groups for the project. However, even then it is best to keep 'control of the knowledge' and use one's own staff if at all possible. In certain circumstances the target population may be such that the research team does not have among them a moderator with the attributes or skill necessary to conduct the focus groups. For example, during the Gulf War much play had been made by the media of anxiety in children as a result of the televised coverage of the conflict, and thus the Institute of Communication Studies study of coverage of the Gulf War wished to include very young children in the project. (Morrison 1992; Morrison and MacGregor 1993) Although we felt confident about designing a national questionnaire for administration to children, no one at the Institute had ever conducted a children's focus group before. Thus, a market research company with experience of running children's groups was employed[1] to assist with the children's part of the study while the Institute's staff conducted the adult focus groups. The only other occasion when we have had to go outside and buy help was for the panel study for the 1992 General election. The groups in that study were too geographically dispersed and needed to be processed at the same time as each other for the resources of the Institute to physically manage the workload. Thus it may be that a university research team has to buy from a market research company in special circumstances; for example, if it was felt necessary as part of some project to have an ethnic minority moderator conduct ethnic minority groups and no suitable individuals were available internally to handle the work. I say 'part of the project' since if the whole project was one involving ethnic minority groups and it was felt that it would be best to have the moderator from the same ethnic background as the participants then it would be best before beginning the project to ensure that such talents were available in-house for the research.

Unless one is conducting focus groups among easily identifiable and self-contained groups, such as Gregg Philo did in recruiting participants within the same occupation or workplace, (Philo 1990) then it is strongly advised to use a

---

1   The company was Counterpoint. Dr Alison Lyon, who is head of the company, and was once an academic herself, ran some of the focus groups.

confidence in the type of textured responses given by group members, even though those textured responses could not be captured by the survey. In other words, if the type of statements that could be measured were representative of a wider audience, then the type of statements that could not be measured were also reasonably likely to be representative of a wider audience – the instrument of one sharpened the instrument of the other.

It is essential in the recruitment of any focus group to screen out by questionnaire at the point of recruitment any categories of people unsuitable for the purpose of the research, or the smooth functioning of the group. Thus in drawing up the sample one may specify, age, class and gender and so on, but then also, if say the topic of enquiry was the political bias in newspapers, screen out anyone who although they fulfilled all the necessary sample categories worked for a media organisation, lectured in media studies, was a local councillor and so on. Such people would bias responses and also skew the discussion by either special pleading or expert knowledge. If one wished to know the views of media personnel towards bias in newspapers then one would recruit a group containing only such people. It is worth while to take pains over the screening process. To have it emerge in the course of the focus group that one has recruited some one 'unsuitable' can be an expensive mistake, severely undermining the value of the information collected. For example, a past colleague in market research informed me recently that a focus group that he had just conducted for a tyre manufacturer on images of high performance tyres could have been an absolute disaster as the screening process had allowed the presence in the group of a motorway policeman. The sample was drawn only on those who drove fast cars, which of course included the policeman. Not surprisingly, perhaps, the responses in the group tended to revolve around the aesthetic appeal of high performance tyres and the occasional comment about the safety of such tyres, but not the safety of grip while cornering at madcap speeds or the traction afforded while sprinting between traffic lights. The policeman's presence was not good for the open exchange of such information, even though he somewhat clumsily attempted to diffuse the tension of his presence by joking that he had checked all the tyre depths of the cars parked in the driveway before the focus group meeting.

Cash incentives to participants are not always necessary, but usually given. This ranges from £12-15, the higher sum sometimes given in the South, a nice reflection of the economic divide in Britain. It is doubtful that this has any influence on proceedings. The money is certainly welcomed by participants, especially since one is asking them to give up one to two hours of their time, usually in the evening. A rainy night, or something good on the television can affect turn out. If a recruitment agency is getting the sample then they will insist that incentives are offered since it makes their job easier and in a professional sense makes them feel less uncomfortable when approaching potential recruits. The only thing to be wary of is not to have the recruits drawn from a panel, ie a list of people that the recruitment agency always use in constructing groups. The professional respondent is more a feature of

American market research, where the agency will have lists of people who have agreed to act as participants to focus groups. Promises are given of course that no panel member has been used in the past so many months and so on, but the whole practice seems undesirable. It might be considered that in consumer research the operation of a panel system of recruitment does not matter. However, I think the opposite is the case. How engaged can one get in judging one brand of toothpaste against another? In such situations it is highly likely that professional response skills will enter, or at least considered thought in responding to questions will be at a minimum since the regular focus group participant can predict the type of questioning coming next from experience of focus groups on vacuum cleaners, shampoo, metal polish and so on. At least in the areas of research dealing with social issues the participants do have to reflect at a deep level on the meanings they have created out of their own social experience. Is there not something 'odd' about people who agree to have their names on such a panel? They ought to be a self-excluding group.

It is not the payment of incentives that ought to raise concerns, but the serial incentive taker. Recruitment is best on an ad hoc basis. It may be that a university research team which does its own recruitment, as we have done on occasion at the Institute, can get away without paying incentives. But it is not good policy. Payment does not create a cash nexus, it simply adds to the friendliness of the exchange in the sense of recognition that people have been good enough to come along to assist with the research exercise when they could well have been doing other things. However, if one was working with very special groups, say those who are HIV positive, or victims of crime, incentives might be totally unnecessary or even inappropriate if they had some burning desire to 'tell their story'. As with everything in focus group research, there are no hard and fast rules. For example, although it has been suggested that to achieve a good sample, and release resources within the research team for other activities, one would be well advised to use a professional recruitment agency, in certain circumstances university researchers would be better at obtaining the sample and perhaps the only body that could do so.

Even in a culture such as England that does not have a high regard for learning, the association of a research project with a university contributes an added value, certainly well above that of having a research project attached to the name of a market research company, no matter how well the name of that company is known. A professional recruitment agency will always, if asked, recruit in the name of the university, but that is not the same as the actual research staff of a university doing its own recruitment. For specialist groups – say political groups such as feminists, or environmentalists, or deviant groups such as joy-riders and drug-takers, or high-status groups such as lawyers or politicians, then to be approached by a university researcher will always be more effective, if done correctly, than by a market research company. Entry is just that much easier if the project is seen to have an integrity uncontaminated by commercial association. In such cases the payment of incentives might be inappropriate.

Before looking at sampling itself, it is worth mentioning perhaps, that academic funding bodies are not keen to find incentives in a research budget. It is agreeable to them to have a university project make payment to market research companies for the provision of services, and often substantial sums at that. But incentives do not easily fit into the accountancy procedures that publicly funded bodies prefer when dispensing grants. The inclusion of incentives in grant applications to academic funding bodies, including philanthropic foundations, needs to be discussed with them. Recruitment costs, using a professional agency for a standard, easily accessible population will be around £250 per group, which with the payment of incentives, and the provision of refreshments will see the research incurring costs of over £400 per group. This does not make focus groups an especially cheap way of conducting research. The alternative of course, is to self-recruit, but it is this self-recruitment, and the limited resources available to the research team, that often results in such discreditable sampling.

The Value of the Sample

For the purpose of focus group research the practice of psychologists who tend to recruit their subjects from amongst the student body is not to be recommended, unless, that is, the subject of enquiry is students. Due to the peculiarity of their experience students cannot be taken to say anything about wider populations. For example, if one found that the showing of a violent film resulted in an increased aggression among a sample of students then one has at least demonstrated that a violent film can cause aggression in a certain population, and one might wish to roll out the research to other populations. One might even conclude on theoretical grounds that there is no need to include further populations since the factors that account for the effect are universal and thus students, because of their location and experiences, are no different from others who do not share their location or experiences. Indeed, that is why experimental psychologists, in particular those involved with the physiological side of psychology, can use very small samples to make general statements. One might, for example, have only a sample of one if measuring some aspect of eye movement in response to a moving image, if it was believed that the neurology of one individual was the same as the neurology of all individuals. Pavlov's dog was not one dog, it was all dogs. However, what is being examined or unearthed in focus group research is not of this order, but rather experiences of the social world, and how individuals express those experiences in terms of the meanings that they bring to various acts, events or ideas. Thus, the sample must be structured so that it can say something about wider populations, either the distinct population from which it is drawn, occupation group, behavioural group and so on, or the wider population in general. This holds true even without statistical representatives, although one sees that once more the question of statistical representativeness is not far below the surface of focus group methodology.

Thus, whilst the employment of a professional recruitment agency may appear an extravagance, it does at least ensure access to a wider population than is available to members of a university department when recruiting. One feels, however, that the lack of attention to the sample is not just because of the lack of financial resources, a reason put forward often for the adoption of the method, but because many qualitative researchers, at least within media studies, wish to disassociate themselves from quantification. To pay attention to the sample, to apply some rigour, may make the qualitative researcher who harbours an enmity towards quantification feel uncomfortable. But to have a good sample does not draw the qualitative researcher into the net of quantification.

No amount of cleverness will overcome the faults structured into the base material by a poor sample. The defence that one is not engaged in quantification and therefore it is not important to focus group research how the sample is drawn does not carry conviction. Birgitta Höijer in the *European Journal of Communication* on viewers' reception of television programmes refers in the course of her article to Peirce, Dewey, Wittgenstein, Vygotsky, and Malinowski – all, one would agree, scholars of serious reputation. Having established the article's credentials we then find that the study was based on a programme, *Life and Death in an Acid Environment*, that was:

> ...shown privately on video to fourteen subjects, nine in their own homes and five in my home. Immediately following the programme in-depth interviews of roughly 45 minutes' duration were carried out. The subjects were selected from among my friends, neighbours and relatives so as to include a broad variety of educational backgrounds, occupations, interests and activities. They ranged in age from 29-78 years old. (Höijer 1990:36)

Friends tend to be drawn from a similar educational and interest background to oneself. Neighbourhoods have a structure that is not randomly drawn – refuse collectors may occupationally visit the leafy groves of Hampstead, but do not, even though they might wish to, live there since the financial rewards of their occupation precludes residency. It is true that through marriage one's in-laws might offer a wider network of 'friendship' than that offered by volitional friendship or neighbourhood associations, but even then there are sociological 'rules' to sexual friendship, as oppose to sexual attraction, that result in rather homogenous family formations. At the most brutal one might say that the sample created by Höijer ran the risk of her talking to herself, but even if this was not the case, then no account is taken of the fact that as the moderator she is inside the circle, that is, she is part of the very group that has been brought into being to examine the messages of the programme. Her attitudes towards the environment is hardly likely to be unknown to her friends, probably known by her relatives and may be known by her neighbours. There is no need here to rehearse the discussion made concerning moderator demand, but in this situation much greater and more complex dynamics are likely to be at work to confound the findings.

Relationships between friends and relatives are constellations of constantly moving emotional exchanges that involve a high degree of strategic manoeuvres which cannot be dumped at the door upon entry into a such a focus group. Höijer attempts to give methodological justification for her sampling arrangement by saying that they were selected to give 'a broad variety of educational backgrounds, occupations, interest and activities'. One might think that this 'variety' could not have been great among only fourteen participants. No reason is even given as to why one might, methodologically speaking, wish for a wide variety of such factors, but the basic point is that given this sample, how do we know what has been measured in the course of the focus group? Perhaps rather than the response to the programme, or attitudes towards environmentalism, what was actually measured or witnessed were attitudes and responses to Höijer, for which the subject of acid rain provided a perfect stimuli. In terms of research procedure the outside observer to the focus group would have been in a more authoritative position to say something about inter-action among friends in the area of political social controversy, than they would have been to say something about viewer response to the programme and the issues that it generated.

Range not Distribution

It is interesting that in a recent Sage textbook, *Research Methods in Psychology*, a section should be devoted to focus group research. As one might expect coming from the discipline of psychology, the author, Lynne Millward, is rigorous in her approach to the area. Quite rightly she makes no claims for the method producing data that can be generalised. As she argues : 'It is not the intention of focus group methodology to yield generalisable data, so random sampling is not necessary'. This does not mean, however, that great care ought not to paid in constructing the groups for the study. She comments: 'None the less, it is important to employ a systematic strategy when deciding on group composition. The sample should be chosen on theoretical grounds as reflecting those segments of the population who will provide the most meaningful information in terms of the project objective'. She then adds, 'Moreover, the participants should have something to say about the topic of interest'. (Millward 1994:279)

One would have no disagreement that the sample should be theoretically grounded in the object of the study. But the type of survey sampling that Millward is referring to here is purposive sampling, that is, a sample which is not representative of a total population, but of some distinct population drawn on the basis of particular characteristics one wishes to examine. In such cases those outside the target area are redundant to the survey. Unless taken out at the analysis stage of proceedings the 'other populations' will bias the study, and thus are best not included in the first place, unless one wished to make some comparative analysis of populations. Thus while strongly agreeing with Millward that careful attention ought to be paid to the sample, I would disagree that it is always necessary that the participants should have something of interest to say on the subject under discussion, unless she means that there is little point in recruiting people who have no interest in the topic under investigation. For example, if one wishes to know responses to Soap Operas, what the enjoyment of them is, there would be little point in recruiting individuals who never watch soap opera. They would have nothing to say and are a self-excluded group. On the other hand if one wished to account for the general popularity of television, then one would want to include viewers whose tastes did not include soap opera, and although they may have little of a substantive nature to say on the intricacies of the genre, they would more than likely give a good account of their objection to it as a form of entertainment. But having nothing to say on a topic in this sense ought to be taken care of by the rigours of sampling; either one wanted viewers of soap operas or one did not. Thus the suggestion appears to be that one should recruit participants who will be vocally active because they have things they wish to say about the topic under enquiry.

It is always hoped that each individual in the group will become actively involved in the proceedings by expressing opinions, that they will 'open up', give judgements, and join in conversation with other members of the group. But one ought not to recruit on the grounds of such 'talent'. To do so is to run the risk of only recruiting a certain type of individual who may not represent the sample area one is interested in. It is true, however, that some people ought to be excluded on grounds of articulation. Unless one is interested in the behaviour of heavy drinkers and the meanings they attribute to drinking and attractions it holds, the drunk ought never to be recruited.

Such categories apart, the danger of recruiting those who will be good performers, especially if recruited by the team actually doing the research, is that assumptions are built into the sample based on the recruiter's own prejudices. Because one can never be entirely sure before any 'test' whether or not a person will add sufficiently to the focus group to deserve inclusion, the chances are that the recruiter will go for those who look as if they will, namely, on outward signs of 'respectability'. Not only does this skew the sample towards ones own biases, but it is not actually necessary that everyone needs to be especially vocal to make a focus group successful. Again, such reasoning lends force to the argument that it is best, in most circumstances, not all, to use the services of a recruitment agency. Whilst the agency has an interest in the focus groups going well, and thus being retained for future recruitment, they are not actually involved in the research. Thus, they are likely, within the categories laid down for selection, to recruit a more varied type of person than that promised by the personal preferences of those working with them in the group.

When recruiting, much depends on the nature of the group to be conducted, but generally it is best to recruit well in advance and re-contact respondents close to the date that the group is to be held. This procedure also allows the replacement of participants should any drop out. This procedure is not easy if the research team, or single researcher, is doing the recruitment themselves, especially if the numbers to be recruited are large and the locations geographically disparate. There is little point recruiting two weeks ahead of time and hoping that all those contacted will turn up on the appointed day and at the appointed hour. If recruitment is made far ahead of time then calls must be made just prior to convening of the group to ensure that attendance will be made. Even if recruitment is close to the point of attendance a call to check that 'everything is okay' is worthwhile; always presuming that the participants are available for contact, which if not underscores the benefit of recruiting as close to the meeting as possible so that respondents do not forget the day or plan something else for the appointed time.

Sample Size

Part of drawing a sample must include consideration of how many groups one needs, never an easy matter. A key factor in deciding the number of groups required is the number of sub-groups that are required. This latter number is determined by the homogeneity of the groups. The principles of sampling in qualitative work are the very same as the principles of sampling in quantitative work: sampling is sampling. However, because what one is doing is focus group research, and thus not making generalisations to larger populations, the actual strictures on sample size do not have to be so tight as those in survey research. This does not mean that anything goes. As Morgan says:

> One important determinant of the number of groups is the different number of subgroups required. The more homogeneous your groups are in terms of background and role-based perspectives, the fewer you need. But one group is never enough: you may be observing little more than the dynamics of that unique set of participants. Even if you only run two and they are highly similar, you are on much safer grounds. (Morgan 1988:42)

Morgan continues:

> In selecting participants, the issue is sample bias, not generalisability: 40 or so participants are never going to be representative of a large population. This is especially important when one's research goal is not to test hypotheses but to learn about others' experiences and perspectives. Using focus groups to learn about the full range of experiences and perspectives in a broad population can be a fool's errand. Indeed, there is no reason to believe that a randomly sampled group holds a shared perspective on your topic. A typical solution, given the small sample size of focus group samples, is to work with theoretically chosen subgroups from the total population. (Morgan 1988:44,45)

A few comments need to be made here. It would be preposterous to run only one group, as Morgan rightly notes. All one might be collecting are observations of one world without being able to check that finding against some other world and thus test for the universality of the truth. Furthermore, the findings themselves are the result of a single group dynamic which may never, even in approximation, occur ever again. But to say that one is on safer ground with two groups prompts the question, safer ground than what?

Morgan states that the focus group does not intend to produce generalisable data to large populations, but some generalisability is necessary, and implied in his statement, otherwise one may be dealing with the idiosyncratic. 'Safety' appears to be given by the regularity of numbers, and regularity of numbers means, and this returns to my basic point about rules and games, quantification, or more accurately, since one cannot go from small numbers to large numbers, focus groups ought to operate as only one plank in a platform built of a variety of methodologies. In this particular argument, another plank must be survey research.

The mistake in Morgan's thinking occurs in his statement that using 'focus groups to learn about the full range of experiences and perspectives in a broad population can be a fool's errand'. It is not the attempt to learn the full range of experiences and perspectives of a broad population from focus groups that makes the exercise a fool's errand, but the attempt to learn the distribution of those experiences and perspectives from focus group research. That is, one might from focus group research gather the range of opinions existing on a topic in a society, but one would not know how those opinions were proportioned, only that they existed in some number or other. For example, one might conduct two focus groups examining attitudes to abortion, consisting of 14 people in total, the number in Höijer's study of an environmental issue,. If the sample is drawn from Cricklewood in North London, a heavily Catholic and Irish part of the capital, we might find that thirteen were against abortion and one was for abortion. Since one can only be for or against abortion this would certainly tell us the range of opinion towards abortion in the country, but it would not tell us the distribution of the range. Indeed, given that the population of Britain is not overwhelmingly Catholic, the split in the range would not help us in determining an abortion policy by democratic voice, if democratic voice is to be judged by weight of opinion. Furthermore, although one can only be for or against abortion, one might be for or against it depending on the context of the pregnancy. The Crickelwood sample, although falling easily into a pro and against abortion split, might raise considerations of when abortion is permissible. Perhaps some of the Catholics siding against abortion would not be 'theologically' pure, and believe a case could be made for abortion if the expected baby was a result of rape, or if continuation of the pregnancy might threaten the life of the mother. Equally the one dissenting voice might consider that abortion should not be permitted if the only reason was that the prospective mother on learning the sex of the baby in pre-natal examination preferred a baby of the opposite sex.

Thus even in an area such as abortion where the range of opinions held on the subject might appear to be only divisible by two, the range of opinion might be larger than previously thought. People can hold the most unexpected views on the most seemingly straightforward matters, and one can never be sure that discussion will exhaust all possible views.

Yet in practice Morgan is wrong that focus groups that attempt to gauge the range of views on a subject are a fool's errand, since that is precisely what they are good at. It is only necessary to conduct a small number of groups before the economic principle of diminishing marginal returns on cost is confronted. That is, every extra group conducted produces less and less new information, until one may as well stop since everything gathered has been heard before. One thus has gathered the range of opinion that exists in the population, but not the arrangements of that range. One knows little about the distribution of the opinions held, that needs survey research to overcome what previously was referred to as the problem of 'limited reference' inherent in focus group research.

The basic principle of sampling in focus groups is to concentrate on those sections of the population that are most likely to provide the information that one wants. If the study is concerned with the spread of HIV in relation to sexual practices there is not much point including in the sample the very old, or nuns. Thus by extension, one might simply include those who are known to be the most sexually active in society, and are therefore likely to be the most 'at risk' groups for the contraction and transmission of the virus through sexual behaviour. If one was interested in how the virus was transmitted through the habits of drug-users, then one would recruit the sample only from among the drug-using community. The result is, as Morgan says:

> ...that focus groups are often conducted with systematically selected samples: either all the participants come from one limited resource, or major groups are consciously omitted from the data collection. Such a bias is a problem only if you ignore it, that is, if you interpret what you hear in the focus groups as representing a full spectrum of experiences and opinions; for example, if gender differences are a major issue, then you might run separate groups of men and women and compare their discussions. To continue the example, if class differences are not a major issue, then your comparisons may be facilitated by using participants who are all blue-collar or all upper- middle class, but you will need to be forthright in recognising and reporting on this sample bias. (Morgan 1988:45)

We have see how the introduction of variables such as age, gender, class, and geographic location can massively increase the number of groups needed for a study, and the effect such variables have on cell size. There is no rule about how many groups are needed to effectively conduct a study; however, it must be said that if focus groups are to be used as a stand-alone method then it is likely that more groups will be needed than if the method is combined with others. One simple factor, however, in determining the number of groups required, as with all sampling, is the diversity of the population. The Glasgow University Media groups AIDS enquiry conducted 52 groups. Kitzinger says:

Many focus group studies rely on no more than 4 or 5 groups, and this may be a perfectly adequate number when working with particular populations. In our case, however, the sample covered a wide range of different 'populations' in England, Scotland and Wales and the groups were selected in order to explore diversity, rather than in order to establish any kind of 'representativeness'. The sample included so-called 'general population' groups such as five women whose children attended the same play group, a team of civil engineers working on the same site, and six members of a retirement club. It also included some groups who might be expected to have particular perspectives on AIDS – groups such as prison officers, male prostitutes, HIV drug users and lesbians. (Kitzinger 1994:105)

Characteristics of the Group

To conduct 52 groups and analyse the data and report on it is no mean achievement, but that is the type of problem confronting the focus group researcher once one starts to diversify populations. Even though the work involved 351 participants, because of the diversity of the populations the study was right not to attempt generalisability.

Morgan, in a very insightful study of responses to widowhood, used the focus group method to address what was a very sensitive area for those who were bereaved. In line with his above instruction on the construction of the sample, he did not bother to isolate class as a variable. The enormity of the emotional upheaval of a loss of a partner submerged class as an experiential divide among the focus group participants:

> ... all the groups were quite mixed with regard to social class, which had little noticeable impact because these widows believed that their bereavement created a fundamental similarity among them that overwhelmed the differences in their background. In other words, their shared beliefs determined what made another's experiences similar or different. (Morgan 1988:47)

It is the homogeneity of a group that increases the likelihood of success, and homogeneity is best ascribed to similar levels of educational attainment or economic status and then factored on gender. Note has already been made of the drawbacks of recruiting people who know each other, and the non-recruitment of strangers tends to be the accepted principle among focus group researchers, but there may be good reason for breaking the rule, as the Glasgow University Media Research Group did in using pre-existing groups, and the Institute of Communication Studies did in its study of reactions to the coverage of the Gulf War when recruiting young children to the focus groups. In that case, it was felt that the support and comfort gained by taking part in an exercise with friends would diminish the strangeness of the situation for the children and assist them to overcome any fear they might have of the 'authoritarian' figure of an adult moderator.

Because the discussants are primarily going to give their opinions, voice feelings and ascribe meanings to actions and behaviour, an essential feature to take note of in recruiting any single group is educational background. Again this cannot be made a general rule because as noted in Morgan's study of widowhood, and this will probably also be the case for deviant sub-groups, the experiences gone through overshadowed other factors in creating a homogeneity of understanding. But Merton, Fiske and Kendall argue, rightly so, that 'educational homogeneity outranks all other kinds in making for effective interviews with groups'. (Merton *et al* 1956:138)

By and large education goes with class, and it is a mistake therefore to have mixed class groups, excluding the type of exceptions already noted. As Hughes and Dumont observe: 'heterogeneity can result in social status differences within a group. Lower status participants may defer to higher status participants.' (Hughes and Dumont 1993:778) It is not, however, just a question of deference that restricts the functioning of such mixed groups; the level of articulation is not likely to be evenly distributed, which can mean the less articulate remaining silent. In addition, differences in background lead to different experiences. Furthermore, a homogeneous group often refer to other 'types' of social groups to illustrate points and make points against, which cannot easily be done if there are members of the highlighted social group present in the focus group. The same principles apply with age, that is, experience of the world differs with age, thus the mixing of very different age groups is not a good idea.

Most social issues have a gender component, or are given a gender attachment by participants, thus the mixing of gender does not allow ease in exploring different gender perspectives on issues. Men in mixed gender groups tend to dominate the conversation. Even though they might say more, it does not follow that they have more to say on an issue. Within all mixed gender groups there exist tensions of sexuality, including the use of discussion as a vehicle for making sexual impressions, and at its most crude outright flirtation. Apart from the very old, which one might wish to mix on the grounds of cost if the topic under examination has no obvious gender implications, such as attitudes to proposed changes to the masthead of the local newspaper, mixed gender groups ought to be avoided.

In so far as the numbers to recruit for each group is concerned, based on experience it is best to over-recruit by 20 per cent. If the group is larger than 10 participants it can become very unwieldy and difficult to control. My own preference is for eight members. Below six it is difficult to generate the type of group dynamic which produces a lively exchange of ideas that is the hallmark of a successfully run focus group. It may on occasion, however, be good practice to conduct mini-groups of say just four people if the topic is one that is particularly sensitive and it is felt that respondents will not share information when faced by a large number of individuals.

It is easier to be clear on the numbers to recruit than to be clear about how many groups one will need to successfully fulfil the goals of the research.

However, Hughes and Dumont observe:

> The number of groups needed to accomplish the aims of the study depends on the problem that is to be addressed and available time and resources. At a minimum, two groups are needed for each subset of the population the researcher intends to study, to ensure that the focus group data do not reflect the idiosyncrasies of a particular group. (Basch, 1987; Morgan, 1988) Some investigators recommend that researchers conduct focus groups until groups are producing redundant information. (Kreuger, 1988) This typically requires three to four focus groups per subset of the population under study. (Hughes and Dumont 1993:778)

This is helpful, but only up to a point. Kreuger's suggestion of continuing the recruitment of groups until material received is redundant, or what I previously referred to as the diminishing marginal returns on cost, is not an option open to most researchers. It presumes an elastic budget. It is unusual in any research enterprise to have an open cheque book, and in raising money the crucial starting point for negotiation, be it an academic funding body or a commercial body, is to know how much one wants, and that is determined by how much the research will cost, which in turn is determined, in this case, by the number of groups to be conducted. A decision must be made on theoretical grounds about how many groups one will need to conduct. Some of the factors to be taken into account have already been discussed, and offered as a guideline in deciding the numbers needed. These numbers, of course, must always be judged against the aims of the research.

As a general rule more groups will need to be undertaken if focus groups are to be used as a stand-alone technique than if they are to be used in conjunction with other methods, but there is no magic safety in numbers since quantification is not the rationale of focus group research. Numbers will increase confidence as diminishing marginal returns on cost (effort) become significant, but the purpose of focus groups is more an exploration in understanding, not certainty.

Seven

Good and Bad Practice in Focus Group Research

There is no set way to conduct focus groups. Mary Brotherson states: 'Design in qualitative research is a recursive process whereby each component of the process informs the next and is therefore continuously emergent and flexible. (Patton, 1990; Tesch, 1990) Thus, there is no set process for conducting focus group interviewing research'. (Brotherson 1994:106) Edward Fern, in fact, casts doubt on some of the assumptions that both academics and market researchers hold in conducting focus groups. Fern was keen to see if the assumptions held by focus group practitioners stood up to empirical investigation. He examined four basic assumptions:

(1) that focus groups provide more information that is qualitatively better than individual interviews;

(2) that the ideal size is between eight to twelve members;

(3) that the moderator plays a crucial role;

(4) within a group, homogeneity of members should be maintained.

Fern argues that the empirical evidence 'casts doubt on the validity of some of these assumptions. Yet other evidence seems to support these assumptions.' (Fern 1983:124) The problem with Fern's empirical evidence, however, is that most of the findings were not taken from focus group studies as such, but from fields such as psychotherapy, the findings of which may not be capable of being carried across to focus group research. Fern recognises this himself: 'In most cases the studies were done in situations quite different from typical focus group interviews. Focus groups are not normally recruited from a population of chronic schizophrenics. And personality is not usually a variable upon which within group homogeneity is sought'. (Fern 1983: 125). Fern is right to search for empirical evidence that the assumptions brought to the conducting of focus groups are sustainable, but any firm conclusion cannot be made from Fern's attempt to do so. However, Morgan and Spanish, writing in *Qualitative Sociology*, provide a thoughtful review of another study by Fern (1982) that addresses the question of empirical evidence for the assumptions upon which much focus group research proceeds:

> Fern compared focus groups of different sizes, moderated vs unmoderated focus groups, and groups composed of strangers vs acquaintances. The current 'tricks of the trade' in market research would call for a group of at least eight, with a professionally trained moderator, and a set of participants who were all strangers to one another. With regard to group size, Fern found that the number of ideas generated did not double as group size increased from four to eight, and that the ideas produced in groups were not necessarily superior in quality to those produced in individual interviews. He also found that moderated focus groups may have some advantages to unmoderated focus groups and that groups of strangers may be preferable to groups of acquaintances, but in neither case were the differences large.... The important conclusion that we draw from Fern's work is that there is nothing sacred (or even necessarily correct) about the current ways that focus groups are conducted in market research. Overall, we see Fern's results as pointing toward a set of dimensions that the researcher can use to decide which form of focus group is best suited to his or her research questions. This flexibility was one of the things that originally attracted us to focus groups. (Morgan and Spanish 1984:255)

The idea of measuring success as advanced by Fern, counting the number of ideas and then questioning the assumptions made about group size because doubling the number of participants did not double the number of ideas, would seem to be a sterile exercise in arithmetic. Even though one might admit that the use of focus groups for brainstorming – the generation of ideas – might make sense, this is not the purpose to which most focus group research is put, nor would one have thought it possible in the arithmetic way suggested to measure the quality of the ideas generated. Of course one might have a panel judging the quality of ideas in the same way that for the construction of some measurement scales one has a panel to adjudicate on the value of the items to be used in the scale, but the judge of the quality of the responses in most focus group research is the researcher herself or himself.

Focus groups are a reflexive operation, and one knows in the course of the discussions if the focus group is moving in directions that are helpful to the research. That is what quality means, whether the data gathered is helpful or not; only the researcher who is in possession of the overall purpose and design of the project is capable of judging the quality of the data achieved. It is not uncommon after conducting a focus group to find researchers saying to one another, 'this is not working', and then examine why it is not working and come up with solutions to make it work. That, as Morgan and Spanish confess, is the type of flexibility inherent in the method that led them into the use of focus group research. Most quantification research does not have that flexibility.

Once the survey questionnaire is in the field the researchers lose all control over its effectiveness as a research instrument. With focus group research knowledge on the part of the researcher is built as the research proceeds. As the learning increases that knowledge might be transferred to new questions for subsequent groups, or the original groups reconvened to gather their views on the researcher's new approach to the issues at hand. It is, in short, a method constantly being constituted, but that does not mean that the researcher need have no set of procedures for exploiting the full dynamic of the process, or that success will be achieved without having formulated a set of procedures on how to conduct the focus group. Preparation is as important for success in focus group research as in any other research, and one of the key factors is preparation of questions, and, unless the groups are being conducted for the purpose of exposing oneself to new territory, knowledge of the area under examination. That is why Merton was keen that a content analysis should be undertaken before subjects registered their responses to programmes using the Lazarsfeld-Stanton programme analyser.

It is the understanding of the area, even if only at a general level, that allows the researcher to place comments made in a wider system of understanding. This familiarity with the area, furthermore, allows the registering of the significance of an 'odd' comment which to the uninitiated might get overlooked but which in fact ought to be followed up. Thus, it is not a good idea for an academic project, even if affordable, to employ a professional moderator to run the groups. Unless the market research company is very specialised indeed, an academic communications researcher ought to have a greater understanding of media processes than a market researcher, and further, the academic is likely to proceed from a body of literature unknown to market research, and it is that literature, as likely as not, that has assisted the shaping of the research question.

Much academic work is an internal discourse, and thus it is very difficult to brief the outsider on its intricacies. Given that the knowledge gained in the course of focus group research is a developing reflexive knowledge, what the professional moderator considers an important avenue to follow the academic may not. In fact, this problem of differences in approach and differences in reception to information received afflicts academic focus group research if conducted by a team of researchers.

Despite Fern's challenge to the importance of the moderator, the success of focus group research is very much dependent on the skills and ability of the moderator. Different researchers will, at the level of performance, approach groups differently to other researchers, based on differences in personality and other factors, but that aside, intellectual differences between researchers in terms of their thinking on a topic will manifest itself in the material gathered. This is not an insurmountable problem, but it does mean that if a team of researchers are conducting the focus group project, close association and sharing of ideas is absolutely essential. Otherwise, quite disparate material is returned which may reflect the individual's interests and thinking, but which does not fit with the material gathered by others in advancing the centrally defined purpose of the study. Indeed, a problem of focus group research is the reliability of the data gathered; hence my argument, following Merton, that focus groups are not very satisfactory research tools when used alone.[1]

Importance of the Moderator

Strange as it may seem the moderator is much more in control of the interview situation in focus group research than the interviewer is in the single in-depth interview. Both situations require the interviewer to have a schedule of some sort, a check list of areas that he or she wishes the interview to address. While it may seem that directing the flow of conversation of eight to ten people to stop it meandering is more difficult than focusing a single individual on the topic of interest, it is not. To begin with, usually in focus group research one has some stimuli material to help focus the discussion; secondly, it is easier to interrupt the individual in a group context without appearing brutish, by asking for comments from others in the group, and thus steer the discussion back to the central ground than it is to interrupt the conversation of a single interview if it strays. Should the single interview falter because the interviewee becomes irritated at not being allowed to say what they want, it is difficult to restart the interviewer and rebuild the familiarity necessary for a good interview, and an absolute disaster if such 'breaks' become frequent. In the single interview there is no one to play the interviewee off against, and any interruption by the interviewer is obviously directed at the interviewee in a most pointed fashion; whereas in the group situation it can be made to appear that the point the participant has made is so interesting that the moderator is only interrupting to collect the thoughts of others on the point. The moderator then only needs to allow the briefest of comments from a person who is not the holder of the original point, and thus does not feel emotionally possessive about it when the moderator shuts

---

1   It must be noted that Lunt and Livingstone in their paper 'Rethinking the Focus Group in Media and Communication Research' would consider this position to be too narrow and depart strongly from Merton's demand for reliability, considering that qualitative research should not be infected by evaluations of data that are used in quantitative studies. They put forward the case that 'qualitative methods compensate for the lack of reliability with greater validity'. Even so, they make a case for the reliability of the data gathered in focus groups by saying: 'Conducting focus groups produces a flood of ideas and information in the early groups, which is then reiterated y subsequent groups until (sometimes sooner than others) no new stories are told. Thus, although there is variation from one group to another, there is a point at which the new information gain drops with each new group. One could argue, then, that the exhaustion of the various things to be said on a given topic is part of the content validity of the method, offering a notion of reliability related not to the identity of two runs of the method, but to the rate of information gain.' (Lunt and Livingstone 1996:92) However, as I have pointed out previously the exhaustion of new information only means that one has collected the range of views in a population, it does not give one the distribution of the views.

down the conversation by asking the opinion of someone else on a point more relevant to the research.

There is no question that the personality of the moderator in the focus group situation, and their skills in social manipulation, is an essential part of the success of the enterprise. In the single interview, especially if conducted with very confident elite figures, it is the interviewer who faces the full force of the successful personality and is the subject of manipulation rather than the interviewee. Within the media, and television in particular, the projection of the personality and the imposition of the ego on others is not only the mark of the successful person, but a characteristic making for success. A strong belief in the self is common to practically all who hold senior positions in the industry, and such people, though courteous and charming – their social skills have been cultivated as essentials for the manipulation of people – do tend to consider that what they have to say is important. Thus to attempt to direct the conversation away from the topic the interviewee is addressing to other topics that the interviewer considers more important can meet with resistance. Charm can easily be dropped when it fails to serve its purpose, to be replaced by a forceful insistence that one takes note of what the speaker is saying, or that the question put is not 'relevant' to the subject at hand. Interviews with elite people tend not to give the researcher more than the interviewee wishes to give. Success in conducting such interviews rests on the interviewer's ability to extract to the limit that which the interviewee is prepared to expose about themselves or the organisation they work for. The negotiation of 'space' is, especially for senior people in the media, a well-honed skill. The situation is not easy to control, especially if the time limit rests with the interviewee, as it almost always does.

The role of personality and the skill of performance should never be underplayed in the conducting of any interview, and no more so than in conducting a group discussion. This is not to say, however, that the moderator ought to impose themselves on the group, but that the moderator must be in control of the proceedings. If control is lost a focus group can become a shambles. Thus, any especially offensive person, someone who repeatedly turns on other members of the group, must be asked to leave. In my experience such offensiveness is usually associated with drink, and sometimes, but not often, with drugs. The best approach is to first try and isolate such people and only as a last resort eject them. If it is necessary to eject someone the group can always be brought back together by some light-hearted banter relating to the ejected participant, and restarted once the tension has been released.

There are some people who just are unpleasant. They must be removed if they become intimidating to other members of the group. A suggestion once in a Northern male working-class group by one participant that some facilities in the town that had previously been a social club for a local football team and had now been turned into a ballet centre subsidised by council funds was a good use of rate payers' money brought a vicious enquiry from another participant of whether or not the speaker was 'queer'. Despite the fact that the focus group had nothing to do with sexuality, the question of 'manliness', accompanied by dark looks towards the individual who had defended the ballet school, entered at a surprising number of points with an inventiveness that was creative in its ingenuity. It was not a successful focus group. In such a situation there is nothing to do but abandon the whole exercise. That is, to bring the focus group to completion as quickly as possible.

By and large focus groups are pleasant experiences for all concerned, and always work best when that is the case. This is not difficult in the area of media research, since people generally like to discuss communication issues. It is in such situations that what might be termed the 'normal' functioning of the moderator comes into play.

As we have seen, Paul Lazarsfeld and his colleague, Robert Merton, attempted to develop a graduate training school for the social sciences at Columbia University in the 1950s. Together they developed a long and carefully thought out document (*Proposal to Establish an Institute for Training in Social Research*, BASR Library 1950) in which they laid out how they considered such training could be given, and what its functions and purposes were. As part of the exercise they addressed themselves to the problem of how one could train researchers for areas of research that depended very much on individualistic 'talent' rather than the performance of set technical skills. It is interesting, therefore, that the article written by Merton and Kendall in 1946 on the focused interview anticipates ideas on qualitative training that surfaced in the 1950 proposal. Indeed, focus group research is an area where it is difficult to say how, in any absolutely precise way, one ought to operate and what skills are required on the part of the moderator for the successful completion of such groups. In fact, it is quite difficult to measure success. At least with survey research one can quickly tell if the sample is wrong, or if the question construction was poor as evidenced by the high number of missing values or contradictory answers to questions, all of which would suggest that respondents had difficulty either following the question routing or in understanding the questions.

Lazarsfeld himself was a keen educator. Educational change and educational instruction formed, along with his fascination with methods, his central intellectual interests. It is reasonable to presume that Merton's exposure to focus group research and the difficulties faced in instructing on their operational principles and practice, found their way into his daily conversations with Lazarsfeld. The partnership of Merton and Lazarsfeld was as intense as it was productive. It is highly likely, therefore, that Merton's involvement in focus group research added substantially to the thinking about research training in the area of qualitative research that went into the 1950 proposal to establish a school of research training. Certainly the following passage from Merton and Kendall's article of 1946 reads as if it been lifted straight out of the Proposal:

> A successful interview is not the automatic product of conforming to a
> fixed routine or mechanically applicable techniques. Nor is interviewing

an elusive, private, and incommunicable art.... There are recurrent situations and problems in the focused interview which can be met successfully by communicable and teachable procedures. We have found that the proficiency of all interviews, even the less skilful, can be considerably heightened by training them to recognise type situations and to draw upon an array of flexible, though standardised, procedures for dealing with these procedures. (Merton and Kendall 1946: 544,545)

Both Lazarsfeld and Merton were enthused with the idea of building up cases for use in student instruction, and their procedures were modelled on medical instruction. In the writings of both one finds frequent medical references, and in the case of the proposed training school students are at times referred to as 'interns'. It is the building up of cases that Merton and Kendall recommend in overcoming the mysteries of transmitting qualitative skills. They remark: 'In his search for 'significant data', moreover, the interviewer must develop a capacity for continuously evaluating the interview as it is in process', and they lay out how this capacity can be instructed. A central instructional technique of Lazarsfeld and Merton was the case; that is, building up a body of work that conforms to good practice, or from which good practice can be deduced:

By drawing upon a large number of interview transcripts, in which the interviewer's comments as well as the subjects' responses have been recorded, we have found it possible to establish a set of provisional criteria by which productive and unproductive interview material can be distinguished. (Merton and Kendall 1946:545)

This procedure led Merton and Kendall to outline four areas of practice:

(1) Non-direction: In the interview, guidance and direction by the interviewer should be at a minimum.

(2) Specificity: Subjects' definitions of the situation should find full and specific expression.

(3) Range: The interview should maximise the range of evocative stimuli and responses reported by the subject.

(4) Depth and personal context: The interviewer should bring out the affective and value- laden implications of the subjects' responses, to determine whether the experiences had central or peripheral significance. It should elicit the relevant personal context, the idiosyncratic associations, beliefs, and ideas.

True to their precise thinking and regard for the process of verification, Merton and Kendal comment that 'since these procedures have been derived from clinical analysis of interview material rather than through experimental test, they must be considered entirely provisional'. (Merton and Kendall 1946:545) As they rightly point out the above criteria although listed out are in fact interrelated, 'merely different dimensions of the same concrete body of interview materials'. However, it is the criteria of non-direction that are worthwhile to examine in more detail, since it is that area, the interaction of the 'observer' with the 'participants', that creates the greatest difficulty in conducting focus group research, and the one where the values, beliefs, and thinking of the researcher infuse the discussion to a degree where it is impossible to decipher what voices are in what discourse. Furthermore, as Merton and Kendal comment in their examination of procedures: 'The interrelations of our criteria at once become evident when we observe that non-direction simultaneously serves to elicit depth, range and specificity of responses. For this reason the tactics of non-direction require special consideration'. (Merton and Kendall 1946:546)

Guiding the Discussion

In discussing the nature of unstructured questions Merton and Kendall note that there are various degrees of structuring, the most unstructured being one that 'does not fix attention on any specific aspect of the stimulus situation or of the response; it is, so to speak, a blank page to be filled in by the subject.' They go on to say that the fully unstructured question is particularly appropriate at the beginning of the interview session, but that it might be fruitfully applied at various points in the overall interview. They consider that at some points it may be necessary for the moderator 'to assume more control' particularly in later stages of the interview, 'if the other criteria – specificity, range, and depth – are to be satisfied'. However, even in such cases where more control is required, they warn that 'moderate rather than full direction is fruitful; questions should be partial rather than fully structured'.

For Merton and Kendall, the focused interview is a vehicle for discovering what participants think and feel, not a hobby horse for allowing participants to discover what the moderator thinks. Under the title, 'Imposing the interviewer's frame of reference', Merton and Kendall, while sympathetic to the strains of the interview situation, offer instruction on curbing the appetite of the moderator to interfere:

> At some points in almost every protracted interview, the interviewer is tempted to take the role of educator or propagandist rather than that of sympathetic listener. He may either interject his personal sentiments or voice his views in answer to questions put to him by subjects. Should he yield to either temptation, the interview is then no longer an informal listening-post or 'clinic' or 'laboratory' in which subjects spontaneously talk about a set of experiences, but it becomes, instead, a debating society or an authoritarian arena in which the interviewer defines the situation.

The consequences of doing so are:

> By expressing his own sentiments the interviewer generally invites spurious comments or defensive remarks, or else inhibits certain discussions altogether. Any such behaviour by the interviewer introduces a 'leader effect', modifying the informant's own expression of feelings. Or should the interviewer implicitly challenge a comment,

the informant will often react by defensively reiterating his original statement. The spontaneous flow of the interview halts while the subject seeks to maintain his ego-level intact by reaffirming his violated sentiments. (Merton and Kendall 1946:547)

The 'leader effect' referred to here is not the same phenomenon as 'moderator demand', although it does have similarities in that both call forth responses that would not have occurred 'naturally'. Moderator demand refers to the situation where the nature of the questions given by the moderator results in an attempt by the participant to feed information that they think would be useful to the researcher, or modify their position in line with the perceived value position of the moderator. 'Leader effect' refers to an interference in the discussion by the moderator that alters the 'quality' of the responses by forcing the participants to recognise the ideas that the moderator holds.

Merton and Kendall are against the interviewer becoming involved in any confrontation with participants through the expression of their own beliefs or opinions, even when the participants might deliberately seek out such information. Without doubt it is best for the moderator not to give an opinion on a topic under discussion, even if asked. Such queries are not difficult to fend off. Comments such as, 'I am not sure what I think, that's why I was interested in what you were saying', are usually sufficient to avoid the moment of 'exposure', especially given that the questioner is surrounded by other people so that the question put to the moderator can be turned straight back to some one else in the group – 'I'm not sure, I wonder what X thinks'. This is not a strategy available to the interviewer in the single elite interview. But then in such interviews it does not matter if one is asked for an opinion no more than can a response be avoided in what is a very directed intellectual exchange. Indeed, such interrogation can act as a stimulus for exploration of the other person's thinking as challenge and counter-challenge takes place, always of course in a probing and not combative way. The major difference, however, between the group situation and the single interview is that the exchange in the latter is private, not public. Thus the interviewee in the single interview has no need to guard their ego or feel that they have been 'exposed', or at least not to the same extent as in the setting of a focus group.

While agreeing that one should not expose one's own position on some topic in the situation of the focus group, matters are somewhat different when it comes to challenging the points made by discussants. As ever, much depends on individual judgement. Focus groups, in the main, are fluid encounters, in which familiarity must be established quickly. The 'friendship' is a very brief affair, lasting only for an hour or two. The skill of the moderator is in her or his ability to quickly make the participants relax so that a minimum of trust is established sufficient for them to feel comfortable in exposing feelings and giving opinion. The moderator, however, does not work alone, but with the people who have agreed to participate in the groups. The atmosphere, therefore, also depends on the personalities of those interviewed. Some groups, for that reason, just work better than other groups. The young, 16 to 18 year olds, are invariably hard-going, having often little to say, or if they do, often affecting a bored look, especially so in the case of male youths.

The struggle for the establishment of self-identity, a mark of that age group, offers a picture of self-centredness that fails to include attention to the world outside their immediate self. Thus, although not always, it is difficult to promote a flowing discussion of broad-based issues. The embarrassed silences often prompt one or two participants to speak in situations where one feels that they would rather not, and thus one is never quite sure if the opinions expressed are genuinely held or the forced classroom response where to say something is better than to say nothing. With such age groups it is essential to have stimuli that will promote engagement and discussion, and not have the proceedings depend simply on the stimuli of verbal prompts. In such a situation one would never challenge the veracity of the statements made by the participants; the whole situation is too fragile to risk disturbance through challenge.

In other groups of older, more confident individuals, especially where the atmosphere is relaxed, usually achieved by the presence of one or two 'characters' who open up the meeting by the sheer warmth of their personalities, challenge to opinion can take place. Even so, such challenge is best reserved until one 'knows' the group and can judge if such interrogation is called for. It all depends on the rapport that has been established, and each group differs in this respect. Moderating is an individual act, in the same way that giving a lecture is an individual act – sometimes one feels good and the performance matches the feeling, other times the reverse is the case. At times, therefore, one may not feel confident or relaxed enough with one's own performance to engage in the delicate judgement of risking challenge. Yet, if the situation is felt to be right, to question the statement of some-one can be very productive. Saying, 'do you really believe that' accompanied by some incredulity in the voice, or presenting a gentle argument against the point made, without giving away one's own position, is powerful tool for examining thought. Disputation, as a method, is always good for establishing truth, but it must not be undertaken in a manner that prevents further reflection and engagement on the discussant's part.

The actual beliefs that people hold are often to be discovered in the qualifying statements that follow the original point that they make. It is often only through challenge to the original point that the qualifying statement is offered. The constant, 'why do you believe that?' or 'why did you say that?' is not always sufficient to excavate meaning. The moderator's skill in offering challenge to statements is in knowing how far to press the challenge. As a general rule one stops the challenge once one feels that the 'interrogation' has gone far enough to allow the participant the opportunity of revealing what they mean by their answers. This exchange, however, must be done in a manner pleasurable to the participant. By doing so, the discussant feels that the moderator has genuinely listened to what they have said, and has taken their contribution seriously. The worst crime is to be dismissive of the discussant, either through verbal expression, or displaying lack of interest in what she or he has to say.

The strain of conducting focus groups is high, especially if several are conducted in the same day, which for the sake of economy often happens. The success of the exercise does depend, to a large extent, on the individual performance of the moderator. Yet this does not mean that the value of focus group research should be all down to the whim of the moderator on the day. A well-prepared interview schedule designed to foster discussion geared to the central interests of the study is one way to ensure success, and a second method is to provide visual or other stimulatory material that will trigger and focus discussion independent almost of the moderator's performance. It ought not to be the case that no other moderator would have received responses that proximate to those recorded. If so, then suspicion must enter that the material had been 'conjured' by the moderator. The skill of the moderator is as a facilitator of discussion, not as the scripter of it, otherwise the data is idiosyncratic and of little social scientific value.

Because of the pressures of the performance, the sheer strain of holding bits of information and mentally noting who has said what means that it is often helpful to have two moderators, one taking the lead and the other acting as a support who can log particularly significant comments for exploration at later points. The support moderator can also relieve the primary moderator by occasionally entering the discussion so that the primary moderator can take quick mental stock of how the discussion is proceeding and re-focus the discussion should he or she consider that 'drift' from the main theme has occurred. The presence of a second moderator is also useful in that following completion of a group each can check notes and generally de-brief each other as to what were the significant trains of thought that might have emerged which had not been expected, but which could usefully be carried over to the next group discussion for further exploration. A word of warning is necessary, however. Focus groups, as they progress, allow the researcher to build up a picture of feelings and responses to the subject matter under enquiry, but the picture is a 'developing one' and may not be clear, or in full focus, at any one point in time. Thus the findings from any one particular focus group, certainly after its immediate completion, can often be deceptive as to their full value or meaning. It is often the case that a group that one thought did not go particularly well, on examination of the transcript in the calm of the office at a much later date turns out to provide more insights than some other focus group that the moderator had judged to have gone very well simply because the discussion in that group flowed. It must also be remembered that although a single focus group can give insight into the question under examination, it is not just individual insights that one is collecting, but the pattern of responses that show that the comments made are related to collective experiences that have, at least for the sociologist, a sociological presence. Here we return to the earlier observation that focus groups are better seen as a beginning and not an end. That is, if one is after a sociological presence, and mostly one is, even the market researcher, having found such a presence, further work using different methods becomes a requirement of the research.

Of course one might simply be interested in using focus groups for concept development, hypothesis construction, to alert the researcher to ways of thinking, for the exploration of language usage, or the possibilities that they offer for the development of theoretical formulation of issues, in which case the pattern of the responses may not be of overriding importance, although they still ought to be of some interest. If this is the case, that they are mere explorations for developmental purposes, the findings of the focus groups should not be published as if they were complete studies. Indeed, it is not surprising, referring back to the comments by Morgan, that the focus group method is not given due publicity by scholars when used as part of a collected set of methods, for the simple reason that they do not deserve great prominence. They are not given prominence because they have served their job as developmental tools, or as illustrations to support more 'powerfully' grounded findings. In other words, in research that uses a variety of methods the results of focus groups are handled with the respect owed the method, and not as stand-alone findings of a generalisable nature. It is only because they have come to be used as a stand-alone method, and thus form the basis of a whole study, that they have assumed the importance they have. But if the habit has developed of having the method form the basis of one's study, it is not surprising that researchers who do so should wish it to be given as much prominence as possible.

For studies that use focus groups as one component in a larger package of procedures, it is not surprising that they will only be accorded the role that they have played in the overall scheme of things. Even then, as important as they may have been in an intellectual creative sense, they often come to be overshadowed in the report stage of the presentation of findings by other methods. The researcher who uses focus groups as part of a package of procedures has no need to 'talk the method up' since the overall methodological strength of the study will speak for itself, perhaps one reason why Merton did not need to signal his use of focus groups in the *The Student Physician*. (Merton 1957)

Building Understanding

In media research, there is a temptation to use the findings as a pattern of responses illustrative of a wider tapestry. But the pattern of responses found in one focus group does not necessarily infer that such a pattern will be found overall when the totality of responses are examined. A simple illustration of this can be given from the quantification approach to knowledge of survey research. Data are often entered into the computer as and when they arrive, and a large sample may take some time before all the returns are in. For various reasons one sometimes makes the first run of the data on the small numbers gathered by the first post-back of responses. It is exciting to read the print out of this first haul. Yet time and again those responses drawn from the incomplete sample, and which on reading one often concludes a pattern, turns out to be wrong when the full data set is received. This underscores the point that it is dangerous to draw general conclusions from the small numbers involved in focus group research, especially given that the form of questioning generally speaking is not designed for quantification. It also warns against making general assumptions about the pattern of responses within focus group research that is itself based on incomplete returns, that is, from groups conducted at an early stage.

Focus group research is a built procedure, this is one of its absolute strengths, but the building only becomes secure as more bricks, in the form of additional groups, are added. But as we have seen, at some point, and usually before too long, the shape of the building can be seen, and unless one wishes to add the fine points of architectural design the conducting of further groups becomes unnecessary. This does not mean that the story is complete once the first storey, to stick with the building metaphor, is constructed. Indeed, to come to conclusions early on in the research about the eventual shape of the building is to construct the building on shaky foundations. That is, the questioning in subsequent groups is framed by the conclusions already made from the initial groups, which entails the danger that the eventually building looks remarkably like the one originally imagined. There is no easy way to overcome this, and this is why focus group research does require checks on findings drawn from additional methodology.

Although the conducting of focus group research is a discursive activity, it is essential that each group covers the same ground, or does so to the extent that the information gained from the groups is comparable. This does not mean that exactly the same questions, put in the very same way, have to be asked of each group. Simply that the same interview guide is followed for each group. One of the great benefits of focus group research is its flexibility. As the researcher's knowledge increases so new elements gained in the course of the groups can be fed in, but these new elements should be variations of the basic elements that formed the foundation of the original interview guide or schedule. Even so one needs to guard against rigidity in the application of the guide; the guide is to ensure that the researcher covers the intended topics with the group. It is not a questionnaire. Merton and Kendall warn:

> The interview guide does, however, lend itself to misuse. Even when the interviewer recognises that it is only suggestive, he may come to use it as a fixed questionnaire, as a kind of interviewing strait jacket.... Though it is convenient for the interviewer not to have to improvise all questions in the course of the interview, predetermined questions may easily become a liability; for, if the interviewer recognises in the respondent's comment an allusion to an area of enquiry previously defined in the guide, he is likely to introduce one of the type questions contained in the guide. This is all well and good *if* the question happens

to be appropriate in the given case. But unproductive interviews are those cluttered with the corpses of fixed, irrelevant queries; for often the interviewer, equipped with fixed questions dealing with a given topic, does not listen closely or analytically to the subject's comments and thus fails to respond to the cues and implications of these comments, substituting, instead, one of the routine questions from the guide. If the interviewer is primarily orientated towards the guide, he may thus readily overlook the unanticipated implications of the subject's remark. (Merton and Kendall 1946:548)

Merton and Kendall's warning is necessary. There is something wrong if the moderator needs to constantly 'read off' from his or her interview guide, certainly after the first one or two groups have been conducted. Having written out the guide the moderator should commit the areas or topics to be covered to memory. This rehearsal of the guide thus frees the moderator in the actual interview to give full attention to what is being said, and respond accordingly with his or her own enquiry for explanations and further comment to points made, always holding in the background the general scheme for the interview.

The basic purpose of the focus group is to get people to talk about what you want them to talk about, but to do so in their own words. There is a great danger of over-complicating what really is a very simple process. Because it is simple, however, does not mean it is easy to do well. Kitziger (1994) mentions the use of various exercises adopted by the Glasgow University Media Group in course of their focus group research:

> At the start of the session, for example, participants were asked to play 'the news game' which involved dividing into two small teams and writing their own news bulletin using a pre-selected set of photographs taken from actual TV news bulletins. Later they were presented with a pack of cards bearing statements about who might be 'at risk' from AIDS and asked, as a group, to sort the cards into different piles indicating the degree of 'risk' attached to each 'type of person'. (Kitzinger 1994:106)

Such a technique would appear to be a very inventive way of having participants work among themselves with very little intervention from the moderator, and at the same time provide base line information which could be carried across for comparative analysis with other groups if it was so wished. It also, one presumes, forms a very good stimuli for conversation. But as Kitzinger herself points out in reference to games in general: 'Unfortunately some people, of course, do not like party games and at worst such games could make people feel uncomfortable and reminded some research participants of school lessons!'. (Kitzinger 1994:107)

Some participant certainly do not like to engage in games or role playing exercises, but it must also be pointed out that neither do some researchers feel comfortable as 'party organisers'. One might believe in the benefit of some game type exercise, but if one feels embarrassed running them they will not work well, and are best left alone. Yet it is in market research that the development of exploratory techniques have been pushed the furthest. Projection techniques have proved particularly popular. The main ones are: personality association, situational association, forced relationships, collage creation, sentence completions, expressive drawings and anthromorphisation. Writing on these techniques Thomas Greenbaum comments:

> Projective techniques are a group of focus group moderating tools that generate information from participants by encouraging them to make associations with other stimuli as a way of expressing their feelings towards the specific conceptual idea, product, service or other entity with which they are being presented. Essentially, these techniques evoke reactions to a familiar stimulus in order to help people share their feelings about a new one. They are not unlike the ink blot tests that psychologists use to get their patients to express their innermost feelings. How a psychologist interprets patients' comments is much more complicated than how a moderator interprets participants' comments, but the principle is the same: They both use a secondary stimulus to elicit the individual's feelings. (Greenbaum 1993:104)

Anyone wishing to follow up in detail these projective techniques ought to refer to Greenbaum directly. It is difficult to see their use in social scientific research. The problem with such techniques is that one really does not know what one is measuring, listening to or observing. Greenbaum, for example, gives the example of a forced relationship exercise using animals, something not uncommon in market research. A bear, so he says, is often associated with caring organisations, ones that are large and friendly. A lion is associated as the king of the jungle, a strong organisation that has great power. A turtle is associated with a very slow-moving or backward organisations. In researching the image that an organisation has in public consciousness one can well see how the technique might be brought into play. But even then, why not ask people how they see a bank, or an oil company, rather than what animal they associate with the organisation? Such techniques would seem only to introduce another variable, the meaning of which one cannot be sure of. Even Greenbaum admits: 'Some participants at first react to this type of exercise with a reasonably negative attitude, feeling that it is silly. (Greenbaum 1993:115)

There may be a temptation by academics to be overly influenced by the success that commercial researchers have had with focus groups and the claims that they make for them. David Morgan in his commentary on the history of focus groups recognises their origins in sociology, but also points to the special role that market research has played in their adoption and development: 'Returning the focus group technique to social science research will thus require considerable borrowing and considerable innovation.' He sensibly notes, however, as if to offer a warning of the danger of straightforward imitation, that the issues market researchers have addressed 'bear little resemblance to the questions that social scientists usually investigate'. (Morgan 1988:10) This is so only to a certain extent. The prefixing of the term market to research understandably conjures images of product research, corporate imagery research and so on, but a lot of research undertaken in the commercial domain, and for which focus groups are used, is social research that has close proximity to work undertaken in the academy. However, it is certainly true that in certain areas academic researchers have little or nothing to learn from their market research cousins.

The adoption of focus groups by market research companies, and the contribution they have made to company revenue, has meant an increased search for new areas of application. For example, one of the more recent additions in America has been their adoption by the legal profession 'as a vehicle to help litigators improve the overall quality of the cases they are preparing for trial.' (Greenbuam 1993:xiii) Market research as a seller of a service as well as a provider of knowledge is constantly on the look-out for new techniques as an aid to sell their services, and not necessarily as a way of improving the quality of the knowledge provided. This is not to say that market researchers are necessarily duplicitous, since they are wrapped up in occupational ideological practices that ferment a genuine belief that the provision of the former assist the creation of the latter, that new techniques will always create not just new knowledge, but better knowledge. Thus it is interesting that in surveying the field Greenbaum notes the many changes that have taken place in the use of focus groups by market research:

> Researchers have come to understand the need for more professional recruiting, better physical plants, and a more of a partnership between the moderator, the client, and the focus group facility. At the present time, the weakest link in the focus group chain is probably the facility.

The term 'better physical plant' is resonant with ideas of truly professionalising a method. The incorporation, furthermore, of a language drawn from engineering helps consolidate focus groups as a specialised activity to be undertaken only by those with access to the means of production. However, a room equipped with two-way mirrors is totally unnecessary for academic researchers, although this is beginning to change along with increasing video taping of groups, and indeed is not all that much used by market researchers in Britain. The two-way mirror, or to use Greenbaum's term, the better 'physical plant', is purely for the benefit of the client who may wish too watch the proceedings, and has nothing to do with the quality of the responses received from participants to the group. In American market research technocratising focus group research has even progressed to a state where the moderator might be equipped with an ear-piece to receive instruction from the client. One can understand this in terms of the moderator-client relationship in market research, but even so to have a client watch focus group in operation is damaging to the method. If one has moderator demand, one now has client demand. That is, 'tricks' are engaged in by the moderator and a performance staged that is for the benefit of the client, not for eliciting information. Indeed, the common practice by some market researchers of always recruiting ten participants, not nine, not eleven, has nothing to do with preferred numbers for facilitating group dynamics or interviewer control, but so that innumerate clients taking notes can easily put percentages on responses.

The requirements of the academic are, in general, different from that of the market researcher. To begin with, practically any location (physical plant) will suffice to conduct focus groups, but in my experience to achieve the most relaxed atmosphere it is better to conduct them in a private dwelling, rather than in a hotel, the upstairs room of a public house, community centre or other such public place. Wherever the focus group takes place the participants need to feel relaxed and be able to offer their contribution in a non-threatening climate. Indeed, focus group discussions can at times become quite heated. Participants can say things that in more calm moments they would not have said, and may later come to regret being so open. Focus group research does in fact throw up special ethical difficulties that require attention.

Eight

The Ethics of Research

Although psychologists sometimes recruit participants to their experiments by providing limited information to disguise the nature of the experiment, it is not good policy, even ethics aside, to do so with focus group research. A psychologist, for example, may recruit respondents by arguing that they are attempting to discover people's ability to recall sequences of numbers, that the test is one of memory, when in fact the test may be to record responses to frustration. Before recall is complete, the subject might be constantly interrupted by the experimenter to break concentration so that after each interruption the subject must go back to the beginning and re-start the whole re-call process again. Only at the end of the experiment is the subject told the real purpose of the research.

It is up to psychologists to work out their own ethical position on 'lying', but they might well argue that without the professional lie many experiments would be impossible. They might also argue that not only is the lie essential for the completion of the experiment, but the fact that the subject is lied to makes no difference to the results. This is not so, however, with the focus group. To lie to the participants about the nature of the focus group at the time of recruitment is only likely to create hostility when they discover that the topic of conversation to be discussed is not the one that they were led to believe. They might feel uncomfortable with the 'real' topic, and had they known what they were to discuss at the point of recruitment refused to attend. Thus even if not on ethical grounds, then on pure methodological grounds it is wrong not to tell participants what the subject is for discussion. This does not mean, and should not mean in all circumstances, that one tells them what the research is about, but it does mean that one should tell them the area or issue that will form the focus of the discussion. Thus if the purpose of the research was to examine people's attitudes to sexist advertising on television, it would be well to say that they are required to examine advertising on television, if not necessarily the exact purpose of the research. If, prior to attendance, participants know the aim of the research they may well discuss it with friends and thus run the risk that the participant's thinking had been 'set' beforehand. Such pre-discussion involves the danger that the participant will respond in the group with the knowledge that what they say will be the subject of enquiry on their next meeting with their friends. In such a situation one could not be sure what responses one was receiving: whether it is their own beliefs, the beliefs of friends, or the beliefs contaminated by the fear of judgmental decision from their friends.

Providing one has informed respondents of the area of discussion, as opposed to the aims of the research, then no ethical issues are really involved. Furthermore, not only has the framework of the agreed discussion been established before participation takes place, but the purpose of the research to some extent unfolds in the course of the discussion. Of course, the full purpose of the research may not become apparent during discussion, and it is a matter for the researcher whether to give a full explanation. Most usually this is done at the end of the discussion, but as ever with focus group research, firm principles cannot be established to cover all situations. For some topics and in some cases it might be best to inform the group in very detailed fashion what the purpose of the research is, but, holding in mind the comments in relation to moderator demand, in general it is best not to do so. If the participants are told the purpose of the research at the end of the session then such 'revelation' can form the focus of an end discussion if the researcher so wishes. It would be a mistake, however, to think that participants to focus groups necessarily share the researcher's enthusiasm for the intellectual purpose of the exercise; they often show a lack of interest in knowing the overall intention of the project.

An ethical problem does arise with focus group research, however, particularly in media research, when material shown is very upsetting or disturbing. The Institute of Communications Research studies examining people's responses to the portrayal of violence in fictional and non-fictional programmes presented this problem. Our study into responses to the coverage of the Gulf War is a case in point. The Institute had material that had not been broadcast by television because the images were considered too horrific. This material clearly upset quite a few participants who viewed it. In one group a sixteen-year-old girl broke down and cried. Up until the showing of the footage of burnt bodies she had been a most lively participant to the group, but after seeing such pictures could not go on. Although we had warned the discussants prior to showing the footage that some of the scenes were very grisly indeed, it afforded no protection in this instance. Following this incident the researchers were much more careful in the type of warning given, and very precise about when, if they wished, participants might avert their eyes. Nevertheless, despite such care, the ethical problem still remained of 'requesting' people to view harrowing footage.

Ethically we felt in the right, but then it was in our interest to feel so. It was our judgement that the issue of the representation of war by television was a socially important matter, especially given the outcry by those against the war that the 'clean' pictures made available to the public sanitised the conflict, and prolonged the war by not leading to public revulsion. The question was, should television companies in possession of pictures showing the absolute horrors of war refuse to broadcast them on the grounds that viewers would find them too upsetting? The Institute repeated such work in relation to the conflict in Bosnia. The reason for doing so was the same. At the end of each focus group conducted about the Gulf War and the Bosnian conflict discussants were asked if we were right to expose them to such material. They considered that it was right of the research team to show such material. In short, they understood the purpose of the research and considered it of sufficient importance to justify showing such material in the context of an 'experiment'.

However, it is not just that the participants to the research that might need 'protection' from the experimenter or moderator; the moderator may require 'protection' from the group discussants. Some hold views that a moderator might find very upsetting indeed. There is also an ethical question of what to do when offensive views are expressed, since by appearing not to challenge them the moderator gives support to those views to the rest of the group, and thus reinforces them through a public circulation of acceptance and non-correction.

Objectional Views

Ellen Seiter presents 'a case study of a troubling interview' where the views of two respondents that she interviewed upset her. She took exception to their views towards television and the manner in which they regarded her. She describes herself as 'an American film and television professor in my early 30s' and her co-interviewer, Hans Borchers, as 'a German American studies professor in his early 40s'. Their subjects were two men aged 62 and 55, retired graphic artists who shared accommodation together. What bothered Seiter and Borchers about the two men was the way they spoke of the 'other', that is, other television viewers. Seiter, close to the beginning of the article, sets the scene:

> Throughout the interview, it was uppermost in these men's minds that we were academics. For them, it was an honour to talk to us and an opportunity to be heard by persons of authority and standing. They made a concerted effort to appear cosmopolitan and sophisticated. For them, our visit offered a chance to reveal their own personal knowledge, and their opinions about society and the media. They had no interest whatsoever in offering us interpretative, textual readings of television programs, as we wanted them to do. In fact, they exhibited a kind of 'incompetence' as viewers in this regard: they were unable to reproduce critical categories common to *TV Guide* and academic television criticism. All fiction shows could be labelled soap opera: situation comedies and medical shows, alike. Yet many television shows were seen by Mr Howe to conform to a more personal, master narrative about the painful relations between generations, which stemmed from his own bitter experience as a father....
>
> This interview made me personally uncomfortable, because of my age and my gender, and because of my status as an academic..... When we

talk about examining our own subjectivities as researchers, we also need to ask what it means to ask someone about television viewing. Television watching can be a touchy subject, precisely because of its associations with a lack of education, with idleness, and unemployment, and its identification as an 'addiction' of women and children. This interview exemplifies the defensiveness that men and women unprotected by academic credentials may feel in admitting to television viewing in part because of its connotations of feminine passivity, laziness, and vulgarity. (Seiter 1990:62)

It is difficult enough to understand why Seiter would expect two retired graphic artists to reproduce critical categories common to 'academic television criticism', but even more difficult to understand why she gets cross at this fact. Seiter does not like what the two subjects of her interview have to say, because they appear not to 'behave' themselves by failing to address issues in the manner that she wishes, and because of the way that they talk about other viewers. The key to understanding the 'problem' that Seiter and her colleague faced in conducting the interviews is given in her statement:

This interview also exemplifies the extent to which television as a 'mass' form is viewed in a very different way by those without access to college education and more authentic bourgeois culture. For working-class and petit-bourgeois viewers, television is alternatively relied on as a source of education and condemned for its failure to confirm and to replicate experience. (Seiter 1990:63)

One would have thought that as categories of organisation the terms bourgeois and petit-bourgeois were singly inappropriate in the context of American society. What could they possibly refer to as descriptive categories either objectively or subjectively in an American setting? They appear to be nothing more than intellectual constructs that Seiter has drawn from European cultural sociology – France in particular judging by her fondness for Bourdieu – to be transposed and imposed as the intellectual framework for her American study. What Seiter displays is an insensitivity to the world around her, and a dismissiveness of the experiences of others who fail to conform to what she approves. It is this imposition of one's own feelings that must be avoided at all costs in doing interview work. In Seiter's case one not only has the imposition of thinking that is misplaced in the context of her subject matter, but a readiness to condemn that cannot possibly be conducive to 'good listening'. At one point Mr H, one of the subjects of the interview, gives an account of his own research activities. Seiter comments: 'This story about research unsanctioned by the academy convinced me that Mr H was a crackpot'. (Seiter 1990:65)

Often in sociological research, particularly in studying cults, one comes across descriptions of the world that as an outsider to the beliefs held by the cult one finds strange. But one would not automatically engage in clinical descriptions of those who held the belief, even the 'common-sense' clinical descriptions denoted by the term 'crackpot'. In my own work with Michael Tracey examining Mary Whitehouse's organisation The National Viewers and Listeners Association, we came across statements referring to 'living in the end times' and 'dark forces at work'. (Tracey and Morrison 1979) Strange as such statements seemed to us as explanations by which to account for social ills, it would have been wrong, on analytical grounds, to label such people as crackpots. There were other and better explanations to be offered as to why members of NVALA should see the world in such ways.

It is when we come to Seiter's account of her two subjects making a joke that the lessons to draw from her article come into full view. Seiter and her colleague, Hans Borchers, asked Mr H and Mr D, the two subjects, if they talked with other viewers about television. Evidently Mr D talked about a friend who was 'a real fan, who arranges her lunch hour around them.' The exchange as recorded by Seiter is as follows:

> *Mr H:*   Well, you know, where the word came from... it's actually true... it's a shortening of the word fanatic.

> *Mr D:*   She was brought up with soaps, because her mother, Mrs Applebaum, a lovely lady, I really love her... she was an avid watcher... she was a housewife and this was her passion.

> *Mr H:*   Is that the lady that every time she coughs or sneezes bubbles come out of her mouth? He said she was brought up on soaps...

Seiter then says, 'Hans, cutting short the joke which we obviously did not find funny, broke in to ask whether soaps have changed, commenting that most of our interviews had been with younger people'. (Seiter 1990:66) Why cut short the joke? And why did they 'obviously' not find it funny? The insertion of 'obviously' to describe their reaction suggests that Seiter and Borchers considered the joke to be in bad taste, and evidence of how uncomfortable the researchers felt in the company of these two men, something that Seiter confesses to and which indeed is the subject of the whole paper, giving rise on her part to 'profound methodological questions' about 'unstructured interviewing'. (Seiter 1990:62)

Although it is difficult on reading the paper to see where the profundity of the methodological questions rest, the point to extract, be it in relation to structured or unstructured interviews, is that a researcher cannot afford the type of 'sensitivity' that Seiter allows herself; one cannot afford to be so insensitive to people's values and judgements simply because they do not square with one's own. One cannot, in other words, afford to be so precious, and certainly not so righteous when engaging with people.

It is not the interviewer's job to 'cure' the world, nor, no matter how offensive one might find the remarks that are made, to adopt a corrective posture towards the subjects. Subjects have given up their time, in the belief that you are interested in what they have to say on a subject, and to let one's displeasure show through is discourteous. More important, such 'hurt intervention' defeats the object of the interview in that one is not getting the subject's actual feelings. In a group discussion the only time to intervene and show that a statement is not acceptable is when what is being said is threatening either physically or emotionally to another member of the group. This situation could not possibly have applied in Seiter's case, where those interviewed were house-mates. One should never intervene to protect one's own sensibilities. If as a researcher one feels so sensitive to statements that offend one's own political values that one cannot bear not to offer corrective statements, then do not do group discussions. In fact, if one is likely to become 'involved' in the manner described, one in effect is disqualified from ever becoming a skilful moderator. If that is the case then some other research methodology ought to be sought that is more in keeping with one's temperament. One is simply not going to get the best out of a group; one may even get 'distorted' data.

Keeping Calm

Before discussing in more detail the role of the moderator when faced by unpleasant comments, two examples will be given from the work of the Institute of Communications Studies. In the most recent study we wished to know reaction to real-life television dramas, and what the limits were in such programmes for the disclosing of personal information. (Kieran, Morrison and Svennevig 1997) We wished in particular to know what rights the media had to 'expose' people, and what right the audience had in receiving information about people's private lives. In nearly all of the focus groups the actor Hugh Grant's encounter with a prostitute surfaced. The question was raised about the right the public had to information about Grant's girl friend, Liz Hurley. It was a question of the right to privacy and the status of the individual involved. There was much clever and funny ribaldry in all groups, both male and female, of a sexist nature. However, one working-class man said: 'I don't understand him. He could go into any bar and tug anyone he wanted. What was he doing going with a 'coon slag'?' The term 'slag' to describe a promiscuous woman is hardly politically correct, and there is no male equivalent, but nevertheless it is a term used by both women and men. Thus one gets used to hearing such a term in group discussion if the conversation drifts to sexual behaviour. But the combination of this word with a particularly nasty racist term gave the statement a brutal offensiveness. Its use did not disturb the rhythm of the group in what was a quick flowing conversation, although one did momentarily detect in one participant a disapproving hesitancy in the way he continued with the point he was making.

From the moment the man had entered the room I had not liked his abrasive brashness, but now, following his sexist racist comment, I distinctly disliked him. I did not register my dislike or, I hope, give any signs of disapproval. No harm had been done: the group was performing well in a relaxed manner, and offering many insightful comments about the subject at hand, privacy and the right of exposure. A mental note was made, however, to freeze him out of conversation should the discussion stray again into an area that would allow the display of such racism. The focus of the group discussion was not race, therefore his racist comments, no doubt genuine expression of his feelings, were of no value to the research, and his contributions in that direction could easily be done without. Despite the dislike I had of him, something that my fellow moderator and I gave vent to together over a drink after the focus group, I did not bar him from contributing to the rest of the session.

Racist and sexist remarks tend to pepper the conversation of working-class men, and indeed, working-class women, even in group discussions that are not designed to examine such attitudes. However, special problems arise when the focus group is organised to investigate racial and sexual attitudes. The statements made can sometimes confront the researcher as an absolute onslaught on his or her sensibilities. If Seiter was made uncomfortable in the interview she described, how she would have fared in the following study is beyond imagination.

The Institute of Communication Studies conducted a study into the presentation of race on television and attitudes of viewers toward such presentations. To do so it was essential that we examined wider aspect of attitudes to race than responses to images appearing on television. A young psychologist, and an expert in scaling, was recruited from the Psychology Department of the university to sit in on the groups. During the ensuing discussions it came as a complete surprise to him that respondents would express themselves in the manner that they did. The participants were not told at the point of recruitment that the study wished to examine attitudes to the portrayal of race on television, but merely that we wished to know their attitudes to various television programmes. Each focus group began by asking participants what changes in the last few years they had noticed in the area where they lived, what they liked about the area where they lived, what were the good points and bad points of the area and so on. Without it having to be directly introduced by the moderator this line of questioning invariably brought to the surface the subject of ethnic minorities.

In one group of women, one of the participants, about nineteen years old, dressed in very modern style, immediately volunteered to the question of what changes had occurred in the area: 'nig-nogs, too many nig-nogs'. The unembarrassed presentation of this observation, plus the forcefulness of the delivery in one who looked so modern came as a surprise, no less than her descriptive category of an ethnic population, since the term she used is practically always reserved for West Indians, of whom there were none in her area, nor for many miles around.

The first problem any moderator faces in such a situation is to gather extra information on how terms are being used but without using the racist descriptors ready at hand as provided by the participants. One cannot say, 'which ethnic grouping are you referring to?' since the term 'ethnic' immediately springs the trap of moderator demand by showing one's own values in speech. Although one must admit that in this case so enthusiastic was she to express her opinions, and so self-confident in her delivery, that the influence of moderator demand may well have got lost in the passion of her own feelings. Yet, the use of the term 'ethnic', and the values associated with such a speech code, may not have been lost on other less forward members of the group. Thus the quizzical statement, 'you've lost me there' was sufficient to avoid her language, but lead to clarification on her part. Her term did not refer to West Indians, but to 'Pakis', a frequent term in the geographic recruitment area of the groups to cover residents from both India and Pakistan. Having established what she took to be a disadvantage of living in the area, questioning followed to establish the basis for her attitudes, in particular whether or not she knew any of the ethnic groups she referred to. Evidently she 'hung out' with quite a few Pakistani boys. To establish her familiarity with Pakistani boys she began a long discourse that would have done credit to a monologue of the most gifted stand-up comic. The rest of the group was riveted by the drama of her life as she unfolded her everyday doings. The most mundane experience was transformed to high drama in the way often only the working class can do in story-telling. She claimed she was a rock musician but had never performed in public because she always fell out with whatever band she joined before taking to the stage. This was not difficult to believe: rehearsals must have been a musical nightmare. She was a most sympathetic character and the rest of the group members who were slightly older than her were clearly warmed by her story-telling. But in the course of this opening account of her friendship with Pakistani youths she said that one day her neighbour had shouted from the upstairs window that she was a slut going with Pakistani lads. Prompted by the moderator to say what her response had been to this observation, since it was felt that she certainly would have had something to say, she informed the group that she had shouted back: 'I don't fuck Pakis, but your daughter fucks them'. Without drawing breath, she addressed the whole group by saying:, 'I mean, I'll fuck anybody, me, but I won't fuck a Paki'.

It was without doubt the most outrageous set of statements I have ever come across in doing focus group research, and a difficult situation to handle. Her statement about her selection of sexual partners made other members of the group drop their jaws. But it had been funny in the way that one knew one shouldn't find it, didn't want to, but couldn't help it. It was her story-telling. One or two of the group sat in stony silence, but most were suffering the shock of forced laughter, embarrassed by their own response.

The problem was not one of approval or disapproval, but of not showing either. After all, this was focus group research about racial attitudes, and she had not threatened anyone else in the group. She had certainly assaulted their sensibilities, but this was accompanied at all times with comic flair. Yet comedy could not, and cannot, disguise the racist nature of the statements, indeed, comedy is one way of 'acceptably' packaging racism, and thus all the more dangerous for that. Her entry into the discussion did open up the group for a discussion of racial representation that would not have been accomplished so well without her presence.

It was not only the white groups who showed virulent racism. The Pakistani men displayed racism allied to sexism. Some of the younger Pakistani men made it very clear what they would do to a white youth who went out with their sister. One or two ran newspaper shops and said that they enjoyed looking at soft porn magazines of naked women, but only if they were white or not of the same race as themselves. It was totally wrong as far as they were concerned, and they were vehement on this point, for Pakistani women to parade their nudity in magazines, but quite acceptable for white women to do so.

The Detached Observer

The moderator when faced by comments that they do not agree with or might even find repulsive has no option but to adopt the role of the detached observer and attempt to capture in the most natural way possible the feelings of those in the group. For the purpose of research the white racist and the black racist or any other must be accorded the same listening rights, even though in private, because of their different access to power, one might be more politically concerned about racist sentiments emanating from one group rather than another.

To be politically correct may endow the individual with feelings of purpose, even with feelings of superiority. It may even allow the individual a certain patrician laziness, as the efforts of rigorous research are deemed unnecessary in the face of a knowledge drawn from the 'ought' of ideology rather than the 'is' of existence. Guilt at a privileged position is one of the sources of political correctness within the academy, especially in America, but the dangers offered by political correctness in focus group research, as shown by the above examples, is clear. One cannot afford, simply because of some notion of correct behaviour, for the moderator to side with a preferred form of linguistic expression, at least not at the site of the research. Nor, it must be added, should critical inspection of what is being said be any less for those groups which the moderator favours or wishes to support than is the case with groups whom the moderator might not favour. Ethnic groups, or marginalised groups such as homosexuals, who might be supposed to be hold politically correct attitudes and who in the course of discussion show politically incorrect attitudes must not have their comments erased or altered to project them in a valorising light. This is one of the great dangers of focus group research, that they easily lend themselves to dishonest usage. To be politically correct is not to be empirically correct.

One might think that through careful attention to language one could help make less difficult the lives of those individuals who failed to share the benefit of personal security offered by normative beliefs or practices, but then find that such individuals themselves transgressed the codes of 'correct' language, and did so to such an appalling degree that if the expressions fell into common usage it would make the lives of those to whom the language refers more difficult. Indeed, this is precisely the case in one such study conducted by the Institute of Communications Studies.

During the course of focus group research into the attitudes of gay men and women towards sexual representations on television, the language used was not politically correct even though these are two groups where politically correct language is supposed to be common. For example, in the course of one discussion with gay men in London one participant referred to lesbians as fish. Although never having heard the term before, even to my untutored ear it struck a none too flattering, even possibly unpleasant, note. Rather than let the comment pass, I enquired to have the term explained. It transpired that it referred to the supposed vaginal odour – fishiness – they associated with lesbians. Had one operated within a framework of sympathy fuelled by sentiments of political correctness towards a sexual group that are the subject of harassment, and not pressed for an explanation of the term, then one would not have unearthed an attitude which then formed the basis of further examination into their attitudes to women in general. Their dislike of lesbians, for some members of this particular group, was revealed as a dislike of a whole category of humanity, women.

Although I had warmed to other groups of gay men that I had talked with in the course of the research project, I certainly did not like this group of London gay men, any more than I have liked racist groups. It was not their reference to other groups of individuals alone that formed the basis of the dislike. I did not find their attitude toward sex attractive, nor did I find the descriptions of their own sexual activity appealing, and this was nothing to do with the fact that they were homosexuals. I would have found the descriptions of their behaviour on Hampstead Heath unattractive in any group of individuals. They were not alone, since I have found other groups' views on sexual practices unattractive. For example, the attitudes of the members of Mary Whitehouse's moralist group, The National Viewers and Listeners Association, towards other groups, particularly homosexuals, I found particularly repugnant. However, the point to stress is that liking or disliking those interviewed, or a dislike of the language used by participants, ought not to interfere with the detached performance of the moderator.

Such detachment does not turn the subject into an object. It is an involved detachment. That is, through the detachment itself – the separation of one's personal identity from that which is being said – the moderator allows the individual to evolve their own story unhindered by the moral involvement of the listener in the story. This is not quite the detachment of the psychoanalyst; the moderator is having the 'patient' reveal things that you wish to know and that are not necessarily of any use to the patient themselves. Indeed, the whole practice of focus groups is selfish; that is, the research is not returned as a benefit to the individual in any direct manner. It may be a public benefit in some generalised sense though the circulation of ideas, or through beneficial policy implementation. But although the subject is the object of enquiry the method does not mean that the subject is objectified. What is being opposed here is an approach in which through political correctness, the individual is regarded as an object, not a reflexive individual whose experiences and accounts of their world are considered worthy of attention and understanding, but instead regarded as an objectified expression of a political position held by the researcher.

Playing with Meaning

The recent upsurge in the popularity of focus groups, and the likely increase in that popularity within media research following the rediscovery of the empirical audience, has within it very real dangers; indeed, it could well become a regressive rather than a progressive step in understanding the audience. For all the reasons given – leading questions, moderator demand, objection to statements made and thus ignoring of statements or not following the offensive statement to explore the meanings behind the statement, downgrading comments by objectionable groups or by objectionable individuals within the group to the status of non-valid informers, the ignoring of certain politically disapproved of comments made by groups that the researcher politically approves of – the focus group is a method that is easily converted, either intentionally or unintentionally, to the political or even theoretical stance of the researcher, especially when used as a stand-alone method.

It is those media researchers who so far have eschewed quantitative methods, but now wish to use focus groups as a stand-alone method, that present the greatest risk to the abuse of the method. For those in cultural and media studies who have contented themselves with the theoretical audience, either as an introspective theoretical construct or arrived at through textual analysis as 'the reader', to now engage in an empirical examination of the audience through focus group research means that they can have their theory and they can have empirical data and neither may touch each other. In other words, to use focus group research as a single method may not produce any advance on understanding the audience over past methods, because unless conducted in a detached manner it will merely reproduce past thinking.

In the fullest sense this is unlikely since to confront real people with real responses as opposed to imagined people and their imagined responses is practically always to be disturbed from existing positions to some degree. It does not of course mean that this 'disturbance' will lead to any great understanding should the researcher not recognise the disjuncture between the 'found' and the 'given' understanding brought to the research site. Nor is it to argue that 'understanding' is given by the participants. The observations made, the presentation of feelings provided, and the subjects' interpretations all have to be made sense of by theoretical formulation. The difficulty of focus group research, however, if used as a single method, is that they are not very good for testing what might be going on in the focus group. For that one needs to bring into play other methods to provide external checks.

Even for testing theory, unless the benefits of the focus group as outlined previously are dispensed with by turning them more into a laboratory experiment, the flow of conversation directed by the moderator, especially if the group is not well focused on a particular stimulus, can confirm most positions the moderator might hold about the subject under discussion. It is like the talking of a young child: they chatter so much that at some point they are going to say something of sense that the loving parent then takes as a sign that their offspring is as clever as they hoped they were, when what needs examining is the number and nature of the stupid remarks they make when offset against the clever remarks, not something most parents would care to engage in but might notice in the child of another parent and use to confirm, by comparison, the cleverness of their own child

While one might not wish to claim certainty as a central principle of social science, it has to be the case that the rendition of what is 'happening' that is attained by the method employed is a superior version than that offered by another method or no method at all. If this is not the case then why use a particular method in preference to some other method? Different methods when applied to the same phenomena will give different understandings of the phenomena, indeed will help construct what the phenomena is, but the method adopted must have some claim to superiority in some direction to be worthy of adoption. This is not say that one does not recognise the pitfalls of the method. But for an empirical worker to over-theorise the problem of knowledge is the death of activity. At times one must proceed, and this would be the case for much scientific activity, with an awareness of the limited or provisional nature of empirical knowledge. That should not, however, simply because of circumscribed confidence lead to a lack of trust in the method or the abandonment of method altogether. If that is not the case then it is better to find a discipline or field of activity where such questioning forms the base of the activity itself and leave empirical investigation alone.

Methodology as a Gender Issue

Although it would be wrong to say that feminist researchers as a whole favour qualitative research over quantification, qualitative research has been proposed as more suitable for a feminist sociology that quantification, and it has even been suggested that quantification itself is masculine. Sheila Riddell states: 'The debate about feminism and the ethics of research starts as soon as a decision has to be made about which methods to use.' After noting that 'the question of what constitutes acceptable working methods for feminists has been hotly disputed', Riddell mentions her own anguish in deciding on procedures:

236

It was some time before I was able to convince myself, through trying out various approaches in the field and reflecting on these experiences, that there was nothing either intrinsically pro-feminist in any of these methods, and what mattered above all were the values implicit in the conduct of the research.... I initially had a very hard task convincing myself that my choice of methods was not at variance with feminist research. Ultimately, however, I felt that my use of quantitative as well as qualitative methods could be justified on the grounds that, far from being mutually exclusive, they could be used in a complementary fashion. Data gathered by the use of multiple strategies can be both sensitive to people's lived experiences, and enable more generalised statements about relationships between variables to be made. (Riddell 1989:78,79,80)

Clearly the question for feminist researchers of what methodology to adopt is far from a settled matter. In other words it would be an injustice to feminist scholarship, and to the variety of thought within it, to force it into a specific practice for the purpose of intellectual argument. Instead, I simply wish to take up certain points of view within feminist scholarship that have important implications for the practice of focus group research. I will draw primarily on the debate on feminist methodology that was carried out in the pages of the spring issue of *Sociology* in 1992 between Martyn Hammersley, Caroline Ramazanoglu and Loraine Geslthorpe.

Hammersley's position is that while some of the arguments are convincing the overall case for a feminist methodology is not. He begins:

It is widely accepted among feminists that feminism implies a distinctive approach to enquiry. Some see this in relatively concrete terms, for instance as a commitment to qualitative and a rejection of quantitative methods. More common, though, has been the argument that it is at the level of methodological and epistemological assumptions that the distinctiveness of a feminist approach to research is to be found. (Hammersley 1992:187)

In support of this last statement Hammersley references Sandra Harding (1987) and Judith Cook and Mary Fonow (1986). Cook and Fonow identify five basic epistemological principles that scholars have discussed in analysing feminist methodology in the field of sociology. They include:

(1)...the necessity of continuously and reflexively attending to the significance of gender and gender symmetry as a basic feature of all social life, including the conduct of research; (2) the centrality of consciousness-raising as a specific methodological tool and as a general orientation or 'way of seeing'; (3) the need to challenge the norm of objectivity that assumes that the subject and object of research can be separated from one another and that personal and/or grounded experiences are unscientific; (4) concerns for the ethical implications of feminist research and recognition of the exploitation of women as objects of knowledge; and (5) emphasis on the empowerment of women and transformation of patriarchal social institutions through research. (Cook and Fonow 1986:5)

Not all the above are 'epistemological principles' as claimed, but rather political goals to be achieved through research. However, the principle that has strict implications for the conducting of focus group research is the second: 'the centrality of consciousness-raising as a specific methodological tool and as a general orientation or 'way of seeing'. Cook and Farrow in unpacking this principle engage in some very mystical thinking indeed, especially in their talk of 'a double vision of reality' as an outcome of feminist scholars 'being in but not of society' – a meaningless statement if there ever was one. We learn: 'Scholars who *possess* [my italics] the double vision of reality are also in a better position to understand various responses to oppression, particularly the contradictions between action and consciousness'. (Cook and Fonow 1986:7) The notion of a contradiction, in the sense of a finding which does not conform to what one expects is of course that which Paul Lazarsfeld criticised Theodor Adorno for when using the term paradoxical: 'Because the fact does not correspond to your assumptions'. Although Cook and Fonow are not against quantification as such they are wary of research 'which overemphasises quantification', that 'forces the researcher to pose structural questions about action while ignoring the subjective dimension of behaviour, as well as the contradiction between action and consciousness'.

Consciousness Raising

Understanding action, which always has a subjective aspect to it, is not something survey research is especially equipped to handle. This is something most methodologists would recognise, be they feminists or not. However, given the emphasis on subjectivity it is not surprising that feminist scholars in general would tend towards qualitative rather than quantitative research, and one of those methods is group discussions, but used for the specific purpose of consciousness-raising. Cook and Fonow write:

> Consciousness-raising as a specific methodological tool has been advocated by a number of feminist sociologists. (Mies, 1983; Stanley and Wise, 1983; Reinharz, 1983) One way this can be done is to examine situations that typically produce changes in consciousness, such as divorce, unemployment, widowhood, infertility, rape, physical abuse, and sexual harassment. Studying crisis situations increases the likelihood that the researcher and subject will relate during a more self-conscious 'click' moment. 'Only when there is a rupture in the "normal" life of a woman... is there a chance for her to become conscious of her condition'. (Mies 1983:125) The rupture with normalcy serves to demystify the 'naturalness' of patriarchal relations and enables the subject to view reality in a different way. (Cook and Fonow 1986:8)

It is difficult here to see where research begins and political agitation ends. It is not absolutely clear whether we are to learn about the nature of society through the experiences of women, or whether women through their own experiences are to learn about the nature of society. Perhaps both. But whichever way, it is to be accomplished by the association of women with the researcher. In such a situation methodology appears to become another word for 'guidance'. Yet the assumption is made that for this 'methodology' to work it is best conducted at specific points that 'typically produce changes in consciousness' so that the 'rupture with normalcy serves to demystify the "naturalness" of patriarchal relations and enables the subject to view reality in a different way'. The situation of widowhood is taken as one of these points of rupture that enables the subject to view reality in a different way.

However, it is not that widowhood 'enables' the widowed to view reality in a different way, but that the death of someone close actually does mean that the bereaved see reality in a different way, for the very reason that reality has shifted to include meanings that were previously absent. What is assumed is that now that the individual is on her own she is in a position to see things that she may not have been in a position to see before, namely, the nature of patriarchal society or rather the mystified 'naturalness' of patriarchal relations. But in fact the centre of her grief is that the world she now exists in is no longer 'natural'. Let us look at this a little bit further. Death is both a physical and a social fact, and it is the social facts of death that can raise problems for the maintenance of reality. Indeed, we often speak of someone going mad with grief at the loss of someone close. That 'madness' is not simply despair born of heartache, but derangement born of not being able to locate oneself any longer in what was once a taken-for-granted certainty of existence.

This unreality, or madness, is not due to the fact that the bereaved contemplates the nature of being and the transient nature of his or her own biography, although that may be the case, but that the world has become unstable by the sudden removal of a point of certainty. The world is no longer firm, but wobbles. The individual is unhinged by the collapse of those structures that provided reality or sense to the world. For sanity to return, reality must be rebuilt, but on the basis of providing meanings that allow the incorporation of the deceased into the present, sufficient to stabilise the personality by anchorage in a set of meanings that are shared by others. The world must become recognisable again, and it becomes recognisable by being given collective authority. The madness, or lack of reality, is brought about by the sudden fracturing of the individual's existence, and in doing so separates him or her from occupation of the same world as others. Sanity returns only when the individual joins once more with the shared reality of others. Chaos becomes normos through common definitions of how the world is constructed, and that is achieved through interaction with others based on collective assumptions about the world. Indeed, the collective assumptions are produced by interaction with others in the common enterprise of living.

Without direction or manipulation of the situation that the widowed occupies, there is no reason to believe that she would come to see the world with a feminist perspective, more likely the opposite. Indeed to 'view reality in a different way', really means no more than to view reality from the perspective of the feminist researcher, and that in crisis periods people who have been hurt are vulnerable to suggestions about how the world really is. This is certainly a research finding, but one which if obtained through experimental method in the psychologist's laboratory, and not clothed in some liberationist terms, would be greeted by howls of protest.

Consciousness-raising 'as a specific methodological tool' is given clarification by Cook and Fonow:

> Another application of this method is through the use of specific consciousness-raising techniques, such as role playing, rap groups, simulations, and psycho-drama, in a more self-conscious, deliberate manner. These approaches have provided feminist researchers with a way to tap women's collective consciousness as a source of data and have provided participants in the research project with a way to confirm the experiences of women which have often been denied as real in the past. (Reinharz 1983) Meis suggests a shift from individual interviews towards group discussions held over a period of time to obtain more diverse data and also to help female subjects 'overcome their structural isolation in their families and to understand that their individual sufferings have social causes'. (Mies 1983:128; Cook and Fonow 1986:8)

What we see in Cook and Fonow's account of consciousness raising as methodology, and especially in the reference to group discussions, is the danger that such an approach may in the future be carried across by feminist researchers into focus group research. Merton and Kendall have already been quoted as saying that the focus group must not become a debating society, or the moderator become a propagandist, (Merton and Kendall 1946:547) but if the 'methodology' suggested above is brought into play the focus group becomes a political debating society whose purpose is to raise consciousness, although admittedly at the same time 'to tap women's collective consciousness as a source of data'.

Focus group research has enough difficulties as a method of procedure without adding to them by a deliberately introduced political purpose, the 'liberation' of the individual. This is not to argue that it might not be a valid hope that through sociological knowledge the individual may benefit in some sense, but it is to argue against seeing methodology itself as a tool of liberation rather than as a set of procedures by which we come to establish understandings of the world.

The Researcher and the Researched?

If we now return to Hammersley we see the real problems that focus group research faces if the moderator moves from the role of 'detached concern' advocated by Merton and his colleagues, (Merton *et al* 1956:179) in the direction of a non-hierarchical relationship between the researcher and the researched that some feminists demand. Hammersley comments, after a discussion of the validity of experience as against method:

> Following on from the previous point is the view that the relationship between the researcher and researched should be a reciprocal one, that 'hierarchical' distinctions between researcher and researched should be broken down. Thus, Oakley criticises prescriptions for interviewing that proscribe the researcher sharing personal experiences with interviewees or providing aid to them. (Oakley 1981) Similarly Reinharz (1983:186) comments: 'as researchers, we should be interested only in information derived from authentic relations', by which she means relationships where 'genuineness is experienced by both parties'. (Hammersley 1992:189)

In this position focus groups as I have discussed them would be discounted on the grounds of a lack of authenticity, indeed, they would probably be seen as exploitative due to the hierarchical relationship structured into the encounter. The solution to hierarchy presented by some feminist researchers is, according to Hammerley's distillation of writing on feminist methodology, an 'equal participation of the people studied in the research process':

> Thus, Rienharz suggests that research subjects should participate in the analysis of the data so that it builds on what is meaningful to them as well as on what is significant to the researcher. (Reinharz 1983:183) And Meis advocates a version of the idea of conscientisation, the key characteristic of which is: 'that the study of oppressive reality is not carried out by experts but by the objects of the oppression. People who before were objects of research become subjects of their own research and action. This implies that scientists who participate in this study of the conditions of oppression must give their research tools to the people'. (Mies 1983:126; Hammersley 1992:189)

Why it should be assumed that the subjects of the research would wish to be involved in the analysis of the results is difficult to say. It is not their job to do so. I cannot imagine many of the women in the focus groups I have conducted, with two or three children and tired out by working full-time in poorly paid jobs, would wish to take on another job. But that is part of an unreality born of political mission. It also presumes that as a 'method' it is an improvement on other methods. That is, that it offers something superior to the situation where the participants clearly understand the situation they are in and freely give information to the researcher in their own words and using their own expressions drawn from their lived experiences. This presumed superiority in non-hierarchical arrangements forms the foundation to better research. But what does better mean?

> There seem to be three arguments underlying this rejection of hierarchy, though under certain conditions they coalesce. One is

> ethical: that only non-hierarchical relationships are legitimate among women, and therefore in research dealing with women. A second is methodological: that the truth will only be discovered via 'authentic' relations, hierarchy resulting in distortions of data. Finally, there is a practical recognition that if research is to be effective in consciousness-raising... then it may be necessary to involve the researched in the research process. (Hammersley 1992:190)

Even if a non-hierarchical situation were desirable it is not achievable in all circumstances. The assumption is, academics having a privileged position, that it is within the researcher's capacity to control the ordering of relationships. The academic may be privileged when compared with working-class women, and may then be in a position to suggest the nature of the research relationship, but the academic is not privileged by comparison with senior women executives in television, advertising or marketing. In facing such people the researcher is certainly not in a position to suggest the relationship that they desire; power is in the hands of the subjects of the research, not the researcher.

Women in senior posts in the media, advertising and marketing, and there are a considerable number, would not see themselves as downtrodden. Furthermore, given their seniority of position within a company there is nothing they would like more than to be involved in the analysis and writing up of the research; the difficulty often is to keep them from being involved, and to resist the pressure to 'change things'. Truth, in other words, would not be best established by their offers of help. It is not just, therefore, that the insistence of a methodology based on non-hierarchical relationships is a general impossibility, but to have it form a stricture of a methodology is to reduce the scope of social enquiry to those areas where it might be possible. What we then have in effect is a restriction on knowledge through the insistence on the adoption of a particular methodological practice; but that is always the danger if one overtly politicises the academy.

Intellectual Authority

From the very outset it has been argued that there is no single methodology by which to understand the social world, and for that reason I have been harsh on those who have even suggested that one type of knowledge – quantitative versus qualitative – is superior to another type. Certain types of knowledge, gained by certain methods, can only be considered better than other types of knowledge gained by other methods depending on the area of enquiry and the intentions of the research. This is not a liberal plea of 'live and let live', but an argument that tolerance in research terms is methodologically sound, and that it works. That is, the object of enquiry is allowed a variety of approaches that is likely to provide a more powerful picture than a single method can provide. It also brings into call, through the use of different methodologies, different forms of intelligence that then allow reflection in general on the process of knowing.

At some point the researcher must claim intellectual authority. As Hammersley states:

> ...we must ask whether the researcher's exercise of control over the research process is necessarily, or even typically, against the interests of others, including those of the people studied. This is only obviously so if it is assumed that 'having a say' in decisions, all decisions, is an overriding interest in all circumstances. And it is not clear to me why we should assume that this is the case. As far as research is concerned, advocacy of this view often seems to be based on the assumption that research findings are simply an expression of opinion by the researcher, and that her opinion is no better than that of any other woman.

Hammersley continues his case for the claim of special authority attached to research, and although he does not say so specifically, he clearly has in mind that one of the reasons for making this claim is the understanding that is offered by method:

> It seems to me that research necessarily and legitimately involves a claim to intellectual authority, albeit of a circumscribed kind. That authority amounts to the idea that the findings of research are, on average, less likely to be in error than information from other sources, and this stems from the operation of the research community in subjecting research findings to scrutiny and thereby detecting and correcting errors.... The point is simply that it is rational to give them [research findings] more attention than the opinions of people who have no distinctive access to relevant information. In short, research is not the only source of intellectual authority and its authority is limited and does not automatically imply validity, but research does inevitably involve a claim to such authority. (Hammersley 1992:197)

Research inevitably involves a claim to authority. One might argue that the role of the academy in 'correcting errors' is somewhat over-played since those whose role it is to correct might well come from the same field of correction as the researcher, and therefore share the same assumptions of correctness as the researcher who submits his or her work for inspection. However, the fact is that the research is open to critical inspection, and inspection is an institutionalised part of research as a social practice. Thus any piece of research has to be defended, even through the bow strings of the archers, for the reasons given, may at times be somewhat slack.

One concern is that focus group research does not leave itself open to good critical inspection. Focus group research involves a relatively private collection of data, but to collapse hierarchy altogether would not just lessen the possibility of critical inspection, but highlight the danger of not knowing who is responsible for the findings, and indeed, what the status of the findings amount to. Consequently Hammersley extends the notion of intellectual authority by suggesting that authority also involves duty or responsibility:

'The other side of the claim to intellectual authority is an obligation on the part of the researcher to ensure that, as far as possible, the information is reliable, and this responsibility cannot be shifted on to the people studied'. (Hammersley 1992:198)

In replying to Hammersley, both Ramzanoglu and Gelsthorpe point out that many of the points that Hammersley makes are subject to intense debate by feminists themselves. It is clear, however, in reading Ramazanoglu's rather sharp rejoinder to Hammersley that different worlds are in operation. She argues that Hammersley:

> ... does not seem to see his own place in the research process as a gendered one, and so treats his conception of reason not as an historical construction but as neutral and presumably gender free.... Hammersley has chosen to evaluate feminist methodologies without even considering the feminist critique of the Enlightenment dualisms on which these methodologies are based, and through which the male dominance of sociological knowing is identified.

> Hammersley's argument depends on a methodological position which feminists have analysed and rejected. That is, on the assumption that while value-neutrality is not possible, objectivity is separable from and superior to subjectivity, just as mind is to body, and reason to emotion. What one means by feminist methodology depends in part on which authors one takes as examples, but it seems particularly insensitive in an appraisal of feminist methodologies to ignore the onslaught by feminists on prevailing conceptions of rationality and objectivity and the whole conception of male-dominated and male defined relevance in the public domain. (Ramazanoglu 1992:208)

A different rationality concerning the approach to knowledge is in evidence here. For Ramazanoglu the project is one of 'seeking ways of knowing which avoid subordination'. Her consideration is that: 'There is no alternative to political commitment in feminist or any other ways of knowing. Since knowing is a political process, so knowledge is intrinsically political'. (Ramazanoglu 1992:210)

While there might not be an alternative to political commitment in feminists' ways of knowing it is difficult to follow why there is no alternative to political commitment in other ways of knowing. One might have thought one alternative would be a commitment to establishing truth by sets of procedures that are taken as capable of establishing truth. The statement by Ramzanoglu that since knowing is a political process then it follows that knowledge is intrinsically political, is wrong; one does not follow from the other. The act of knowing may be a political process in that it involves interventions with others, but that does not mean that the knowledge which is obtained is political by virtue of the act of obtaining it. For example, the activity of organising a laboratory physics experiment might be considered political in that it consists of a hierarchy of relationships among the team of experimenters, but it is difficult to see how that then makes the knowledge gained political. Even if it is said that something has a political loading that does not mean it is fully loaded with the political. The danger of such reasoning is that because social research often does have political implications, then research is seen as a political act and scholarship a political activity. Once that has occurred then a different logic comes into play and anything goes in the pursuit of the political goal.

However, my purpose in entering the choppy waters into which Hammerseley plunged was not to comment on feminist methodology in any general way, but to draw attention to an aspect of it that has relevance for focus group research, namely, the non-hierarchical arrangement of research. Gelsthorpe, in her response to Hammersley, comments:

> In some respects I am puzzled as to why Hammersley does not begin his discussion of hierarchy with his concluding points, that some feminists recognise the complexity of issues. Indeed, there is some potential for assuming from his writing that there is *a* feminist position on *all* these issues and to this end Hammersley may not be doing them justice. This reflects his overall conclusion that there isn't a convincing case for a feminist methodology. Who said there was? Feminists have expressed methodological preferences, some of which are more obviously in sympathy with feminists' aims, but as within different disciplines, there has been no widely acknowledged consensus on methodology. Hammersley has thus demolished a case that never really was. (Gelsthorpe 1992:217)

It would be as surprising if feminists researchers did have a consensus on methodology, as it would be that they had a consensus on feminist politics; such matters are always the subject of critical inspection and debate. But part of what Hammersley was attempting was to elucidate what he saw as some of the central distinctions of feminist methodology, one of which was the non-hierarchical relationship of the research setting. Gelsthorpe, even here, although not disagreeing that such a situation is a preferred one, points to awareness within feminist scholarship of the difficulties and problems raised by such an approach:

> They [feminists] are aware that the dismantling of power differentials between women is one thing; between female researchers and men who are the researched potentially quite another. (Morris and Gelsthorpe 1991) Thus whilst an 'interactive methodology' which abandons hierarchies may have obvious value in research on, by and for women, it is difficult to envisage feminist research which will change its aims, objectives and ways of proceedings because of the men involved (spouse batterers or rapists, for example). Others have highlighted the dilemmas and difficulties involved in the democratisation of the research process with considerable force. (Poland 1985; Barker 1986)

Indeed, Barker suggests that we are in danger of creating a 'false-equality' trap whereby feminists negate their possession of knowledge and skills in order to minimise differences between women. (Gelsthorpe 1992:216,217)

The creative work by feminists in the realm of methodology should not be ignored, but it is hoped that the idea of non-hierarchical research will be ignored by focus group researchers who wish to apply this 'recently' re-discovered method to areas of social research, and by media researchers in particular who have 'recently' re-discovered the empirical audience. The situation of the focus group, the informality of the proceedings, the provision of refreshments, and the friendly atmosphere that usually ensues, should not disguise the fact that to be successful they must be structured, and that the moderator or researcher is the key figure who guides the proceedings along a path that she or he wishes followed. It is not a situation for sharing experiences. There must be a separation of the researcher and the researched, although that does not exclude an 'involved distancing'. The distance is necessary to protect against the contamination of the findings by moderator demand, and the involvement is only the limited one of attempting to 'get inside' what is being said in order to understand the emotional and experiential wells from which the comments might come. And such understanding is achieved by giving regard to the significance of what they are saying. This does not mean that one respects the views that are presented. Indeed, in some of the examples given of statements made by participants, it would be difficult to respect such views. The situation itself, the research setting and the procedural ground of the method, must, however, be respected and that includes not attacking, seriously questioning or showing disdain for what participants say.

Changing the World

The purpose of the focus group is not to raise the political consciousness or political awareness of the participants, although that might occur as a by-product of proceedings. The purpose of the focus group is not liberation in any sense. Even though practices within focus group research are subject to change and evolution, the basic rationale is not one that can accommodate non-hierarchical relationships. It is true, however, that some clinical use of focus groups, where change in the consciousness of the participants is the aim of the exercise, do flout the relationship principles laid out, as indeed do 'self-managed groups, (Morgan 1988:51-53) and in doing so place themselves outside the rubric of focus group research. In such cases the similarities of the method to focus group research should not disguise the differences.

Focus group research is not there for therapy, awareness-raising, or problem-solving, but exists as a qualitative method for gathering interpretative data. The closeness to the participants in the research, especially if the focus groups are organised on a panel basis so that repeat groups are conducted, undoubtedly puts the researcher in a position rarely encountered in quantitative research. The researcher is on display to the subjects of the research and faces the difficulty of colluding through silence with views and attitudes expressed. This may be personally difficult, but it should not be made into a research problem. Beverly Skeggs says:

> What does a feminist researcher do when a debate on abortion arises and you are asked for your views? When you continually experience dominant ideological views and remain silent you give these views a legitimacy. Griffin (1991) and Troyna and Carrington have experienced similar dilemmas with research on racism. Both racism and sexism are reproduced and legitimated every day through the process of collusion. Should the researcher be part of that process? (Skeggs 1992:17)

For the ethnographer the moral question can also become a research question, but not for the focus group researcher. For the ethnographer, often 'living' closely with his or her subjects, not to answer questions can produce a resentment on the part of the questioner. Friendships may develop in the course of ethnographic work and at the very least both the subject and the researcher will have spent sufficient time with each other so that for the researcher not to engage in the answering of queries looks unfriendly, and this may damage the special relationship that is often so essential to such research. In our work on moral protest, Michael Tracey and I would often be asked by Mary Whitehouse, whose views on so many things we did not share, questions that demanded agreement or disagreement. We would even be telephoned at home for our 'advice' about certain issues. We had no rule on this apart from the research one of keeping the relationship with Whitehouse going for the benefit of the research. Certain linguistic games can be employed in such a situation so that committal to a view is not given, but since the view presented is not obviously denied or contradicted such 'silence' must be to the benefit of the original holder of the view. For the ethnographer this type of situation is something that has to be lived with. Of course the 'situation' might become so uncomfortable for the researcher, especially in the course of participant observation, that the project has to be abandoned.

However, this 'research dilemma' does not arise in focus group research. The meeting is too transitory for the researcher to be forced into a position of agreement or disagreement with a statement. It can always, with skill, be avoided. The moral difficulty still remains, but that is based on an empirical premise, namely, that by not contradicting a racist statement then through silence or agreement such collusion furthers racism. The fact is, however, that anything one says by way of agreement or disagreement in the course of a focus group would not impact either way on someone who held racist views. Racism is not overcome like that.

While not disagreeing with Skeggs that by remaining silent racist views are given a legitimacy, it is wrong to equate silence in the 'open public domain' of everyday life with silence in the 'closed private domain' of the research setting. In the former the circulation of racist views has a different power of address than the latter, since that is where real political struggle takes place. In the setting of the focus group the power of address of the racist statement is muted by the 'unnaturalness' of the experience. The research setting is not part of the individual's naturally occurring world, and thus the play of ideas are not embedded to the same degree as they are in everyday life. It is the weaving of racist ideas and terminology in the very fabric of existence that gives them their power, and that fabric cannot be unpicked by the act of research.

Of course it would be wrong to consider that what I have described as the 'open public domain' of everyday life, and the more 'closed private domain' of the research setting, can be entirely separated from each other as if on leaving the research setting the memory tapes are wiped clean. Even the brief act of engagement in a research activity becomes part of the individual's biographical experience. It is certainly open to strong question, however, whether the racist statement which might have bothered the moderator, and made him or her consider if the statement ought to be challenged, is carried as a significant 'effect' by other participants to the world of everyday existence. Neither for the racist or others in the group is it likely that by not challenging a racist statement the moderator has made any contribution one way or the other to views held prior to the participants joining in the research.

What ought not to be over-looked in examining the ethics of research and the researcher's response to racist statements is that the researcher is much more likely to take notice of and register the exchanges that occur in focus group research than the participants. This is not surprising, given that it is the very job of the moderator to pay keen attention to what is being said, but such attention is likely to lead the moderator to over-emphasise the dramatic impact of such statements. Furthermore, if racist views are an absolute anathema to the researcher, and they probably are to most social scientists, then it is highly likely that they not only give the racist's statement more attention than the participants in the group, but more readily register the statement as a matter for concern. That is, shocked by the sentiment, they over-dramatise the event and feel political action on their part is required. Most academics' private lives are so arranged that they are protected against exposure to crude racist statements. It is direct contact with the ugliness of a language that in their non-professional capacity they are not likely to meet that shocks the researcher and demands action on their part.

It is agreed that the private domain of the research setting and the public domain of everyday life cannot in practice be entirely separated, but even so the researcher cannot accept responsibility for the entirety of the historical and contemporary situation that has resulted in racism in society, or hope to correct such a situation by intervention through brief encounters with participants in focus groups. But what they can do in the research setting is to accept their responsibility as researchers to find out the best they can what the nature of the sentiments are, and what factors may be at work that have given rise to the sentiments. It is that basis, the fulfilling of the research demands rather than being a political actor, which then allows the creation of knowledge from the private domain of the research setting to be transferred over as knowledge to the public domain of discourse, where distinct political action might be effective.

The position here taken goes right back to Merton's formulations on focus groups over half a century ago; namely, that the method must be made as rigorous as possible without giving up any of the benefits associated with the flexibility that they offer in gathering the subjective meaning to responses. His position was quite clear: focus groups should be used in conjunction with other techniques to ensure the reliability of the findings. The idea that the researcher should take on other responsibilities – the moral responsibility for the ideas expressed – that will interfere with responsibility of the researcher towards the reliability of his or her data is not sustainable.

Focus groups suffer from special difficulties which make them prone to questions concerning the reliability and validity of the data collected. It is this lack of reliability and validity in the findings that is a worrying feature of their ready reception and acceptance by media researchers wishing to examine the audience, especially so when the method is used as a stand-alone technique. There is a further worry about the method, especially when not joined by other techniques that might act as a check on the findings; that there might be straightforward fraud in the writing up of the results.

The focus group is very much a private act. It is not open to critical inspection to the same extent as the survey questionnaire. One might ask to see the interview guide, but that would tell one very little about what went on in the actual situation of the focus group. There is simply no way of checking if pointed leading questions were put to encourage the support of a particular view the researcher wished to have affirmed. Nor does one know if friendly support and encouragement was given by the moderator to those individuals showing lines of enquiry favoured by the researcher. True, transcripts might be asked for, but that could be refused by the researcher on grounds of participant confidentiality. Thus one very much has to take on trust that what is published does capturing the proceedings and what was actually said. It is very easy in reporting the results of focus groups, especially when used as a single method, to distort the overall findings and even to concoct statements.

While it is always hoped that intellectual training will lead to intellectual honesty, it cannot be guaranteed. Intellectual fraud may take place knowingly – either in the conducting of the groups or in reporting them – but distortion may occur not out of intentional fraud, but because of the selective use of quotes that favour a particular theoretical position held by the researcher which could not, unless one was blinded by enthusiastic commitment to a position, be extracted from the findings. In short, the quotes used to support the theoretical or conceptual position of the researcher could not, on examination of the transcripts when set against the whole of the proceedings, support the presented position.

There is no absolute protection against this type of fraud. Science must, and does, proceed on trust. There is very little rigorous policing of research. In the absence of a visit to the relevant archive, which might not be easy, the historian's reproduction of a document in support of an interpretative stance on some event must be taken on trust. One may disagree with the interpretation given, but one hopes, and that is part of the historian's methodological training, that sufficient documentation is provided to support his or her position or allow others, through sufficient documentation, to contest the interpretation.

Although it might not be easy to visit the archive to check the document by which the historian has supported his or her work, especially if the archive has a practice of restricting access or is in a geographically remote location, in principle one can. More to the point, the historian knows that others can, should they wish, visit the source. But one cannot visit the focus group discussion, and one really cannot inspect the proceedings of the focus group in a very satisfactory way. This again is an argument against using the method as a stand-alone technique, but it is also to argue for the use of long extracts from the transcribed conversations in the presentation of reports. The use of the long quote at least provides some protection against the faults of privacy, and in a vicarious way takes the reader into the research performance itself. The long quote also allows the reader to contest the interpretations that the researcher puts on the findings. The one or two line quote, unless it is simply to keep a narrative point going that has already been established by a previous long quote, is a dangerous practice. The less hidden in research the better.[1]

In the reporting of focus groups as full a space as possible must be given to what has been said, especially if the researcher wishes to make some fundamental point or observation about the subject of enquiry. Not to allow the participants full voice by the use of the long quote, and instead to use only a few lines of transcript to support a point that the researcher wishes to make, is indeed to turn the subject into an object, the supporting actors to the researcher's story.

John Corner in looking at new audience studies says, '...one of the most striking points of development in the media research of the last decade has centred on the question of 'reception'. (Corner 1991: 267) Corner is right and in his own empirical work on the audience reactions to the issue of nuclear power has

---

1   John Corner asks for more computer-applied controls on the data selection to guard against a 'selectivity' of quotes. 'A final methodological issue to note here is the question of how respondents' accounts should be used to provide "*evidence*" of interpretation. The temptation to select "telling quotes" from a range of speech transcribed is only too obvious. Not only does this run the classic risk of simply confirming researcher hypotheses but it is also likely to ignore the possibility of inconsistencies and contradiction between group members. Despite the requirements of space, the citing of as complete a transcript as possible provides the only useful guard (and only then a partial one) against selectivity and analytic skew'. (Corner 1996:291) Of course, this is much more of a problem if the whole weight of the research rests on focus groups, and not so much of a problem if accompanied by other methods to support the findings, or act as a check on the findings.

employed focus group research. (Corner, Richardson and Fenton 1990) This attention to the empirical audience is welcome, but the move towards employing focus group research as a method of exploring audiences is not so welcome. It is a way forward for those who have an antipathy, even dislike, of quantification, but as a hope for full understanding of the subject area, it is a hopelessly incomplete method.

Afterword

Market Research and University Social Science Research

Ido not wish to become embroiled in consideration of a epistemology or the benefits of one approach to knowledge over another – enough has been said in the main body of the book to show that I do not favour a single approach and that I take issue with those who do. Instead I wish to use the opportunity of this afterword to continue the 'story' of the focus group by reflecting on some aspects of the organisation of the production of knowledge.

My main concern is, as argued previously, that focus groups are in danger of becoming the tyrant of communication research, but I am also concerned that the embracing of focus groups represents a deeper malaise within the academy, namely, a preference for a method that protects the scholar from having to deal with the financial issue of research as an enterprise. Empirical research requires money, and in large sums if it is not to become parochial. Big does not necessarily mean good, but some issues are of a type that require address on a large scale, and this requires substantial sums of money. Time and again I have been taken aback at industry meetings and conferences by the sums of money spent on research into the changing nature of mediated change. Of course, it is in companies' own self interest to protect their survival by understanding that which might affect their performance, but this means that the amounts spent by academics on media research look increasingly insignificant. The small sums spent by academics on research into mediated change and cultural performance, despite recent initiatives by the ESRC in the field of communication research, reduce their voice when compared to industry on how change might be managed, and what the consequences of those changes might be for how we live our lives.

The Source Of Funds

C Wright Mill's attack on Lazarsfeld for 'abstracted empiricism' was also an attack on Lazarsfeld for the sources of his research funds. But where else, if not from commercial sources, was Lazarsfeld to get the money for expensive empirical work? As Lazarsfeld said: 'I got money from the industry – everything depended on that'. For example, The Decatur Study which formed the basis of Personal Influence (Katz and Lazarsfeld, 1955) was aided by money from True Story magazine who were interested, for obvious reasons, in the reception of 'messages'. Such support did not make the study any less academic and, true to Lazarsfeld's insistence that even 'trivial' consumer studies (although Decatur was far from that) could be used for the construction of concepts, the two–step flow model of influence was honed from this study, along with the notion of opinion leaders.

The fact is, no money is pure. It always comes attached with 'interests', and that includes ostensibly pure money from research councils. Increasingly ERSC grants are 'directed' money given to address identified problems, and the manner in which the problem is defined or constructed is very much drawn from the politics of administration of a particular political culture, a culture far removed from the tradition of radical social criticism. However, whatever ones political/philosophical position on social arrangements, I take it as axiomatic that knowledge must be for something, and that a part of that something, although not all, must be, at least in terms of media research, to have some influence on how the media are either managed or thought about.

In terms of funding for research then one of the advantages of working within communication research is that it is not without an industrial, commercial and government regulatory base. Furthermore, this base is interested in many of the questions that academic researchers are interested in. Admittedly, to share an interest in questions with the media industry and regulatory agencies may not be to share the same interests in sets of arrangements one might like to see, or to share similar power in the ability to arrange interests, but that is no reason to dismiss involvement with those outside the groves of academia who are direct actors in change, or with those who are responsible for supervising change.

The True Cost of Research

A basic fact of research life is that empirical work costs money, and survey work tends to cost a lot of money. It is not surprising that Lazarsfeld, with his industry contacts, should say that his work, and a large part of the work of the 'Bureau', depended on money raised from that quarter.

I am not advocating a Lazarsfeld style of research, nor am I advocating the adoption of a Lazarsfeld style of research management, but I am saying that the question of research funding for communication research is a pressing one, and that not to secure funds of a substantial nature involves the danger of a restriction in growth and influence at the very time when rapid and far reaching changes are taking place in the communication industry. Research within the academy must not come to consist of understanding audiences based on knowledge gained only from focus groups. Politically, intervening voices in the management of change have little effective force if drawn from a study talking to a few people in a few focus groups, nor, it must be said, given my criticism of them, are they a very strong method if used on their own for establishing 'truth'. Indeed, unlike survey data, findings from focus groups have little cumulative veracity.

The Attraction of Focus Groups: An Easy Way?

A method may be attractive for many reasons, but we must be very clear about the nature of that attraction. It is one thing to hold to a method because of its perceived intellectual strengths, but it is quite another matter to hold to a method because it avoids the necessity of having to engage in extensive fund raising. It may be tiresome to have to raise funds for research, even seen as a rude interference in research itself, but practically all research involves fund–raising as an essential component, be this in physics, medicine or whatever. Raising money is part and parcel of being a researcher, although such skills are rarely taught as part of gradate training.

Thus, in understanding the attraction of focus groups what cannot be overlooked is that, compared to surveys, they are cheap to do, and require few research managerial skills. We must question how far the popularity of the method owes itself to the perceived intellectual benefits and how far it owes itself to the avoidance of the fund raising reality of research. There is no question that the discovery of a method capable of addressing the empirical audience by non-quantitative methods has proved popular among sections of media researchers, but one feels that focus group's popularity have been perpetuated by the fact that they can be cheap to conduct and 'easy' to do. Of course, an 'easy' methodology is always attractive. Indeed, the ease with which a method can be employed can be seen as one of the benefits or strengths of a method. Such qualities, however, can never justify the abandonment of other methods simply because they are difficult to execute or might require extensive resources and the development of skills to ensure those resources. It would be ironic indeed if a method that owed its birth to a situation structured by Lazarsfeld's ability to gain research contracts was held to, beyond any intellectual merits it may have, simply because it absolves the researcher from having to raise serious levels of research funds.

I have argued that focus groups are of restricted value, but the real danger is that, if they are accepted as 'The method' for addressing the audience, the development of communication research, or one section of it, will be restricted by being condemned to small-scale studies. Perhaps more worrying still, in the light of points discussed earlier, is that to adopt focus groups as the method for studying the audience re-defines the nature of the field itself. Subjects or disciplines are judged by their methods, indeed, it is the methods or language of research used, that shape the subject. It is not simply, therefore, that the adoption of focus groups as a stand-alone method ought to be guarded against on grounds that it is an incomplete method, but guarded against because if focus groups come to dominate research proceedings then the nature of the field comes to be altered. This is perfectly acceptable if the new configuration is accepted as an advance in the creation of knowledge. But, if it is accepted that focus groups are an incomplete method, this will mean that one area of communication research will be transformed into an incomplete activity incapable of saying much of much importance.

The Production of Knowledge

In examining the history of focus group research, and their emergence from a particular style of research operation associated with Lazarsfeld, I have attempted to ground the story of the method through an approach that sees research as a social process. Attention was given therefore to the historical situation that Lazarsfeld faced in Vienna, and the manner in which he began to create a new form of research setting which he later successfully developed in America – the research institute or bureau. Lazarsfeld broke the mould of the humanistic tradition of scholarship, where the single researcher operated within a teaching department to create a much more formal framework, and re-formed it with research involving teams of workers. Projects were broken down into parts, with tasks, roles and duties allotted to various individuals under the control of a project director. It was, in a sense, the rationalisation of the production of knowledge, which for a time gave Columbia University a pre-eminent position within American sociology. The research institute, bureau, or research centre is now an established part of higher learning. Yet nowhere has this rationalisation of the production of knowledge gone further than in market research companies. In fact the extent of the rationalisation is such that one can refer to the production of knowledge within market research as the industrialisation of knowledge. What one sees within market research companies is a rhythm of production that fits with the rhythm of the industries that they serve. There is an inexorable logic to the type of knowledge demanded and the development of structures to provide that knowledge.

I now, therefore, wish to provide some observations on the operation of market research organisations and university departments in relation to the production of knowledge. I wish to do this for a few reasons. One, to consider if there are any lessons to be learnt from how market research companies organise their practices, and secondly to provide some insight into that world which took focus groups out of the academy and made them their own. My main purpose, however, in looking at market research is to show the type of operation that is required if industry funds of any substantial amount are to be obtained by academic communication researchers. At no point, however, do I wish to suggest that the academy should model itself on the operations of market research companies – the rationales of the market research company and a university are entirely different. The purpose of the exercise is to show the type of expectations of performance that the media industry expects as they have already been generated by the performance of market research companies.

Forms Of Knowledge Production: A Case In Point

Many areas of research that the media and related industries are interested in addressing would not be of interest to the academic because they are often too narrowly related to technical performance rather than social questions. Many areas do, however, offer common interest. One such area is technological change. For example, the Institute of Communications Studies at the University of Leeds has established 'The Research Centre for Future Communications'. The Centre is focused around a project known as futura.com which receives funding of close to a million pounds from industry sources. The primary sponsor, the Independent Television Commission, has contributed a quarter of a million pounds over three years and the remaining funding comes from a variety of industrial and commercial sources. The study is based on a longitudinal panel initially made up of 13,000 adults in nearly 7000 households who are surveyed every six months. Further to the quantitative research, a variety of qualitative techniques are used for a detailed exploration of the results. Raising these funds, running the project and providing data to the sponsors whilst maintaining the central intellectual direction of the study, has necessitated putting the research on an industrial footing. Thus, before moving on to document the operations of pure industrial production witnessed within a market research company, I will briefly describe what this has meant.

The sheer managerial complexity of such a large scale project, and the complexity of the funding, has required a pattern of work resembling a cross between the structure of operations within a market research company and a university department. Amongst other things this has involved the selection and appointment of fieldwork suppliers and monitoring of their performance and subsequent data output, designing of questionnaires, meeting deadlines, presenting to sponsors on request, responding to requests for data quickly, establishing billing and payment mechanisms, drawing up contracts between the University and each individual sponsor, taking action to protect intellectual property rights, employing consultants to give specialist advice on particular aspects of the study and seeking new sponsors when more money was needed to extend the study to include emerging groups such as Internet users and so on. The running of such a project has required a completely different approach to the organisation of the production of knowledge from that obtaining to any of our current ESRC grants, but as a consequence we now have access to information, both quantitative and qualitative, beyond anything that we might have hoped for without recourse to industrial funding. Based on a joint inquisitiveness of people's attitudes and responses to new technology, the combination of our interests as university researchers and the interests of

257

the industry and commercial backers has meant that the interests of all have been satisfied albeit through different levels of analysis and interpretation.

In discussing the institutionalisation of knowledge earlier, Lazarsfeld was quoted as explaining what he did by reference to Marxist notions of the sociology of knowledge. His position was that new ideas – empirical sociology – required new structures for their practice – research bureaux, and also a new type of academic personnel, the managerial scholar. We may as well keep with dialectical thinking: if new forms of knowledge call for new structures for their practice, the structures then instituted play back into ideas themselves, or at least they do in the manner in which knowledge is approached. In some ways this is no more than an extension of adopting a certain method, that is, the method restricts the possibilities of how one thinks about the topic, although equally, and again one cannot escape the dialectical nature of thought, how one thinks about a topic decides the method for processing the thought. Yet organisation itself has to influence, to some degree thinking itself. I cannot give precise examples of this, and it would probably be best for an outsider engaged in non-participant observation of the production process to provide them, but one knows that lines of enquiry are dropped because the structure of processing knowledge has its own routines. These routines are geared for mechanical efficiency, the wheels of which turn when the switch of the production cycle is thrown. An intellectual problem can only be given so much time for resolution before the structure created becomes impatient for input. It is always the hope that before the 'switch is thrown' intellectual questions have been addressed reasonably satisfactorily at the creative stage of the cycle, but this is rarely the case. In terms of the market research industry, then as stated, its rhythm of performance is locked into the performance rhythm of the industries that they service. The industries serviced by the market research companies generate problems that they require quick research answers to, but they rarely give enough notice to the market research company for it to creatively address the problem before the switch of the production cycle must be thrown. It is worth noting in this context that the industry has shifted towards operating on what is known as 'just-in-time' research.

Indeed, there appears to be a direct and significant parallel with the increasing trend in manufacturing and other industries for companies to order components on this basis, rather than stockpiling – known as just in-time manufacturing. The suppliers of the goods, though, it is most likely, do not see any benefit in this practice – the sharp end of just-in-time methods mean stress, problems with quality control and cash flow. Similar pressures must be expected if this industrialising trend continues within the research fraternity. It this just-in-time practice that has lead to the increasing attractiveness of focus groups in that they can often give back 'answers' quicker than survey research despite the increased mechanisation of interviewing and data processing. The results from focus groups are often subject to hardly any reflection at all, and the client is simply given a debrief the day after the completion of the groups. This is a classic case of the misuse of focus groups that Merton chastised the market researchers for: 'One gains the impression that focus group research is being misused as quick-and-easy claims for the validity of the research are not subjected to further, quantitative tests'.

Market Research And The Industrialisation Of Knowledge

Given my call for university based communication research to form closer links with the communication industry and regulatory authorities as a way of financing research, and hopefully at the same time assist in shaping, no matter how slight, the communication landscape, it is ironic, given what I have had to say about focus groups, that it is in the realm of focus group research that universities are likely to be more attractive sites for placement of that type of research than they are for the placement of survey research. The following will explain why, but basically the discrepancy in opportunities for attracting funds rests in differences in the organisation of knowledge between market research companies and universities, at least in the area of quantification.

British university departments are not geared to handle survey research on anything like the favourable terms that exist in market research companies. Nor should it be assumed that universities are methodologically superior to market research companies when it comes to the practice of research itself. It is hardly surprising, therefore, that the media industry's first port of call for survey research are market research companies, and not universities.

Technically, there is no such thing as a perfect sample. When it comes to survey research as a practice, experience is of the utmost importance, not just in deciding the sample but in deciding the feasibility of the application of the research instrument. A senior market researcher in a large company may well have several surveys running at the same time, and in the course of his or her working life expect to conduct hundreds of surveys of varying degrees of complexity. The university researcher on the other hand is unlikely, even if a survey specialist, to complete a fraction of the number of surveys as their market research cousins. It is, furthermore, market research that has taken survey research to its rational conclusion and industrialised production. I will explain why.

This industrialisation of knowledge by market research companies has been made possible not by intellectual advances in statistics, but by technological advances, namely, the introduction of computers. Through the development of the computer the social world has been opened to 'mass conversation'. The researcher instead of 'talking' with a few people can with ease, no matter how staccato, now talk to whole populations. Advances in computer technology have allowed, with the sophisticated interrogation of data, complex 'conversations' to take place with an ease and rapidity only dreamed of by early survey researchers such as Lazarsfeld using a Hollerith machine. However, although the computer has been significant for the industrialisation of knowledge through the speed by which information could be processed and analysed, the real industrialisation has been managerial rather than technical.

The Organisation Of Production

The actual unit working on any particular project within a market research company is smaller than might be imagined, perhaps no more than four people. The company itself, however, is organised on a factory-like basis that allows an efficient and swift processing of information. Deadlines are met even if it means that the 'factory' is put onto night work. Each stage of the production process is carefully controlled to avoid slippage in one department resulting in blockages and problems further down the assembly line. Once the account (grant in university terms) has been secured, depending on the complexity of the job, any single project might involve: a sampling expert; conceptual design of the questionnaire by the project director; questionnaire layout and design by junior executives, and maybe even question construction by junior executives; a fieldwork buyer; a specification writer for analysis; a statistician for any complex analysis of data; data entry by teams of workers; a controller of fieldwork; interviewers; dispatch personnel; junior executives checking tables and graphics production; and in some cases a client manager. In so far as possible within a creative activity, nothing is left to chance. Contracts are drawn up not simply specifying 'the agreement to act' but detailing what is expected and when – for example, the amount of data analysis within the cost, and the cost of extra data analysis should it be required. A punishment clause is not uncommon should the company fail to meet the agreed conditions, most usually covering late delivery of results.

The outcome of this activity, the final report, is usually written by the project director, who, as indicated above, will not be involved at every stage of the research. The cycle of production must, however, be accomplished within the stipulated budget, created from the costings carefully calculated at the time of the initial tender for the project. Any unforeseen problems can cost dearly, turning an erstwhile profitable account into a non-profitable one, or one with margins unacceptable to the finance department – the finance department feeds the research unit's performance figures to the board of management on a regular basis. Projected targets, not just of an individual account, but the project revenue of a units overall performance must be met. Not surprisingly such a factory form of knowledge production demands, as far as functionally possible within a creative enterprise, rather strict demarcation of authority and power, the like of which would not be possible, or accepted, within a university. Such a set-up means that the call on any individual's time, should a problem arise, is unquestioned. It is expected that this is given without dissent; this is not surprising given that the whole purpose of a market research company is that of production. The corollary of this is that the staff are looked after in a way that would be the envy of academic researchers.

Market research companies, especially the larger ones, are very streamlined organisations, structured so that as little time as possible is given to activities not directly related to the production of research. The senior staff within a market research company may well have to attend board meetings, but no one attends a fraction of the committees that a senior academic within a university does. It also goes without saying that few market researchers have to consult the teaching timetables of colleagues before acting on some demand, or at least if timetables of other personnel are consulted they are subject to a greater degree of flexibility. Money, furthermore, is flexible. The financial outlay on a project is under the director's control who can shift it around on the spur of the moment without complex negotiations with others; the profitability of the job can be redefined as the project runs – a job may even be sold at a loss or an extremely low profit margin to encourage further accounts, or to keep the opposition from establishing a market foothold with a valued or prospective client. The research director, in other words, has a financial freedom, and hence an ability to act swiftly should a research problem arise not shared by his counterpart in a university. Above all, those within a market research company have a clear understanding of the function of the organisation, and can get on with satisfying the goals of performance in a way which cannot be said of those employed within a university. This is not meant as a criticism of university based research, rather a description of differences between the operating basis of knowledge between the two spheres of production. Indeed, no matter how much the Research Centre for Future Communications had to move to an industrial footing necessitated by the size and complexity of the futura.com research and the relationship of the research to the funding base, the space we managed to create, tolerated by our backers because they wished to have the reflective and theoretical input of university learning, falls into insignificance compared to the industrialisation of knowledge achieved and witnessed within the market research industry.

The Point of Existence

Universities do not have a single function, and increasingly in the flux of change have difficulty in deciding what their functions ought to be. Even where functions are identified there exists confusion over how they can be achieved without the satisfaction of one function hindering the achievement of another. In terms of the satisfaction of goals, universities are complex organisations compared to market research companies. It is the 'competing' interests within a university that detract from the single minded pursuit of any one interest. This, perhaps, is how it should be, and is to be expected given the position of universities within the political and cultural life of the country. Yet the frequent 'outside' interferences in the operation of universities – changes in financial funding bases, the research assessment exercise, the teaching quality assessment and so on – require a constant re-jigging of performances to the extent that, when it comes to the satisfaction of a sponsor's requirements, no researcher within a university has the freedom of operation that his or her colleague in market research has.

As with any organisation, a university must put its own organisational purposes first, and since the satisfaction of the demands of the media industry could never be its primary goal this means that disappointment of the sponsor's expectations are practically structured into the research operation from the outset. The satisfaction of a sponsor's demands cannot be the prime rationale of a university and meeting the whims of a sponsor must be resisted, but this runs the risk of being seen by sponsors used to dealing with the market research world as 'unprofessional'. To a commercial sponsor of research you work for them, and not for some further cause no matter how laudable in some wider social sense that might be. It is in this area that C Wright Mill's criticisms carry validity.

Even the smallest client of a market research company treats the company as if its whole purpose is the satisfaction of his or her own needs, refusing to see that other clients also demand service and that not everything can be readily met at once. But the definition of professionalism within the market research industry is to meet all demands at once, and the company is structured to ensure such compliance. Having said that, not all clients are 'human'. Some are less reasonable than others, and some just downright unreasonable. It is one of the duties of the research director, therefore, if he or she wants anything approximating a pleasant life, to educate the client into what can be expected and when. The cash nexus, however, alters all relationships (this is something that universities to their cost may shortly discover through the introduction of tuition fees). Thus, within the business sector of research the demand by a client for a hurriedly arranged meeting, which may well be reasonable given some problem within their own organisation, must be met no matter how difficult it is for the researcher to arrange. The diary of a market researcher is as flexible as the situation demands, usually determined by the value placed on the client. The absolute impossibility of making a meeting because those handling the 'account' have to teach at that time, or have some vital administrative deadline to meet does not apply to the market researcher.

Given the wide range of duties that an academic must perform within a university setting the consequences of instant demand on an academic's time are not understood by buyers of research, and what is not understood is rarely tolerated. Market researchers do not have administrative deadlines, only research deadlines, or more accurately, the research deadline and the administrative deadline are one and the same. It is, in other words, the clear identification of a single goal within market research that allows all resources to be ploughed into achieving that goal and gives an efficiency the likes of which a university cannot match.

However, it is perhaps in the realm of staff costs that a market research company has the advantage over a university research operation in attracting funds. The through-flow of work in a market research company means that any researcher is working on several accounts at the same time, thus his or her salary is not drawn from any single account. Money for salaries is of course reflected in the price that is charged for any piece of work, but the break-down of the project into distinct tasks means that junior executives do much of the routine work at a vastly lower salary than that of the director, a fact that helps to feed profits. Production, in other words, is rationalised.

It is this structure of performance within the commercial sector of research that enables staff to be retained on a permanent basis with relative ease, offering clear advantages in terms of stability of production over the university department. Whilst the large long term research contract is attractive to market research and is highly valued, the long-term project is essential for university performance. Not only does size confer prestige, but it also provides the lengthy employment contracts without which it is difficult to attract staff. The suspicion is that 'tenders' for research projects by universities are falsely stretched to ensure that they last for a year or more, not because of the length of time it takes to do the research, but for the length of the employment contract that this makes possible. Even when the award has been given, the lengthy process of advertising for staff must be gone through with no guarantee that suitable candidates will be found, or that those found once appointed will perform satisfactorily. Once in post, staff often have to be trained, most usually by the senior personnel, which then takes time away from his or her other research duties. Compared to market research companies, research within a university is not an efficient system of operation.

Within market research formal training is given to junior staff, either in house, or through attendance at courses in research methods. The most valuable training, however, is provided by working in a highly pressured environment on a range of projects. Mastery of one level of research practice leads to promotion and the mastery of higher levels of practice. Training in management will also be given, and more importantly, practised. If staff are considered to be performing poorly they are not retained, or simply not moved onto a stage of performance considered to be outside their competence. Performance is thus guaranteed. In addition, the repetitive performance of tasks by the junior staff makes each of them extremely efficient at their allocated jobs. Furthermore, no researcher within a market research organisation works on tasks that are deemed to be below his or her salary level. No senior person would dream of doing the routine research tasks on a regular basis that one sees senior staff in a university do. To do so would not be considered efficient, or economical.

Why a University?

Given my observations about the absence of the appropriate infrastructure within the academy by which to industrialise the production of knowledge, and acknowledging that industrialisation is aimed at keeping the cost of research down, it is not surprising that, for most buyers of research, universities are not attractive sites for the fulfilment of their research needs. Furthermore, leaving aside the possibility of using postal questionnaires, no university department has a field staff of sufficient size to conduct national surveys. Thus, a university department wishing to conduct large-scale empirical work, must sub-contract field world to a market research company.[1] Not surprisingly, this prompts the question to most research buyers, why bother going to a university in the first place, why not go direct to the research supplier?

An area where universities face a particular difficulty in attracting industry money, especially in the realm of media research where there is no absence of expertise, is the costing structure of a university. If market research companies appear expensive suppliers of research, then universities can sometime appear more so. For a buyer to have to pay a university's direct staff costs – often the whole of an individual's or several individuals' salary – and then be charged an on top of salary costs makes any tender not only high, but appear to the buyer as unjust, especially if a surplus or profit is also to be taken, which is often expected. Why should they, as they argue, pay for the upkeep of a university?

It may be government policy to direct university research towards helping industry and national economic performance. However, it is not its policy to make university expertise a gift to industry. Yet it is one thing to force a policy on university researchers, but it is quite another matter to have failed to educate industry about its policy; namely that universities are not to be regarded as a free gift to industry. This lack of education makes for extreme difficulties when it comes to selling research. In the commercial sector that I know best, the communication industry, universities are seen as part of the commonweal to turn to for help, not part of the market keen to make a return on investment. The industry does not expect university research to be as expensive as, or even more expensive than, commercially based research.

Existing outside of the academy, most buyers of research have little understanding of the changes that have taken place within universities, judging life in the academy still as a leisured existence removed from harsh economic realities. Of course, they understand the general financial strictures facing universities, but that problem is seen to rest at the door of government policy and they see no reason for them to pick up the 'tab' for something that is not of their doing. One might speculate that the introduction of student fees, once they bite into the middle-class buyers of research, may result in one of two things. On the one hand it may provide the educational lesson that is currently missing, that universities have moved onto a business footing and therefore funds for research ought to be viewed in the same way as buying from commercial contractors, or, and I feel this is more likely, it will produce an over-extension of an existing condition. Namely, that since the education of their

---

1   The Bureau did not maintain a permanent interview staff on the grounds that Lazarsfeld realised that to do so would mean that to keep them fully employed he would have to accept contracts of little research interest. For the same reason sampling and coding staff were also avoided. This meant designing samples and gathering interviewing staff as Charles Glock states '*de novo* for each new study, or where not feasible, as with national samples, of having fieldwork done by other research organisations'. Glock makes the interesting point that this reluctance to develop a structure that could operate on a more complete basis '...probably meant that some interesting opportunities for research did not come the Bureau's way'. (Glock 1979:27)

off-spring is no longer free, why should they also, through expensive research, assist with the upkeep of a university?

To overcome this 'problem' of the cost of university research, and the puzzlement about the costing mechanism, a considerable amount of added value has to be assured to persuade a media company wishing to buy survey research to favour a university over a market research company. As matters stand value appears to rest with the university in what looks like an unfair trading deal. If the perceived high cost of research was not sufficient to make universities unattractive places to commission survey research from, the working practices of universities seal their fate. The most bitter and common complaint by the industry against universities is that they fail to deliver the results within the agreed time.

It is difficult for most university researchers, having never been locked into the rhythm of industrial production, and used to the practised excuse of why their contribution to a book will be late, to fully appreciate the value placed on time by people within a fast-moving industry such as the media. To be late with results can often mean that the data is past its sell-by date; the meeting for which the data was demanded has come and gone, to the discomfort of those who have commissioned the work. Failure to deliver results on time by the research staff of a media company to their management, no matter whose fault it is, reflects badly on their commissioning competence.

Why Bother With Industry Funds?

From what has been said it might be assumed that universities are well rid of such work. I would argue that to adopt such a position is wrong. Certainly it is difficult for a university to generate much profit from commercially contracted survey work. The lack of an appropriate industrial base means that a very small amount of revenue remains within the 'building' as profit, with most of it having to be spent on the research itself. However, in any system of accountancy arrangements differ as to how profit is calculated. Although it is unusual to include staff payment in profit one might argue that within a university setting the payment of staff could be taken as profit. But the main reason why such work is important for a university is not the money that it might generate, but the necessity for academics, especially within media research, to engage in empirical research that is of value to academic knowledge, and of value to the media industry also. This is not to say that all knowledge generated by a commercially funded project ought to be of value to the commissioning agent, but some of it ought to be. Indeed, if one looks at academic media work then although much is of a high standard, what is missing are large-scale studies, and they are missing, in part, through lack of finance. The academic development of the field has suffered because of this.

Academic media researchers ought to re-appraise their relationship with the media industry, especially in light of restricted research council funds. It may be difficult, for all the reasons given, to persuade buyers of research to place large-scale quantitative work with a university research centre, but it is not impossible and ought to be attempted if media research in Britain is to break out of its pursuit of the small, and its over-reliance on research council funding. To depend on council funding is bound to lead to frustration and disappointment for many given the limited pot of money to go around.

Market Research and Focus Groups

The organisation of focus group research within market research companies is invariably on a small scale, be it in the realm of consumer research or social research. The largest market research companies usually house a specialist qualitative wing, but even within the big companies offering such specialist services many survey researchers will also conduct focus groups, often because the client wishes to have some exploratory focus group work attached to the main survey and the researcher wishes to be involved in the entire programme of research. Because very few direct research costs are involved in focus group research they can appear to be very profitable. Most of the money received falls straight through to the bottom line to be taken as profit. Given that a single group is charged at anywhere between £1,000 to £1,500, more if the groups are particularly difficult to recruit or execute, it takes very few groups to show a healthy return on effort. Yet all is not as it seems, and it comes down once more to the question of the management of research, or the institutional organisation of knowledge.

It is difficult to successfully mix industrial production with craft production, or in this case quantification with qualitative production methods. The financial returns from focus group research may appear high, but the activity itself is very labour intensive, often requiring the researcher to spend reasonably long periods away from the 'factory'. They cannot, furthermore, really be conducted successfully by junior executives, although they sometimes are. Thus all the advantage of factory production, the breaking down of tasks into specialised units of production, and the working on several accounts at once by a single individual, are lost. In the case of survey research staff move in and out of a project when and as needed. A large account, say a £500,000 survey, may at a particular point only engage a single junior researcher, and at other times, for example when the survey is in the field, no researchers at all might work on the project, apart from someone occasionally checking with field control that all is running to plan. At other times the director himself or herself may give all their time to the account. It is the fine control of the production cycle of a project that allows the processing of a number of projects together. It is not difficult to see, therefore, that although the returns on focus group research may look attractive, the fact that the activity itself cannot be put on an industrial footing does not make them, in comparative terms, profitable for a survey research company, but they are very profitable for specialist companies. One needs, furthermore, to do a significant number of focus groups to compete with a £500,000 survey. In addition, qualitative report writing demands special skills, and is time-consuming; most usually it is the time of the most senior and hence most expensive researcher that is engaged. With the case of survey research, even the task of report writing can be broken down among the research team, especially as it is most usually the case that only literal description of the figures is required. Clients have paid for the skill of the researcher in designing and planning the survey and for the reputation of the company in being able to successfully conduct and complete the work, not for the mind of the researcher in giving his or her deep interpretative understandings of the data. Interpretation is given, but such interpretation generally remains very close to the data.

The very nature of qualitative work, its lack of amenability to the type of industrial production capable with survey research, means that even within large companies boasting a specialist qualitative arm, such operations remain small. The qualitative branch of a market research company with ten researchers would be considered a large operation. Most focus group research is done not inside the big market research companies, but by quite small outfits, many consisting of no more than two or three people. In fact, companies consisting of no more than a single person are common. There is little benefit to be had in qualitative work from economies of scale, indeed, scale is often inverse to performance. As explained in the body of the book, the success of focus group research depends very much on the skill, talents and intelligence of the moderator. It is difficult, therefore, to institute controls on quality in the sense of correcting poor performance. Furthermore, because such work is not characterised by team performance, clients tend to insist on the top person in the company, or a known 'star', to undertake the work. No one wants a junior researcher to handle the account. Not surprisingly focus group researchers in specialist qualitative divisions within the large market research companies often command higher salaries than their quantitative counterpart; even so, it does not take much arithmetic for a good qualitative researcher with a strong client list to work out that they could earn considerably more money establishing themselves as a company rather than see their efforts siphoned off as profits for someone else. Consequently the establishment of new qualitative companies, often with fanciful names to denote some piercing intelligence, is common. Breakaways on the quantitative side of operations are much more rare, since without the whole complex industrial infrastructure to support the activity, success is unlikely. In the realm of survey research the individual cannot, with great efficiency, work alone. Services can be bought, that is true, and a whole satellite industry exists offering data preparation and analysis, the drawing of samples, fieldwork staff and so on. However, even presuming that through the buying-in of services one could compete with the large companies in terms of performance, the lone survey researcher, or even the small survey company, is at a distinct disadvantage when it comes to selling their own services.

Statistics offer the appearance of certainty. Buyers of research do not want that certainty diminished by having a study associated with a company whose name does not have recognised public authority. Well known companies such as MORI, NOP, Harris, Gallup have a ready advantage in securing accounts, especially in those cases where the results of a survey are intended for public display. Gallup, or rather Gallup UK, is in fact quite a small company, but universally known owing to its polling activities, as indeed are the other three mentioned companies. Other market research companies within the rather closed world of media research buying have a high reputation and are commissioned for research, but the point is that the locking together of the cultural prestige awarded to statistical knowledge and the social prestige attached to high-profile companies offers a powerful block to the challenge of findings. Although universities are not outside the circle of authority spun by the leading research companies and will sometimes, but not often for all the reasons advanced, be commissioned to conduct work, most usually where the commissioning organisation does so for 'political reasons' and where high value is placed on the perceived independence of the research, the trend towards the concentration of resources disadvantages all but the big players in the survey game. The sheer economics of production, therefore, leave most university departments, and even designated research centres, at a disadvantage in attracting commercial money for survey research. This, however, is not the case when it comes to qualitative work. Indeed, the inability to industrialise qualitative research shifts the balance in attracting research funds away from market research companies and towards universities. Perhaps the only competitive advantage that market research companies have in the area of qualitative work over universities is their practised skill at 'pitching' for accounts, and in the presentation of results. This is no small benefit. The presentation of the self and the presentation of results, especially in the area of qualitative work which lacks statistical certainty, is essential for establishing trust between the researcher and the commissioner of research. But then the academics, especially if holding some title of distinction, and better still if they also come from a prestigious university, have a great deal of cultural capital to be cashed in for the creation of trust.

The basic reason that universities are not disadvantaged when compared to market research companies in the realm of focus group research is the resistance of qualitative work to the logic of industrialisation. This resistance means that universities are ideal settings for such work. In terms of focus group research, universities can keenly compete with market research companies in terms of cost, and can turn around such studies, or ought to be able to do so, in a time equivalent to that of market researchers. Universities also have existing staff for such work, and in addition can draw upon a body of theoretical knowledge that affords an added insight into the meanings generated within a focus group. Indeed, the academic researcher is better placed than the market researcher, to relate the findings of focus groups to more general states of affairs, or, in other words, to place the findings within a wider context than that bounded by the research site.

The Attraction of Focus Groups to the Media Industry

The rise in the popularity of focus groups for academic researchers is matched by their popularity within the media industry. From what has been said it is clear that the one area where the university-based researcher can relatively easily enter into conversation with the media industry through the language of research is by way of focus group research, and can do so because of the scale of operation involved. Most industry financed focus group research projects usually involve the commission of about six to eight groups. This may not seem many, but for most purposes it is sufficient. I have already discussed the determinants of numbers of groups needed for a project in the methodology section of the book so will make no further comment; the point to register here is that focus group research is not expensive to commission – on the basis of conducting six groups it would cost about £8,000. This is because focus group research does not involve an elaborate research infrastructure so much of the advantage of using special market research companies falls away. The lone scholar can easily conduct such research on his or her own, indeed, as I have suggested, for many communication scholars part of the popularity of the method is precisely that their execution requires low-level organisational and managerial skills. They may be used in conjunction with survey research, but as often as not are employed as a stand-alone technique.

Through BARB, the joint industry-funded research body measuring audience size and reach, and viewers' appreciation of programmes, the industry is not short of statistical data on the audience, but such statistics have their limitations. This type of joint industry research provides a wealth of information on the audience, but lacks rich detail. Thus, focus groups are often brought into play precisely in those areas where a quantification of responses to a question would be inappropriate because of the degree of uncertainty that exists, most usually where pre-coding responses would not be possible or where idiosyncratic factors would defeat the statistical examination of regularities. It must be said, and this relates back to the discussion of just-in-time-manufacturing, that an unfortunate trend has arisen within the media industry of using focus groups as quantification, especially as the market research industry has gained in confidence of using statistics based on small numbers. One might say, however, that such 'confidence' has been bolstered by the pressure to deliver generalisable results from small numbers forced on them by the demand from the media industry for rapid results.

There is little question that focus groups will continue to form an important part of the research mix employed by the industry. It should not be presumed, however, that focus groups are used merely for programme research; they are often employed to explore audiences' attitudes and opinions towards issues that programmes raise, to explore attitudes towards media policy, or even such general questions as the place of television in people's lives.

By and large, despite the comments above concerning cheap quantification, focus groups are in demand to gain a deeper and more textured understanding of the audience than is possible through survey research. This demand requires interpretative understanding, and a theoretical or conceptual input of some sort - the exact type of activity that a university based researcher ought to be

269

well equipped for. Indeed, coming from the field of media research, the academic ought to have an understanding of the way that the complexities of social issues relate to individuals' relationship to the media, and be in a position to detect lines of enquiry that help focus the questions the client wishes to address. By comparison, most market researchers are not specialists, nor do they have the time to give unqualified attention to issues. Their knowledge tends to be research led, and not informed by wide reading of journals or books relating to media issues or theoretical developments within communication and media studies. They are too busy doing research to bother much with anything other than keeping abreast of the technical or methodological issues of research. This concern with 'doing research' does not make market researchers unreflective, but it does restrict their reflective ability.

The Attraction of University Researchers

Many of the areas that the industry uses focus groups for are the very same areas, as outlined above, that the academic might approach a funding council for support for. Thus, when allied with the benefits of commissioning focus groups from university departments focus group research offers a much more solid basis than survey research for bridge-building between the academy and industry. What is more, focus groups are used, or should be, in those areas where uncertainty exists about the likely responses to issues, programmes and so on. In other words, focus groups are intended to clarify a situation, not to provide certainty and to provide confidence that existing thought is correct. Thus, a significant amount of freedom is given to the researcher, more than with survey research, in terms of how he or she addresses the issues to be covered. Furthermore, because of its very nature, focus group research nearly always includes questions from the client about why it is that such beliefs are held, or why views are articulated in the way that they are especially at the stage where findings are presented. This forces the researcher back into using more basic knowledge to explain the findings, or if one prefers, a more theoretical interpretation of the results. Discussion nearly always centres on the social significance of the findings, and not, as often the case in presenting survey data, the statistical significance of the findings. It is this appreciation of the social meaning of the findings drawn from focus groups that makes the university researcher well placed to compete with the market researcher. Much of this appreciation for the 'social' as opposed to the 'statistical' is due to the rapid changes that are taking place in the communication landscape, changes that make the future appear uncertain. The industry needs to know the audience at a new level and depth, hence their increased reliance on focus groups.

A Rapprochement with the Media Industry

The discussion of the relationship of the media industry to their suppliers of knowledge, and the discussion of the structure of market research companies has been offered to provide insight into how the industry research requirements are served and what organisational strategies have been constructed in the production of knowledge. As well as providing insight into the manner in which a substantial amount of knowledge is produced in contemporary society, my intention has been to offer academics a glimpse at the organisational practices of an industry that is in many ways in direct competition with educational institutions in the provision of understanding. Centres of learning must compete with the new providers of knowledge if they are to reclaim their influence on cultural life. To accept research monies from the communication industry does not spell the death of independent thinking. David Morely's work, 'Family Television' (Morely, 1986), for example, was funded by the Independent Broadcasting Authority, and Philip Schlesinger's study 'Women Viewing Violence' (Schlesinger *et al* 1992) was funded by the Broadcasting Standards Council. These were qualitative studies, but the Institute's survey research into responses to the coverage of the Gulf War (Morrison, 1992) was financed by money from the Independent Television Commission, the Broadcasting Standards Council, and the BBC. The content analysis side of the study was funded by money from the Social Science Research Council. In this case the Institute approached the industry to finance the research, and not the other way around. What one notices about the mass of work on the Gulf War is a virtual absence of nationally representative data on audience response to the War, one presumes this is because the swiftness of events prohibited the raising of large funds in such a short time. It was only by approaching the industry, and not a research council, could the money necessary for a survey, and focus groups, be raised quickly enough to conduct the study almost co-terminant with events. The industry, unlike many other possible sources of funds, can and will make decisions to back research, providing the money can be found within existing budgets, within days, and not months, should it be necessary.

It is worth observing, furthermore, in making a plea for closer collaboration between academics and the communication industry, that to have research questions set by others can be intellectually productive for the academic, forcing the researcher to consider issues and problems that they would normally not encounter – the researcher is forced out of existing paths of enquiry and sometimes forced to re-think existing procedures. Indeed, the new method of video editing groups, mentioned previously, was developed directly out of industry commissioned research to assist the resolution of problems that the commissioning agent had set us.

Having argued for closer association between universities and the media industry, it must be stressed that universities cannot and should not turn themselves into the docile research arm of the industry by providing it with routine information; that is the job of market research. In any case, especially on the quantification side of research, they are ill-equipped to face the competition posed by market research for that type of research, and secondly, the inability to compete with market research companies in terms of controlling costs will increase as media owners purchase research companies and engage in economies of scale beyond the scope of a university. The research setting that I have described within the market research industry, the industrialisation of knowledge as I have termed it, will continue apace.

In fact changes are taking place in line with general change in the way the industry is beginning to organise itself that will increase efficiency and reduce costs. In recent years economists have been bemused by the 'productivity paradox' (Krugman, 1994:59-63, 277-79; Magnet, 1994:35-39) that rising spending on information and communication technology has not, as expected, produced significant improvements in productivity, and hence living standards. The reason for this has been that the largest sector of advanced economies is in services which have proved resistant to improvements in productivity. The call centre phenomenon is representative of a new effort to rationalise the handling of information. The emphasis given to home working as a result in changes in technology has over-looked the reverse process, namely, that technology is driving white collar workers into 'factories'. It is not, in many ways, the growth of home working that has been the revolution, but the re-industrialisation of sites of knowledge through the creation of 'call centres' where the owner of the technology can achieve the advantage of factory production – standardisation, quality, high productivity and so on. The rate of this process has been staggering. Call centres barely existed five years ago, but now account for two per cent of the British workforce. This process of industrialisation has not escaped market research. Major companies such as WPP and media owners such as United News and Media have begun to buy ever more research companies in order to obtain the benefit of both vertical and horizontal integration for their clients. It is this concentration of resources that has further facilitated their ability to build more complex technological factories on the basis of work that can be generated within their own group of companies. For example, CATI – Computer Assisted Telephone Interviewing operates as an outward call centre, and CAPI – Computer Assisted Personal Interviewing – where the interviewer sends to data electronically captured to a data caption centre by phone lines, are both examples of the factory method, or the call centres, of the market research world. The real danger is that, without the asked for rapprochement, market research, for all the reasons given, will increase its dominance as a provider of not just information, but of the type of knowledge that feeds into cultural decision making.

If universities are not well positioned in terms of survey research to attract industry funds for their research, then as I have stressed, this is not the case with qualitative work. It might be ironic, indeed it is, given the objections I have raised against the practice of focus group research, to now suggest that focus group researchers should use the advantages of a university setting and seek funding from the communication industry. The danger here, from my position, is that an existing practice will be given further encouragement through an injection of funds into that area. Focus group research, however, is a point of entry into influencing cultural decision making not so readily open to the survey researcher. In other words, it is only at the qualitative level that the march of the market research companies can if not exactly be halted, then limited.

A Rapprochement with Market Research

I have argued in the main body of the book that a suspicion exists within the academy towards their market research neighbours. This is not as it should be, despite my concern over the position that market research has gained in providing cultural intelligence. There is a good argument to be made for academics to use, or part use, the expertise and infrastructure for research that exists within the market research world. In short, for the qualitative researcher, and indeed the quantitative researcher, but particularly the former, to join in collaborative projects with market researchers where the academics conduct the focus group side of a study and the market research company handle any survey aspect would be a beneficial relationship.

Indeed, it is not an uncommon industry practice in awarding research to employ more than one agency. Often the focus group research will be awarded to a specialist qualitative company and the survey research to a survey research company. In one of the Institute's studies into audience responses to violent imagery commissioned by the Broadcasting Standards Council (Morrison and MacGregor, 1993c), the Institute conducted the focus group part of the study and a market research company, MORI, conducted the survey side of the research. This involved us working closely with staff at MORI to determine the possible level, degree and distribution of the principles governing response that we had constructed from the focus group findings. MORI then took several of the conceptual principles we had developed and operationalised them for survey instrument use. It was a very successful partnership. In fact, most market research companies would be only to happy to liase with academics in raising funds for research. Thus, if the qualitative researcher wished to conduct large scale empirical work that would benefit by the application of a survey, then the sharing of the idea with a market research company not only means that the university researcher is relieved of the administration of the survey, but in addition can draw on the close contacts that any company has with possible funders to arrange meetings and so on. Indeed, the market research company will even assist in preparing and attending the presentation of the proposal – practically all media industry funded research requires a written proposal, no matter how brief, followed by a presentation and verbal interrogation.

For academic researchers wedded to or only familiar with qualitative research, such involvement could only be beneficial. It would be enlightening for those advocating stand-alone focus group methodology to have their findings verified. At the very least it would protect against the worst excesses of a focus group researcher making claims based on small numbers. What is required is not a separation of methods, but a convergence of methods advocated by Merton at the very beginning of the history of focus group research.

Bibliography

Adorno, Theodor W. (1941) (a) 'On Popular Music' in *Studies in Philosophy and Social Science* Vol. IX , No. 1, (1941), pp17-48.

Adorno, Theodor W. (1941) (b)'The Radio Symphony' in Lazarsfeld, Paul F. and Stanton, Frank N. (1941) *Radio Research*. New York: Duell, Pearce and Sloan.

Adorno, Theodor W. (1945) 'A Social Critique of Radio Music' in *Kenyon Review*. Vol.11, No 2 (Spring), (1945), pp 208- 17.

Adorno, Theodor W. (1969) 'Scientific Experiences of a European Scholar in America' in Fleming, D. And Bailyn, B. 1969 *The Intellectual Migration* Mass. Harvard University Press.

Allison, Scott T. and Messick, David M. (1987) 'From Individual Inputs to Group Outputs and Back Again: Group Processes and Inferences About Members' in Hendrick, Clyde. (ed.) (1987) *Group Process* Newbury Park: Sage.

Allport, Floyd Henry. (1924) *Social Psychology* Boston, M.A.: Houghton Mifflin.

Barker, H. (1986) 'Recapturing Sisterhood: A Critical Look At "Process" In Feminist Organising and Community Work' in *Critical Social Policy* Vol.16, (1986), pp80-90.

Barnes, H. E. (Ed) (1958) *An Introduction to the History of Sociology*. Chicago: University of Chiaago Press.

Basch, C.E. (1987) 'Focus Group Interview: An Under-Utilised Research Technique for Improving Theory and Practice' in Health Education. *Health Education Quarterly* 14,(1987), pp411-448.

Bauer, Otto. (1925) *The Austrian Revolution*. (Trans. Stenning, H. J.) London: Leonard Parsons.

Benney, M. and Hughes, E.C. (1956) 'Sociology and the Interview' in *American Journal of Sociology* Vol. 62, (1956), pp137- 142.

Bentwick, Norman. (1967) 'The Destruction of the Jewish Community in Austria 1938-1942' in Fraenkel, J (1967) *The Jews in Austria: Essays on their Life, History and Destruction*. London: Vallentine and Mitchell.

Berelson, Bernard. (1959) 'The State of Communication Research' in *Public Opinion Quarterly* Vol. 23, No 1,(1959), pp1-6.

Berger, M. (1954) *Freedom and Control in Modern Society* New York: Van Noestrand.

Bertrand, Janet T., Brown, Judith E. and Ward, Victoria M. (1992) 'Techniques for Analyzing Focus Group Data' in *Evaluation Review* Vol. 16, No 2, (1992), pp198-209

Blau, Peter M.(1964) 'The Research Process In The Study Of The Dynamics Of Bureaucracy' in Hammand, Phillip E.(ed) (1964) *Sociologists At Work: Essays On The Craft Of Social Research* Garden City, New York: Doubleday/Anchor books.

Blumer, Herbert. (1948) 'Public Opinion and Public Opinion Polling' in *American Sociological Review* No. 13, (1948), pp549-61.

Bogardus, Emory S. (1926) 'The Groups Interview' in *Journal of Applied Sociology* Vol. 10, (1926), pp372-382.

Booth, Charles. (1903) *Life and Labour of the People in London (5 Vol.s.)* London: Macmillan.

Borden, Richard J. (1975) 'Witnessed Agression: Influences Of An Observers Sex and Values on Aggresive Responding' in *Journal of Personality and Social Psychology* Vol. 31, No. 3, (1975), pp567-573.

Bottomore, Tom. and Goode, Patrick. (1987) *Austro-Marxism* Oxford: Oxford University Press.

Boudon, Raymond. (1972) 'An Introduction to Lazarsfeld's Philosophical Papers' in Lazarsfeld, Paul F. (1972) *Qualitative Analysis: Historical and Critical Essays* Boston: Allyn and Bacon.

Bowles, G. and Duelli, Kline R. (1983) *Theories of Women Studies* London: Routledge and Kegan Paul.

Brailsford, Henry. (1945) Introduction to Braunthal, Julius. (1945) in *In Search of the Millenium* London: Gollanz.

Breakwell, G. et al. (eds) (1994) *Research Methods in Psychology* London: Sage.

Bristol, Terry. and Fern, Edward F. (1993) 'Using Qualitative Techniques To Explore Consumer Attitudes: Insights From Group Process Theories' in *Advances in Consumer Research* Vol.20, (1993), pp444-8.

Brotherson, Mary J. and Goldstein, Beth L. (1992) 'Quality Design of Focus Groups in Early Childhood Special Education Research' in *Journal of Early Intervention* Vol. 16. No. 4, (1992), pp334-342.

Brotherson, Mary J. (1994) 'Interactive Focus Group Interviewing: A Qualitative Research Method' in *Early Intervention. Topics in Early Childhood Special Education*. Vol. 14, No 1, (1994), pp 101-118.

Bullock, Malcom. (1939) *Austria, 1918-38(microform); A Study in Failure* London: Macmillan.

Burgess, Robert G. (ed.) (1989) *The Ethics of Educational Research* London: Falmer Press.

Burns, Tom. (1969) *The BBC: Public Institution and Private World* London: Macmillan.

Buttinger, Joseph. (1953) *In the Twilight of Socialism: A History of the Revolutionary Socialists of Austria* New York: Praeger.

Cantril, Hadley. and Allport, Gordon. (1935) *The Psychology of Radio* New York: Harper.

Cantril, Hadley., Gaudet, Hazel. and Herzog, Herta. (1940) *Invasion from Mars* Princeton: Princeton University Press.

Carr, Edward H. (1961) *What is History?* New York: Vintage Books.

Carver, Charles S. (1979) 'A Cybernetic Model of Self-Attention Processes' in *Journal of Personality and Social Psychology* Vol.37, August (1979), pp 1251-1281.

Cashmore, Ellis. (1994) *...And There Was Television* London: Routledge.

Chibnall, Steve. (1974) *Law and Order News* London: Tavistock.

Coleman, James. (1980) 'Paul Lazarsfeld: The Substance and Style of His Work' in Merton, Robert K. and Riley, Matilda W. (eds) (1980) *Sociological Traditions from Generation to Generation: Glimpses of the American Experience* New York: Columbia University Press.

Coleman, James. (1982) Introduction to Kendall, Patricia L. (1982) *The Varied Sociology of Paul F. Lazarsfeld* New York: Columbia University Press.

Cook, Judith A. and Fonow, Mary M. (1986) 'Knowledge and Women's Interests: Issues of Epistemology and Methodology' in *Feminist Sociological Research Sociological Inquiry* Vol. 56, No 1, (1986),pp 2-29.

Corner, John., Richardson, Kay. and Fenton, Natalie. (1990) *Nuclear Reactions. Form and Response in Public Issue Television* London: John Libbey.

Corner, John. (1991) 'Meaning and context: the problematics of 'public knowledge' in new audience studies' in Curran, James. and Gurevitch, Michael. (eds) (1991) *Mass Media and Society* London: Edward Arnold.

Corner, John. (1996) 'Reappraising Reception: Aims, Concepts and Methods' in Curran, James. and Gurevitch, Michael. (eds) (1996) Second Edition *Mass Media and Society* London: Edward Arnold.

Coser, Lewis A. (1982) *Refugee Scholars in America: Their Impact and Their Experiences* New Haven: Yale University Press.

Crankshaw, Edward.(1974) *The Fall of the House of Habsburg* London: Cardinal Books. Crossman, Richard H. (1962) Introduction to Laquer, Walter Z. (1962) *Young Germany: A History of the German Youth Movement* London: Routledge, Kegan Paul.

Crawford. W Rex. (ed) *The Cultural Migration: The European Scholar in America* Philadelphia: University of Pennsylvania Press.

Curran, James. (1990) 'The New Revisionism in Mass Communication Research: A Reapraisal' in *European Journal of Communication* Vol. 5, No. 2-3,(1990), pp133-164.

Curran, James. and Gurevitch, Michael. (eds) (1991) *Mass Media and Society* London: Edward Arnold.

Curran, James. and Gurevitch, Michael. (eds) (1996) Second Edition *Mass Media and Society* London: Edward Arnold.

Dennis, W. (ed.) (1948) *Current Trends in Social Psychology* Pittsburgh: University of Pittsburgh Press.

Duval, Shelley. and Wickland, Robert A. (1972) *A Theory of Objective Self Awareness* New York: Academic Press.

Elliot, Philip. (1972) *The Making of a Television Series - A Case Study in the Production of Culture* London: Constable.

Faulkner, R.R. (1982) 'Improving On a Triad' in Van Maanen, J., Dabbs, J.M. and Faulkner, R.R.(eds) (1982) *Varieties of Qualitative Research* London: Sage.

Fern , Edward F.(1982) 'The Use Of Focus Groups For Idea Generation: The Effect Of Group Size, Acquaintanceship and Moderators In Response Quality and Quantity' in *Journal of Marketing Research* Vol.19, (1982), pp1-13.

Fern, Edward F. (1983) 'Focus Groups: A Review of Some Contradictory Evidence, Implications, and Suggestions for Future Research' in *Advances in Consumer Research* Vol. 10, (1983), pp121-126.

Festinger, Leon. (1954) 'A Theory of Social Comparison Processes' in *Human Relations* No.7, May (1954), pp117-140.

Fischer, Ernst. (1974) *An Opposing Man* (Trans. P. And B. Ross). London: Allen Lane.

Fleming, D. And Bailyn, B. (1969) *The Intellectual Migration* Mass. Harvard University Press.

Florance, Ronald. (1971) *Fritz: The Story of an Assassin* New York: Dial Press.

Fraenkel, J. (1967) *The Jews in Austria: Essays on their Life, History and Destruction* London: Vallentine and Mitchell.

Freedman, Jonathan L. (1986) 'Television Violence and Aggression: A Rejoinder' in *Psychological Bullitin* Vol. 100, No. 3, (1986), pp372-378.

Freud, Martin. (1967) *Who was Freud?* in Fraenkel, J. (1967) *The Jews in Austria: Essays on their Life, History and Destruction* London: Vallentine and Mitchell.

Gauntlett, David. (1995) *Moving Experiences: Understanding Television Influences and Effects* London: John Libby.

Gay, Peter. (1969) 'Weimar Culture: The Outsider as Insider' in Fleming, D. And Bailyn, B. (1969) *The Intellectual Migration* Mass. Harvard University Press.

Gelsthorpe, Loraine. (1992) 'Respone to Martyn Hammersley's Paper 'On Feminist Methodology' in *Sociology* Vol. 26, No 2, (1992), pp213-218.

Gitlin, Todd. (1978) 'Media Sociology: The Dominant Paradigm' in *Theory and Soceity* Vol. 6, (1978), pp205-253.

Glock, Charles Y. (1979) 'Organizational Innovation for Social Science Research Training' in Merton, Robert K *et al* (1979).

Glasgow University Media Group (1976) *Bad News* London: Routledge and Kegan Paul.

Glasgow University Media Group. (1980) *More Bad News* London: Routledge and Kegan Paul.

Goethals, George R. and Zana, Mark P. (1979) 'The Rule of Social Comparison in Choice Shifts' in *Journal Of Personality and Social Psychology* Vol.37, Sept, 1979, pp1469-1476.

Golding, Peter. and Elliot, Philip. (1979) *Making the News* London: Longman.

Greenbaum, Thomas L. (1993) *The Handbook for Focus Group Research* New York: Lexington Books.

Greenberg, Bradly S. and Gantz, Walter. (eds) (1993) *Desert Storm and the Mass Media* Cresskill, N.J.: Hampton Press.

Griffin, C. (1991) 'The Researcher Talks Back: Dealing With Power Relations in Studies Of Young People's Entry Into The Job Market' in Shaffir, W. B. and Stebbins, R.A. (eds) (1991) *Experiencing Fieldwork: An Insiders View of Qualitative Research* London: Sage.

Grossberg, Lawrence. (1993) 'Can Cultural Studies Find True Happiness in Communications?' in *Journal of Communication* Vol. 43, No 4, (1993), pp 89-97.

Gulick, Charles A. (1948) *Austria: From Hapsburg to Hitler* Berkeley, California. (2 Vols)

Hall, Stuart. (1973) *Encoding and Decoding* Stencilled Paper 7, Birmingham Centre for Contemporary Culture studies, University of Birmingham.

Hall, Stuart. (1980) 'Introduction to Media Studies at the Centre' in Hall, Stuart. et al. (1980) *Culture, Media, Language: Working Papers in Cultural Studies 1972-79* London: Hutchinson.

Hall, Stuart. *et al.* (1980) *Culture, Media, Language: Working Papers in Cultural Studies 1972-79* London: Hutchinson.

Hammand, Phillip E. (ed.) (1964) *Sociologists at work: essays on the craft of social research* Graden city, New York: Doubleday/Anchor books.

Hammersley, Martyn. (1992) 'On Feminisit Methodology' in *Sociology* Vol. 26, No 2, (1992), pp187-206.

Harding, Sandra. (ed.) (1987) *Feminism and Methodology* Bloomington: Indiana University Press.

Hendrick, Clyde. (ed.) (1987) *Group Process* Newbury Park: Sage.

Herzog, Herta. (1941) 'On Borrowed Experience in Studies' in *Philosophy and Social Science* Vol. IX, No. 1, (1941), pp65-95.

Herzog, Herta. (1944) 'What do we really know about daytime serail listeners?' in Lazarsfeld, Paul F and Stanton, Frank N. (1944) *Radio Research 1942-43* New York: Duell, Pearce and Sloan.

Hilter, Adolf. (1975) *Mein Kampf* (trans. Manheim,R) London: Radius Books/Hutchinson.

Hoggart, Richard. (1961) *The Uses of Literacy* Boston: Beacon Press.

Höijer, Birgitta. (1990) 'Studying Viewer's Reception of Television Programmes: Theoretical and Methodological Considerations' in *European Journal of Communications* Vol. 5, (1990), pp 29-56.

Hugentobler, Margrit. (1991) Review of Morgan, David L. 1988 and Review of Krueger, Richard A. 1988 in *Health Education* Vol. 18, No 2, (1991), pp253-256.

Hughes, Diane. and Dumont, Kimberly. (1993) 'Using Focus Groups to Facilitate Culturally Anchored Research' in *American Journal of Community Psychology* Vol. 21, No 6, (1993).

Hunt, Morton. (1961) 'A Profile: Robert K. Merton' in the *New Yorker* January 28th 1961.

Ickes, William John., Wickland, Robert A. and Ferris, Brian C. (1973) 'Objective Self Awareness and Self Esteem' in *Journal of Experimental Psychology* Vol.9, May (1973), pp202-219.

Inglis, Fred. (1993) *Cutural Studies* Oxford: Blackwell Publishers.

Jacobs, N. (1959) *Culture for the Millions: Mass Media in Modern Society* Boston: Beacon Press.

Jahoda, Marie., Lazarsfeld, Paul F. and Zeisel, Hans. (1933) *Die Arbeitslosen von Marienthal: Ein Soziographisher* Leipzig: Hirzl.

Jahoda, Marie., Lazarsfeld, Paul F., and Zeisel, Hans. (1971). *Marienthal: The Sociography of an Unemployed Community* Chicago: Aldine-Atherton.

Jameson, Frederic. (1967) 'T.W. Adorno or Historical Tropes' in *Salmagundi* Spring, (1967).

Jankowski, Nicholas W. and Wester, Fred. (1991) 'The Qualitative Tradition In Social Science Enquiry: Contributions To Mass Communication Research' in Jensen, Klaus B. and Jankowski, Nicholas W. (1991) *A Handbook of Qualitative Methodologies for Mass Communiction Research* London: Routledge.

Jay, Martin. (1973) *The Dialectical Imagination. A History of the Frankfurt School and the Institute of Social Research 1923-50* London: Heinemann.

Jedlicka, L. (1966) The Austrian Heimwehr in *Journal of Contemporary History* Vol. 1, No 1, (1966), pp127-144.

Jenks, Chris. (1993) *Culture* London: Routledge.

Jensen, Klaus Bruhn. (1993) 'The Past in the Future: Problems and Potentials of Historical Reception Studies' in *Journal of Communication* Vol. 43, No.4, (1993), pp20-28.

Johnston, W.M. (1972) *The Austrian Mind: An Intellectual and Social History* Berkeley: University of Califonia Press.

Jones, Ernest. (1953) *The Life and Work of Sigmund Freud Vol. 1: The Formative Years and the Great Discoveries 1856-1900* New York: Basic Books.

Kann, R.A. (1951) 'Karl Renner' in *Journal of Modern History* Vol. 23, No 3, (1951), pp243-249.

Kaplan, Martin F. (1987) 'The Influencing Process in Group Decision Making' in Hendrick, Clyde. (ed.) (1987) *Group Process* Newbury Park: Sage.

Katz, Elihu. and Lazarsfeld, Paul F. (1955) *Personal Influences: The Part Played by People in the Flow of Mass Communication* Glencoe: Free Press.

Kieran, Matthew., Morrison, David. and Svennevig, Michael. (1997) *Regulating For Changing Values* a Research Working Paper London: Broadcasting Standards Commission.

Kitzinger, Jenny. (1994) 'The Methodology of Focus Groups: The Importance Of Interaction Between Research Participants' in *Sociology of Health and Illness* Vol. 16, No 1, (1994), pp103-121.

Knoll, A. (1959) 'Austria' in Roucek, J. S. (1959) *Contemporary Sociology* London: Peter Owen.

Koestler, Arthur. (1955) *Arrow in the Blue* London: Collins with Hamish Hamilton.

Koestler, Arthur . (1974) *The Case of the Midwife Toad* London: Pan Books.

Komarovsky, Mirra. (1940) *The Unemployed Man and his Family: The Effect of Unemployment in 59 Families* New York: Dryden Press.

Konig, Rene. (1959) 'Germany' in Roucek, J. S (1959) *Contemporary Sociology* London: Peter Owen.

Kripendorff, Klaus. (1980) *Content Analysis: An Introduction to its Methodology* Beverely Hills: Sage.

Krueger, Richard A. (1988) *Focus Groups: A Practical Guide for Applied Research* Beverly Hills: Sage.

Krugman, Paul. (1994) *Peddling Prosperity: Economic Sense and Nonsense in the Age of Diminished Expectations* New York: Norton.

Lalane, Bibb. and Nina, Steve. (1980) 'Social Impact Theory and Group Influence: A Social Engineering Perspective' in Paulus, Paul B. (ed.) (1980) *Psychology of Group Influence* Hillsdale. N.J.: Lawrewnce Erbaum.

Landheer, B. (1958) 'The Universalistic Theory of Society of Othmar Spann and his School' in Barnes, H. E. (Ed) (1958) *An Introduction to the History of Sociology* Chiago: University of Chiaago Press.

Laquer, Walter Z. (1962) *Young Germany: A History of the German Youth Movement* London: Routledge, Kegan Paul.

Lazarsfeld, Paul F. (1941) 'Remarks on Administrative and Critical Communication Research. Studies' in *Philosophy and Social Science* Vol. IX, No. 2, (1941).

Lazarsfeld, Paul F. and Stanton, Frank N. (1941) *Radio Research* New York: Duell, Pearce and Sloan.

Lazarsfeld, Paul F. and Stanton, Frank N. (1944) *Radio Research* 1942-43 New York: Duell, Pearce and Sloan.

Lazarsfeld, Paul F., Berelson, Bernard. and Gaudet, Hazel. (1944) *The Peoples Choice: How the Voter Makes Up His Mind In a Presidential Campaign* New York: Duell, Pearce and Sloan.

Lazarsfeld, Paul F. (1949) 'The American Soldier: An Expository Review' in *Public Opinion Quarterly* Vol. XIII, No. 3, (1949), pp377-404.

Lazarsfeld, Paul F. (1950) 'The Obligation of the 1950 Pollster to the 1984 Historian' in *Public Opinion Quarterly* Vol.XIV, No.4, (1950), pp617-38.

Lazarsfeld, Paul F. and Merton, Robert, K. (1950) *Proposal to Establish an Institute for Training in Social Science* (BASR library).

Lazarsfeld, Paul F. and Merton, Robert K. (1954) 'Friendship as a Social Process: A Substantive and Methodological Analysis' in Berger, M. (1954) *Freedom and Control in Modern Society* New York: Van Noestrand.

Lazarsfeld, Paul F. (1959) Introduction to Jacobs, N. (Ed) (1959) *Culture for the Millions: Mass Media in Modern Society* Boston: Beacon Press.

Lazarsfeld, Paul F. and Theilens, Wagner. (1958) *The Academic Mind: Social Scientists in a Time of Crisis* New York: Free Press.

Lazarsfeld, Paul F. (1961) 'Notes on the History of Quantification in Sociology, Trends, Sources and Problems' in *ISIS* Vol. 52, June, (1961), pp277-335.

Lazarsfeld, Paul F. (1962) 'Sociology of Empirical Social Research' in *American Sociological Review* Vol. 27, No. 6, (1962).

Lazarsfeld, Paul F. and Sieber, S.D. (1964) *Organising Educational Research: An Exploration* New Jeasey: Prentice Hall.

Lazarsfeld, Paul F. (1969) 'An Episode in the History of Social Research' in Fleming, D. And Bailyn, B. (1969) *The Intellectual Migration* Mass. Harvard University

Lazarsfeld, Paul F. (1972) *Qualitative Analysis: Historical and Critical Essays* Boston: Allyn and Bacon.

Lederman, Linda C. (1990) 'Assesing Educational Effectiveness: The Focus Group Interview as a Technique for Data Collection' in *Communication Education* Vol. 38, April, (1990), pp117-127.

Leser, Norbert. (1966) 'Austro-Marxism: A Reappraisal' in *Journal of Contempory History* Vol. 1, No 2, (1966), pp117-133.

Lindhof, Thomas R. (ed.) (1987) *Natural Audiences: Qualitative Research of Media Uses and Effects* Norwood, N.J: Ablex.

Livingstone, Sonia. (1990) *Making Sense of Television: the Psychology of Audience Interpretation* Oxford: Permagon.

Livingstone, Sonia. (1993) 'Research: An Old Story With a New Ending' in *Journal of Communication* Vol. 43, Autumn No 4, (1993), pp5-97.

Lunt, Peter., and Livingstone, Sonia. (1996) 'Rethinking the Fous Group in Media and Communication Research' in *Journal of Communication* No.46(2) Spring, pp79-98.

Lynd, Robert S. (1939) *Knowledge for What?* Princeton: PrincetonUniversity Press.

Lynd, Robert S. and Lynd, Helen M. (1929) *Middletown. A Study in American Culture* New York: Harcourt Brace.

Macdonald, Mary. (1946) *The Republic of Austria 1918-1934: A Study in Failure of Democratic Government* London: Oxford University Press.

Macrea, Donald G. (1974) 'Review of Adorno's Negative Dialectics' in *New Society* Vol.28, March, (1974), pp786.

Madge, John. (1963) *The Origins of Scientific Methodolgy* London: Tavistock Publications.

Magnet, Nyron. (1994) 'The Productivity Payoff Arrives' in *Fortune International* 27 June, (1994), pp35-39.

Markus, Hazel. (1978) 'The Effect of Mere Presence on Social Facilitation: An Unobtrusive Test' in *Journal of Experimental Social Psychology* 14, July (1978), pp389-397.

Mayhew, Henry. (1851) *London Labour and the London Poor* London: Griffin.

McCartney, C. A. (1926) *The Social Revolution in Austria* London: Cambridge Universtity Press.

McIver, Robert M. (1968) *As A Tale is Told* Chicago: Chicago University Press.

McQuarrie, Edward F. (1989) 'Review of Kreuger, Richard A. 1988' in *Journal of Marketing Research* Vol. 26. No 3, (1989), pp371-372.

Meis, Maria. (1983) 'Towards a Methodology for Feminist Research' in Bowles, G. and Duelli Kline, R (1983) *Theories of Women's Studies* London: Routledge and Kegan Paul.

Merton, Robert K. (1938) 'Social Structure and Anomie' in *American Sociological Review* Vol. III, (1938), pp 372-682.

Merton, Robert K. and Kendall, Patricia L. (1946) ' The Focussed Interview' in *American Journal of Sociology* No. 51, (1946), pp541-557.

Merton, Robert K., Fiske, Majorie. and Curtis, Alberta. (1946) *Mass Persuasion: The Social Psychology of a War Bond Drive* New York: Harper and Bros.

Merton, Robert K. (1948) (a) 'The Bearing of Empirical Social Research upon the Development of Social Theory' in *American Sociological Review* Vol. XXIII, No. 3, (1948), pp505-515.

Merton, Robert K. (1948) (b) 'The Social Psychology of Housing' in Dennis, W. (ed) (1948) *Current Trends in Social Psychology* Pittsburgh: University of Pittsburgh Press.

Merton, Robert K. (1948) (c) 'Discussion of Parsons' in *American Sociological Review* Vol. XXIII, No. 2, (1948), pp164-168.

Merton, Robert K., Fiske, Majorie. and Kendall, Patricia. L. (1956) *The Focussed Interview* A Report of the Bureau of Applied Social Research, Columbia University. New York: Free Press.

Merton, Robert K., Reader, George., and Kendall, Patricia, L. (1957) *The Student Physician: Introductory Studies in the Sociology of Medical Education* Cambridge M.A.: Harvard University Press.

Merton, Robert K. (1979) 'Remembering Paul Lazarsfeld' in Merton, Robert K., Coleman, James S. and Russi, Peter H. (eds) (1979) *Qualitative and Quantitative Social Research: Papers In Honour of Paul F Lazarsfeld* New York: Free Press.

Merton, Robert K., Coleman, James S. and Russi, Peter H. (eds) (1979) *Qualitative and Quantitative Social Research: Papers In Honour of Paul F Lazarsfeld* New York: Free Press.

Merton, Robert K. and Riley, Matilda W. (eds) (1980) *Sociological Traditions from Generation to Generation: Glimpses of the American Experience* New York: Columbia University Press.

Merton, Robert K. (1987) 'The Focussed Interview and Focus Groups. Continuities and Discontinuities' in *Public Opinion Quarterly* Vol. 51, (1987), pp550-566.

Mills, Wright C (1959) *The Sociological Imagination* New York: Oxford University Press.

Millward, Lynne J. (1994) ' Focus Groups' in Breakwell, G. et al (eds) (1994) *Research Methods in Psychology* London: Sage.

Millwood-Hargrave, Andrea. (ed) (1993) *Violence in Factual Television* Annual Review of the Broadcasting Standards Council. London: John Libbey.

Morely, David. (1986) *Family Television: Cultural Power and Domestic Leisure* London: Comedia Publishing Group.

Morgan, David L. (1988) *Focus Groups and Qualitative Research* Newbury Park: Sage Publications.

Morgan, David L. and Spanish, Margaret T. (1984) 'Focus Groups: A New Tool for Qualitative Research' in *Qualitative Sociology* No 7, Fall, (1984), pp 253-270.

Morgan, David L. (1993) *Successful Focus Groups. Advancing the State of the Art.* Newbury Park: Sage Publications.

Morris, A. and Gelsthorpe, Loraine. (1991) 'Feminists Perspectives in Crimonology: Transforming and Transgressing' in *Women and Criminal Justice* Vol. 2 (2), (1991), pp3-26.

Morrison, David E. (1978) (a) 'Kultur and Culture T.W. Adorno and P.F. Lazarsfeld' in *Social Research* Vol. 45, No 2, (1978), pp 331-355.

Morrison, David E. (1978) (b) 'The Beginnings of Modern Mass Communication Research' in *European Journal of Sociology* Vol.XIX, (1978) pp 347-359.

Morrison, David E. (1988) 'The Transference of Experience and the Impact of Ideas: Paul Lazarsfeld and Emigration' in *Communications* Spring,(1988), pp 185-209.

Morrison, David E. (1992) (a) *Television and The Gulf War* London: John Libbey.

Morrison, David E. (1992) (b) *Conversations With Voters* (1992 General election) - report to the BBC and ITC.

Morrison, David E. and MacGregor, Brent. (1993) (a) 'Anxiety, War and Children: The Role of Television' in Greenberg, Bradly S. and Gantz, Walter. (eds) (1993) *Desert Storm and the Mass Media* Cresskill, N.J.: Hampton Press.

Morrison, David E. and MacGregor, Brent. (1993) (b) 'Detailed Findings from Editing Groups' Section 2 in Millwood-Hargrave, Andrea. (ed.) (1993) *Violence in Factual Television* Annual Review of the Broadcasting Standards Council. London: John Libbey.

Morrison, David E. and MacGregor, Brent. (1993) (c) 'Viewer's Response to Violence in Non-Fictional Programmes' a *Report to the Broadcasting Standards Council*.

Morrison, David E. (due Autumn 1999) 'The Late Arrival Of Television Research: A Case Study In The Production Of Knowledge' in Tumber, Howard. (ed.) (due Autumn 1999) *Media Power, Professionals and Policies* (provisional title)

Moser, Claus A. and Kalton, Graham. (1971) *Survey Methods in Social Investigation* Aldershot: Gower.

Mowlana, Hamid., Gerbner, George. and Schiller, Herbert I. (1992) *The Triumph of the Image: The Media War in the Persian Gulf - A Global Perspective* Boulder: Westview Press.

Murdock, Graham. (1989) 'Cultural Studies - Missing Links' in *Critical Studies in Mass Communication* Vol. 6, No. 4, (1989), pp 436-440.

Noble, Grant. (1975) *Children In Front of the Small Screen* London:Constable.

Nuemann, Franz L. (1953) 'The Social Sciences' in Crawford, W Rex. (ed) (1953) *The Cultural Migration; The European Scholar in America* Philadelphia: University of Pennsylavania Press.

Nyamthi, Adeline. and Shuler, Pam. (1990) 'Focus Group Interview: A Research Technique For Informed Nursing Practice' in *Journal of Advanced Nursing* Vol. 15, (1990), pp1281-1288.

O'Brien, Kerth. (1993) 'Using Focus Groups to Develop Health Surveys: An Example from Research on Social Relationships and AIDS-Preventive Behaviour' in *Health Education Quarterly* Vol. 20, No 3, (1993), pp361-372.

Oakley, Ann. (1981) 'Interviewing Women: A Contradiction in Terms' in Roberts, Helen. (Ed) (1981) *Doing Feminist Research* London: Routledge and Kegan Paul.

Ogg, Frederick.(1928) *Research in the Humanistic and Social Sciences* New York: The Century Co.

Orwell, George. (1959) *The Road to Wigan Pier* London: Secker & Warburg.

Parsons, Talcott. (1948) The Position of Sociological Theory in *American Sociological Review* Vol. XXIII, No 2, (1948), pp 156-164.

Parsons, Talcott. (1956) *Department and Laboratory of Social Relations Harvard University : The First Decade 1946-1956* Harvard: Harvard University Press.

Patcher, Henry. (1970) 'A Memoir' in *Salmagundi* Fall-Winter, No 10-11, (1970), pp 12-52.

Patton, M.Q. (1990) *Qualitative Evaluation Methods* Newbury Park CA: Sage.

Pauling, C. (1974) 'A Bibliography of the Frankfurt School' in *Cultural Studies* Vol. 6. Centre for Contemporary Cultural Studies, University of Birmingham.

Paulus, Paul B. (ed.) (1980) *Psychology of Group Influence* Hillsdale. N.J.: Lawrewnce Erbaum.

Philo, Greg. (1990) *Seeing and Believing: The Effects of Television* London: Routledge.

Poland, F. (1985) *Breaking the Rules* Manchester: University of Manchester, Department of Sociology, Studies in Sexual Politics No. 4.

Pulzer, Peter G. J. (1964) *The Rise of Anti-Semitism in Germany and Austria* New York: Wiley and Sons. Inc.

Ramzanogulu, Caroline. (1992) 'On Feminist Methodology: Male Reason Versus Female Empowerment' in *Sociology* Vol. 26, No 2, (1992), pp 207-212.

Reinharz, Shulamit. (1983) 'Experiential Analysis: A Contribution to Feminist Research' in Bowles, G. and Duelli Kline, R (1983) *Theories of Women's Studies* London: Routledge and Kegan Paul.

Rex, John. (1973) *Discovering Sociology: Studies in Sociological Theory and Method* London: Routledge and Kegan Paul.

Riddel, Sheila. (1989) 'Exploiting the Exploited? *The Ethics of Feminist Educational Research'* in Burgess, Robert G. (ed.) (1989) The Ethics of Educational Research London: Falmer Press.

Roberts, Helen. (Ed) (1981) *Doing Feminist Research* London: Routledge and Kegan Paul.

Rock, Paul. (1979) *The Making of Symbolic Interactionism* Totowa, N.J: Rowman and Littlefield.

Rogers, Everret M. (1994) *A History of Communication Study* New York: The Free Press.

Rose, Gillian. (1978) *The Melancholy Science. An Introduction to the Thought of Theodor W. Adorno* London: Macmillan.

Rosenmayr, Leopold. (1966) 'Vorgeschicte und Entwicklung der Soziologie in Osterreich bis 1933 in *Zeitschrift fur Nationalokonomie* Vol.XXXVI, (1966), pp268-282.

Roucek, J. S. (1959) *Contemporary Sociology* London: Peter Owen.

Rowntree, Seebohn B. and Lasker, Bruno. (1911) *Unemployment, A Social Study* London: Macmillan.

Rowntree, Seebohn B. (1901) *Poverty: A Study of Town Life* London: Macmillan

Rowntree, Seebohn B. (1941) *Poverty and Progress* London: Longmans.

Schlesinger, A.M. (1949) 'The Statistical Soldier' in *Partisan Review* Vol. 16,(1949), pp 852 - 856.

Schlesinger, Philip. (1978) *Putting Reality Together: BBC News.* London: Constable.

Schlesinger, Philip. et al. (1992) *Women Viewing Violence* BFI: London.

Schramm, Wilber (1952) 'Comments on Berelson' *Public Opinion Quarterly* Vol. 23 No. 1 pp6-10.

Serge, Viktor. (1963) *Memoirs of a Revolutionary 1901-1941* (tras. Sedwick, P.) Oxford: Oxford University Press.

Shaffir, W. B. and Stebbins, R.A. (eds) (1991) *Experiencing Fieldwork: An Insiders View of Qualitative Research* London: Sage.

Shaw, Martin. and Carr-Hill, Roy. (1991) *Public Opinion, Media and Violence. Attitudes to the Gulf War in a Local Poplation.* Gulf War Project. Report No. 1. University of Hull.

Shaw, Martin. and Carr-Hill, Roy. (1992) 'Public Opinion and Media War Coverage in Britain' in Mowlana, Hamid., Gerbner, George. and Schiller, Herbert I. (1992) *The Triumph of the Image: The Media War in the Persian Gulf - A Global Perspective* Boulder: Westview Press.

Shepherd, B. G. (1961) *Dollfuss* London: Macmillan and Co.

Shils, Edward. (1970) 'Tradition, Ecology and Institutions' in the *History of Sociology* Daedalus Vol. 99, No. 4, (1970) , pp760-828.

Siegert, Michael. (1974) 'Numerus Juden Raus' in *Neues Forum* June.

Skeggs, Beverly. (1992) 'Confessions of a Feminst Researcher' in *Sociological Review* Vol. 2, No 1, (1992), pp14-18.

Slater, Phil. (1974) 'The Aesthetic Theory of the Frankfurt School' in *Cultural Studies* Vol.6 Autumn (Centre for Contemporary Cultural Studies. Univesity of Birmingham)

Stadler, Karl R. (1968) 'Austria' in Woolf, S. (1968) *European Facism* London: Weidenfeld and Nicholson.

Stanley, Liz. and Wise, Sue. (1983) (a) 'Back into the Personal or: Our Attempt to Contruct Feminist Research' in Bowles, G. and Duelli Kline, R (1983) *Theories of Women Studies* London: Routledge and Kegan Paul.

Stanley, Liz. and Wise, Sue. (1983) (b) *Breaking Out: Feminist Consciousness and Feminist Research* London: Routledge and Kegan Paul.

Stein, Maurice R. (1964) 'The Eclipse of Community: Some Glances at the Education of a Sociologist' in Vidich, A. J. (1964) *Reflections on Community Studies* New York: Wiley and Sons.

Stewart, David W. and Shamdasini, Prem N. (1990) *Focus Groups. Theory and Practice* Newbury Part: Sage.

Story, John. (1994) *The Study of Popular Culture Within Cultural Studies* Harvester Wheatsheaf.

Stouffer, Samuel A. (1962) *Social Research to Test Ideas: Selected Writings of S.A. Stouffer* Glencoe: Free Press.

Stouffer, Samuel A. et al. (1937) 'Depression and the Family' in *Social Science Research Council Bulletin 29 of Studies in the Social Aspects of Depression.*

Stouffer, Samuel. A. et al. (1949) *Studies in Social Psychology in World War II Vol. 1- 4* Princeton N.J. Princeton University Press.

Swenson, Jill D., Giswold, William F. and Kleiber, Pamela B. (1992) 'Focus Groups. Methods of Enquiry/Intervention' in *Small Group Research* Vol. 23, No. 4, (1992), pp 459-474.

Terry, Bristol. and Fern, Edward F. (1993) 'Using Qualitative Techniques to Explore Consumer Attitudes: Insights from Group Process Theories' in *Advances in Consumer Research* Vol. 20, (1993), pp 444-8.

Tesch, R. (1990) *Qualitative Research : Analysis Types and Software Tools* New York: Falmer Press.

Thomas, William. and Znaniecki, Florian. (1927) *The Polish Peasant in Europe and America* New York: Knopf.

Thomson, E.P. (1963) *The Making of the English Working Class* London: Gollancz.

Torrance, John. (1976) 'The Emergence of Sociology in Austria 1885-1935' in *Arch. Europ. Social* Vol.XVII, (1976), pp185-219.

Tracey, Michael. (1977) *The Production of Political Television* London: Routledge and Kegan Paul.

Tracey, Michael. and Morrison, David E. (1979) *Whitehouse* London: Macmillan Press.

Trotsky, Leon. (1965) *The History of the Russian Revolution Vol. III* London: Gollancz.

Troyna, B. and Carrington, B. (1989) 'Whose side are we on? in (Ed) (1989) *The Ethics of Educational Research* London: Falmer Press.

Tunstall, Jeremy. (1971) *Journalists At Work* London: Constable.

Van Maanen, J., Dabbs, J.M. and Faulkner, R.R.(eds) (1982) *Varieties of Qualitative Research* London: Sage.

Vidich, A. J. (1964) *Reflections on Community Studies* New York: Wiley and Sons.

Vinokur, Amiram. and Burnstein, Eugene. (1974) 'Effects of Partially Shared Persuasive Arguments on Group induced Shifts; A Group Problem Solving Approach' in *Journal Of Personality and Social Psychology* Vol.29, March, (1974), pp305-315.

Vinokur, Amiram. and Burnstein, Eugene. (1978) 'Depolarization of Attitudes in Groups' in *Journal of Personality and Social Psychology* Vol.36, August, (1978), pp 872-885.

Ward, Victoria N, Bertrand, JanetT, and Brown, Lisanne F. (1991) 'The Comparability of Focus Group and Survey Results: Three Case Studies 'in *Evaluation Review* Vol. 15, No 2 (1991), pp 266-283.

Wartella, Ellen. (1987) 'Commentary on Qualitative Research and Chidrens Mediated Communication' in Lindhof, Thomas R. (Ed) (1987) *Natural Audiences: Qualitative Research of Media Uses and Effects* Norwood, N.J: Ablex.

Westphalen, Ferdinand A. (1953) *Sociology and Economics in Austria: A Report on Post-War Development* Library of Congress Reference Department, European Affairs Division, Washington.

Whitney, John C. and Smith, Ruth A. (1983) 'Effects of Group Cohesiveness on Attitude Polarization and the Acqusition of Knowledge in a Strategic Planning Context' in *Journal of Marketing Research* Vol.20, May (1983), pp167-176.

Whyte, Willian F. (1943) *Street Corner Society* Chicago: University of Chicago Press.

Wiggershaus, Rolph. (1994) *The Frankfurt School* (trans. Robertson, Michael). Cambridge: Polity Press.

Williams, Raymond. (1958) *Culture and Society*, 1780-1950 New York: Columbia University Press.

Williams, Raymond. (1961) *The Long Revolution* New York: Columbia University Press.

Willis, Paul E. (1980) 'Notes on Method' in Hall, Stuart. et al. (1980) *Culture, Media, Language: Working Papers in Cultural Studies 1972-79* London: Hutchinson.

Woolf, S. (1968) *European Facism* London: Weidenfeld and Nicholson.

Zanjonc, Robert B. (1980) 'Compresence' in Paulus, Paul B. (ed.) (1980) *Psychology of Group Influence* Hillsdale. N.J.: Lawrewnce Erbaum.

Zeisel, Hans. (1968) ' L'Ecole Viennoise des Recherches de Motivation' in *Rev. Fanc. Sociol.* Vol.IX, (1968), pp 3-12.

Zeisel, Hans. (1969) 'Der Anfang Moderner Sozialforschung in Osterreich. Die Osterreichische Wirtschaftspsychologische Forschungsstelle, 1925-1938' in *Soziologie Forschung in Osterreich Verlag Hermann Bohlaus, Vienna*

Zeisel, Hans. (1979) 'The Vienna Years' in Merton, Robert K., Coleman, James S. and Russi, Peter H. (eds) (1979) *Qualitative and Quantitative Social Research: Papers In Honour of Paul F Lazarsfeld* New York: Free Press.

Index

291

293